Psychology: A Science in Conflict

Psychology:
A Science in Conflict

HOWARD H. KENDLER

University of California, Santa Barbara

New York   Oxford
OXFORD UNIVERSITY PRESS
1981

Copyright © 1981 by Oxford University Press, Inc.

Library of Congress Cataloging in Publication Data
Kendler, Howard Harvard, 1919–
   Psychology: A Science in Conflict
   Bibliography: p. Includes index.
   1. Psychology–Philosophy. I. Title.
[DNLM: 1. Psychology–Methods. BF38.5 K33p]
BF38.K43   150′.1   80–22613
ISBN 0–19–502900–3   ISBN 0–19–502901–1 (pbk.)

Printing (last digit): 9 8 7 6 5 4 3 2 1

Printed in the United States of America

Preface

This book is a direct outgrowth of my career in psychology. I became committed to psychology after experiencing the excitement of doing original research under the tutelage of Solomon E. Asch. I chose to go to the University of Iowa for graduate training because of my interest in Gestalt psychology. There, more by accident than by design, I took an advanced seminar with Kenneth W. Spence that inspired me to do research with him. It gradually became apparent that the differences between Gestalt theory and the neobehaviorism of the Hull-Spence-Miller paradigm were not simply a consequence of competing theoretical assumptions. To fully understand the differences, one had to comprehend varying conceptions of science, strategies of research and theorizing, and even views about the role of science in society.

My methodological interests expanded during World War II when I served as an army clinical psychologist. Being a psychotherapist, interpreting a variety of psychological tests, participating in psychiatric staff meetings, and supervising a ward of patients forced me to confront new methodological issues that had not been met in the laboratory.

My interest in methodological problems in psychology soon developed into a professional responsibility. In order to help unify a graduate program at New York University, I was asked to prepare a course (Psychology 201: Conceptual Problems in Psychology) to be required of all incoming students that would acquaint them with the methodological structure of psychology. My plan was to reveal the alternative methodological decisions that have been and can be made in psychology and to analyze the implications of these decisions on research, theory, and social applica-

tion. I aspired to do this in a detached manner in order to illuminate the various alternatives without prescribing any particular
approach. Admittedly this neutral stance was difficult to maintain because of my commitment to the particular set of methodological assumptions and strategies that governed my own research
program. But realizing that there was no one *valid* approach to
psychology I tried to inhibit any missionary zeal to persuade
others to adopt my orientation. And I might add that this zeal
subsided as a result of repeatedly teaching Psychology 201.

My position on many of the issues analyzed in this book have
changed from the time the course was initially taught at New
York University. That was inevitable. The vigorous and exciting
discussions and debates with the talented N.Y.U. students forced
me to rethink my positions and modify some of my views. I also
profited from teaching the course at the University of California,
Berkeley; The Hebrew University of Jerusalem; and the University of California, Santa Barbara. One methodological assumption,
however, has remained firm. The final support for any theoretical
or interpretive psychological statement must be linked to empirical evidence. This does not imply that all questions, especially
those directed at many significant problems of human existence
and social organization, can be answered by empirical means
alone. Empiricism has definite limits. But those limits cannot be
overcome by a priori philosophical reasoning.

Numerous debts have to be acknowledged. Being a Fellow
at the Center for Advanced Studies in the Behavioral Sciences
helped me plan this book. Tracy S. Kendler offered many cogent
criticisms and suggestions at various stages of the project. Gerald
Zuriff submitted a penetrating critique of the manuscript that
proved to be most valuable in the preparation of the final version.
Discussions with Roy Lachman, usually dominated by disagreements, proved enlightening. Many useful suggestions were offered by David Messick, John Foley, and T. S. Krawiec. Naturally,
I am obligated to many scholars whom I cite. In some cases, I decided against citing a specific reference because of the context in
which a particular idea was embedded. Isolating the notion that
interested me might be seen as a distortion or an oversimplifica-

tion. Rather than risk a debate about whether I was misstating a particular position, I thought it best to deal with the idea alone. Finally, to protect the innocent, I must acknowledge full responsibility for the views expressed in this book.

Many different secretaries worked on this project. The major contributions were made by Christine Whitehead, JeNeal Bradford, Carolyn Scherr, and Chris Clark. I appreciate the care they devoted to their task. Finally, I would like to express my indebtedness to Melanie Miller at Oxford University Press.

Santa Barbara   Howard H. Kendler
January 1981

Contents

To those echoes of the past
that still ring clearly.
Dedicated to the memory of my brother:
Joel J. Kendler (1918–1935)

Psychology: A Science in Conflict

Plans and Purposes

1

1. Several interpretations of the nature of psychology are possible. An understanding of contemporary psychology demands an appreciation of both the different methodological assumptions that underlie various interpretations and the distinctive kinds of knowledge they produce. Such clarification can best be accomplished by analyzing psychology as it is rather than as it should be. In this chapter the orienting attitudes of the proposed epistemological analysis are described.

PROBLEMS

Psychology is an ambiguous science. Arguments rage about the nature of the discipline: what it is and what it should be. This book aims to clarify some of the basic issues of this continuing debate by analyzing three interrelated problems: the nature of psychology's empirical methods, the criteria employed to arrive at psychological truths, and the principles that govern the application of psychological knowledge.

To reveal the structure of psychology requires a systematic plan, and yet no predetermined set of logical or empirical operations are available for such a task. Therefore, one is forced to make personal decisions to guide a rational analysis while recognizing that these decisions cannot command acceptance in the same sense that a logical proof or an experimental fact can.

To compensate for this inevitable arbitrariness of any methodological plan, it is necessary to make clear its goals and orienting attitudes. My intention is to offer a detached analysis of the structure of contemporary psychology that will identify both common themes and discordant notes. This analysis will be guided by five predilections, which will presently be elaborated. First, psychology will be described as it is and not in any idealized version. Second, the goal will be illumination and not prescription. Third, the methodological analysis will be that of a psychologist rather than of a philosopher of science. Fourth, since knowledge is an end-product of human behavior, the psychology of the scientist and the sociology of the community of psychologists will at times be considered when analyzing the nature of psychology. Fifth and last, my aim is not to achieve unanimous agreement about the epistemological decisions that are appropriate for psychology, an unrealistic and perhaps undesirable goal. Instead, my desire is to encourage collective understanding—the comprehension by all members of the community of psychologists—of the competing and contrasting methodological decisions that different groups of psychologists have made and can make in the future.

These five predilections will now be clarified and justified:

1. *Contrasting views of psychology.* The history of psychology testifies clearly to the fact that different conceptions of psychology are possible. More often than not, these contrasting positions have been justified on the basis of representing the real essence of psychology. Probably the most controversial question, and the one with the widest-ranging impact, has been whether psychology is the science of the "mind" or "behavior." Is there a true answer to such a question? Does some Platonic notion of psychology exist that has to be discovered? I think not. The nature of psychology can best be clarified by being both democratic and operational. Psychology is what psychologists do. If psychologists do basically different things, then there are basically different kinds of psychology.

2. *Methodological decisions: illumination versus prescription.* Methodological analyses of psychology in the past have frequently resulted in prescriptions that unhesitatingly offer eternal truths as to how research is to be done, what dependent variables to measure, what problems to investigate, what psychological

processes are fundamental, what questions are relevant, what answers are trivial, and what constitutes true explanation. In evaluating these prescriptions, some modestly proposed, others messianically, it must be noted that no universally accepted guidelines presently exist that specify the proper procedures a scientist should follow in the pursuit of "truth." From data collecting to theoretical interpretations, the scientist is constantly required to make many decisions that cannot be defended by appeals to truth or logic. To understand what these decisions are, what considerations encouraged their adoption, and what their consequences are, can be helpful in identifying and clarifying significant methodological issues in contemporary psychology. The aim of such an analysis will be illumination, not persuasion.

3. *Different perspectives in analyzing the methodology of psychology*. Though I am not a philosopher of science, this book might suggest that I am functioning as one. Such a conclusion would be based upon the assumption that an analysis of the structure of psychology is intrinsically a philosophical task regardless of who performs it. Such an assumption can be questioned. Although the philosophical and psychological orientations overlap in both sphere of interest and method of analysis, they are nevertheless far from equivalent in technique or purpose. Without denying Feigl's point that "philosophical analysis [is] continuous with scientific research" (1967, p. 160) one can nevertheless recognize that a philosophical perspective will yield a different view of psychology than will a research orientation. Perceiving psychological issues primarily within an empirical context, and for the moment the term *empirical* will be used in the broad sense of referring to any form of observation, encourages the isolation and identification of problems capable of empirical resolution. This does not mean that all methodological issues, even those that demand only linguistic clarification, will be fitted into an empirical mold, however inappropriate. Instead, many issues that will engage our attention will be perceived more in terms of their empirical substance than in terms of their philosophical content or background. For example, the mind-body problem, which has been pursued interminably in the history of philosophy, has led

to numerous competing resolutions such as interactionism, parallelism, epiphenomenalism, monism, and the identity hypothesis. From the viewpoint of many contemporary psychologists, these philosophical positions are irrelevant to the science of psychology, while to others they represent unnecessary prejudgments about empirical issues. Although such views may be considered by some philosophers to be excessively parochial, they do suggest that a methodologically oriented analysis of the nature of psychology by a psychologist will differ from that conducted by a philosopher. This is not surprising considering that the methods, purposes, and goals of the two disciplines differ.

The thrust of these comments should be obvious. This book is written from the perspective of a psychologist whose purpose is to reveal the structure of psychology. For the purpose of this book, being a a professional psychologist and at best an amateur philosopher has two advantages. Viewing psychology from within allows one to detect problems and issues not apparent from without. Ignoring subtle philosophical issues prevents one from becoming entangled in those that have no bearing on one's action as a psychologist. *In sum, my analysis may not be sufficient for the philosopher, but it may be necessary for the psychologist.*

4. *Psychological insights into methodological issues.* The relationship between a methodological analysis of science and the psychological analysis of a scientist is a source of much confusion. Two contradictory, oversimplified views illustrate how science is perceived when objective methodological criteria or subjective psychological factors are emphasized to the exclusion of the other. At one extreme is the completely rational view of science that states that from theoretical formulation to empirical investigation (or vice versa) every decision made by a scientist can be judged by objective "logical" considerations. The entire scientific enterprise is governed by completely rational rules that, if understood and implemented, will inevitably lead to "truth." Therefore to understand psychology one needs only to identify the rational rules that govern the scientific enterprise and determine whether they are being obeyed by the psychologist. The contrasting view is that the practice of science is governed by the personal tastes of

the individual scientist. The selection of one theory over another is not determined by rules of evidence but instead by personal preference. Understanding science depends not upon a logical analysis of its methods but instead upon a psychological comprehension of its practitioners.

Both views, objective and subjective, are oversimplified and obviously wrong, although they have been attributed to sophisticated and well-known interpretations of the philosophy of science, e.g., logical positivism is perceived as having tried to uncover an infallible recipe for conducting science in such a way that progress is guaranteed; Thomas Kuhn, in his widely read *The Structure of Scientific Revolutions* (1962) is interpreted as espousing the view that science is without rules and that only personal tastes dictate the acceptance and rejection of theories.

In addition to being distorted by oversimplification, these objective and subjective characterizations of science suffer from two fundamental misconceptions. First, they fail to recognize that the scientific method consists of a variety of activities not necessarily governed by the same standard of conduct. Although rules of logic govern one activity such as deducing the empirical consequences of theoretical assumptions, personal taste will determine the choice of a particular research problem (e.g., mother-child relationships or hypothalamic functioning) to investigate. Second, some scientific activities involve both rational choices and personal preferences. For example, in selecting a criterion for explanation, one may adopt a deductive framework with its implicit logical demands while simultaneously rejecting the deductive rigors of mathematics for a looser informal logic in order to obtain a wider explanatory scope for one's tentative theoretical hunches.

In discussing the relationship between a methodological analysis of science and the psychological analysis of the scientist, it becomes essential to clarify the meanings of subjective and objective scientific standards. On the most fundamental level, science is a sociopsychological enterprise, which simply means that all its activities are expressions of principles that govern human behavior. But this does not mean therefore that all decisions are subjective in the sense of reflecting personal taste. Consider a game of chess. A person decides to play chess in preference to checkers. Without going too deeply into the psychological reasons underlying his choice, we can nevertheless attribute it to a personal preference. Attributing the choice to personal preference does not mean that it is arational or irrational in the sense that the choice is without reason or unreasonable. The person finds chess more interesting and challenging, he enjoys reading chess magazines, he is an outstanding player, his father encouraged him to play chess, etc. All these reasons can be summarized in the simple statement that he prefers chess to checkers and therefore when given a choice he opts for the former. Although his choice is reasonable, it is not *demanded* by some explicit rule. An example of rule-governed behavior would be the restrictions placed upon the chess player when he moves the various pieces, e.g., bishop can be moved only along a diagonal while rooks are limited to moves along ranks and files. Whereas the choosing to play chess instead of checkers was an example of behavior controlled by personal preference, the decision to move a bishop along a diagonal is dictated by a socially adopted rule. Society demands that a bishop be moved along a diagonal and if one insists on moving it along a file, he will be prevented from playing the game that is conventionally called chess. Socially adopted rules clearly separate chess from non-chess, chess from checkers, and checkers from non-checkers.

The rules governing the movement of chess pieces do not control what pieces will be moved, only that they be shifted from one square to another in a specified way. The actual movement of pieces is not simply an expression of preference because some moves (e.g., opening the game by moving the King's Rook pawn) are counterproductive if one aims to win a chess game. The actual moves of a reasonable sophisticated player are controlled by principles of strategy. Although these principles are not as automatic and restrictive as the rules that govern the movement of pieces, they nevertheless place restraints upon behavior.

My intention is not to suggest that the scientific method is completely analogous to chess but instead to illustrate different kinds of behaviors that operate in science as well as in chess. Because science is completely and exclusively a human enterprise, the actions of scientists can be viewed solely within a sociopsychological framework. This does not mean, however, that all scientific behaviors are similar. As a first approximation I have suggested that a distinction can be made among three kinds of behavior that lie along a dimension of increasingly restrictive rules of conduct. At one extreme is behavior that is regulated by no rule but is simply an expression of preference. At the other extreme are rigid rules that must be strictly obeyed, while in between are behaviors governed by principles of strategy that allow some options.

The acknowledgment of science as a sociopsychological enterprise and the distinction among different kinds of preference-governed and rule-governed behaviors provide a frame of reference to discuss the role of the psychology of the scientist in analyzing the science of psychology. Although, in principle, deeper understanding of any human activity can be achieved by comprehending its psychological origins, this generalization has certain limits. Popper (1949), for example, thought it necessary to "distinguish sharply between the process of conceiving a new idea, and the methods and results of examining it logically." In the same vein, Reichenbach (1938) used the terms *context of discovery* and *context of justification* to distinguish between the form in which knowledge is subjectively created and the form in which the knowledge is communicated to others. The purpose of this distinction is to separate from empirical propositions, expressed either as statements of fact or as theoretical principles, those events that are irrelevant to the task of judging the proposition's meaning and validity. For example, when evaluating the electromagnetic theory of light, one does not have to understand all those psychological characteristics of Maxwell, such as his personality and thinking style, that were responsible for his famous formulation. To understand and judge the electromagnetic theory of light requires only knowledge of the theory itself. Consider an extreme example. A psychologist, under the influence of alcohol, formulates a new theory of reinforcement. Let us assume that the effects of alcohol played a major role in his "creative" act in the sense that the novel notion would not have occurred if he were sober. The theory cannot properly be rejected because the theorist was drunk. Such information is irrelevant, even when we know that alcoholic consumption can interfere with problem solving. The theory must be judged within the context of justification in its ability to integrate the facts of reinforcement.

Now that some limit has been set upon the psychological analysis of the scientific enterprise, attention will be directed to two ways in which the structure of psychology can be clarified by considering the psychology of the scientist. The first concern is with the motives and aspirations of the scientist that influence his adoption of specific methodological assumptions about the nature of psychology: its subject matter, mode of explanation, social role, etc. Psychology has become what influential psychologists have thought it should be. If the notion is rejected that various interpretations of the nature of psychology can be evaluated by how close they come to some single Platonic ideal, which must and can be revealed, then the competing conceptions can be better understood when the personal psychological reasons for their adoption become known. An attempt to understand the psychology of the psychologist need not be as difficult or complex as it would appear initially. Psychologists have usually been uninhibited about expressing the philosophical commitments underlying their views of science and society, and these commitments in turn have typically shaped their conception of psychology. Thus in trying to understand the structure of psychology, it not only becomes desirable but also necessary to comprehend the motives and aspirations of psychologists.

Nobody should be surprised to discover that conceptions of psychology have not always been articulated with such clarity that no doubt remains about their meaning. To overcome this ambiguity historians and methodologists frequently project their own biases into an original formulation, thus achieving explicitness at the expense of accuracy. An alternative method of clarifying a vague position is to interpret it consistently with the author's scientific style. An example of such an effort is Ghiselin's (1969) attempt to illuminate Darwin's evolutionary theory by reconstructing Darwin's methodological commitments to the hypothetico-deductive approach. Such efforts are psychological in nature because a person's methodological preferences are revealed by the analysis of the total range of his scientific behavior.

The second manner in which psychological analysis can be brought to bear upon methodological clarification is to consider behavioral evidence that is relevant to the scientist's data-collecting activities. For example, the question has been raised as to whether observations are biased in the direction of what the scientist expects or hopes to observe. In support of certain methodological positions (Hanson, 1958; Kuhn, 1962) the results of psychological experiments investigating perceptual processes have been cited. If evidence about the perceptual behavior is available, it would seem only proper that such information be used to clarify methodological issues. The question is not whether it is proper to use psychological evidence in analyzing methodological issues but instead whether the information is being used properly.

This brief discussion relating psychological and methodological analyses does not exhaust all possible sources of interaction. The point here is that in *some,* but not *all,* cases methodological discussions can profit by considering the psychology of the scientist.

5. *Collective understanding by psychologists of different methodological positions.* What is badly needed in contemporary psychology is a collective understanding about the present structure of psychology. Some perhaps do not share this view or value its goal. But it should be emphasized that collective understanding does not require unanimous agreement about what methodology is appropriate for psychology. Understanding, for example, the reasons for adopting conscious experience as the dependent variable in psychology does not require accepting such a decision. But intelligently rejecting this choice does demand an appreciation of the reasons for its acceptance. Collective understanding of the different methodological decisions not only should expose psychologists to alernatives that have been ignored or misunderstood

but also holds the promise of elevating the quality of methodological controversies.

PROLOGUE

The plan of this book is to analyze successively three basic and interrelated questions that face all psychologists: What is the subject matter of psychology? What are the criteria for understanding psychological events? What ethical principles underlie the application of psychological knowledge?

There is no one valid answer to these questions. Instead each question poses a "choice point" that permits alternative responses. These responses in turn raise further options. In essence, psychologists are confronted with a methodological maze that ultimately can lead to incompatible conceptions of psychology. The purpose of this book is to explore the various paths through this maze and to disentangle the numerous methodological and empirical issues associated with each path. This examination of the structure of psychology, which reveals a diversity of methodological assumptions and ultimate goals, inevitably raises questions about the future of psychology. This topic will receive attention in the last chapter.

Now that the orienting attitudes and the goals that will guide this effort to reveal the structure of contemporary psychology have been presented the analysis can begin.

The Data Base and *2*
Subject Matter of Psychology:
Part One

1. Psychology can be viewed as the science of the mind or as the science of behavior or as some combination of both. Whatever concept is chosen the data base is the observation of the scientist. The observational base of studying conscious experience or behavior is intrinsically subjective. Although equally subjective, the study of behavior is qualitatively different from the study of the mind. Behavior can be observed by many individuals thus permitting intersubjective agreement about behavioral events. In contrast, intersubjective agreement about conscious experience is doubtful because the event is available only to the scrutiny of the experiencing individual.

2. Behavior, an observable event independent of theoretical preconceptions, can be defined directly as an activity of an effector or indirectly as an event that modifies the environment. This dual-classification system is capable of incorporating certain forms of "meaningful" behavior.

3. The psychologist who wishes to systematically study consciousness has several options ranging from using trained introspectors to naive observers and from analyzing the mind into basic elements or processes to considering it a holistic entity. The history of psychology suggests that phenomenological research is incapable of achieving consensual agreement about the nature of mental events. Methodological preconceptions about the manner in which the mind is to be investigated determine what is observed.

13

4. The question is raised as to whether the unresolved phenomenological controversies in experiential psychology are methodologically
similar to unresolved theoretical disputes in behavioral psychology. This
similarity is denied because the roots of the experiential disagreements
result from observational differences while those of behavioral psychology are a consequence of theoretical limitations. In other words,
the observer and what is observed are separable in behavioral psychology but not in experiential psychology.

PSYCHOLOGY'S SUBJECT MATTER

Although academic psychology has passed its hundredth anniver-
sary, agreement about its proper subject matter has yet to be
reached. Is this state of affairs due to the absence of a sufficiently
penetrating and persuasive analysis that someday will be forthcoming? Or does the failure result from the problem itself: the
subject matter of psychology cannot be determined by any logical
or factual means that in the foreseeable future will lead to any
consensus among the members of the community who call themselves psychologists. By identifying and analyzing the decisions
that have led to various conceptions of psychology, this chapter
will offer arguments in favor of the second alternative.

The possibility will also be raised that a universal concurrence about the subject matter of psychology may be unachievable in principle because different subject matters are possible.
Although such a conclusion might sadden those who desire an
integrated discipline, a frank recognition of its intrinsic disunity
would do much to minimize those unnecessary and destructive
debates that have plagued psychology's past.

CONSCIOUS EXPERIENCE AND BEHAVIOR

Two extreme views have prevailed about the subject matter of
psychology: it should be solely conscious experience or solely be-

havior. Numerous compromises have been offered that, in one form or another, express the notion that psychology should study both. The roots of this argument are deeply embedded in the history of philosophy, an examination of which would no doubt help clarify the issues but would not lead to any meaningful resolution. For that, psychology must examine itself and discover the alternative solutions within its own historical and methodological frameworks.

Descartes (1596–1650) most clearly represents the dualistic heritage that influenced the development of the science of psychology. For Descartes the human being is a union of a psychological mind with a mechanical body. The mind is a thinking substance, conscious of itself and capable of being studied by self-observation. The body requires for its study the methods of natural science. Whereas the mind is free, the body is constrained by principles of physics. To overcome the separation between the mind and the body, Descartes postulated a mechanism for their interaction: the pineal body, which lies in the brain, is controlled by the mind, and in turn controls the body.

Descartes' conceptions touch upon fundamental epistemological and methodological problems that have continuously remained at center stage in the history of psychology. First, by postulating two worlds, one of the mind, the other of the matter, Descartes raised the question whether knowledge about each derives from different sources. Second, the Cartesian system anticipated the distinction between conscious experience and publicly observed behavior as the subject matter for the science of psychology. Third, the issue of appropriate methods for investigating mind and body was raised by Descartes with the suggestion that different procedures are required: introspection, observation from the inside, is needed to examine the mind while observation from the outside, the procedure of natural science, is required for the study of the body. Fourth, Descartes recognized the significance of the problem of the relationship between mind (conscious experience) and body (behavior). Although his proposed solution based upon the activities of the pineal gland possesses only historical interest, it must be recognized that the problem itself is still important and unresolved. Finally, Descartes suggested, consistent with Platonism, that the mind contained innate ideas such as notions of time and space as well as the existence of God. Whether ideas were innate or acquired became a source of debate among philosophers, and this argument was transformed for psychologists into a debate concerning the relative contributions, within their discipline, of heredity and environment.

The history of philosophy relevant to psychology since the time of Descartes has been concerned for the most part with variations of his ideas. My attention now will be focused on the source of empirical knowledge of mind (conscious experience) and body (behavior), and the subject matter of psychology—problems that are distinct but unfortunately have become muddled.

Data Base Versus Subject Matter

Many philosophers who rejected Cartesian dualism, particularly some of the British empiricists, stressed the priority of phenomenal experience—raw observations, sense data—as the foundation of all knowledge. Berkeley (1710), for example, concluded that events, objects, and sensations do not have "any existence out of the minds or thinking things which perceive them." This kind of philosophical speculation led to the conundrum familiar to most college freshmen: "Is there a sound in an uninhabited forest when a tree falls to the ground?" To anticipate future discussion the question becomes clarified when the distinction is made between physical and psychological measurement, between sound waves and sensations of sound. Within this context the appropriate answer becomes "Yes and No!"

From Berkeley's skepticism not too much intellectual distance had to be traversed to arrive at Mach's conclusion that all sciences, including physics and psychology, share a common data base—the sensory experience of the scientist. Mach's judgment anticipated positions adopted by apparently irreconcilable orientations: structuralism and behaviorism. Titchener (1910) states: "It is plain that all sciences have the same sort of subject matter;

they all deal with some aspect of the world of human experience."
Pratt, expressing a position consistent with methodological behaviorism (Bergmann, 1956), a position that asserts that behavior
can be investigated and explained without direct examination of
mental states, writes: "No science is capable of definition in terms
of subject matter, for the subject matter of all sciences is the
same. Some person, some scientist, makes a report on something
which he has observed . . . The physical sciences, the biological
sciences, and the mental sciences all make use of the same observational data. Psychology is a division of scientific labor, not a
subject matter" (1939, pp. 22–32).

How can such agreement be achieved by methodological
positions—structuralism and behaviorism—that expound such contrasting views of the subject matter of psychology? This agreement is partly illusory because it stems from the failure to distinguish between two possible meanings of the term *subject matter.*
Both Titchener and Pratt use *subject matter* to refer to the data
base of science, and both reach the same conclusion that the rock-
bottom foundation of all sciences is the phenomenal experience
of the observing scientist. But *subject matter* can be interpreted
within another context, that of characterizing the phenomena that
identify a discipline. Just as a course in French has a different
subject matter than a course in German, so does physics possess
a different subject matter than psychology. Although students in
introductory French and German courses are both learning,
among other things, to associate foreign words with their English
equivalents, the types of words involved are different. Similarly,
investigating the speed with which balls roll down an inclined
plane or the trajectory of a spacecraft involves a different set of
events than the study of a dog salivating to a tone or an adult
human solving a mathematical problem. The former deals with
the movements of inanimate objects while the latter deals with
the behavior of organisms, a discrimination that can be made in
a highly reliable fashion.

It could be argued, although not very persuasively, that the
behavior of organisms cannot be distinguished fundamentally
from physical principles that govern objects in motion because

ultimately behavioral principles can be reduced to laws of physics. Although a discussion of reductionism will be postponed until later (Chapter 4), it should be sufficient for the time being to state that even if the optimistic claims of reductionism were to be accepted, the discrimination between physical and behavioral phenomena—their observational characteristics—is still highly reliable. The concern with differences in subject matter, from the viewpoint of characterizing a set of phenomena, is not one of theoretical reductionism but instead one of being able to discriminate reliably between distinctive features of different sets of phenomena. (Editors of physical and psychological journals rarely if ever get confused about which discipline a manuscript properly belongs to.)

Subject matter, defined as the distinctive characteristics of a set of phenomena, is being emphasized because it identifies a central problem in the history of psychology. Whether psychology should have one or two subject matters—private conscious experience and/or objective behavior—has been a source of controversy for the major part of its history. Although both the structuralist and behaviorist schools agree that scientific knowledge is based upon a foundation of phenomenal experience, a discrimination was made between two kinds of such experience: the observations of one's private experience, such as feeling happy, and the observation of the public behavior of another organism, the recall of a list of words.

In preparing to deal with the practical problem of selecting an appropriate subject matter for psychology, it might be useful to shift from a historical-philosophical framework in judging the mind-body problem to the perspective of an empirically oriented psychologist who, while freeing himself of methodological preconceptions, seeks to assess the research potential of his discipline as the science of the mind or of behavior. The examination from this vantage point is not designed to resolve perennial disagreements concerning the mind-body problem either in psychology or philosophy, but instead to identify the options that are available to a psychological investigator who aspires to draw conclusions acceptable to his peers.

As noted, scientific choices are frequently an expression of "volitional decisions." These decisions can exert profound effects upon the structure of a science when they lead to a "volitional bifurcation" (Reichenbach, 1938), a choice between irreconcilable alternatives as was presumably the case when Wundt opted for psychology to be a science of the mind while Watson chose behavior to be the dependent variable in psychology. The term "volitional bifurcation" is particularly appropriate to characterize such decisions because it emphasizes the divergent directions that such choices force a science to take.

The Distinction Between Private Experience and Public Behavior

Is the distinction between mind, for the moment equated with phenomenal experience, and behavior, defined as publicly observed actions, valid or does it represent a conceptual confusion? One way of dealing with such a question is to transform it into a query about the independence of two kinds of observations: mental events and publicly observed behavior. This question has two components: (1) Can conscious experience be distinguished from public behavior? (2) If so, does it differ in its epistemological characteristics? Although these two issues cannot be completely isolated they will be analyzed separately.

The Observational Base of Experience and Behavior

The distinction between conscious experience and public behavior can be viewed from two observational perspectives: the person who is examining himself and the person who is examining another.

I can reliably distinguish between my observations of my conscious experience and my observations of my public behavior (sometimes only with the assistance of recording instruments)— my feelings of affection and my affectionate behavior, my intense anger and my angry outbursts. In other words, I am aware of the difference between my inner experience directly accessible only to myself and the behavioral acts that I and others can observe.

Unlike the case of a person distinguishing between his own conscious experience and public behavior, the individual who is examining another person can justify the distinction under consideration only by inference. I can directly observe another person's public behavior but can only infer his inner experience from introspective reports or some other form of public behavior.

One can easily be persuaded that the distinction is valid because one can observe it directly, plus the fact that others report a similar discrimination. On this basis it can be argued that it would be wise for psychologists to accept the validity of the distinction between private experience and public behavior without qualifications and leave any subtle epistemological issues to philosophers.

Accepting such a pragmatic conclusion appears both reasonable and desirable as long as one does not overextend its implications. First and foremost one must recognize that the ready acceptance of the consensual agreement about the distinction between one's own private experience and public behavior in no way elevates the observational base of private experience into the public domain. No matter how many individuals report that they have private experience, the fact remains that any particular private experience is accessible to only one person, the experiencing individual. To highlight this point consider the hypothetical example of a person who denies experiencing private feelings or thoughts. Although one would be encouraged to reject such a statement as mistaken or pathological one must recognize that such a rebuttal is not based upon direct contradictory observations. In other words, I cannot look into his mind to obtain contrary evidence. I cannot therefore conclude that his mindlessness is factually incorrect in the same sense that I can reject statements about his public behavior. If this mindless chap for example maintained that his reaction time fails to be increased by alcoholic consumption, I can prove him wrong (or perhaps correct) by a simple laboratory demonstration. We could both observe his public behavior but only he could observe his own private experience. Thus the assumption that all individuals have a mental life becomes less compelling when we seriously entertain the possibility of mindless persons. In the final analysis, the only mind whose existence I can be sure of is my own.

Within this context acceptance of the distinction between human minds and public behavior becomes a matter of choice since it is not demanded by logic, and its factual basis could conceivably be open to an unresolvable dispute. I may be overcautious in not rejecting the possibility of mindless humans and overconcerned with the problem of "other minds"; yet a greater danger than excessive prudence is that of disregarding special methodological problems entailed in researching other minds.

In any case, the psychologist, unlike the philosopher, must go beyond his analysis of the mind-body problem; he must cope with it both empirically and theoretically. In regard to the private experience/public behavior distinction, he can deny, ignore, or deal with it.

I choose the last alternative not because it is demanded by the dictates of science but because it simply seems to be a reasonable decision. I do not wish to be pushed from the reasonable concession that other minds cannot be directly observed to what I consider the unreasonable doubt that other minds exist. In short, I accept the existence of my own mind and intuitively trust the verbal reports of *the existence* of other minds. But I cannot ignore the decisionlike quality of my choice, a recognition that makes me particularly aware of problems associated with "other minds" and of methodological decisions that differ from my own.

The Epistemological Status of Experience and Behavior

Accepting the distinction between "subjective" experience and "objective" behavior raises the question as to whether these two kinds of events are epistemologically different. To clarify the issue consider a pedestrian example: I generate an image of a rat responding at a choice-point of a T-maze. Compare such an image with that of my observing a "real" rat in the "same" kind of situation. In one fundamental sense the "observations" of the imaged rat and the real rat are the same. Both observations are strictly subjective in that they are both experientially private, *directly* accessible to no one else but myself.

Although fundamentally similar in terms of their intrinsic

subjectivity, the two kinds of observations differ in an important pragmatic way. The observation of the image of the rat is strictly *intra*subjective in the sense that it is encased in my conscious experience, incapable of being perceived by anyone else. I am the *only* source of knowledge about his choice behavior, whether he turns left or right. I can transmit to somebody else information about the choice, but then the information becomes second-hand, no longer based on direct observation.

Observing a real rat at a choice-point allows for reaching *inter*subjective agreement. A group of observers with adequate vision, a knowledge of what is *left* and *right*, and a reasonable level of sobriety, should have no difficulty in reaching a unanimous agreement about the rat's choice. Of course, factors could operate to prevent achieving unanimous agreement: the criterion of a right or left response could be poorly defined thus producing disagreement when the rat darts into the right alley and then retraces and enters the left alley. Or false evidence could be reported: an observer could be a compulsive liar or a theoretically biased observer might "unconsciously" record a response to the left when in fact the rat went right.

These possible sources of disagreement or distortion of intersubjective evidence have important philosophical implications and raise practical problems for the experimenter. But these problems are of limited significance to the experimenter because they are so easily handled. Any competent and honest investigator will have no difficulty in arranging an experimental situation in which observers, regardless of theoretical persuasion, can achieve complete agreement about the choices of rats in a T-maze. And if incompetence or dishonesty were operating, subsequent replications would overcome the mischief created by the initial misleading results.

This analysis suggests that observations of "inner" and "outer" events are equally subjective but qualitatively different. Because of the nature of the world and the structure of our bodies, agreement about the occurrence of outer events can be achieved more easily than those of inner events. It is not the experience itself that distinguishes private from public observations but instead the availability of the observed event to the personal scrutiny of other observers. When an event can, in principle, be observed by more than one person, socially agreed upon criteria can be adopted to encourage observational agreement.

Admittedly, my treatment of the pragmatic advantages of observing "outer" as compared to "inner" events suggests the existence of a real world—an assumption that most scientists make implicitly or explicitly—but this *need* not lead to any conceptual confusions in regard to research or theorizing.[1]

Implications of the Distinction Between Experience and Behavior. A misconception common among many psychologists who accept the distinction between phenomenal experience and public behavior, and most do, is that the science of psychology is required to investigate both. Accepting the distinction implies nothing more than the distinction itself, i.e., private experience and public behavior are distinguishable, and each or both are possible subject matters for psychology. It does not follow that both are required to be investigated. A number of arguments could be offered to encourage the investigation of one subject matter to the exclusion or subordination of the other. One could argue: that public behavior can be profitably analyzed by the "methods" of natural science, or that human consciousness distinguishes man from animals and therefore should be the fundamental subject matter of psychology, or that both subject matters need be studied but with the realization that one is basic to the other in the sense that knowledge of it can lead to accurate predictions of the other, or that one should be studied because strategic considerations suggest that the understanding of one subject matter precedes the comprehension of the other, and so on.

All of these arguments can be defended rationally and convincingly. One cannot, however, demand acceptance of one and the rejection of the others on the basis of logic although at some future date, with the benefit of hindsight, the relative fruitfulness of the different orientations might become apparent.

1. The thorniest methodological problems created by the assumption of an external reality are involved with the criteria for explanation (see p. 117).

Once again this analysis identifies a significant volitional decision that psychologists have to make at the very beginning of their efforts. This decision typically is made with little or no thought, being more a result of educational training than personal deliberation. Regardless of the basis of its adoption, the decision exerts a profound effect on the character of a psychologist's psychology.

POSSIBLE SUBJECT MATTERS IN PSYCHOLOGY

Up to now my treatment of two possible subject matters for psychology[2] has been very general. No attempt was made to describe in any detail these subject matters—private experience and public behavior—beyond delineation for the purpose of mere identification. *Private experience refers to the raw phenomenal feelings, thoughts, and images that are directly observable only to the experiencing individual. Public behavior refers to the actions of an individual organism that can be observed by others.*

To understand these concepts and speculate about their possible interrelationships requires a more analytic treatment of private experience and public behavior. In the history of psychology

2. A modern cognitive psychologist might dispute the notion that psychologists are limited to a choice between two subject matters: conscious experience and behavior. He could argue that the true subject matter of psychology is "the functional organization of the mind," which strictly speaking cannot be reduced to either conscious experience or behavior. The mind's organization, according to this argument, is not totally revealed in conscious experience and so it could not be reflected in introspection. In a similar vein, even though behavior can serve as an indicator of the mind's organization, the two are not identical. The fallacy in this argument stems from the conflation of a theoretical statement with an observational one. "The functional organization of the mind" is not simply an observational statement but instead is a theoretical inference in the same sense as is the following statement: "The subject matter of psychology is the formation and strengthening of stimulus-response associations." "Behavior" and "conscious experience" refer directly to certain kinds of observations; "the functional organization of the mind" and "stimulus-response associations" refer to theoretical inferences about observational events.

the initial concern was with the mind followed by a shift of interest to behavior. This analysis begins in the opposite order first because the problems of analyzing public behavior are simpler than treating private experience and second because some special problems of analyzing private experience can be illuminated by knowledge of the methods used to describe behavior.

The Nature of Behavior

A one-sided debate has prevailed in psychology about the meaning of *behavior*. Critics of behaviorism insist that behavior is an ambiguous concept and therefore cannot serve as a satisfactory dependent variable for psychology. Behaviorists, for the most part, ignore these criticisms and go about their task of systematically studying behavior. If precise empirical laws involving behavior as a dependent variable can be discovered, then the concept of behavior is sufficiently clear. No additional rebuttal appears necessary to the argument that behavior cannot serve as a dependent variable for psychology. In reaction to such a defense critics of behaviorism suggest that perceiving behavior only in the context of specific response measures, such as the amount of salivation or frequency of bar pressing, is at the root of the behaviorist's failure to appreciate the ambiguity within a *general* concept of behavior that presumably applies to all forms of behavior. Thus although specific illustrations of behavior can be offered, no systematic, consistent definition can be formulated.

There are many problems in defining behavior, more than the typical behaviorist realizes, but the significance and extent of these difficulties depend on whether the concept of behavior is treated solely as a dependent variable completely isolated from efforts to explain it or as something embedded in a theoretical network.

In order to analyze the meaning of behavior it first becomes necessary to eliminate the confusion that springs from linking behavior in some fashion to conscious experience. A decision to investigate behavior does not imply that mental events are unreal.

Nor does it suggest that behavior can be employed as a mirror to reflect the inner workings of the mind. The adoption of behavior as the dependent variable has absolutely no implications for the role of conscious experience in psychology or for the relationship between experience and behavior.[3]

Early behaviorists, such as Watson, equated behavior with bodily movement. The notion of bodily action as the criterion of behavior immediately raises the issue of intent. Is a person behaving when his body is moved forward by some external force such as a fierce wind? Or is there any difference between the behavior of two persons who descend a flight of stairs, one by stepping down on the successive steps, the other by tripping at the head of the stairs and falling to the bottom? If these responses are treated solely as dependent variables, then the questions posed are not concerned with defining behavior but instead with explaining it. If one were to research the behavior of these two persons, defining behavior only in terms of an end product of going from location A to B, one would discover that the same change in position could be governed by different principles. Getting from the top of a staircase to the bottom need not result from a common cause, and no one who measures a particular form of behavior is automatically committed to the assumption that the same processes operate whenever a common response occurs. The questions concerning intent appear trivial to the empirically oriented behaviorist, who would immediately recognize that the pattern of behavior of being pushed by the wind is different from intentionally moving forward, or that falling downstairs involves different responses

3. It is also important to recognize that the choice of behavior as the subject matter of psychology has no implication for other methodological decisions such as the meaning of concepts, the nature of explanation, or the role of science in society. Historically, the selection of behavior as the dependent variable in psychology has been associated with the behaviorist movement, which seeks to make psychology a natural science in the same sense that biology, chemistry, and physics are. In the ensuing discussion of the nature of behavior, the relationship between behavioral phenomena and natural science principles will sometimes be mentioned; however, this does not imply that the choice of behavior as the subject matter of psychology demands a natural-science orientation.

from walking downstairs. Although these questions may be of interest to philosophers, they are of no immediate significance to the psychologist who studies behavior with a natural-science orientation.

A much more relevant concern with employing behavior as a dependent variable is the ease with which behavioral descriptions can be contaminated by phenomenological interpretations. Take, for example, the following behaviors: a boy throws a snowball at his teacher, a child writhes in pain in a dental chair. The behavior that is being observed in the first example is the throwing of a snowball that covers a trajectory from the boy's hand to the teacher's head; no intent is perceived. Similarly, in the second example the child is squirming, but no pain is observed. The observer reads into these situations an explanation of the behavior in line with his own past experience and phenomenology. If a boy hits somebody with his snowball he probably intended to, and if a child is writhing in the dental chair he is no doubt experiencing pain. Of course, the boy could have had defective aim and hit the wrong target, or perhaps he threw the snowball without any intent to hit anybody. The child may be writhing not from pain but perhaps from restlessness. The initial explanations offered are reasonable in the sense that they are probably true. Human beings learn to interpret behavior on the basis of their own phenomenological experiences, which they attribute to the person whose behavior they seek to explain. These experiences aid, at times, in interpreting the world, but such attributions are neither essentially true nor necessarily equivalent to a natural-science theory.

The problem raised by contaminating a description of behavior with phenomenological states is not a result of some intrinsic defect with behaviorism as a methodology but rather a consequence of the psychological difficulty of limiting descriptions of behavior to directly observed characteristics of responses. The difficulty is not insurmountable, but it can generate confusion and self-deception, especially when the mentalistic descriptions of behavior are uncritically accepted as explanations.

A final criticism of the decision to employ behavior as the sole dependent variable in psychology is that it eliminates from study such significant human events as contemplation, fantasy, and dreaming. What would life be without an inner life? This question raises profound issues that are better postponed until the concepts *behavior, understanding,* and *values* are clarified. First I will turn to the analysis of the meaning of *behavior*. It should be recognized that the agreement among behaviorists to study behavior does mean that they also share other methodological assumptions and strategic decisions as to how behavior should be investigated and understood. My sole concern will be with behavior itself as a dependent variable for the science of psychology.

Defining Behavior

Behavior, as defined by some dictionaries and the early behaviorists, refers to any activity of the organism. A moment's reflection reveals the unmanageable breadth of this definition. Numerous activities occur simultaneously ranging from movements of neural impulses along sensory nerves to gross muscular movements; from biochemical changes in the retina to hormonal secretions in the pituitary; from coping with the physical environment to interacting with the social environment. To search for laws or principles that would apply to such a variety of phenomena is an invitation to disaster. A more reasonable approach is to select a circumscribed definition of behavior that would have a fair chance of serving as a dependent variable for a large set of fruitful empirical relationships. Such a definition emerges not so much from rational prejudgments as from laboratory procedures. Conditioning, a popular methodology for most early behaviorists, was particularly influential in explicating the meaning of behavior.

There are basically two kinds of behavioral measures in conditioning—direct and indirect. Classical conditioning illustrates the former; changes in the activity of some effector organ, gland, or muscle, are directly measured. Pavlov demonstrated that a hungry dog exposed to repeated pairings of a tone with food would finally salivate at the sound of the tone alone. This salivary action, the conditioned response, is measured in terms of the amount of glandular secretion. Another example that uses a direct measure is the classical conditioning paradigm involving the pairing of a light (conditioned stimulus) with a faradic shock (unconditioned stimulus) applied through an electrode attached to a leg of a dog. After repeated pairings the light alone elicits muscular contractions in the leg. In both cases of direct measurement of salivation and muscular contraction, the performance of a specific organ is observed.

Indirect measures of behavior are illustrated in the instrumental conditioning procedures made famous by B. F. Skinner with the use of the so-called Skinner Box. An animal's response is instrumental in producing a reward, e.g., a pellet of food is delivered after a rat presses a lever or a pigeon pecks a disk. Although muscular changes are inevitably involved in such behavior, they are nevertheless ignored in the psychologist's observations. Electronic gadgetry records the movement of the lever or the disk, and such changes define the response. In other words, the behavior of the organism is measured indirectly in terms of its effect upon the environment.

Thus, conditioning provides two clear kinds of behavioral measures that lend themselves to high intersubjective agreement: a direct measure that reports effector activity and an indirect measure that describes what a response accomplishes.[4]

Evaluation of the Direct and Indirect Classification Schema

Are these measures of behavior satisfactory? Satisfactory for what? They are certainly satisfactory for providing reliable measures of conditioning, and satisfactory also for the accumulation of a large amount of information about conditioning. Heart rate, pupillary dilation, and other measures of effector functioning are

4. Some behaviorists would question the validity of the distinction between direct and indirect measures because both ultimately depend upon their environmental effects. A muscular movement, or the amount of salivation, is determined by its effect on some recording instrument. This reservation ignores the point that direct measures reflect specific effector activity whereas indirect measures do not. This distinction has both empirical and theoretical significance.

commonly used behavioral indices of attention, emotion, social processes, etc. Indirect measures, in turn, blanket the entire spectrum of experimental psychology, e.g., key-pressing responses in a concept identification problem, picking up and holding a snake in desensitization therapy.

Is satisfactoriness, in the sense of being intersubjectively reliable, the only standard by which direct and indirect measures of behavior can be judged? Two other criteria—inclusiveness and fruitfulness—might be considered in evaluating the adequacy of behavior measures. As used here, an inclusive classification schema would encompass the entire range of behavioral events; no form of behavior would be eliminated from consideration. It might be argued that meaningful behavior is excluded from the direct-indirect behavior classification schema.

Inclusiveness of the Dual-Classification Schema: Meaningful Behavior

What does "meaningful behavior" mean? Something is meaningful if it makes sense, if it can be translated into some language that is comprehensible. Behavior can be interpreted as meaningful in several different ways.

Operational Meaning Versus Theoretical Meaning. Perhaps the most important distinction in analyzing the meaning of *meaningful behavior* is that between operational and theoretical meaning. This distinction can be clarified by reviewing the criticism leveled against associationistic theories of learning by Gestalt psychologists who argued that the theories were based upon artificial tasks that lacked meaning to the experimental subjects. Thorndike's research on animal intelligence (1898) is one example. To study the course of learning of cats, dogs, and chickens, Thorndike designed a puzzle box that enclosed an animal and gave it full view of food located on the outside. The animal could escape and obtain the food by making an instrumental response such as pulling a loop, pressing a lever, or stepping on a platform. According to Thorndike, the subject learned to make the correct response "by trial and error with accidental success" (1898, p. 105). A cat, for example, tried a variety of responses such as pressing against the door, sticking its paw through the slats, and other "erroneous" acts that failed to open the door. Then by "accident" it would emit the appropriate instrumental response, escape, and consume the food.

Gestalt psychologists argued that there was no meaningful relationship between the act of pressing the platform and escaping from the box. There was no more reason to press on the platform than to insert the paw through the slats or lie down. Instead, meaningful behavior depends upon being able to perceive the rational relationship between the structure of the problem and the behavior required to solve it. Problem solving depends upon understanding, not "accidental success." An example of a meaningful problem is the task employed by Köhler (1925) in studying insight. In one of his experiments a banana was suspended from the top of a cage out of a chimpanzee's reach. Several boxes were scattered around the floor. The animal repeatedly jumped for the fruit without success. Eventually these futile leaps ceased, giving way to restless pacing. Then according to the report, the pacing stopped, and after some apparent contemplation the animal pushed the boxes below the banana and stacked them, enabling him to climb to the top and grab the fruit.

Köhler used the term *insight* to describe the problem-solving behavior of his chimpanzees. He assumed that *insight* was a consequence of a sudden change in the chimpanzee's perception of the problem. Instead of seeing the boxes and banana as isolated objects, the chimpanzee suddenly perceived them as related parts of the problem. As a result of *insight* (perceptual reorganization) problem solution occurred.

Gestalt psychologists essentially argued that a qualitative difference existed between learning based upon an arbitrary association and learning resulting from understanding rational relationships. An organism from his knowledge of the world had no reason to expect that the pressing of the platform would lead to escape, but he could anticipate that stacking the boxes would enable him to grab the bananas. The implication of this position is that a theory of learning based upon the formation of arbitrary associations that occur in puzzle boxes, and conditioning as well, would be inadequate to the task of explaining learning by understanding.

Although the Gestalt position has theoretical merit, it does not follow that methods of measuring behavior based upon "meaningless" behavior cannot be applied to the study of "meaningful" behavior. Such a conclusion results from conflating the issue of the validity of the theoretical distinction between two kinds of learning with the methodological issue of the inclusiveness of the direct-indirect classification of behavior. The dual-classification schema refers to observable characteristics of behavior (operational), not to causal factors (theoretical). There is no epistemological difference between observing a cat pressing a platform or a chimpanzee stacking a set of boxes even though the principles governing each form of behavior may differ. Meaningfulness, in the context discussed, is not an observable property of behavior but instead is an interpretation of the behavior that is observed. In other words, the insight of Köhler's apes was not in the responses of *stacking the boxes and grabbing the banana* but in the theory proposed to explain that behavior.

If the theoretical distinction between meaningful and meaningless processes in learning is made, then methods of measuring meaningfulness can be developed. It is important to recognize that the operational measures of meaningfulness are not equivalent to the theoretical processes that are assumed to influence them. Consider the case of clustering in free recall (Bousfield, 1953). Clustering can be demonstrated by presenting in random order sixty words, each word from one of four different conceptual categories, (e.g., animals, vegetables, men's names, and professions), to subjects. If immediately thereafter the subjects would list as many of the sixty words as they could recall, their lists would fall into clusters of concept-related words (e.g., lion, tiger, giraffe, pig; corn, pea, carrot; Dick, Jack, Paul; etc.). Assuming that the input order of the words from the different conceptual categories is random, the degree of clustering is determined by how closely the order of the subject's recall coincides with the distinct conceptual categories. The measure of clustering is a dependent variable that presumably reflects a rational principle that operates to determine memory. In the case of clustering the rational principle is the linguistic organization of words into conceptual categories. A subject, however, could behave rationally in a manner that would *reduce* the amount of clustering. For example, he might recall the sequence "plumber, Adam, garlic" because the name of his plumber is Adam whose breath frequently smells of garlic. For this subject the idiosyncratic rational principle underlying the sequence of his recall of these three words exerts more of an effect in determining this sequence of behavior than does the rational principle of clustering. This does not imply that clustering is a defective measure. It only emphasizes the distinction between clustering as an operationally defined attribute of behavior and as one of many theoretical processes that organize information into meaningful patterns.

Does our analysis of meaningful behavior extend beyond the laboratory to behavior in everyday life? Can the direct-indirect classification be applied, for example, to the behavior of a paranoid? His meaningful, but unjustified, paranoiac reactions can be measured indirectly by the discrepancy between his persecutory responses (e.g., hiding because "X is trying to kill me") and the objective social situation (e.g., X is his therapist who is attempting to help him). Direct measures may be possible in the future if, and when, neurophysiological correlates of paranoia are discovered.

In sum, the analysis offered distinguishes between operational and theoretical definitions of "meaningful behavior." This advances the argument that the direct-indirect behavioral classification is sufficiently broad to include meaningful behavior of the sort that is an expression of rational processes. However, it is important to recognize that no guarantee can be offered that measuring techniques designed to reflect rational processes will yield fruitful empirical relationships and lead to satisfactory theories. Scaling techniques to measure behavior are always experimental and tentative in nature, and their usefulness or "validity" cannot be prejudged. The value of such methods can only be discerned in relation to their empirical and theoretical yield.

The claim that the dual classification system is adequate for meaningful behavior does not imply the absence of practical and technical difficulties. Consider the question of when does a child emit his first word. A word in this context is not merely a sound; it possesses referential meaning. When does the sound *mama*, which is a common babble, first acquire meaning? The absence of criteria that would discriminate between the babble *mama* and the first occurrence of the word *mama* does not, however, reflect any intrinsic limitations of indirect measures of behavior; instead, it illustrates one of the many complexities of language development. In principle, there is no reason to believe that the discrimination between babbling and word formation can never be made, although more complicated measures of behavior (perhaps combinations and sequences of direct and indirect measures) may have to be developed. In addition, it may be discovered that the transition between the babble *mama* and the word *mama* is gradual, not discontinuous.

Phenomenological (Subjective) Meaning. The meaning of meaningful behavior that has just been described refers to a theoretical position that postulates the operation of certain rational processes that govern behavior. These rational processes, if they are to meet the demands of the dual classification system, must yield predictions or estimates of behavior that are intersubjectively defined. Another possible interpretation of *meaningful behavior* stems not from the perspective of the observing scientist but instead from that of the organism who is behaving. This kind of meaning emphasizes the meaning a situation has for the organism. It can be labeled a *phenomenological* or *subjective meaning*, and like theoretical meaning, can be explicated by reference to the Gestalt interpretation of insight. Recall that Gestalt psychologists suggested that a perceptual reorganization is required to achieve insight; the essential elements of the problem have to be perceived as related, not isolated, events. One possible interpretation of this assumption is that only by understanding the internal viewpoint of an organism is it ever possible to understand its actions. This position insists that the conscious experience of the organism cannot be bypassed if behavior is to be fully comprehended.

Although at first glance phenomenological (subjective) meaning appears to be excluded from behavioristic psychology, a moment's reflection would suggest otherwise. The central issue is the manner in which the phenomenological meaning is ascertained. Behavioristic psychology accepts the distinction between intrasubjective and intersubjective evidence and insists that psychological data meets the requirements of the latter. If phenomenological meaning is defined *intra*subjectively, unavailable to the inspection of others, then it fails to meet the demands of the direct-indirect classification schema and therefore is excluded from behavioristic psychology. As previously noted, behavioristic psychology need not deny the existence of conscious experience, but it does recognize methodological limitations associated with *direct* investigations of the mind. If phenomenological meaning is viewed from a different methodological perspective, not from direct raw experience but instead as an inferred "state of mind," then its admissibility into a behavioral psychology based upon public observation becomes possible and, as some would argue, desirable. Verbal reports of inner states are the most likely candidates, but certainly not the only, upon which to infer a model of the mind. Such reports of a person's inner state are epistemologically no different from any other kind of publicly observable behavior, but it must be recognized that the verbal report, not the conscious experience, is the basic sense observation.

The position of raw phenomenal experience in a behavioral psychology that demands publicly observable events as the foundation of its knowledge is a source of much controversy as well as confusion in the history of psychology. Too often behaviorism is conceived of as a monolithic orientation instead of as a group of methodological positions that share common principles. The fundamental assumption is that the subject matter of psychology is publicly observed behavior. Adopting that position leaves a wide variety of options in regard to the treatment of phenomenal experience. At one extreme would be an *epiphenomenal behaviorism* that rejects as unnecessary all inferences from mental processes; at the other extreme would be a *subjective behaviorism* that strives to explain behavior in an objective fashion on the basis of a model of the mind. In between would be a variety of forms of *pragmatic behaviorism* that would infer phenomenal processes only when the demands for explaining a particular kind of behavior requires it.

Transcendental Meaning. One kind of "meaningful" behavior remains to be discussed, *transcendental meaning*. This concept refers to the general notion that life has a meaning: human beings individually and collectively strive toward certain goals and seek appropriate standards of conduct. Such ambiguous and popular phrases as "life's meaning," "self-fulfillment," "meaningful relationship," and others are used to express the idea that life has a purpose. Transcendental meaning, in the above sense, expresses a common theme in most, if not all, religious doctrines. Within this context, the statements implied by transcendental meaning are not falsifiable in that empirical evidence can, in principle, be obtained to deny their validity.

Transcendental meaning is obviously antithetical to a behaviorist psychology, which is designed to employ natural-science methods in order to arrive at psychological truths. However, like phenomenological meaning, it is important to recognize that some feature of transcendental meaning might be able to be incorporated within an empirically oriented behaviorism. To do this, one must understand that a behaviorist methodology is not wedded to a strong environmental or hereditary position; although leading behaviorists, for social and personal reasons, have tended to align themselves with the former. When the problem of transcendental meaning is removed from its ethical and spiritual context, it can be interpreted in terms of genetic predispositions in regard to human motivation and social behavior. If the idea is accepted that human behavior is not completely malleable, then one can suggest that certain classes of behavior are more likely to occur and be maintained than others. Thus the empirical question can be asked as to whether certain ethical positions and forms of social organization are more in tune with the genetic preprogramming of human behavior than are others. Presumably, if such questions are stripped of ethical and cultural biases—and one cannot overestimate the difficulty of accomplishing this—then empirical issues will remain, the implications of which can be checked by investigations employing direct and indirect behavioral measures.

A Closing Comment on Inclusiveness. In concluding this discussion of the inclusiveness of the dual-classification schema, it should be noted that although direct and indirect measures of behavior emerged from the early behaviorists' devotion to conditioning, there are no a priori reasons to believe that such kinds of measures are inappropriate for investigating any other form of behavior. One could suggest that measures of behavior that are used to study "meaningful behavior" should emanate from theoretical considerations instead of being borrowed from a research problem that was initially conceived as being devoid of cognitive involvement. Such a criticism is based upon the faulty notion that the dual-classification system represents an a priori prescription as to how the initial work in conditioning could, and should, be conducted. In actual fact, the direct and indirect conceptions of behavior did not emerge from rational considerations but instead from an ad hoc methodological analysis of how behavior was defined in conditioning. The fact that the dual-classification schema is an effective representation of behavior in conditioning in no way limits its applicability to other forms of behavior.

Fruitfulness of the Dual-Classification System

The answer to the question about whether direct and indirect measures of behavior are fruitful depends upon a criterion of fruitfulness. Various orientations in contemporary psychology do not share a common goal for psychological inquiry. Consequently, before the query about fruitfulness can be answered, an appropriate yardstick must be adopted. Such yardsticks will be the topic of discussion in Chapters 4 and 5. For the time being, however, the conclusion can be drawn that direct and indirect measures have served the aims of two different streams of behavioristic psychology, the one concerned with formulating abstract theories of behavior, the other with describing behavior with an eye to control it. This, of course, does not rule out the possibility that a more suitable and fruitful behavioral classification than the direct-indirect system can be developed in the future.

Some Final Comments about Behavioral Measures. Two additional points must be made. The first concerns the relationship between direct and indirect measures of behavior, the second concerns a possible misinterpretation of the sequence of topics of this methodological analysis.

Distinguishing between two forms of measuring behavior immediately raises the question of the relationship between the two and the possibility that one is more basic than the other. These are not methodological issues but empirical and theoretical ones. The empirical relationship between direct and indirect measures can only be revealed by empirical investigations that monitor changes in both types of responses. For example, in instrumental conditioning it would be possible to discover the relationship, as conditioning progresses, between muscular movements and a lever-pressing response. Which measure is more basic is purely a theoretical issue assuming that one accepts as the goal of scientific inquiry the formulation of a satisfactory theory. The more basic measure, for any empirical phenomenon, is the one that is employed in a theory that can explain the empirical laws involving the other measure. For the present, however, the question of which is more basic is not an immediate issue and would be best sidetracked until it becomes one. It would seem that certain empirical problems are more easily investigated with one than with the other measure. Pragmatic considerations often serve as the best guide for methodological decisions.

The reader may get the impression that all psychologists are confronted with an orderly sequence of methodological issues beginning with a choice of subject matters, proceeding to a selection of a suitable dependent variable, and followed by the adoption of a criterion of understanding, and so on. The intent of my analysis is not to construct a methodological maze with a predetermined succession of choice points that must be traversed by all psychologists. That would be misleading. Methodological questions are highly interrelated, and the order of making decisions can vary from psychologist to psychologist. In some cases, all the significant decisions are made simultaneously, while in other cases some decisions are isolated from others. My aim is not to prescribe the order in which the significant methodological decisions should be made. Instead, my concern is to rationally reconstruct psychology in a systematic fashion so that the fundamental decisions are laid bare. It is conceivable that a similar analytic effort could be made that would proceed with an entirely different order of issues. Starting from the data base of psychology seems to be an appropriate beginning.

The Nature of Consciousness

The behaviorist revolution in America was successful in directing psychologists' attention from the study of the mind to behavior. Although the study of consciousness (sometimes referred to as phenomenology or experientialism) was discouraged, it was never abandoned. A topic that permeates human existence and is of central concern to both the worlds of art and religion inevitably had to attract the interest of some psychologists.

Interest in the *systematic* study of consciousness has waxed and waned over the years. It was given a boost more than a decade ago when an internal immigration to the examination of the mind took place in an attempt to escape from the apparently, or truly, insoluble problems of the "real" world. Fascination with "mind-expanding" drugs and a reawakened interest in religion were expressions of this renewed interest in consciousness. At the same time, modern behaviorists, freed of the need to polemicize the conflict between subjective experience and public behavior, began to view the problem of the subject matter of psychology more tolerantly. The issue shifted from whether conscious experience should be investigated to whether it could be investigated without sacrificing a natural-science approach. This is the issue that will now be analyzed, not to legislate the fundamental ingredients of science in order to excommunicate "unscientific" approaches, but rather to identify conflicting methodological positions that establish different standards for evaluating knowledge.

As was the case for behavior, *consciousness* will be treated as an entity in itself. My first concern will be with pure phenomenology. Then the possible relationships between conscious experience and behavior or neurophysiology will be explored.

Two related questions come to the fore when contemplating the study of mind. Can conscious experience, which up to this point has been dealt with in a global manner, be analyzed into some fundamental scheme analogous in inclusiveness to direct and indirect measures of *behavior?* How can the mind be systematically studied if a given mental event is accessible to only one observer?

Options in Experiential Research

My qualifications to cope with the problems of describing conscious experience may be immediately challenged on the basis that for such a task only an experienced phenomenologist is competent. However, my aim is not to propose a phenomenological description that will lay bare the essential characteristics of the mind. That is an empirical problem to be solved by phenomenological research. Instead, my purpose is to examine the problem of describing conscious experience in some systematic fashion. If the issues are not strictly parochial then presumably they can be analyzed by a general psychologist.

Numerous options confront the investigator who initiates experiential research. Not only can he look at the mind in different ways, but he also can sense different mental events. The phenomenologist can insist that the perception of mental events demands a trained observer who can impartially sense the evidence of immediate experience. Or he can adopt an opposing view by "assuming" that consciousness can only be accurately observed in a naive and relaxed fashion in the absence of any presuppositions. He can divorce his self-observation completely from physical stimulation or systematically attempt to relate the two. The mind can be conceived as consisting of basic elements of experiences, such as sensations, images, and feelings; or as an activity in which all psychic events contain an act and an object; or as an undifferentiated, inchoate mass of experiences that can be described and interpreted both in an analytic and holistic fashion.

This brief enumeration of possible methods and conceivable mental events demonstrates, as any history of psychology (e.g., Boring, 1950) will show, that different frames of reference, both in regard to the method of observation and the kinds of mental events observed, are possible.

What are the implications of these differences? Will these differences inevitably produce conflicting pictures of the mind or merely varying views that can potentially be combined into a single integrated portrait? The answer to these questions will depend upon the criteria adopted to evaluate the validity of various conceptions of the mind.

Phenomenology or Phenomenologies?

In judging the adequacy of different conceptions of consciousness one can pursue a dialectical approach and conclude that a universal agreement about the nature of the mind is *in principle* beyond reach. Three completely different reasons for this conclusion are possible. First, everybody is endowed with a unique mind, and therefore, the formulation of general principles that apply to all minds is impossible. Second, phenomenal experience is not independent of the method used for observation; and consequently, different methods of phenomenological research must yield different descriptions. Third, the language used to describe mental experience will influence its content, and even if a common method is utilized, descriptions employing different languages will yield fundamentally different pictures of the mind.

Arguments that invoke the notion that some goal is *in principle* unachievable usually leaves this writer cold because of their strong commitments to untested prejudgments and to the limits they place upon human ingenuity. Perhaps such restrictive positions should be reserved for obvious logical impossibilities such as the construction of a triangular rectangle. A more reasonable way of judging the possibility of formulating a single valid conception of mental events would be to base one's inference on historical evidence. When this is done the conclusion drawn is that a universally agreed-upon representation of the mind, although not impossible, is highly improbable.

Such a position would accept the notion that general mental principles may operate but recognize the overwhelming obstacles that are in the path of achieving consensual agreement about their identification. The conceptual framework one adopts to examine the mind influences the verbal description of consciousness, and consequently divergent views will result as long as different presuppositions are adopted. In opposition to such a position one can argue that observing the mind, or any other phenomenon, demands some prejudgments in order to make empirical observations. But when such prejudgments are considered as heuristic rather than final positions, they can be modified, and even abandoned, in the face of evidence. If observations of mental events are pursued with diligence, one would hope that the empirical results will ultimately reshape the initial prejudgements in the direction of developing methods of observations that will be capable of achieving consensual agreement.

Does history offer any optimism for the claim that an open-minded, diligent pursuit of the problems of the mind will yield a picture of the mind capable of achieving consensual agreement? Although past failures cannot rule out future successes, prior controversies about the nature of the mind do not leave much room for optimism that the study of the mind as an entity in itself will ultimately yield any generally agreed-upon interpretation.

Titchener proclaimed that his sensationalistic orientation to the study of the mind was "simply an heuristic principle, accepted and applied for what it is worth in the search for the mental elements" (1909, p. 34). Although suggesting an open-minded view, the important restriction of the methodological "search for the mental elements" should not be overlooked. In the controversies that structuralists in general and Titchener in particular engaged in, disagreements with their own positions were attributed to faulty methods of self-observation by their critics. This does not mean that the structuralists were incapable of changing their descriptions in light of empirical evidence. Modifications of descriptions of the mind occurred frequently, and disagreements among structuralists were common—e.g., Nafe (1927) rejected Titchener's distinction between *feelings* and *sensations,* concluding that the former mental event could be reduced to the latter. But such modifications and disagreements did not extend beyond the methodological commitment to analyze consciousness into basic elements or processes.

It will be informative to briefly review some controversies about the nature of the mind in order to achieve an appropriate perspective for judging the source of such disputes. Brentano conceptualized consciousness as consisting of psychical acts instead of the elementary sensations of the structuralists.[5] An implication of Brentano's view is that psychical events can be analyzed into act and content, a view that did not jibe with the introspective reports of others. Whereas Brentano maintained all psychical acts had to have a content, others maintained that affective acts could be experienced independent of any content. To be specific, Brentano felt you had to be happy about something; others (e.g., Külpe, 1909) concluded you can just experience happiness. Titchener suggested that Brentano's conception of the mind was generated by an inappropriate methodology: "The act-and-content psychology . . . [is] a psychology not of observation but of reflection" (Titchener, 1909, p. 53). That is, Brentano was not accurately observing conscious experience; his reports were contaminated by an inappropriate perspective.

Another disagreement exhibited a similar pattern; the partici-

5. Although the distinction between conceptualizing consciousness as sensations or as acts is embedded in subtle and complex philosophical and phenomenological issues (Boring, 1950), I feel that this distinction represents a difference similar to that between *stimulus* and *response;* sensations are psychical stimuli that represent the mental environment, while acts are psychical responses that refer to the activity of the mind. For a sophisticated behaviorist turned naive phenomenologist, it would appear that a complete understanding of consciousness requires not only an adequate description of the content of mental experience but also a comprehension of the principles governing the production of these sensations (Kendler, 1970; Skinner, 1969). In other words, there are two aspects of consciousness: its content and its activity.

pants explained away conflicting phenomenological descriptions by attributing them to defective methods of self-observation. Boring recounts the vitriolic controversy between Wundt and Stumpf on the topic of tonal distance.

> The clash seemed to have arisen because Stumpf leaned heavily upon his own musical sophistication, while Wundt relied on the laboratory results with apparatus and the psychophysical methods. Whatever is obtained under unprejudiced, carefully controlled experimental conditions must be right, Wundt virtually said. If the laboratory yields results that are obviously contrary to expert musical experience, they must be wrong, was Stumpf's rejoinder (Boring, 1950, p. 365).

William James, who some consider the greatest introspector of all times,[6] noted difficulties in observing the transition between successive experiences in the stream of thought. "When the rate is slow, we are aware of the object of our thought in a comparatively restful and stable way. When rapid, we are aware of a passage, a relation, a transition *from* it, or *between* it and something else." Consciousness, "like a bird's life, seems to be made up of an alternation of flights and perchings." James thus distinguishes between the substantive and transitive parts of the stream of thought.

> Now it is very difficult, introspectively, to see the transitive parts for what they really are . . . The rush of the thought is so headlong that it almost brings us up at the conclusion before we can arrest it . . . The attempt at introspective analysis in these cases is in fact like seizing a spinning top to catch its motion, or trying to turn up the gas quickly enough to see how the darkness looks (1890, pp. 243–44).

The fleeting quality of the transition that James describes does not reflect what truly is in consciousness, Titchener argued, but instead defective observation. "If James had looked away

6. This claim, in itself, highlights fundamental difficulties in interpreting phenomenological research. What is James' presumed superiority a result of? An abnormal sensitivity to conscious events, an ability to have more subtle experiences than others, or an exceptional writing style that encourages an empathic response in the reader? Phenomenological research would have difficulty in disentangling these various possibilities.

from 'awareness of object' and 'awareness of relation' and had looked toward the actual content of consciousness, we should not have heard of the top and the gas jet" (1909, p. 29).

The discussion about the nature of the mind will be concluded by referring to the debate about "imageless thought" (Woodworth, 1938). Several experimenters independently reported that some subjects, when responding to simple word-association tasks or when interpreting Nietzsche's aphorisms, failed to observe any images in their consciousness. Wundt considered these results to be invalid; images do occur while thinking. Imageless thought, for Wundt, was an outcome of a defective methodology; one cannot observe thought while thinking. Nevertheless, thought experiments were conducted in Titchener's laboratory. The results indicated the presence of images in consciousness. Titchener concluded that imageless thought was a consequence of defective introspection. Woodworth, in reviewing the controversy, suggested that "the whole question may well be shelved as permanently debatable and insoluble" (1938, p. 788). The controversy about imageless thought led to a disenchantment with the introspective method and encouraged the emergence of behaviorism.

The Source of Unresolved Phenomenological Controversies. One could add countless other examples of unresolved controversies about reports of self-observations. History demonstrates that no general phenomenological method was ever adopted that could resolve these controversies for the entire psychological community. In light of this historical evidence one can conclude that pure phenomenology, unlike natural science, can never yield universally valid conclusions. That is, any proposed picture of the mind will never be accepted as "universally" valid in the same sense that evolutionary theory or the theory of relativity is. The justification for this conclusion could be either a radical subjectivist assumption that every phenomenological description is valid regardless of its incompatibility with others or a methodological position that decrees that every method employed to observe consciousness is based on some presuppositions and these presuppositions will inevitably influence what will be observed.

In rebuttal, the argument can be advanced that this pessimism about phenomenology is based upon a fundamental mis-understanding. A universally valid description of human con-sciousness is a false goal because human minds do differ in their sensitivities, content, feelings, etc., and therefore differences in phenomenological descriptions are bound to occur and persist just as do individual differences in behavior.

In support of this line of argument one can offer the results of psychophysical investigations that meet the methodological standards of a behavioristic psychology. They reveal that indi-viduals do differ in their sensory capacities. Those with acute color vision can form a language community (Koch, 1964) and discuss among themselves esoteric aspects of color sensations and delicate differences in hue that would possess no meaning for others. Phenomenology within this context, it can be argued, is no different from behavioristic psychology, which obviously rec-ognizes individual differences.

Although this argument, at first glance, appears reasonable, it overlooks an important difference between pure phenomenol-ogy and behavioristic psychology. Whereas the abnormal color sensitivities can be publicly displayed by psychophysical meth-ods, experiential sensitivities (e.g., beauty) that have not been correlated to publicly observed stimulus events cannot. This does not automatically mean that such sensitivities do not operate, but one cannot be sure that they do. Is the "hypersensitive" art critic at a gallery exhibition who is reporting rhapsodic experiences in fact having them or indulging in social gamesmanship encour-aged by prior social reinforcements? In sum, unresolvable con-troversies in experiential psychology do not possess the same epistemological status as individual differences do in behavioral psychology; they fail to meet the standards of intersubjective agreement.

Another possible interpretation of the phenomenological dis-putes is that they represent unresolved theoretical differences, which are certainly not peculiar to phenomenology since they occur with great frequency in behavioral psychology. One can point to the controversies of latent learning, perceptual defense, one-trial learning, continuity versus noncontinuity conceptions of discrimination learning, racial differences in intelligence, operant conditioning of verbal responses, the organization of attitudes, and many others, all of which have been contested within behavioral psychology and all of which have failed to yield an unqualified conclusion supported by consensual agreement of the scientific community. In rebuttal, a behavioral psychologist would argue that theoretical differences are not methodologically equivalent to disputes about basic observational events. The latent-learning controversy, in which I was involved during the early period of my research career, entailed a host of theoretical issues about which the competing theories (of animal learning), the Hull-Spence S-R model and the Tolman cognitive map formulation, were not articulated with sufficient clarity to yield unambiguous implications for all of the empirical problems studied. Some of the concepts that proved to be unclear were *zero reinforcement, drive satiation, perceptual awareness,* and *fractional anticipatory goal responses.* The point at issue is whether the theoretical disputes in behavioral psychology spring from disagreements about basic empirical observations, e.g., whether a rat turned left or right in a T-maze or entered or did not enter a blind alley in a multi-unit maze. If these observations are the source of the disagreements, as they are in phenomenological psychology (e.g., does one experience images when responding to the word *chair* or *grass* in a simple word-association task?), then the conclusion can be drawn that the unresolvable disputes in phenomenological psychology do not set off this discipline from behavioral psychology.

In the larger context of the philosophy of science, we have become enmeshed in two controversial issues: whether observational terms can be distinguished from theoretical terms and whether we can ever know if one theory is true and another is false. These are exceedingly controversial and complex issues in the philosophy of science. Consistent with the plan of this book I will avoid the philosophical problems that are not immediately relevant to the problems under scrutiny. This does not mean that psychologists do not have much to learn from various conceptions of the philosophy of science, past and present, but instead it means that for the active researcher and theorist, viewing the methodological issues within a restricted psychological framework may have special advantages.[7]

Observational Purity

My present concern will be with the problem of whether a scientist's perceptions are immaculate, whether his observations are free of influences from his experiences and preconceptions (the issue of the "truth" of theories will be treated in Chapters 4 and 5). To cope with this general problem effectively it must be analyzed into separate issues. This can be done by examining the statement that denies that perceptions can be immaculate: "Observer and observed are not separable" (Kessel, 1969, p. 1002).

There is no question that an observer's experience and preconceptions will determine what is observed. This can be accomplished in three major ways: (1) observers can observe different situations; (2) observers can attend to different events in the same situation; and (3) their preconceptions can determine what they observe when attending to the same event. Let me now analyze each of these alternatives and then examine their implications for the problem of achieving consensual agreement about basic observational evidence.

It may appear trivial to note that a scientist's interest will determine what he will observe. But it does represent an exam-

7. A common ploy in some current methodological discussions (e.g., Koch, 1964) is to disparage a particular psychological orientation (e.g., behaviorism) by claiming that it is based upon an inappropriate philosophical position (e.g., logical positivism) that has long been rejected by the philosophical community. The implications that flow from such a criticism are: (1) if a particular conception of science is not completely right, it must be completely wrong and hence possesses no value for psychology; (2) a unanimity of opinion about specific philosophical positions prevails among philosophers of science; (3) different philosophies of science and methodological orientations in psychology represent fixed positions resistant to all change; (4) some philosophical paradigm is appropriate to all sciences at all stages of development; and (5) psychologists would be well-advised to seek Good Housekeeping-type Seals of Approval for their methodological positions from philosophers of science who are currently in vogue.

ple of how observations are influenced by the observer. The observer's interest patterns are basic to the division of psychology into different research areas: learning, cognition, personality, social behavior, and so on. They are responsible for what events a psychologist observes: pigeons pecking disks, children choosing cards in a visual-learning discrimination task, patients ventilating their emotional hang-ups in psychotherapeutic sessions, and social groups behaving in natural settings.

Observers' in the same situation can also observe different events. This point has been demonstrated repeatedly in discrimination-learning problems in which organisms are required to choose one of two visual displays. Such learning can be accelerated or retarded depending upon whether or not the subject is observing the features of the stimulus displays that are correlated with reinforcement (e.g., Ehrenfreund, 1948). In a similar vein it has been demonstrated that older children perform in a superior manner to younger children in a perceptual-learning task because they scan the visual displays more systematically and hence are better able to detect the important similarities and differences (Vurpillot, 1968).

Now if we shift our perspective from that of an experimental subject observing stimulus displays to that of an experimenter observing behavior, we find similar processes at work. In the same experimental situation different experimenters can be observing different events. A noted example in the history of learning theory is the different observations made in instrumental bar-pressing conditioning situations by a "Skinnerian" and a "Guthrien"—the former observing whether the bar is depressed and the latter, the subject's pattern of movement when depressing it. This difference in what is observed is an expression of the theoretical preconceptions of the observer as to what are the significant data.

I learned early in my research career that what the experimenter observes, or fails to observe, can be at the heart of a theoretical dispute. One aspect of the latent learning controversy, which raged during the 1940s and early 50s, illustrates this point. The empirical question at issue was whether rats who traversed a multiunit maze but who were not fed when they reached the goal box learned as much about the maze pattern as those who were fed. The initial California latent learning studies (Blodgett, 1929; Tolman & Honzik, 1931) offered an affirmative response; when food was introduced into the goal box for the previously nonfed subjects, their maze performance (blind alley entrances) on the next trial matched those who had consistently received food. Such evidence was interpreted to be consistent with Tolman's cognitive theory of animal learning, which postulated that reward was not necessary for learning. The subjects not fed in the goal box learned as much about the structure of the maze as did the food-rewarded group; the inferior performance of the former during the time they were not fed was due to the absence of an incentive to utilize their knowledge.

An underlying assumption of this analysis was that the equal performance of blind-alley entrances exhibited by the two groups *following* the introduction of food for the previously nonfed animals reflected equal amounts of learning (Kendler, 1952). I encouraged a doctoral student, Joseph Kanner, to test this assumption. His first chore was to replicate the California latent learning phenomenon, no easy task considering that other attempts had failed (MacCorquodale & Meehl, 1948; Reynolds, 1950). After several failures Kanner (1954) nevertheless was able to discover some of the fundamental variables in the California latent learning phenomenon and was then able to replicate the original finding. Of great interest were the striking differences observed, aside from blind-alley entrances, in the maze behavior of the food and nonfood groups, the latter exhibiting marked signs of "fearfulness" suggesting that the motivational incentive conditions of the two groups were strikingly different. Additional research (Kanner, 1958) indicated that contrary to Tolman's original interpretation the two groups had *not* acquired "equal knowledge" about the structure of the maze.[8]

8. Kanner's study (1958) had little impact upon the latent learning controversy because at the time of its publication, interest in the problem had petered out as a consequence of the exhaustion of the combatants. As a result, a study for which I had predicted instant notoriety largely went unnoticed. Kanner still has 273 reprints of the 300 I encouraged him to purchase.

The point of the above is not to revive interest in the latent learning controversy (although it is still relevant to some fundamental theoretical issues) nor to argue in favor of one position over the other. All the issues in the controversy were not resolved because the competing theoretical formulations were much vaguer than initially thought and some of the participants failed to distinguish between separate theoretical problems. The latent learning data and the attempts to interpret them revealed the stark inadequacies of the competing theoretical structures. The psychological community, rightly or wrongly, finally decided that possible payoffs in new data and theoretical clarification did not justify continued efforts. In short, the controversy died at its own hands.

A close examination of this historically interesting dispute reveals that it did not concern disagreements about the same observational events. True, some phenomena were difficult to replicate, not because of any observational confusion as to what behavioral event occurred, but because of the combined effects of ignorance about the influence of some experimental operations and sloppy methods of replication. And the compulsion of many experimenters to prove competing theories wrong rather than clarify theoretical issues added to the general confusion. But fundamentally, the core of the difficulty lay with the imprecision of the competing formulations and the primitive state of knowledge about the effects of a large number of experimental operations, not with the theoretical pollution of observational statements.

Two ways in which a scientist's experiences and preconceptions can influence his observations have been noted. He can select different phenomena to observe, or he can limit his attention to certain features of an experimental situation while ignoring others, perhaps of greater potential importance. The first does not pose any special obstacle to the scholar who seeks to identify the different observations to which the different conceptions of behavior are linked. Distinguishing an operant-conditioning conception of behavior from one based upon a Piagetian model requires reconstruction of the observations from entirely different situations. Doing this may cause difficulties because of inadequate reporting of what is actually observed or contamination of observations with theoretical preconceptions. But with diligence and persistence, and the cooperation of the scientists who work within these conceptual frameworks, it should be possible for a scholar to identify the different observations made that are basic to these theoretical differences and to reveal the nature of the links (e.g., clear, vague, or nonexistent) between observational and theoretical statements.

Similarly, the observational support of conceptions that use the same experimental paradigm but that are interested in different events should provide no insurmountable obstacle for the scholar who desires to trace these conceptions back to observational events. Again it need be noted that the point of this analysis is not to argue that such observational reconstructions are easy or always possible. The argument advanced is that, in principle, in either of the two cases described—events in different empirical situations or different events in the same empirical situation—there should be no confusion between the two sets of observations underlying the different theoretical conceptions.

The influence of different backgrounds of scientists upon their observations of the *same event* is at the heart of the problem of distinguishing between observational and theoretical statements, i.e., deciding whether observational statements are unavoidably polluted by theoretical preconceptions. If they are then judging the relative merits of competing formulations that seek to interpret the "same" observations could be a hopeless task because the observers would be unable to agree about the basic evidence for which they are offering competing formulations. Behavioral psychology would be in almost the same predicament as experiential psychology; consensual agreement about basic facts would seem to be an unobtainable goal.

The study of perception provides information that is *relevant* to the methodological issue of whether observational statements must inevitably be contaminated or whether consensual agreement about observational events is a realizable goal for behavioral psychology. The problem in deciding between these two alternatives is determining what perceptual evidence is relevant and what interpretation is appropriate.

Figure 2.1

Numerous perceptual phenomena demonstrate that different observers looking at the same stimulus display will perceive different events. A reversible figure-ground design is one example of a visual pattern that can generate different perceptions. Figure 2.1 illustrates a stimulus display that can either be perceived as a vase or two faces in profile. What is it really? More about that, later.

Kuhn (1962), in his influential book *The Structure of Scientific Revolutions,* cites an experiment of Bruner and Postman (1949), to demonstrate the influence of a person's preconceptions on his observations. College students were briefly shown individual playing cards with instructions to identify them. Mixed in with the regular cards were incongruous ones such as a *black four of hearts*. Most students identified such a card as a *red four of hearts* or a *black four of spades*. That is, their perceptions were not determined *exclusively* by the physical characteristics of the cards but also by the conceptual categories that they had previously learned, black spades and red hearts.

A similar finding was obtained in an experimental demonstration of the influence that perception exerts on memory (Carmichael, Hogan, & Walter, 1932). Different subjects were shown the same outline figure (e.g., two circles connected by a straight line) each coupled with a different label (e.g., *eyeglasses* or *dumbbells*). Later the subjects were asked to draw from memory the figures they had been shown. Their drawings tended to be distorted in the direction of the label that was assigned to the drawing, i.e., the drawings were not remembered as they really were but rather were distorted in the directions as to how they were conceptualized.

Many other perceptual phenomena can be reported that are consistent with the principle that preconceptions *can* influence observations. We must conclude that the principle that an observer's perceptions can be influenced by his past training and present set is beyond debate. Quite obviously the facts of psychology are consistent with the notion that a scientist's observations can be contaminated by his preconception.

The significant question that should be raised about these and related studies demonstrating that a person's preconceptions can influence his observations is whether they are representative of the observations of a scientist. Is there empirical data from behavioral research similar to the reversible figure-ground relationship in which one observer can perceive one event, a vase, while another an entirely different one, two profiles? It would be mistaken to argue that the reversible figure-ground problem is such an example. *One must distinguish in behavioral research between the experimenter and the subject.* Although subjects, for brief periods of time, might observe different events (a vase or two profiles), two experimenters would have no difficulty in agreeing that the stimulus display was a pattern with borders that serve as outlines of either a vase or two profiles. This stimulus display, as described by the observations of the experimenter, will evoke a perception of either a vase or two profiles when observed by a subject for a brief time period. And when subjects continue to fixate upon the reversible figure-ground display, they observe a sequence of perceptions of a vase and two profiles in which the two percepts alternate. But from the viewpoint of the experimenter no confusion has ever occurred as to whether the stimulus display was a vase or two profiles. It was neither. It is only what appears in Figure 2.1, which can be easily described and reproduced without difficulty. Thus the analysis of the reversible figure-ground phenomenon itself provides absolutely no difficulty for research psychologists who aspire to achieve consensual (intersubjective) agreement as to the nature of an environmental situation and the resultant behavior.

An analysis of the Bruner-Postman study (1949), which demonstrates that an observer's preconceptions can distort his perceptions, also raises the question as to whether such an experiment is an appropriate model of scientific observations. The dramatic effects obtained occurred when the anomalous playing card was briefly exposed. Longer exposure times enabled most subjects to correctly identify the anomalous card. One can speculate as to what would have been the results if the experiment had been designed to reflect actual research practices. Presumably, efforts would have been made to observe the significant event, the red four of spades, under optimal conditions that would have encouraged accurate identification. And if an error were made, and no doubt observational errors are more likely to occur when events are at odds with prevailing expectations, then the self-correcting procedures of good research practice such as the use of several observers and/or the replication of the study would uncover the observational error. In sum, although preconceptions may influence empirical observations they do not necessarily have to, especially when precautions are taken.

Although careful research practices are important in reducing the possible contamination of the experimenter's observations by his preconceptions, it must be noted again that the proper perspective with which to interpret the relevance of the Bruner-Postman study to the problem of immaculate perceptions is not from the position of the subject but rather from that of the experimenter. From this perspective it should be noted that Bruner and Postman did not encounter any difficulty in specifying clearly to the psychological community the actual characteristics of the anomalous display that was employed in their study. Any experimenter would be capable of replicating their anomalous playing card.

An obvious implication of this line of analysis is that a clear demarcation between observational statements and theoretical statements is always possible. Yet I am reluctant to accept such a strong conclusion. I am not qualified to judge the appropriateness of such a distinction for physics, the science that usually serves as the model for philosophical analyses. Although logical positivism, the dominant school of the philosophy of science in the second quarter of the twentieth century, proposed an absolute distinction between theory and observation, its position has since been frequently and vigorously attacked. Many distinguished philosophers of science (e.g., Popper and Lakatos) deny that such a distinction is possible.

In spite of this I can offer two reasons to encourage psychologists to try to maintain the distinction between observational and theoretical events. The first has to do with the nature of the distinction from the perspectives of the philosopher and the psychologist, and the second with practical considerations.

Linguistic Representation of Scientific Observation

The observational-theoretical distinction for the philosopher is embedded in a complicated linguistic problem that may be best ignored, at least for the present, by the psychologist. The problem is essentially one of whether a language can be formulated that accurately mirrors the observations of the scientist, free of any bias that theoretical preconceptions might encourage. Logical positivists thought that such an ideal language was possible. They assumed that fundamental to all observations were a finite set of elementary sensations linked either to psychological or physical measurement. Complex observations (e.g., rate of responding, aggression), according to this conception, were essentially combinations of these elementary observations. A language consisting of terms coordinated to these elementary sensations could therefore, in principle, describe accurately any set of scientific observations.

Although efforts to construct such a pure observational language were attempted, none succeeded. The reasons for these failures are open to debate. Some argue that the psychological assumption that complex "scientific" perceptions are simply combinations of elementary sensations is invalid; holistic perceptions are different than the sum of their parts. Others question whether all scientific observations can be reduced to a finite set of elementary sensations. Is there not an infinite number of possible elementary sensations when observing an empirical situation? Consider what would be involved in a *complete* description of an operant-conditioning situation or an experiment designed to investigate obedience (e.g., Milgram, 1963). If one wanted to describe *every* detail of the entire situation one would be involved in a never-ending task. Still others would argue that the so-called elementary sensations are not the basic elements of observation; instead, they are the products of perceptual analysis. Our observational knowledge emerges from perceptions of integrated entities (e.g., levers, individuals) that can be analyzed into smaller components.

It should be apparent that the linguistic orientation pursued by many philosophers in their attempt to analyze the validity of the distinction between observational and theoretical events is most complex, containing many important empirical questions that presumably (or perhaps just hopefully) will be illuminated by future research in both perception and psycholinguistics. However, the important issue of an observational-theoretical distinction need not be put aside until a deeper understanding of the psychological problem is achieved. The needs of psychologists can be met by viewing the problem of the observational-theoretical distinction from a purely pragmatic viewpoint. What procedures can be followed that would yield the highest degree of observational (consensual) agreement among researchers? What methods can be pursued that will permit one psychologist to reconstruct the observations that are basic to another's conclusions?

Possible Volitional Decisions in Dealing with Problems of Observational Purity

If one takes the position that an observer and what he observes are inseparable, then one must be pessimistic about achieving any consensual agreement among psychologists about empirical evidence except in those cases when the two observers share common theoretical commitments. This extreme position is obviously wrong, as any historical review of research areas such as memory, sensation, ethology, and others would show. True, there are theoretical arguments about what experimental design is most appropriate to test a particular hypothesis. And as already mentioned, disputes exist as to what results a particular experimental design produces. But one must also consider the numerous instances where scientists with different theoretical commitments are able to communicate in a completely satisfactory manner the observations of experimental design, procedure, and results without ambiguity; when replications are desired they can be executed without confusion. The debate about the validity of the distinction between theoretical and observational terms has been one-sided, overconcerned with the difficulties encountered in maintaining the distinction at the expense of ignoring the more frequent occasions when such difficulties are not met.

In my own experiences as a research psychologist, I have not encountered insuperable difficulties in distinguishing between my own observational and theoretical statements. I have also been able to make a similar distinction with regard to efforts of a large number of other researchers. This is not to say that in my case, or in theirs, the theoretical concepts are always unambiguous and clearly coordinated to experimental operations. Nor is it to deny that some psychologists hopelessly conflate theoretical statements and empirical evidence either because they ignore or reject the distinction. The argument that is being advanced is that consensual agreement, in principle, can be attained about empirical observations free of theoretical contamination, assuming that investigators are interested in achieving such a goal. To be specific, no fundamental difficulty will be encountered when one reports the rate of responding under different schedules of reinforcement, the stimulus display confronting preschoolers in their discrimination-learning task and the mean number of trials they require to execute a reversal shift, the description of a set of line drawings and the percentage of subjects of different age groups that make categorical, overgeneralized, and overdiscriminated classifications. Some of these observational terms (e.g., overgeneralized, overdiscriminated) have their origins in theoretical concepts, but their operational meaning can be traced back to their observational foundation (Kendler, 1980). No confusion need occur about these observational events among observers of different theoretical persuasions. And even when theoretical implications get embedded in empirical descriptions (e.g., the Ptolemaic-inspired statement that "the sun rises in the east") one can frequently link the statement to an observational base.

It may be that the kinds of research problems that have been described are not representative of all areas of psychology. Perhaps reading EEG records is contaminated by theoretical preconceptions. Discriminating between grammatical and ungrammatical sentences may be another illustration of theoretical pollution of observational statements. Theoretical commitments may taint observations in Rorschach testing, and probably did in my efforts as a clinical psychologist. I believe, however, that improved recording procedures and increased concern with problems of reliability among observers would reduce, if not eliminate, theoretical pollution of observational statements.

In spite of my belief that careful empirical practices can produce immaculate perceptions,[9] I cannot offer any infallible meth-

9. There is another sense in which theoretical preconceptions can become imbedded in observational statements, but this issue is unimportant. If an observer reports that a subject had a reaction time of a certain mag-

odological rule that will guarantee, either for the empirical investigator or the scholar who is attempting to reconstruct knowledge, the complete separation of observational events from theoretical conceptions. Therefore, I am forced to entertain the possibility that perhaps in some empirical areas that the observational-theoretical distinction may be difficult, or even impossible, to maintain.

Accepting this possibility raises the question as to whether the distinction loses all relevance to scientific practice. If some notion is not completely right must it be completely wrong? Consider this problem within the practical framework of building a boat with primitive equipment that is inadequate to the task of preventing all leaks; one would nevertheless make every effort to minimize potential leaks. Is not the scientist confronted with a similar problem? His tools of epistemological analysis are inadequate but he nevertheless strives, as best he can, to keep his observational statements uncontaminated.

Nagel expresses a similar point of view:

> It would be idle to pretend, however, that there are no difficulties in drawing a distinction between observational and theoretical statements; and I certainly do not know how to make such a distinction precise. Nevertheless, I do not consider that this distinction is therefore otiose any more than I believe that the fact that no sharp line can be drawn to mark off day from night or living organisms from inanimate systems makes these distinctions empty and useless (1971, p. 19).

The argument that a sharp distinction between theoretical and observational statements should serve as an ideal of scientific practice, even if unrealizable, would seem to be at odds with my disclaimer about offering methodological prescriptions for *all* to

---

nitude, the accuracy of that observation is based upon the validity of the theoretical principles of physics, which are assumed to account for the functioning of the equipment. In this context every observational statement is influenced by theoretical preconceptions. But these theoretical preconceptions are not those under investigation and hence are not relevant to the significant issue of whether observational statements are contaminated by those theoretical principles *that are being investigated.*

follow. Such a recommendation, strictly speaking, is not being made. A researcher must make some decisions to govern his scientific activities. Considering the general philosophical and methodological problems that have been discussed in regard to the distinction between theoretical and observational statements, I conclude that a productive strategy to pursue is to strive to maintain the distinction as best one can, an effort that I have not found difficult.

Other volitional decisions are possible. One possibility would be that since no rule can be stated that clearly separates observational statements from theoretical preconceptions, attempts at maintaining such a discrimination will inevitably prove misleading and confusing; science would be unavoidably distorted by attempts to maintain a fictitious distinction. Adopting this line of reasoning suggests that one should go about one's scientific business without any self-conscious efforts to distinguish between observational and theoretical statements. Such a methodological decision cannot be faulted if one denies the reality or the usefulness of the observational-theoretical distinction. But one can raise the question whether such a decision encourages an excessive amount of subjectivity in science and creates unnecessary obstacles for scientists who are trying to discover the relative merits of competing theories.

This is an appropriate point in my analysis of the observational purity of behavioral psychology to return to the question that initiated such a discussion: Was the inability to achieve consensual agreement about mental events by phenomenological (experiential) psychologists comparable to the unresolved theoretical differences in behavioral psychology? If one accepts the assumption that the observational-theoretical distinction in behavioral psychology is relevant and useful, even if not always sharp and clear, then one must answer the question in the negative. Phenomenological psychology is apparently confronted, at least for the present, with the insolvable task of isolating its observational events from the presuppositions of the methods used to observe them. One can speculate that different methods of self-observations do not represent different perspectives for observing the same event but instead they bring into existence different phenomenal events. If true, then we really do not have different phenomenological methods but instead different phenomenologies in the sense that different experiential worlds are created by different methods of phenomenological exploration.[10]

In rebuttal, it might be argued that the same situation prevails in behavioral psychology; theoretical preconceptions determine what is observed. For example, if one assumes that movements are learned in instrumental conditioning, then one observes the manner in which an animal presses a bar; but if one assumes that acts are acquired, then one notes only whether the bar is depressed. Such an argument overlooks fundamental differences between behavioral and experiential observations. In the example cited it would be possible to observe both events (movements and acts) simultaneously, achieve intersubjective agreement about the observational events, and ultimately determine the relative merits of the competing conceptions of instrumental conditioning. None of these would be possible in pure phenomenology; the intrasubjectivity of the experiential event prohibits recordings of the event, intersubjective agreement about its occurrence, and resolution of theoretical differences.

If one denies the pertinence of the observational-theoretical distinction to behavioral psychology, one need not be compelled to accept a methodological equivalence between pure phenomenology and behavioral psychology. One can acknowledge that the theoretical disputes in experiential psychology bear a resemblance to those in behavioral psychology in that they emerge from contamination of observational data by theoretical preconceptions. At the same time one can recognize that the contamination can be qualitatively different or significantly greater in one case than in the other. If this is true, then one would expect that history would demonstrate that agreement about observational events would be more difficult to achieve in experiential psychology than in behavioral psychology. I would suggest that historical evidence supports this expectation.

---

10. This speculation must remain a conjecture because no method of phenomenological analysis is available to evaluate its validity.

In shifting the frame of reference from methodological analysis to historical examination, one must entertain the possibility that improved methods of phenomenological research are possible. One need not accept the convenient assumption that experiential analyses are infallible and incorrigible. One can suppose the opposite; a person's self-observations can be mistaken and are correctable. The concept of *stimulus error* identified a possible source of error in observing mental events—confusing physical characteristics with psychological experience. One can also argue that just as illusions occur in the perception of the outer world so are they possible when observing the inner world. Conceivably, a tense person can "mistakenly" believe he is experiencing *inner serenity* when in fact he is feeling a sense of relaxation following physical exertion.

Many, if not all, phenomenological methods operate on the assumption that self-observations can be fallible and corrigible. In essence, graduate training in departments of psychology with a structuralist orientation, as was the case at Cornell when Titchener was chairman, was designed in part to teach future psychologists methods of self-observation that would be free of errors. It is interesting to note that a similar problem is posed for the patient in psychoanalysis who must learn to examine and report his phenomenal experience in an "accurate" and forthright way. Even if one adopts the position that self-observation should be executed in a naive fashion, in the absence of preconceptions (assuming that is not a presupposition), one will nevertheless learn, as is suggested by the author's experience (self-observation can be fun!), that increased sensitivity to the events of phenomenal experience seems to occur with increased practice.

In essence, the suggestion that the "accuracy" of self-observations can be improved with training supports the notion that introspection is fallible and corrigible. The question is immediately raised as to whether persistent efforts to improve observations of mental events would not yield a level of consensual agreement about the nature of the mind that heretofore has not been achieved.

The discussion up to this point does not offer any optimism about such a possibility. The reason seems obvious. The assumption of fallibility and corrigibility applies only to experiential data but not to the methods employed to obtain them. Although it might be possible to resolve differences about experiential data when introspectors are in agreement about the appropriate method of self-observation, no standards are presently available to resolve differences about which introspective method is the valid one. If we accept the historical conclusion that different methods of phenomenological research provide different pictures of the mind, we are once again led to the conclusion that we do not really have different methods of phenomenology, but different phenomenologies. Within this context, the conclusion seems inevitable that consensual agreement about the nature of conscious experience by methods of pure phenomenology is an unobtainable goal.

Shared Experience

Before leaving the analysis of the mind as an independent enterprise, reference to the important concept of *shared experience* needs to be made. Interestingly, this concept, which is of great importance for humanistic psychologies, can be elucidated by reference to some comments of Titchener, the American leader of structuralism who said:

> I turn now to the topic of visual imagery, which is always at my disposal and which I can mould and direct at will. I rely, in my thinking, upon visual imagery in the sense that I like to get a problem into some sort of visual schema, from which I can think my way out to which I can return (1909, p. 10).

He goes on to discuss the experiential meaning of "visual schema":

> The term "visual schema" is, of course, itself equivocal. Those of you whose minds are built on the same general plan as my own will know well enough what it means. But I must warn the others, to whom this sort of imagery is unknown, not to think of a geometrical figure printed black on white, or of anything a hundredth part as definite (ibid., p. 12).

Later on, after offering other examples of his visual imagery, Titchener concludes: "All this description must be either self-evident or as unreal as a fairy-tale" (ibid., p. 14). In other words, what he is proclaiming is that if the reader has had phenomenal experiences similar to Titchener's, the reader would "understand" Titchener's mind, at least that portion involved with visual imagery. Without such experience, Titchener's mind would remain beyond others' personal apprehension.

Shared experience then becomes a vehicle for "understanding" another person's private experience. The concept of shared experience, however, does not overcome any of the methodological difficulties previously discussed in regard to attaining consensual agreement about the basic data of private experience. An obvious question is how does one know that the same kind of experience is being shared. One evidently does not look into another person's mind and observe that his own experience is being shared by another. The psychological basis of the shared experience is that a verbal description of one's own experience (or that of a character in a novel) can arouse in another an empathic response, which signifies that he has had a similar experience. The sharing itself cannot be proved to have occurred by methods of pure phenomenology unless the weak methodological requirement of merely the testimony itself is accepted as sufficient.

The concept of "shared" experience (in quotes to emphasize the speculative nature of the sharing) has significance outside of the range of phenomenology. The concept represents a commonly used index of understanding the behavior of others, e.g., if a clinician can empathize with his patient he can understand the patient's actions. Also, "shared" experience can presumably function as a causal link in a behavioral chain, e.g., if a person can empathize with someone he will be altruistic toward him (Krebs, 1975). In sum, "shared" experience as a phenomenological event has implications for the understanding and control of behavior, which will be returned to later (page 94).

The Data Base and 3
Subject Matter of Psychology:
Part Two

1. Behavior and conscious experience can each be investigated independently of each other or in combination. The resulting information from any one of these three approaches (behavior, experience, behavior and experience) can serve as the subject matter of psychology.

2. Phenomenologists, in their effort to reveal the nature of the mind, can rely exclusively on verbal descriptions, or they can attempt to coordinate these descriptions to public events. When coordination is successful "quasi-objective" knowledge results. Such knowledge does not guarantee a veridical account of consciousness, but it does contribute a degree of objectivity not possessed by the phenomenological report itself.

3. Behavioral psychology can deal with phenomenal experience using a variety of strategies ranging from choosing to ignore it to constructing a theoretical model of the mind that meets the demands of methodological behaviorism.

4. An operational approach in behavioral psychology is desirable if it is understood that the entire meaning of a concept is not limited to its operational meaning. An operational definition links a concept to its observational base thus facilitating communication about empirical knowledge. The empirical meaning of a concept is represented by the total number of empirical relationships within which the operationally

defined concept is involved. The intuitive meaning of a concept refers to the hunches and ideas a scientist has when attempting to think creatively about a concept while its theoretical meaning is contained in the totality of theoretical statements that are proposed to account for the empirical relations involving the concept.

5. The kinds of knowledge yielded by studying public behavior and private experience are fundamentally different although future technical developments may make it possible to investigate conscious experience in an objective fashion. At present, psychologists are confronted with convergent and divergent paths in investigating conscious experience and behavior. What path one selects will depend on both the goal one sets for psychology and the criterion one accepts for understanding.

RELATIONSHIPS BETWEEN BEHAVIORAL AND EXPERIENTIAL PSYCHOLOGY

My analysis of the subject matters of psychology, behavior and private experience, has suggested that the study of the former can stand alone as an independent natural-science discipline. This means that it would be possible to interpret behavior, even human behavior, on the basis of empirical relationships and theoretical construction without any reference to direct observations of mental events. A broad consensual agreement among a community of behavioral psychologists could be achieved about the meanings of the underlying observational and theoretical statements. Again, this does not mean that such statements would be completely free of ambiguity but rather that with scholarly dedication possible sources of ambiguity or confusion would ultimately be revealed. Thus it should be possible for one behavioral psychologist to understand another in spite of theoretical differences. And when clarification is not easily forthcoming, historical pressures inherent in the scientific enterprise (e.g., experimental replications, epistemological clarification) will bring to the surface the facts and confusions inherent in unresolved theoretical disputes. Behavioral psychology has the capacity to be "objective" in the sense of dealing with events, observational and theoretical, that are available to public scrutiny.

The idea that it is possible to adopt objective behavior as a dependent variable without any reference to mental events does not imply that such a decision is strategically desirable, only that it is methodologically feasible. Introspective reports need not threaten behavioristic purity if the reports themselves are considered basic observational data and not direct reflections of conscious experience. The point at issue for the behaviorist is to discover whether such reports possess heuristic value as sources of significant data or fruitful hypotheses.

Experiential psychology, with conscious experience as its subject matter, can also stand alone as an independent discipline. However, its foundations appear too insubstantial to support a discipline capable of achieving broad consensual agreement about the *facts* of conscious experience and the means by which theoretical differences to account for them can be resolved. By broad consensual agreement is simply meant that the accord extends across boundaries of the variety of methodological orientations that have and can be employed in pure phenomenological research. Both historical evidence and epistemological analysis support the opinion that consensual agreement is an unobtainable goal for pure phenomenology. As a consequence, pure phenomenology is incapable of employing a natural-science approach.

Is such a verdict final? Are mental events forever beyond the pale of objective (intersubjective) knowledge? I think not. But only when one accepts the intrinsic methodological limitation of raw phenomenal experience can one creatively cope with it. Acknowledging the intrasubjective isolation of experiential data encourages one to develop means to compensate for its privacy. What is obviously needed is an epistemological prosthetic that will provide public support for the tenuous methodological underpinnings of private experience. This can be accomplished by relating verbal descriptions of private experience to other publicly observable events. By doing so, confidence can be increased that the verbal reports that presumably reflect private experiences do so with some degree of accuracy.

Phenomenal Experience and Public Events

A simple example of the advantages that accrue from relating experiential reports to public events can be demonstrated by reference to the popular pastime of wine tasting. Suppose some self-assured connoisseur, who happens to be a dean, in his infinite wisdom proclaims a particular wine to be "amusing but honest." Viewed within the framework of pure phenomenology we can either accept the description as possessing some degree of validity in that he is having a distinctive experience, or we can entertain the suspicion that he is showing off. The significant point is that if we do not proceed beyond the evidence of his introspective report, we will forever remain in the dark about which of these two alternatives is correct.

One way of resolving the issue is to challenge him to a blindfold test (assuming he does not rule on salary raises) in which he is instructed to identify from a variety of wines those that are *amusing but honest*. You would be led to the conclusion that the dean is a phony about wine tasting if his judgments are inconsistent: several different wines are *amusing but honest* on one occasion but not on another. Suppose, however, he is consistent: of all the wines he swishes in his mouth, he identifies only two, a Portuguese rosé and a California rosé, as amusing but honest. If the blindfold test is executed effectively so that the only cue to his response is the taste of the wine, one is encouraged to conclude that these wines produced a distinctive experience for him.

No doubt, such an example will be immediately labeled, by some, as trivial—unrelated to significant human experiences such as the feeling of self-worth, human dignity, and other experiential concepts that are thought to be at the core of human existence. This kind of reaction obstructs methodological clarification and frees those who deal with life's vital issues from meeting demanding standards of evidence when drawing conclusions.

The point of my wine-tasting example was not to suggest that all problems of phenomenological research would collapse to a psychophysical approach in which verbal reports of conscious experience are related to publicly observable characteristics of the environment. Obviously that is not the case for several reasons that will subsequently be identified. For the moment, the important consideration is that the problems of experiential research take on an entirely new cast when considered within the context of relating phenomenal experience to publicly observable events (e.g., different kinds of wine).

When the dean is successful in consistently selecting the same wines as *amusing and honest,* our confidence increases that his introspective reports reflect phenomenal events. The consistent relationship between the reports and publicly observable events indicates that the former are not solely linguistic expressions in that they are unrelated to conscious experience and are *simply* an expression of social gamesmanship. Of course, the characterization *amusing but honest* itself is not demanded by the underlying experience. It could be that another individual, a new assistant professor, whose discriminations were as consistent as those of the dean, would describe the two rosés as *light, moderately full-bodied,* and *relatively dry.* The difference between the two characterizations could possibly be linguistic in that different words are used for the same or similar experience. Such a possibility could be explored by subjecting the two to additional wine-tasting tasks to determine the similarities in their discriminative abilities along with attempts to discover whether the linguistic dimensions used to represent the dean's experience (e.g., *amusing, honest*) are translatable into the terms used by the assistant professor (e.g., *lightness, body, dryness*).[1]

1. Cain (1979) has reported that odor identification is vastly improved when the observer has labels to identify his olfactory experiences. This raises the interesting phenomenological question as to whether the labels influence the experience directly by making the olfactory sensations more distinctive or serve only as convenient terms with which to associate unchanging experiences. Because the experiences cannot be publicly observed, the question does not lend itself to a universally acceptable answer by methods of *pure* phenomenology.

I am not trying to suggest the rough outlines of a proposed research project in experimental phenomenology nor to imply that at the end of such a project the strong conclusion could be drawn that two individuals are sharing a common phenomenal experience. I am only suggesting that a quantum leap in reliable knowledge is achieved when phenomenological reports are in agreement with each other and correlate with some publicly observable external referent. To return to an underlying theme, such a conclusion is based upon the assumption that introspective reports go beyond phenomenal experience itself. The raw experience is transformed into an introspective report, and a fundamental task for experiential psychology is to tease out from the introspective report the purely linguistic components (*amusing but honest* versus *light, moderately full-bodied,* and *relatively dry*) that are unrelated to the phenomenal experience itself. By discovering that a relationship prevails between the report and a publicly observable event, one surmises that the verbal reports are not only linguistic; they do, in fact, reflect some characteristics of phenomenal experience. And perhaps the most compelling argument in favor of such an interpretation is that one could possibly predict the kinds of verbal descriptions that would be forthcoming when novel forms of stimulation (e.g., new wines) are presented. If the self-observers who had previously agreed now also report similar introspections, then confidence increases in the similarity of their experiences.

One must be exceptionally guarded, as I have tried to be, in drawing any conclusion about the similarity of the phenomenal experiences of two different individuals. There are two main reasons for this. First, and foremost, the phenomenal experiences of the two individuals cannot be directly compared, and thus at best, the presumed similarity must remain a tenuous inference. Second, the implication of the absence of a psychophysical relationship is ambiguous in regard to drawing inferences about phenomenal experience. Consider once again my hypothetical dean. Suppose his introspective report, *amusing but honest,* was not correlated with any particular wines. Could one therefore deny that he had a distinctive phenomenal experience when he uttered such statements? One could not! Perhaps his verbal reports reflected a distinctive experiental state, but such states are a function of a constellation of variables and therefore are not simply tied to a taste of a particular wine. Another possibility is that the dean is indulging in deception; he is merely using words for their social effects, and they have nothing to do with his inner experience. I cannot deny the former interpretation although my intuition favors the latter.

In essence, if a psychologist opts to become a phenomenologist in order to reveal the nature of the mind, he has a choice between being a pure phenomenologist who depends exclusively on verbal communication to reflect conscious experience or being an experiential psychologist who seeks to overcome the intrinsic limits of the privacy of the mind by coordinating introspective reports to public events. The knowledge obtained from these two different positions is qualitatively different; a shift from the first orientation to the second results in a shift from purely subjective knowledge to quasi-objective information.

The conclusion that the relationship between introspective reports of "conscious experience" and publicly observable environmental events represents only quasi-objective knowledge applies *only* to the efforts of experiential psychology. The qualifier *quasi* is added to emphasize the point that such knowledge, as already argued, has limitations for drawing definitive conclusions about the mind. The same kind of information—introspective reports related to environmental events—is objective (intersubjective) for the behavioral psychologist because he is not burdened with the task of revealing the nature of the mind. His task is restricted to behavioral analysis, and introspective reports can be considered simply another form of public behavior, free of any inferential content for the nature of the mind. The same knowledge—a psychophysical relationship—has different meanings depending upon whether the investigator is studying the mind or behavior.

Some phenomenological experiences need not or cannot be coordinated solely to environmental events. Physiological measures can also provide the coordination required to qualify "conscious experience" as quasi-objective knowledge. This point is illustrated by the phenomenon of meditation.

In meditation one restricts one's perceptual experience and concentrates fully upon an apparently insignificant event, such as counting breaths; or pondering intuitively rather than logically a riddle, known as a *koan* (e.g., "How can I attain enlightenment by driving on the Los Angeles freeway?"); or repeating certain significant words over and over again; or contemplating an object such as a vase for long periods of time; or repeating monotonous chants. Confirmed meditators describe their phenomenal experience as *pleasurable detachment, no mind, one-pointedness, inner serenity,* and other characterizations that suggest a lack of responsiveness to the outside world and an expanded consciousness of the self.

Obviously the question arises, particularly among the tough-minded variety of behaviorists, whether such phenomenally descriptive terms mean anything? Do meditators merely learn new verbal responses or do they actually acquire new experiences? To answer this question a number of investigations have sought to determine whether meditation has an effect on physiological processes. In one well-known study (Wallace & Benson, 1972), representative of others, an affirmative answer was found. Electrical skin resistance, a commonly used measure of "emotionality" (the higher the skin resistance, the greater the "relaxation"; the lower the measure, the greater the "tension" and "anxiety") changes during periods of meditation. For a representative experienced meditator, skin resistance rises rapidly when meditation begins and drops when it terminates. Other findings are that meditation, compared to periods of nonmeditation, decreases oxygen consumption, carbon monoxide elimination, the rate and volume of respiration, heart rate, and blood lactate level. The intensity of slow alpha waves also increases during meditation. The entire pattern of physiological changes resulting from meditation indicates a wakeful, highly relaxed, hypometabolic state.

The epistemological status of such results are no different from those of the psychophysical relationship between introspective reports and wine tasting. Assuming that phenomenal experience is related to physiological processes, one is encouraged to use such evidence to demonstrate that meditation in fact produces a distinctive kind of mental event. If this physiological pattern is distinctively different from that exhibited during sleep or hypnosis, and some investigators deny this, one can also conclude that the meditative experience has unique phenomenal properties that distinguish it from other relaxed states. However, consistent with my previous analysis, relating physiological events to phenomenal reports does not *guarantee* that persons who are exhibiting a common physiological pattern are in fact having the same mental experience; nor can it be demonstrated that those who are not exhibiting a common physiological pattern are also not experiencing similar mental events. Thus the conclusion must be drawn, as in the case for environmental-mental relationships, that physiological events coordinated with phenomenal experience produce only quasi-objective information.

What is obviously true is that the physiological pattern is *not* the conscious experience. If, for example, a group of meditators described their experience as *inner serenity* and such a report was perfectly correlated with a distinctive pattern of physiological and environmental measures, nonmeditators would know nothing about how the experience of *inner serenity* feels. The subjective experience of *inner serenity* cannot be confused with public events to which reports of the experience are coordinated. This distinction has been touched upon by many philosophers. Schlick made a distinction between *to have an experience* (e.g., *inner serenity*) and *to have knowledge* (e.g., the introspective report of *inner serenity* is related to a distinctive pattern of physiological and environmental events). Dewey similarly distinguished between *having* and *knowing*. One can *have* a toothache and one can *know* that toothaches are "caused" by a pattern of neurophysiological events.

Behavioral psychology is concerned with *knowing* about behavior while experiential psychology is involved with understanding *having*. Understanding, in this context, can be achieved in two possible ways. One can understand a phenomenal experience (e.g., toothache, inner serenity) by having it, or one can understand a phenomenal experience by knowing the publicly observable conditions that produce it. I do not understand labor pains in the former sense but do in the latter sense.

A pure phenomenologist could turn his back on possible relationships between phenomenal experience and environmental or physiological events because such information, he could argue, is irrelevant to the task of discovering a veridical account of human experience. Therefore, adopting the epistemological standards of the natural sciences is self-defeating because the richness of everyday experience cannot be revealed by the scientific method, by *knowing*.

If one acknowledges that a veridical account of human experience is possible, but that it cannot be evaluated by standards of empirical verification (or falsifiability), then one must propose some method capable of capturing the quality of phenomenal experience with great fidelity. But what method? This question comes back to the problem of establishing rules by which one can judge the relative merits of different methods of observing phenomenal experience. Numerous methods have been employed, ranging from highly structured analytic procedures to those that encourage a naive, natural, "presuppositionless" attitude.

In the absence of any objective criteria, the pure phenomenologist must resort to subjective standards. Since the knowledge forthcoming from the enterprise of pure phenomenology is completely insulated from any refutation, one can conclude that it is unscientific, a judgment that some phenomenologists would proudly accept. For our purposes not much is gained from the attribution "unscientific" because of the lack of agreement that prevails about demarcation lines between science and nonscience. Of greater relevance to psychology than explicating the boundary between science and nonscience is examining the possible relationship between purely subjective and objective knowledge.

Consider the hypothetical case of describing conscious experience by a method of pure phenomenology. Suppose the effort produces an ideally descriptive language that coordinates distinctive phenomenal events (e.g., ecstasy, happiness) to distinctive public events (e.g., patterns of physiological events). If each term of the phenomenal vocabulary that was generated by pure experiential research was coordinated to a particular pattern of public events, one would be in a position to formulate a theory in which phenomenological constructs, defined in terms of coordinated public events, could serve both as "causal" agents for subsequent behavior (e.g., empathy toward members of minority groups will reduce prejudice) and as a dependent variable (e.g., empathic feelings toward others can be acquired by special training procedures). In addition, the phenomenological language, with its coordinated public measures, could serve as a bridge in the attempt to relate, both in terms of similarity and differences, one phenomenal experience with another. Even experiences that could not be shared (e.g., maternal and paternal love, male and female orgasms) could be analyzed in terms of their phenomenal similarity.

At this point warnings and qualifications are demanded to protect my methodological flanks. I have not argued that the results of pure phenomenological research, even of the highest quality, *can* be incorporated into an objective psychological theory involving environmental, behavioral, and physiological measures. I have only suggested that they *might* be. In other words, no insurmountable obstacle precludes the possibility that accounts of human experience from pure phenomenological research could be integrated with an objective psychology. I mention this possibility, although I am not optimistic about its occurrence in the foreseeable future, in order to identify potential points of contact between the apparently incompatible methodological orientations of pure phenomenology and behavioral psychology. The most likely possibility is that these distinctly different kinds of psychological orientations will remain disparate, thus contributing to a fundamental disunity within psychology.

If extremist methodological positions are rejected by experiential and behavioral psychology, then a number of different lines of reconciliation become possible. Experiential psychology, without abandoning its primary concern with mental events, can nevertheless acknowledge the possible relevance of environmental, behavioral, and physiological events. If this is done then some methodological decision must be made concerning the relative value of subjective verbal reports in comparison to objective indices of environmental, behavioral, and physiological events for understanding the mind. By considering the objective indices, the experientialist acknowledges the insufficiency of verbal reports alone. An obvious strategy for an experientialist to pursue is the one already described—a quasi-objective approach in which the accuracy of phenomenal reports are judged within the context of their coordination to publicly observed events. Such events provide a framework for developing a mutually agreed-upon vocabulary to describe phenomenal experience. The more objective measures one can relate to private experience, the greater is the likelihood of achieving consensual agreement about the nature of the mind. At present, this opinion represents more an article of methodological faith than a demonstrated fact. The current interest in the relationship between physiological states and mental events should demonstrate soon whether this expectation is justified.

Phenomenal Experience and Behavioral Psychology

Behavioral psychology can deal with phenomenal experience in a number of different ways that will now be described and evaluated. The major decision is either ignore it or deal with it. Justification of the first position can take one of three forms.

Metaphysical Behaviorism

Metaphysical behaviorism (Bergmann, 1956), denies the existence of mental states. Watson's aggressive polemics against structuralism finally encouraged him to favor this extreme position. It is one thing to point out the methodological difficulties inherent in analyzing subjective experience; it is quite another matter to deny its existence. This distinction seemed to have been lost in Watson's energetic attacks on the conception of psychology as the science of the mind.

Epiphenomenalism

By adopting the philosophical position of epiphenomenalism some psychologists feel justified in ignoring conscious experience.

A major assumption of this position is "that experience is simply a nonfunctional derivative of certain physiological processes taking place in the nervous system" (Wagoner & Goodson, 1976). According to this argument then, conscious experience could not be responsible for changes in behavior any more than the movement of a person's shadow is responsible for his walking. If true, why bother with conscious experience when analyzing behavior?

The trouble with this gambit is that it oversimplifies the problem of causation, prejudges empirical issues, and ignores practical considerations. The assumption that conscious experience does not play a functional role in determining behavior is hopelessly enmeshed in the problem of causation, a topic that has failed to yield any universally accepted solution since the days of the ancient Greek philosophers. It is important to recognize that accepting the notion that conscious experience is an expression of neurophysiological events and has no existence apart from them does not rule out the possibility that knowledge about experience, regardless of its inferential status, can account for behavior or even neurophysiological events. The macrogenetic concept of gene had no *existence* apart from the microgenetic sequence of rungs on a DNA ladder; yet we know that the former concept of gene effectively helped predict a variety of hereditary phenomena.

Another tack that can be taken in questioning the nonfunctional status of conscious experience that is consistent with epiphenomenalistic doctrine is to note that assuming experience to be a "derivative" of neurophysiological processes does not necessarily imply that the two are equivalent. Being embarrassed is not identical to the neurophysiological events to which the embarrassment is coordinated. This does not mean that embarrassment exists apart from the neurophysiological changes but only that the two are operationally distinct because they are based upon a different set of observations. From this point of view, one can argue that conscious experience under certain circumstances (e.g., limited knowledge of neurophysiological events, the nature of the behavior that is to be predicted) will be more closely correlated with certain forms of behavior than available neurophysiological information.

The relationship between conscious experience and behavior can be perceived by the psychologist as a purely empirical problem. Rather than adopt a traditional philosophical resolution of the mind-body problem such as epiphenomenalism, parallelism, or identity, or some other position, a more productive strategy would be to transform specific experiential-behavioral problems into theoretical questions with determinate empirical consequences. Accepting this approach would discourage embarking on a search for a single general answer to experiential-behavioral relationships that may be unobtainable simply because the nature of the relationship may vary for different kinds of experiences and physiological events. The empirical approach, at least for the time being, would focus on specific experiential-behavioral relationships with the realization both that the conclusion drawn about one need not apply to others and that any specific conclusion is susceptible to modifications with additional information.

The simplest, and perhaps the most compelling, argument against ignoring introspective reports is that significant data can be excluded. Even a shadow, a noncausal agent of behavior, can provide useful information. A detective who wants to watch the movements of a person under surveillance, without being seen himself, can focus on his target's shadow and thus be able to predict his movement.

The Incompatibility Between Phenomenology and Behaviorism

Instead of rejecting conscious experience because of its unreal or nonfunctional status, one can choose to ignore it because of the conviction that a behavioral analysis will inevitably become corrupted, contaminated, and confused when consideration is given to mental processes. Even in the absence of interest in phenomenology many behaviorists seem unable to resist employing phenomenological interpretations of behavioral events. Tolman (1932), a sophisticated behaviorist, created theoretical ambiguities by using phenomenological terms to express his behavioral hypotheses. Even Skinner (1969), a hard-line behaviorist, succumbed to phenomenological descriptions when he stated that when contingencies of reinforcement are arranged in a hospital for psychotics the "patients make fewer demands on the staff and yet display as much dignity and happiness as their pathology permits." The solution to the threat of phenomenology would be to adhere to a strict behavioral analysis similar to that required for the treatment of the psychology of infrahuman organisms. Only a rigorous mentally free strategy in psychology, the argument goes, will be capable of meeting the standards of a natural-science methodology.

Arguments Against a "Mentally Free" Strategy in Behaviorism

A "mentally free" strategy is unnecessary and self-defeating. The objectivity of a behavioral psychology can be preserved by treating introspective reports as directly observable events. Such reports can and have had heuristic value for developing a behavioral psychology.

Introspective reports can be time-savers. Psychophysical methods and operant conditioning methods involving simple *yes* or *no* responses or key-pressing reactions can reveal that a human responds to the two lines of the Müller-Lyer illusion as unequal in length. But is it necessary to go through so much trouble to discover what a simple introspective report would reveal in a second? This does not mean that psychophysical and operant conditioning methods might not be useful later on when precise psychophysical laws are desired, but rather, that introspective reports can provide useful information in identifying interesting problems, especially in the field of perception.

Introspective reports can be a source of useful hypotheses. Learning a list of nonsense syllables (e.g., BEW, ZUR, VOD) was once thought to be acquired by rote memory. Each syllable was presumably memorized as a meaningless sequence of letters until the subject mastered each item. Introspective reports of many subjects would not reflect such processing. Instead, one strived to make sense out of nonsense; nonsense syllables were encoded into words and meaningful relations were established among them. For example, the above string of three nonsense syllables could be encoded as part of a sentence: BEWare of ZURich and VODka. If introspective reports are systematically obtained from adult human subjects, the results of most, if not all, would be at odds with a simple rote-learning model.

Phenomenological Interpretations of Behavioral Theories

Behavioral theories are not required to be consistent with phenomenal experience. They have to be compatible with publicly observable evidence. The reason for rejecting a simple rote-learning model is not that it fails to jibe with phenomenal evidence but instead that it is inconsistent with available data (e.g., Postman, 1971; Tulving & Osler, 1967). Recent theoretical developments have suggested that an adequate theory of serial learning must include mechanisms of encoding and organization, processes that are suggested by introspective reports.

But why should not the demand be made that behavioral theories reflect phenomenal experience? The reason is obvious. Processes that determine behavior are not always represented in phenomenal experience.

A familiarity with the history of psychology of thinking will immediately dispel the illusion that introspective reports, which presumably reflect consciousness, can provide a complete account of human thinking. One of the most significant problems in developmental psychology, the relationship between language and thought, provides ample evidence that introspective reports are unable to reflect the cognitive processes that are operating (e.g., Anglin, 1977). This conclusion is true for adult behavior as well. For example, Binet (Reeves, 1966) concluded from the analysis of introspective reports of two expert arithmetical calculators and several creative writers that unconscious processes were operating in thought. The same conclusion is supported by the introspective analysis of thought by psychologists of the Würzburg school. Little conscious content in thought was noted. In certain tasks, such as associating a superordinate word with a subordinate one (e.g., *chair-furniture*), thought occurred without any conscious deliberation. "One does one's thinking before one knows what he is to think about" (Boring, 1950, p. 404). In the more demanding task of concept identification, subjects appear unaware of their cognitive processes. Hull (1920) found that some of his subjects could classify linear patterns (Chinese ideograms) into correct conceptual categories without being consciously aware of the critical cue. Even creative efforts at the highest intellectual level can suddenly occur without any premeditation. Henri Poincaré, the famous French mathematician, described an episode in which he decided to go on a vacation after working unsuccessfully for some time on a mathematical problem. Travelling from his home to another town, he completely forgot about his mathematical problem until he arrived at his destination and boarded his bus. At the moment he put his foot on the bus, the solution to the problem that had plagued him for weeks suddenly became clear.

The above evidence is a compelling argument against basing theoretical processes of thinking exclusively on reports of conscious experience. Something more is needed.

Another limitation of introspective reports is that they can be misleading. This is a cardinal assumption of many, if not most, personality theorists and clinical practitioners. A person can consciously believe that his behavior is determined by one factor when in reality another factor is responsible. Posthypnotic suggestions illustrate one such example: a person falsely explains a particular act because he is unaware of the command given to him while under hypnosis. Numerous kinds of phenomena, which have been described by concepts such as repression, rationalization, ambivalence, amnesia, projection, motivated forgetting, reaction formation, and overreaction, all suggest that conscious experience can be a misleading source of information for understanding behavior. Although psychologists disagree as to the appropriate theoretical conceptualization of such phenomena, the evidence, some experimental (e.g., Latané & Darley, 1968; Latané & Rodin, 1969) but mostly clinical, denies the assumption that introspective reports will accurately reflect behavioral causation.

Do I contradict myself? I first suggest that introspective reports can have heuristic value and then argue that important behavioral processes can be absent from such reports and that they can actually be misleading. Although these two conclusions are in opposition they are not contradictory for the simple reason that no single relationship operates for all cases in which comparisons are made between introspective reports and behavior. The two in some cases can dovetail, in others be related, and still in others be antagonistic. A uniform strategy for dealing with introspective reports in a behavioral analysis would therefore be unwise.

Behavioral psychologists have a variety of strategies to choose from in dealing with introspective evidence. They range from one extreme of ignoring it to the other of using it for constructing a theoretical model of conscious experience. In evaluating such strategies three important principles must be remembered for dealing with introspective evidence within a behavioral framework: (1) the ultimate value of the strategy must be demonstrated rather than prejudged; (2) phenomenal experiences must be considered an inferred construct and not basic datum; and (3) introspective evidence need not reflect fundamental behavioral processes (and vice versa). In regard to the final point, Tolman, one of the leading theorists in the early history of cognitive psychology, offered the following warning about the value of introspection for formulating theoretical constructs, which he referred to as *intervening variables:*

> Is not introspection after all, at least in the case of men, a significant method by which one can get at and define these intervening variables in a direct and really reliable fashion? I doubt it. I believe that introspection is a form of social response—a type of final behavior . . . one which has very complicated conditions. . . . The very essence of introspection lies in the fact that it is a response to audiences—external and internal. And such being the case, it seems less likely to mirror most types of intervening variable so directly and correctly as do more gross nonsocial forms of behavior (1936, p. 101).

Although Tolman can be accused of overstating his case by suggesting a universal principle that belittles the heuristic value of introspective reports, his comments nevertheless serve as a useful warning to those who believe that introspective reports can serve as the royal road to the understanding of human behavior.

One last point. This discussion has revolved around the relationship between a subject's introspective report of his phenomenal experience and his behavior. Another mind-behavior relationship prevails in behavioral psychology; the phenomenal experience of the psychologist serves as the source of theoretical ideas. Tolman, who expressed disdain for the theoretical value of introspective reports of subjects, admitted to exploiting his own phenomenal experience in order to develop theoretical constructs of the learning behavior of rats. Unless a human's phenomenal experience has some special advantage for interpreting rat behavior, Tolman could be accused of being inconsistent. If introspective reports, which he argued are responses to an internal as well as an external audience, are inferior to gross behavior for suggesting theoretical notions, why should his own experience possess a special value for the behavior of rats?

Tolman's apparent inconsistency is a side-issue; the significant problem concerns the merits of a theorist's phenomenal experience as a source of theoretical notions. This problem is equivalent to that of evaluating the theoretical potentialities of introspective reports of subjects; pragmatic considerations are the only reasonable guidelines. It would be difficult to justify any a priori argument that *mining one's own mind* possesses some intrinsic validity for formulating behavioral hypotheses.

Mining one's own mind might be helpful in generating theoretical insights. The effectiveness of the strategy could probably be increased by appreciating its limitations. An obvious limitation for constructing theories of infrahuman behavior (as well as that of young children) is that of anthropomorphism—attributing mechanisms of behavior reflected in the theorist's consciousness that are not available to the subject. Darwin, who attributed humanlike feelings and highly intelligent behavior to dogs, illustrates one such example. My own opinion is that Tolman (1936) and Krechevsky (1932) made similar errors on a much smaller scale. Although they both tried to be operational in defining their mentalistic-sounding concepts of *cognitive maps* (Tolman, 1932) and *hypotheses* (Krechevsky, 1932), their theoretical terms rapidly acquired surplus meaning that exceeded by far the learning capacities of their rodent-subjects.

Two other risks in extrapolating theoretical processes from one's own inner experience should be mentioned. These also can be discussed within the context of Tolman's theory of animal learning, but unlike anthropomorphism, these interfere with interpreting human behavior. First, phenomenally descriptive concepts (e.g., *cognitive maps*) are intuitively appealing, providing a sense of understanding that is not matched by their explanatory power; in Dewey's terminology (page 74) a sense of *having* is mistakenly interpreted as *knowing*. Second, is the tendency for theories involving terms that reflect mentalistic processes to ignore principles of performance. This was pointedly expressed by Guthrie, who accused Tolman's cognitive theory of leaving the rat "buried in thought" (Guthrie, 1952, p. 143). Tolman's rats, like Hamlet, had the capacity to think but not to act.

A similar problem prevails in psychotherapy. Psychotherapists frequently assume that if a patient becomes consciously aware of his psychological problems, his pathological behavior will disappear. Unfortunately, insight into one's own difficulties often seems to have no effect upon behavior. Therapists who postulate that behavioral improvement follows the attainment of insight can, and do, defend their position by arguing that if behavior fails to improve following insight, "true" insight has not been achieved. (Theoretical defense mechanisms will be discussed in the next chapter.)

Once again, let me clarify my basic point. Formulations that seek to interpret behavior with theoretical concepts that presumably reflect phenomenological processes are not intrinsically defective. Rather, they involve potential sources of difficulties that can be best avoided by becoming aware of them.

In concluding my discussion of the role of phenomenal experience for behavior theory, whether based on the conscious experience of subjects or the theorist, one particular problem must not be overlooked. A frequently repeated truism for many psychologists is that the key to understanding a person's behavior is to know how he perceives the world. The whole problem of psychological explanation would be solved, the truism goes, if only we had a key to unlock the secrets of the mind. There is no question that if we had direct access to a person's conscious experience our ability to predict his behavior would improve. Nevertheless, such information would be far from perfect for the reason already mentioned; there is not necessarily a one-to-one correspondence between inner experience and outer behavior. But even of greater significance is the problem of understanding why a person's conscious experience is the way it is. Surely we can better understand a person's bizarre behavior when we appreciate that he is a victim of paranoid thoughts? But that for such a person a vast explanatory problem still remains is summarized by the simply-stated question, "Why does he have paranoid thoughts?" This question, if one desires to understand the behavior of paranoids, with the aim of reducing the incidence of paranoia, is of much greater importance than discovering and describing how a paranoid feels. Bergmann expressed a similar view when discussing the concept of *psychological environment*, which represents a subject's personal perception of the world:

> But even so, what is the predictive value of the suggestive metaphor "psychological environment"? Is it not the business of science to ascertain which objective factors in the past and present states of the organism and its environment account for the difference in response, so that we can actually predict it instead of attributing it, merely descriptively and after it has happened, to a difference in the psychological environment? (1943, p. 133).

In sum, one can strategically opt for interpreting behavior within a phenomenological framework. To achieve success, more is required than formulating theoretical concepts that reflect inner experience.

Consensual Agreement about Basic Observations in Behavioral and in Experiential Psychology

The conclusion thus far is that two distinct and legitimate subject matters are available for study, conscious experience and objective behavior. The methodological principles governing behavioral and experiential research differ in regard to the capacity of each discipline to approach consensual agreement about basic observations; because the basic observations of behavioral psychology are open to public (intersubjective) scrutiny, consensual agreement is more easily achieved than is the case for experiential psychology.

In my attempt to structure the fundamental methodological issues I have ignored two problems related to consensual agreement of basic observations: operationism in behavioral psychology and the *direct* comparison of the conscious experience of two persons in experiential psychology. The foundation has been laid for the profitable discussion of these two problems.

OPERATIONISM

My analysis of the distinction between observational and theoretical statements has been approached pragmatically within the operating procedures of behavioral psychologists who are interested in communicating experimental procedures and results, and theoretical notions. Although recognizing that terms that describe the scientist's observation can be contaminated by theoretical preconceptions, in the absence of any precise linguistic rules to distinguish between theoretical and observational statements, a psychologist's efforts should be governed by the ideal of maintaining the distinction. In actual practice, this means the psychologist is confronted with the problem of conveying sufficient information about his research so that others will know exactly what he did and, if desired, replicate his efforts. Although misunderstandings can and do occur, such failures must be judged against the frequency of successful communications.

Operational Meaning

In essence, what is being argued is that the *operational approach* is not only desirable but also feasible. Such a statement demands analysis, both because of the variety of meanings that have been assigned to operationism and the failure of many operationalists to appreciate that operational meaning does not encompass all of the meaning contained in a scientific concept.

In its most limited sense operationism represents a simple recipe to further meaningful discourse about empirical results. Misunderstanding could be reduced and, it is hoped, eliminated by tracing the meaning of a term used to report experimental evidence back to its observational base via the operations of the scientist. For example, operationally the statement that "The two groups of children were equated for intelligence with the Peabody Picture Vocabulary Test" means that a particular test of intelligence was administered properly and the statistical evaluation revealed that the obtained differences between the IQ scores of both groups could reasonably be attributed to chance.

Although the statement that "The two groups of children were equated for intelligence with the Peabody Picture Vocabulary Test" is simple and would constitute a minute portion of an entire experimental report, it is nevertheless an exceedingly complex proposition in that it summarizes a large number of experimental operations and implicit assumptions. The operations range from the numerous procedures required to administer the intelligence test to the appropriate statistical evaluation to appraise the difference in IQ scores. Can such a brief statement accurately summarize all these observations? Yes. The communication is taking place between psychologists who are presumably suitably trained to understand the observational references of such a simple statement. If questions or confusions arise (e.g., What were the variances of the IQ scores for each group? Did some of the subjects suffer from a language handicap that would make the intelligence test inappropriate?) direct communication between the author and the reader may be required for a "complete" understanding of the observational base of the experimental report.

Conceptualizing operationism in this limited sense (e.g., the operational definition of intelligence as given in the description of the technique of intelligence testing) seems to reduce it to the trivial. Quite obviously, prior to the advent of operationism scientists were being operational. Scientific communication demands it. If this is all that operationism means, why was a fuss created when operationism appeared on the psychological scene in the 1930s? If we remember that structuralism and other methodological orientations employing mentalistic concepts were plagued with imprecision and unresolved theoretical disputes, then we can understand the enthusiastic reception operationism initially received. A faith was generated, particularly among psychologists who aspired to a natural-science methodology, that conceptual ambiguities would dissipate, theoretical differences would disappear, and progress would be ensured. This hope was based upon a misconception of operationism. As Bergmann aptly noted, "The root of the trouble was that some psychologists in their enthusiasm mistook the operationist footnote for the whole of the philosophy of science" (1954, p. 210).

Critics of operationism also exaggerated its role; shortcomings were attributed to operationism for its inability to solve problems for which it was not designed to cope. In the field of intelligence, which suffers from more conceptual confusions than it needs or deserves, the role of operationism is frequently misunderstood. One example is the criticism that operationally defined intelligence—*what the intelligence test measures*—both renders the formulation impregnable to attack and contributes nothing toward the validation of the intelligence scale (Pennington & Finan, 1940).

Empirical Meaning

There are several kinds of meanings of intelligence of which operational meaning is only one. The validity of an intelligence test refers to empirical meaning, how test scores are related to other operationally defined concepts such as academic success, achievement tests, and job performance. A clearly operationally defined concept need not have empirical meaning. That is, operationism does not guarantee the fruitfulness of a concept. For example, *cephalic index*, the ratio multiplied by 100 of the maximum breadth of the head to its maximum length, is operationally defined when the techniques of measuring maximum breadth and length are clearly stated. Nevertheless, its elegant clarity has failed to give psychology a concept of any importance for the simple reason that no one has been able to involve the concept of cephalic index in any significant psychological law.

The fact that cephalic index is operationally defined but empirically empty in no way detracts from the communication value of its operational meaning. Knowing that an operationally defined concept is empirically empty provides significant information. It indicates at that time that the concept is not fruitful, and the investigator has the option of dropping the concept, persisting in his attempts to discover some empirical meaning or modify its operational meaning.

The possibility of altering a concept's operational meaning has been overlooked by some critics of operationism. A common complaint against operationism is that it tends to freeze the meaning of a concept before it could be developed into a fruitful construct. Such a criticism is inappropriate if the proper scope of operationism is realized. An operational definition is not permanent. Its meaning can evolve by the addition of new or the elimination or modification of old operations. Nevertheless, at any *given* time its operational meaning can be discerned:

> A statement such as this, . . . Operationism requires that all the conditions be taken into account, can be quite misleading. For a construct which unwittingly leaves out a relevant factor (or determining condition) just leads to a different formulation of the empirical laws. For example, by telling us what manipulations he performs, what pointers he reads, . . . and what computations he carries out with the numbers thus obtained . . . , a primitive physicist would give us a methodologically correct definition of his *empirical construct* "density of a liquid." And this in spite of the fact that he might not have given any attention to the temperature in his laboratory, one of the conditions upon which, and as we know, and as he might not know at that state of his investigation, the results of his manipulations and computations depends. The point is that we are able to trace back the terms of his lan-

guage to the immediately observable. He has laid down all the conditions under which he is going to say: "This liquid has the density 1.3." Therefore, we know what he means, and that is all general methodology can insist upon at this level of the so-called *operational definition of empirical constructs* (Bergmann & Spence, 1941, p. 3).

Intuitive Meaning

Another criticism frequently heard is that operationism places an unnecessary burden on the creative scientist. Demanding a set of operations when one is forming vague ideas of a concept may be too much of a burden for the creative process. Again we find a criticism that is not aimed at the proper target. Operationism does not offer a prescription for productive thinking. Operational definitions are the results of creative thought, not necessarily the means by which it is accomplished. A psychologist may have only a vague, imprecise notion of a concept (e.g., intelligence, motivation) when first thinking about it. When he is "thinking through" the concept, indulging in *intra*subjective communication, the requirements of operational definitions need not be considered, and certainly not be met. In actual fact, it is not inconsistent for a researcher who is investigating intelligence to use an IQ test as his operational definition of intelligence while simultaneously entertaining an intuitive conception of intelligence that is much broader and more complex, involving such notions as symbolic representations, cognitive structures, intellectual operations, and other concepts that one might consider to be fundamental in intellectual functioning. To underline this distinction *intuitive meaning* must be contrasted with *operational meaning*.

Critics of operationism argue that the richness of the *intuitive meaning* of a concept is destroyed by the narrowness of its operational meaning. Such a conclusion emerges from the misconception that the two kinds of meaning need to be at odds when in fact they can be complementary. Intuitive notions can be enriched by surveying relevant empirical evidence, which of necessity contains the ingredients of operational definitions. Although an investigator may not self-consciously formulate an operational definition when conducting research, such a definition can be extracted from an examination of his procedures.

I find it difficult to imagine that a psychologist interested in interpreting intelligence within a broad theoretical framework would fail to be stimulated by the wealth of data that has been collected from intelligence testing designed to predict academic and job success. The evidence obtained as a result of wide-scale intelligence testing reveals important developmental changes that must be accounted for by any theory of intelligence.

Theoretical Meaning

At this point a fourth meaning of a concept, *theoretical meaning,* must be added to conclude this discussion of operational definitions. Again using intelligence as an example it can be viewed neither as: (1) an operational definition referring to the procedures of a particular instrument of measurement; nor as (2) an empirical law relating operationally defined concepts (e.g., intelligence test scores with academic success); nor as (3) a set of intuitive reflections and ideas entertained by a scientist when thinking creatively (hopefully) about the psychological nature of intelligence; but instead as (4) an explicit theory of intellectual functioning. In essence, the *theoretical meaning* of intelligence is contained in the totality of theoretical statements that are proposed to account for the empirical relations involving intellectual functioning. Such a theory, if it aspires to any breadth, would seek to go beyond the facts of intelligence testing. The intelligence test movement, it must not be forgotten, was not conceived for the purpose of collecting data about fundamental processes of intellectual functioning or for formulating a general theory of intelligence. A broad theory of intelligence would have to cope with many processes such as symbolic representation, conceptual development, memory, intellectual operations, and inference. The theory would have to account for the facts of learning sets, hypothesis testing, conservation, discrimination-shift behavior, stages of information processing, and so on. Within such a broad theoretical and empirical context, intelligence means much more than what the intelligence test measures. Whereas operational meaning is designed solely for purposes of communication, theoretical meaning serves the need for understanding.

After distinguishing between operational, empirical, intuitive, and theoretical meanings, it should be apparent why Bergmann assigned operational meaning the status of a footnote in the philosophy of science. A primary aim of science is to provide understanding, and the really difficult tasks in achieving this goal are the formulation of some guiding notions (intuitive meaning), collection of significant facts (empirical meaning), and development of fruitful hypotheses (theoretical meaning). In contrast, operational meaning assumes minor importance. But it should be understood that the search for these four kinds of meaning are not independent efforts, insulated from each other. Rather they represent different components of a single venture, and even though operational meaning may be of secondary importance when compared with the other forms of meanings, it nevertheless serves an essential function in the entire enterprise of behavioral psychology.

There is no doubt that much criticism and resistance to operational definitions was encouraged by the exaggerated claims and oversimplifications advanced by its proponents. Even P. W. Bridgman, the physicist-philosopher who fathered operationism (1927), disassociated himself from the inflated claims of naive operationists by admitting to feelings of having sired a "Frankenstein."

> I abhor the word *operationalism* or *operationism*, which seems to imply a dogma, or at least a thesis of some kind. The thing I envisaged is too simple to be dignified by so pretentious a name; rather, it is an attitude or point of view generated by continued practice of operational analysis (1954, p. 224).

At the same time he recognized a fundamental opposition to even his modest conception of operationism:

Any person can make an operational analysis, whether or not he accepts what he supposes to be the thesis of "operationalism," and whether or not he thinks he is wasting his time in so doing. So far as the "operationalist" is to be distinguished from the "nonoperationalist," it is in the conviction of the former that it is often profitable and clarifying to make an operational analysis, and also, I suspect, in his private feeling that often the "nonoperationalist" does not want to make an operational analysis through fear that it might result in a change in his attitude (1954, pp. 224–26).

Bridgman's clinical judgment could be extended a bit further. The nonoperationalist may resist an operational analysis not for fear of a change of attitude but rather because of an unshakable faith in the validity of his intuitive conceptions. He is convinced that all operational definitions will fall short of the true meaning of his intuitive notions and, if employed, might lead to a premature "disproof" of an idea that is intrinsically sound. The nonoperationalist is correct in believing that operational definitions cannot possibly reflect the full range of his intuitions for the simple reason that the latter are much broader and more intricate than the former. But what he fails to realize, or refuses to acknowledge, is that intuitive notions can only evolve into viable theoretical conceptions via the employment of some operational definitions. Theoretical development cannot occur in the absence of empirical evidence, which of necessity, implicitly or explicitly, contains operational definitions. In essence, the nonoperationalist employs a protective shield to defend his intuitive ideas from possible refutation and by so doing stunts their scientific growth.

DIRECT COMPARISON OF THE CONSCIOUS EXPERIENCES OF DIFFERENT INDIVIDUALS

The major obstacle to achieving consensual agreement in experiential psychology is that conscious experience is private, accessible to only the experiencing individual. As a result, even when the subjective reports of two individuals are in essential agreement and are buttressed by a similar pattern of common physiological measures and/or environmental events, a nagging doubt prevails about whether the two are really sharing a common experience. There appears to be no way of getting around the possibility that common verbal descriptions coupled with common objective indices need not reflect common experiences (or even the obverse that different introspections combined with different objective measures may occur in combination with a common experience). It is because of this possibility that phenomenological investigations seeking to correlate introspective evidence with publicly observable behavior and/or physiological events are characterized as quasi-objective. The inability to *directly* examine the conscious experience of different individuals necessitated the adjective *quasi.*

The question that I would like to raise now is whether the highest level that can possibly be achieved by a natural-science approach to experiential psychology is quasi-objective. To answer this question one must face up to the problem of whether it can be demonstrated directly that two individuals are sharing a common experience. If so, experiential psychology could achieve a level of objectivity that is presently unobtainable.

One answer to the question concerning the feasibility of directly comparing the inner experiences of two individuals is that it cannot be done; the privacy of mind cannot be penetrated by any physical means. An alternative response is that although a comparison is presently impossible, technical developments could make it feasible.

Over the years I have presented this issue to graduate classes concerned with methodological issues in psychology. The question is posed in the context of a "game" I played with my younger son, Kenneth, who at the age of seven responded to questions about visual images by admitting that he was capable of seeing "clear pictures" in his head. On one bitterly cold winter day I asked him to close his eyes and imagine High Lake, an idyllic spot in Vermont where we spent our summers. I then closed my eyes and said, "I'm 'seeing' High Lake also. Are our 'pictures' of High Lake the same?" (I forget his answer although I sometimes wonder whether questions of this sort encouraged him to become a psychiatrist.) After describing this anecdote I challenged my class to design an experiment, unimpeded by any technical limitations, capable of answering the question that was posed to my son.

My own position has been that the direct comparison of inner states is neither logically nor physically impossible but rather, at present, technically impossible. Consistent with this position, the following research design was proposed replete with science-fiction apparatus.

The first piece of equipment that is needed is an apparatus that publicly and accurately displays a person's visual image. To demonstrate its accuracy, the subject, by appropriate means, would be placed in a state in which he would be unaware of whether he is observing his own image or observing his image on the display. By appropriate psychophysical techniques it could be demonstrated that the subject cannot discriminate between the two.

Once the adequacy of such equipment is demonstrated then the significant comparison can be made. Ken and I would simultaneously image High Lake from a common vantage point. Our brains would be connected to the visual display that could accurately reproduce either image. We then, individually, would be subjects of a psychophysical experiment to determine whether we can discriminate our own image from that of the other. By systematic research of this sort it should be possible to determine whether common visual images do occur and with what frequency.

Most students accept the appropriateness of this design although a majority argue, as is always the case in designing experiments, that some variation in procedure would be preferable. These reservations, however, are not critical because they do not question the fundamental assumption that such research is feasible given that certain technical breakthroughs were achieved. Some argue, for reasons that are unclear, that the proposed kind of research is physically or logically impossible. Perhaps their disagreement stems from a confusion of peripheral issues with the fundamental problem of the direct comparison of conscious experiences of different individuals. In order to minimize that confusion the three following clarifications are offered: (1) The proposed experimental design is not based on the assumption that visual images are "floating around the head" and are perceived by a "mind's eye." Although visual images can be observed phenomenologically their occurrence depends upon neurophysiological events. (2) The proposed design does not imply that all prob-problems of comparing phenomenological experiences such as feelings, will be as "simple" as investigating shared imagery. But the basic argument is that if private visual images can be made public, appropriate procedures could be developed for other forms of private experience. (3) The proposed design in no way implies that the linguistic problem of describing inner experience will automatically be solved by demonstrating that similar images or feelings can be shared. The problem of coordinating a linguistic system to represent the basic observations of what were previously private events is no different from making observational statements about public events. In essence, what would be accomplished if the proposed science fiction project were successful would be the eradication of the epistemological boundaries between what is currently described as private experience and public behavior. The problems of developing an appropriate language system for publicly observed "private" events and determining whether such a system would be insulated from theoretical preconceptions bring us full circle to the problems of discussing observational statements about public behavior. The issues are identical and, therefore, the answers should be the same.

SUMMARY

Has anything been gained by this excursion into science-fantasyland? Not if the entire issue of the relationship between behavioral and experiential psychology is simply put aside until the miracle of achieving direct access into the minds of others is realized, assuming it ever will be. The point of my analysis is to lay out the possible methodological choices confronting the psychologist when deciding upon which subject matter(s) to investigate. The conclusion reached is that the independent entities of public behavior and conscious experience yield two fundamentally different kinds of knowledge: the criterion of consensual agreement for observational statements is attainable in behavioral but not necessarily in experiential psychology. Such a conclusion in no way justifies restricting the subject matter of psychology to public behavior. It does suggest, however, that consensual agreement among phenomenologists about the facts of conscious experience will at best be limited to communities of psychologists that share a common parlance and investigatory procedures.

Psychologists are not confronted with an "either-or" choice when choosing between public behavior and private experience as subject matters. One can seek to investigate both, but if one strives for methodological consistency one must adopt a single epistemological framework to judge the validity of all kinds of observational statements. An obvious and common choice has been to select the public framework of behavioral psychology while viewing private experience as an inferred state from directly observed events (introspective reports, responses to personality inventories, environmental stimulation, etc.). Viewing conscious experience as a theoretical construct, in preference to ignoring it or conceiving it as a directly observable event, must be considered a strategic decision. Its value must be demonstrated rather than taken for granted.

Within the epistemological framework of a psychology that adopts public behavior as its subject matter, the phenomenal experience of the psychologist possesses no intrinsic validity for any formal interpretation of behavior. That is, the validity of a theoretical construct cannot be justified on the basis of any apparent correspondence with the phenomenal experience of the theorist. It has for behavioral psychology no factual content although it certainly can serve as a source, and perhaps a fruitful one, of potential hypotheses. This is cogently represented by the title of Max Meyer's book (1921), *The Psychology of the Other One,* that illustrates the methodological isolation of the behavioral psychologist from the subject matter he investigates and interprets.

Up to this point, conscious experience, as reported by subjects or directly observed by psychologists, has been perceived as ancillary to the major task of understanding publicly observed behavior. Without changing the underlying epistemological framework of behavioral psychology, it becomes possible to expand the discipline to include the analysis of experiential processes, to investigate "subjective behavior." This can be accomplished by "objectifying" subjective experience—by relating experiential reports to publicly observable events, particularly physiological processes, because of the presumed intimate relationship between the two. The underlying assumption of such an effort is that the accuracy with which introspective reports reflect conscious experience is in some way proportional to the number and variety of independent publicly observed events to which they are coordinated. These correlated public events, then, serve as anchor points to coordinate a phenomenally descriptive language with conscious experience.

In sum, this analysis offers both divergent and convergent paths for psychology, with its dual subject matter, to pursue. The particular choice selected will be determined not only by the goals psychologists set for their efforts but also by the conceptions they adopt for *understanding* psychological events, a topic that is examined in the next two chapters.

On Understanding: Part One

4

1. Understanding is a psychological concept that refers to the manner in which empirical phenomena are comprehended. Psychologists have employed different criteria to achieve understanding: deductive explanation, interpretive consistency, comprehension by behavioral control, and intuitive understanding.

2. Deductive explanation is achieved when an event is logically deduced from a set of assumptions that have empirical implications. Deductivism as a form of understanding must be distinguished from deductivism as a research strategy that encourages the formulation of formal deductive models at all stages of theoretical development. There is no methodological recipe that indicates at what stage of theoretical development a formal deductive model should be introduced.

3. Successful deductive theories cannot be automatically created by an "inductive logic." Although logic can get one from theoretical assumptions to empirical statements, it cannot provide passage from empirical statements to theoretical assumptions.

4. The natural-science approach to psychology has usually been associated with the use of deductive explanation to achieve understanding. Some psychologists have argued that the scientific method must be modified to meet the needs of the social, behavioral, and humanistic sciences. If the scientific method is considered as a systematic procedure used to arrive at warranted theoretical statements regardless of content, then the method transcends the borders of various scientific disciplines.

5. Deductive theories can be conceptualized as representing reality or as convenient fictions that enable discrete events to be interpreted in a coherent manner. In both cases, the structure of the deductive theory is essentially the same. Nevertheless, the strategic consequences of neurophysiological theories, as contrasted to "black-box" theories, may be quite different, particularly in regard to the resolution of theoretical disputes.

6. Reductionism has several meanings in regard to the reduction of behavioral to neurophysiological events: relating behavior to neurophysiological variables, adopting a model of behavior based on physiological evidence, and coordinating a behavior theory to a physiological theory. The theoretical reduction of psychology to neurophysiology is not necessarily inevitable.

7. The "truth value" of deductive theories can be evaluated within three different frameworks. The traditional view assumes that scientific knowledge is accumulated in a progressive, linear fashion and that theoretical disputes are resolved by critical experiments that validate one theory and disprove its competitor. The subjective view, an extreme version of Kuhn's analysis of the history of science, assumes that there are repetitive patterns of normal science and revolution. During normal science, a global methodological-theoretical orientation —known as a paradigm—guides empirical and theoretical development. A revolution occurs when a prevailing paradigm is supplanted by a new one. This revolution does not occur suddenly and decisively but instead takes many years to accomplish because the competing paradigms are incommensurable, and the choice of one paradigm in preference to another is subjectively determined. The historical view assumes that competing research programs are commensurable, and the adoption of one program in preference to another can be defended on the basis of explicit standards such as one program is progressive (e.g., predicting novel events) while another is degenerating (e.g., adding ad hoc assumptions). The historical view is the most appropriate framework for evaluating deductive theories in psychology.

THE SEARCH FOR MEANING

Aristotle, in the opening sentence of his *Metaphysics*, postulates that "all men by nature desire to know." Today, many psychological theories (e.g., Maddi, 1970), make a similar assumption, viz., humans possess a motive for meaning—the need to understand and interpret their world in a consistent manner. Clinical evidence suggests to these theorists that failure to achieve a meaningful existence is a prime cause of psychological disturbances. The laboratory also provides evidence for a need to know. Experiments that investigate cognitive processes find that humans persist in their attempts to extract regularities from sequences of environmental events. One example is the behavior of human subjects who are confronted with the task of predicting which of two alternative events will occur. When the events are randomized the subject, unaware of the chance order, persists to an extraordinary degree in producing hypotheses to account for the sequence of occurrences (Feldman, 1963). When the binary events are generated by some rule that is not excessively complex, the principle that underlies the regularities is usually discovered with little difficulty.

My intent is not to argue for any universal human motive to seek meaning. I personally find it difficult to deal with a hypothesis that ignores environmental, or hereditary, components in behavior. At the same time, I am willing to admit (at least I like to believe) that psychologists as a group are motivated by a need to understand the problems with which they deal.

Many scientists accept the notion that a valid interpretation of the world can only be achieved by the scientific method. Implicit in this position is the denial that a "true" understanding can be reached in nonscientific disciplines—art, the humanities, theology, philosophy—and that only one form of understanding prevails in science. My position will be more subjective. A sense of understanding can be achieved in a variety of ways. That understanding can only be achieved by empirical methods is essentially denied by those, including myself, who seek to understand science by epistemological analyses.

To understand understanding, within contemporary psychology it becomes necessary to identify and analyze different modes of "explanation." If we accept the notion that understanding can be achieved by different kinds of knowing, we can more easily understand the apparent diversity of "explanations" that are offered by different psychologists. For example, childhood autism has been interpreted by some as a frustration response to a mechanistic environment (Murray, 1974) and by others as resulting from a particular schedule of reinforcement (Ferster, 1961). In evaluating such contrasting views one could rationally argue for, or arbitrarily select, a model of scientific explanation that would serve as a standard to judge interpretative efforts. Although such standards are helpful for one's own work, they can nevertheless render incomprehensible the efforts of others who fail to adopt a similar interpretive framework. Since our aim is illumination, not persuasion, four different kinds of understanding will be identified: deductive explanation, interpretive consistency, comprehension by behavioral control, and intuitive understanding. Though not necessarily mutually exclusive, they are each characterized by a dominant feature that makes them distinctively different.

DEDUCTIVE EXPLANATION

The form of understanding usually associated with natural-science methodology is deductive, which assumes that natural events can be interpreted in the form of logical order. Understanding is achieved when an event is deduced from one or more general propositions. In essence, the deductive process is analogous to mathematical proof with the precision varying from mathematical verification to the rigorous use of ordinary language.

The medium for deductive explanations is a "deductive theory"—a system of propositions that are logically organized and are coordinated to empirical events in such a manner that legitimate deductions (predictions or postdictions) about the phenomena can be made. The essential characteristics of a deductive theory possess an empirical content and are capable of generating deductions that could, in principle, be at odds with the evidence.[1] In line with my refusal to don the robes of the philosopher of science, I will neither suggest that all deductive theories share a fundamental conceptual structure nor adopt what appears to be a more reasonable position that they can assume a variety of theoretical forms (Suppe, 1974).

Deductivism as a Form of Understanding and as a Theoretical Strategy

To clarify the discussion of deductive explanation a distinction must be made between two different features of deductivism. Deductivism can be considered as a methodological decision to adopt a deductive model of understanding. It can also be considered as a strategy to formulate highly formal deductive models at all stages of theoretical development. Deductivism as a model of understanding does not necessarily imply deductivism as a methodological strategy. The conflation of the two is illustrated in the efforts of Clark L. Hull, who passionately argued for the necessity of hypothetic-deductive theories of behavior. Of interest is the following quotation from his autobiography:

> The study of geometry proved to be the most important event of my intellectual life; it opened to me an entirely new world—the fact that thought itself could generate and really prove new relationships from previously possessed elements. Later in the writing of a prep school paper in English composition, I tried to use the geometrical method to deduce some negative propositions regarding theology (Hull, 1952, p. 144).

1. The discussion of this crucial point must be postponed until later (pages 135–151). For the time being a strongly worded interpretation of this essential characteristic is that the deductive theory could be falsified; weakly expressed it means that the deductive theory could be embarrassed by certain kinds of empirical evidence.

Although Hull obviously understood the distinction between logical proof and empirical prediction, his failure to mention this difference reflects the high premium he always placed in his theoretical efforts on a formal deductive structure, often to the detriment, some believe, of empirical content. That is, sometimes he was more concerned with formalism than empiricism.

An overall evaluation of Hull's efforts, I believe, would indicate that he exerted salutary effects upon theoretical practices in psychology, particularly in regard to the explication of the supporting logic underlying theoretical predictions. I am reminded of a comment made to me by M. E. Bitterman, a frequent and severe critic of Hull's work. He took upon himself, during one sabbatical, the task of reading successive volumes of the *Psychological Review* in order to obtain deeper insights into the history of psychology. He remarked that Hull's articles in the 1930s "were like a breath of fresh air" when contrasted with the muddy conceptualizations of that and previous eras. In his early articles Hull formulated theoretical models of "complex" forms of animal learning based upon principles of conditioning. The models were cleverly conceived, possessing clear deductive implications that served to guide future research. The whole effort was modest in scope and lucid in content. Later on his theoretical formalism seemed to get out of hand. Elegance of formal style began to operate as an end in itself; the empirical evidence required to support the formal superstructure tended to be ignored. The prime example of this excessive formalism was the *Mathematico-Deductive Theory of Rote Learning: A Study in Scientific Methodology* (Hull, Hovland, Ross, Hall, Perkins & Fitch, 1940), which was expressed in symbolic logic, mathematics, and stilted English prose. Hull was so impressed with its formal structure that he was led to make the following "modest" evaluation:

> At the very least [it] is believed to represent in a clear manner the form which the more scientific work on behavior of the future should take (1952, p. 158).

History offered another evaluation. *The Mathematico-Deductive Theory of Rote Learning* was largely ignored and quickly forgotten. It generated little research and failed to encourage theoretical attempts with the same formal characteristics.

Why the abysmal failure? First and foremost, the *Mathematico-Deductive Theory of Rote Learning* was based upon an inadequate assumption, viz., principles of conditioning could alone handle the facts of verbal learning. The question raised is whether this oversimplified and distorted view was encouraged by the ceremonial formalism that dominated Hull's thinking. My historical interpretation suggests an affirmative answer; concern with theoretical style was at the expense of empirical content. This, however, need not be the inevitable consequence of the search for deductive explanation. Deductive explanations can be mediated by modest theoretical proposals as Hull and many of his co-workers demonstrated (e.g., Spence, 1936; Miller, 1944). Spence, I believe, was much more sensitive to the fine nuances of experimental data than was Hull and more aware of the provisional nature of psychological theorizing. Spence felt no compulsion to offer anything resembling a final theoretical solution. Imprecision or incompleteness in model building did not bother him as long as his conceptions could generate empirical predictions, the defining characteristic of a deductive model.

The criticism of excessive formalism could be directed, but with less force, against Hull's most significant effort, *Principles of Behavior* (1943). The title is misleading in that the book deals primarily with conditioning phenomena. (Hull thought they would provide sufficient evidence for principles that would apply to all forms of behavior, including social.) *Principles of Behavior* proved to be successful both in identifying significant variables and proposing fruitful hypotheses about learning. The book generated much experimental research, probably more than any other single publication in the history of psychology. In spite of its heuristic value the argument could be advanced that Hull's theory was degraded by his overconcern with ceremonial formalisms. Formal considerations outweighed empirical ones in the selection of primary assumptions. Take, for example, his treatment of the delay of reinforcement gradient mainly as a function of passage of time. No consideration was given to the animal's reactions during the delay period, a factor that was later demonstrated to be significant (Spence, 1956). One possible reason for Hull's oversight is that it enabled him to express the delay of reinforcement principle in the elegant mathematical style that he desired.

One could generally agree with the criticism of "ceremonial formalism" that has been directed at Hull but still side with his strategy. Psychology, at that time, had a pressing need for theoretical hypotheses that could in principle be falsified. Although Hull's formalism may have been excessive for his own theoretical task, it was pitched at the right level to attract the attention of the psychological community who had to be "shown" the virtues of deductive explanation. (A disconcerting aspect of the history of psychology is that all its "great men" overstated their cases—as did many who were not so great!) Hull's efforts, in fact, served as an impetus to the development of mathematical models of learning. Although the post-Hullian mathematical models of learning were much more sophisticated, particularly in regard to the clarity of their empirical implications, they also can be faulted for sacrificing empirical content for formal elegance. At the time of their formulation many mathematical interpretations of probability learning, concept identification, prisoner-of-war game, and selective attention, seemed to be primarily formal exercises that distorted by oversimplification the behavioral events they sought to explain.

As an aside it should be noted that diametrically opposed evaluations of a common methodological effort are possible without necessarily being contradictory. Particular mathematical models of learning can be faulted as theoretically naive and of limited empirical relevance and at the same time be praised for encouraging the raising of explanatory standards in psychology.

The point of my historical excursion has not been to evaluate the relative benefits of deductive precision or explanatory breadth but instead to underline the difference between the formal aspects of deductive explanation and the strategic methods used to achieve that goal. Hull, in essence, argued for the strategy of rigorousness at all stages of theoretical development. In contrast, I have suggested (Kendler & Kendler, 1975) that deductive ambiguity in the early stages of theoretical development, when the empirical evidence is sparse and many theoretical alternatives are possible, may be a more productive strategy than premature precision that is overcommitted to one of several reasonable theoretical options. Feigl (1970), a distinguished philosopher of science, concludes: "It is a matter of controversy just how fruitful or helpful strict axiomatizations are for the ongoing creative work of the theoretical scientists."

Other strategies are also possible. One of the great surprises of my professional life occurred in 1970 during a conversation about the unity of psychology with Abraham H. Maslow, who was one of the major promoters of humanistic psychology and for whom I served as an undergraduate assistant at Brooklyn College in the late 1930s. I was at that time preparing an essay, along with Janet T. Spence, entitled *Tenets of Neobehaviorism,* for a memorial volume dedicated to Kenneth W. Spence (Kendler & J. T. Spence, 1971). In analyzing the epistemological assumptions of neobehaviorism, we identified the deductive model of explanation as a primary one. I raised the question to Maslow whether humanistic psychology aspired to this kind of explanation and was flabbergasted to hear an affirmative answer. He suggested that it would be achieved when the physiological aspects of consciousness were more fully understood and thought the research of the kind in the book Tart edited, *Altered States of Consciousness* (1969), would lead ultimately to deductive theories in humanistic psychology. As far as I know, Maslow never put such notions in print, and there is much published in humanistic literature that is at odds with it. Whether his comments in our conversation were an expression of a temporarily expansive and optimistic feeling or the beginning of a new direction in his thinking is something that will never be known. But his position at that time does illustrate the possibility of adopting a goal of deductive explanation while simultaneously being concerned with issues (e.g., the nature of human experience, self-actualization) that appear to be far removed from deductively structured formulations. Although Maslow could have been accused of harboring inconsistent concerns (deductive explanations versus a humanistic interpretation) the fact of the matter is that deductivism, as a method to achieve understanding, does not specify at what stage of a research program the demands of deductive explanation need be considered and at what stage they should be met. The sole requirement seems to be that the goal is acknowledged, which implies an intention to achieve it. Conceivably more than a lifetime of work might be required to obtain and transform information about conscious experience and physiological processes into a deductive theoretical system relevant to humanistic psychology.

Although I find it difficult to imagine how one could adopt the goal of deductive explanation while ignoring it completely in day-to-day practice, I cannot formulate any rule that would specify exactly when one should become concerned about the deductive capacities of one's theoretical conceptions. (It should be clear by now that the standard I am using for a deductive principle is minimal: some logically determined prediction, expressed in ordinary language that could be embarrassed by inconsistent findings.)

The difficulty in specifying at what stage of a research program deductive practices should begin, and the level of rigor they should possess, should not cause any surprise. Constructing a successful deductive theory is purely an exercise in creative thought. At the present we are unable to extract principles from our knowledge of creative thinking that would suggest a step-by-step plan for constructing a successful deductive theory. It is questionable whether psychological principles of such power could ever be formulated because the growth of knowledge, including the formulation of novel theories, may be beyond prediction (Popper, 1957). In any case, at least for the present, if not forever, we cannot evaluate the strategy employed to construct a deductive theory. We are limited to judging the explanatory ability of the theory itself.

Social criteria can be applied with reliability to assess the logical correctness of a particular prediction. Although mathematicians may entertain some disagreement about the logic of a specific deduction, for the most part, consensual agreement about its correctness can be achieved. The further one gets from forms of mathematical representation, or the closer one gets to ordinary language as the medium for deductive explanation, the greater will be the disagreement about the logical legitimacy of a particular explanatory deduction. But these disagreements are usually resolvable when the issues are clarified by discussion. And even when a deadlock is reached historical pressures will begin to operate to demonstrate either that the deduction is true or false or so ambiguous as not to deserve further consideration.

Inductive Processes in Deductive Theorizing

Is there an inductive logic that can guide the efforts of a theorist in his attempt to formulate valid assumptions, that is, postulates that will generate predictions in line with empirical evidence? The answer depends upon what is meant by the term *logic*. If the term is used in the conventional sense, reasoning according to a set of explicit rules, then the notion of an inductive logic that inevitably leads from empirical evidence to valid theoretical assumptions must be rejected. Although one can logically get from theoretical assumptions to empirical statements, one cannot logically get from empirical statements to theoretical assumptions. The main reason is that theories say more than the data they purport to explain. They not only summarize available evidence, but they also possess implications for data not yet obtained. A theory is more than the evidence it is designed to explain; the data are less than the theory that interprets them. In essence, a theory has something extra and that extra emerges from the creative efforts of the theorist.

It is a mistaken notion to liken the problem of theory construction to an inductive logical problem that can be solved by *deductive* means. Identify a preselected number from one to eight after asking only three questions that can be answered by "Yes" or "No." By halving remaining alternatives (Five or above? Seven or above? Eight?) the correct answer *must* be forthcoming after the third query. Although the solution appears to be achieved by inductive means, in reality it represents the deductive consequences of a simple probability model.

Empirical theories do not deal only with specific events or a finite set of events. A theory limited to the interpretation of the influence of practice on the acquisition of classical conditioned responses deals with an infinite number of empirical events. One can never exhaust all possible experimental designs involving all combinations of conditioned stimuli, unconditioned stimuli, and response measures. Nor can one exhaust the infinite number of conditioning trials. Thus no matter how well a given theory can account for available evidence, no guarantee is possible that it will be successful in interpreting new experimental data.

Hull (1943), influenced by Tolman's tactics of theorizing (1936), operated on the assumption that an inductive logic could be used to determine the mathematical properties of theoretical concepts. By investigating the influence of practice (number of reinforced trials) in some ideal experimental situations in which the influences of other significant variables were presumably controlled, it would be possible to conclude that the observed behavior reflected without distortion the properties of the theoretical process of *habit formation.* Hull, in fact, formulated his law of habit growth from curve-fitting procedures applied to results of parametric studies that measured behavioral changes (e.g., amplitude of the conditioned response) as a function of the amount of training.

In principle there is nothing wrong with the procedure of using experimental results as direct sources of theoretical notions. But there is a world of difference between considering the results as logical inductions and as mere suggestions about the properties of the theoretical process. In the former case one concludes a fait accompli: the theoretical principle is valid and nothing remains but to spin out its implications. In contrast, considering the evidence only as suggestive and tentative encourages one to critically examine the adequacy of the theoretical assumption and prevents one from becoming overcommitted to it.

Explanation in Physics and Psychology

Experimental psychologists have frequently been accused of succumbing to scientism, the adoration of the methods of the natural sciences, a false god for psychology. The argument offered is that the methods of the natural sciences may not be appropriate for those of the social, behavioral, or humanistic sciences; the "scientific method" must be adapted to the special needs of each discipline.

The essence of such an argument revolves about the meaning of *method*. If one understands *method* to represent specific kinds of research tools and techniques, then quite obviously each scientific discipline must develop its own particular investigatory procedures. Psychology needs standardized tests and operant conditioning apparatus; physics requires cloud chambers and low temperature laboratories. However, if scientific method is considered a systematic mode for arriving at warranted empirical conclusions, then the *method* transcends the borders of various scientific disciplines. Regardless of the particular procedures of investigation used, the criteria of empirical truth remains the same.

Psychologists who employ the deductive model of understanding, for the most part, freely admit to the adoption of what they consider to be the natural-science approach to psychology. The accusation that their behavior as psychologists is being motivated by their desire to emulate physics appears to them to be irrelevant to the problem of arriving at warranted conclusions. If one maintains, they would argue, that psychology requires a different conception of understanding than does physics, one is obligated to articulate the difference between "natural science" understanding and "psychological" understanding. Although it is difficult, if not impossible, to draw a precise demarcation line between science and nonscience, this does not suggest that the division between the two should be blurred beyond any distinction.

Productive methodological discussions within psychology will become impossible if the term *science* is robbed of all its significant meanings. An analogous, though extreme, example occurs in a discussion about art in Tom Stoppard's play *Travesties*.

TZARA: Doing the things by which is meant Art is no longer considered the proper concern of the artist. In fact it is frowned upon. Nowadays, an artist is someone who makes art mean the things he does. A man may be an artist by exhibiting his hindquarters. He may be a poet by drawing words out of a hat. In fact some of my best poems have been drawn out of my hat which I afterwards exhibited to general acclaim at the Dada Gallery in Bahnhofstrasse.

CARR: But that is simply to change the meaning of the word Art.

TZARA: I see I have made myself clear.

CARR: Then you are not actually an artist at all?

TZARA: On the contrary. I have just told you I am.

CARR: But that does not make you an artist. An artist is someone who is gifted in some way that enables him to do something more or less well which can only be done badly or not at all by someone who is not thus gifted. If there is any point in using language at all it is that a word is taken to stand for a particular fact or idea and not for other facts or ideas. I might claim to be able to fly . . . Lo, I say, I am flying. But you are not propelling yourself about while suspended in the air, someone may point out. Ah no, I reply, that is no longer considered the proper concern of people who can fly. In fact, it is frowned upon. Nowadays, a flyer never leaves the ground and wouldn't know how. I see, says my somewhat baffled interlocutor, so when you say you can fly you are using the word in a purely private sense. I see I have made myself clear, I say. Then, says this chap in some relief, you cannot actually fly after all? On the contrary, I say, I have just told you I can. Don't you see my dear Tristan you are simply asking me to accept that the word Art means whatever you wish it to mean; but I do not accept it (Stoppard, 1975, pp. 38–39).

The natural-science oriented psychologist favors the deductive model of understanding because of its value in achieving *publicly* warranted empirical conclusions; the explanatory statements contained in a deductive explanation are available to all rather than being merely in the minds of the person asserting them.

Even if one were interested in uncovering the motive for selecting a deductive model of understanding, other hypotheses, besides the frank desire to mimic physics, are possible. For example, Brodbeck (1962) argues that accepting the deductive model does not mean that physics is being imitated but instead that physics is being admired. The most compelling point about the deductive model of explanation, she argues, is in its conclusiveness. The persuasiveness of deductive explanation became apparent to me when a schoolboy. Gravitation finally became understandable when I was exposed to the story of the discovery of a planet in 1843. It had been noted that the planet Uranus followed a peculiar and variable path around the sun. Astronomers deduced from the theory of gravitation that some unknown body must be exerting a gravitational pull on Uranus. As a result, the location of a heretofore unknown planetary body, later to be named Neptune, was predicted and discovered.

Particularly important for later discussion is the distinction between two different aspects of the "conclusiveness" or "persuasiveness" of a deductive explanation: the public logico-empirical component and the private intuitive sense of understanding. It is difficult for me to recall exactly what weight each component had in my achieving a sense of understanding of gravitation except to note that the latter component was operative. That is, the deductive explanation was phenomenologically fulfilling; it generated a compelling sense of understanding. I am not suggesting that every confirmed prediction gives rise to as dramatic a case of intuitive understanding as did the discovery of Neptune for me. Nor am I implying that for all individuals deductive explanations are intuitively persuasive. My proposal is that deductivism, as a public method of arriving at warranted conclusions about empirical events, can provide a phenomenologically satisfying sense of understanding.

The Role of Laboratory Experiments in Deductive Theorizing

The example of the discovery of Neptune should put to rest any argument that deductive explanations are possible only for an experimental science. Darwin's theory of evolution is another case.

According to Ghiselin (1969), Darwin, in his naturalistic observations of animal and plant life as well as coral reefs, was guided by the goal of deductive explanation. Although the logical form of his theories can be criticized, they did basically represent a deductive system that was testable by empirical evidence. Darwin, himself, argued in favor of the deductive model of explanation by emphasizing the importance of hypotheses in the collection of empirical evidence. In one of his letters he wrote:

> About thirty years ago there was much talk that geologists ought only to observe and not theorize, and I well remember someone saying that at this rate a man might as well go into a gravelpit and count the pebbles and describe the colours. How odd it is that anyone should not see all observations must be for or against some view—if it is to be of any service (Darwin, 1903, p. 195).

Perhaps Darwin's most acute statement concerning the relationship between theory and observation was, "I have an old belief that a good observer really means a good theorist" (1903, p. 176).[2]

Analysis of clinical data can also be organized into a deductive explanatory system; an example is the attempt to explain the changes over the years that have occurred in the incidence of peptic ulcers among men and women. Studies conducted before 1900 indicated that peptic ulcers occurred more frequently among women. About 1910 the incidence for both sexes became equal; since 1910 there has been a progressive rise in the occurrence of peptic ulcers among men, with a decrease in the incidence among women. In the 1960s four times as many men as compared to women had peptic ulcers. It has been suggested (Rosenbaum, 1967) that these changes can be accounted for by changes in social attitudes about dependency and aggression for men and

2. Darwin was at times inconsistent in describing his scientific strategy. In an autobiographical sketch, he confessed to working "on true Baconian principles, and without any theory collected facts on a wholesale scale" (Darwin, 1887). Nevertheless, in numerous other comments, including the above two, and more importantly in his actions, Darwin (Ghiselin, 1969) demonstrated the significant role that hypotheses with deductive consequences played in his scientific efforts.

women; the inhibition of the needs to express dependency and aggression encourages peptic ulcers.

In the freer and more independent socioeconomic society of the nineteenth century, men were not inhibited about expressing dependency and aggression. It was socially acceptable for them to be active and aggressive in work and to be mothered by their wives at home. In contrast, women could satisfy their dependency needs at home, but being aggressive was considered unfeminine and therefore unacceptable. After the turn of the century, more men found jobs in large organizations with many superiors, and consequently they were forced to inhibit aggression. It also became less fashionable to be dependent, both in the eyes of other men as well as women. On the other hand, it became more socially acceptable for women to express aggression along with dependency. It follows from such an analysis that if the women's liberation movement is successful in freeing women from their conventional social roles, then the incidence of peptic ulcers among them will increase. Discouraging ʹdependency while not modifying dependency needs is one important factor. In addition, opening jobs to women in large organizations that inhibit aggressive behavior is another variable that should, if Rosenbaum's theory (1967) is valid, increase the incidence of peptic ulcers among women.

This is not to say that the logical rigor of the dependency-aggression formulation as it applies to the women's liberation movement is free of all ambiguity nor that clearcut measures of needs to be dependent and aggressive are readily available. Nor does it imply that if operational definitions were available to test the theory and that if the predicted increase in the incidence of peptic ulcers among women occurred, then the theory would be confirmed, and if not, falsified (pages 142–151). Nor is it being stated that deductive theories of natural-occurring events in the behavioral sciences can achieve the same predictive capacity as theories of experimental phenomena. The only point being made here is that a deductive theory that applies to clinical events in a historical perspective can be formulated and tested.

The major thrust of my analysis is that the deductive model

of understanding can be adopted for behavioral events whether in the form of experimental, clinical, or naturalistic evidence. If one accepts the notion that understanding is achieved by deductive means, then a way can be found to formulate psychological hypotheses that can be checked against observational events.

The Reality of Deductive Theories

Should deductive theories be conceptualized as representing reality or treated as man-made fictions? Arguing for the former position, William Whewell (1794–1866), the English philosopher expressed a realist position:

> The cultivation of ideas is to be conducted as having for its object the connexion of facts; never to be pursued as a mere exercise of the subtilty of the mind, striving to build up a world of its own, and neglecting that which exists about us. For although man may in this way please himself, and admire the creations of his own brain, he can never, by this course, hit upon the real scheme of nature. With his ideas unfolded by education, sharpened by controversy, rectified by metaphysics, he may *understand* the natural world, but he cannot *invent* it. At every step, he must try the values of the advances he has made in thought, by applying his thoughts to things (1858, pp. 184–85).

Louis L. Thurstone (1887–1955), the famous mathematical psychologist, takes an opposite view:

> The constructs in terms of which natural phenomena are comprehended are man-made inventions. To discover a scientific law is merely to discover that a man-made scheme serves to unify, and thereby to simplify, comprehension of a certain class of natural phenomena. A scientific law is not to be thought of as having an independent existence which some scientist is fortunate enough to stumble on. A scientific law is not a part of nature. It is only a way of comprehending nature (1935, p. 44).

This argument has been with us for centuries. It is still being pursued, perhaps because it can be so much fun, especially over cocktails. The fundamental issue within the pragmatic framework of this book is whether the choice to view a deductive theory as a reflection of reality or as pure fiction has any effect upon one's activities as a scientist. Let us examine some of the implications of adopting either of these apparently competing views.

Adopting the realist position requires the assumption of a reality existing beyond one's sensory observations. This conjecture can be accepted without necessarily becoming entrapped in metaphysical quicksand. One can, in a sophisticated manner, accept a naive realist view that a reality exists beyond sensory observation but admit to the impossibility of demonstrating it. If only this is done then the practical effect of the difference between the two views, uncovering truth or superimposing order, becomes negligible. By examining most scientists' empirical and theoretical practices, one would find it difficult to distinguish between those who intuitively hold an "uncovering" versus "superimposing" orientation toward theory construction.

If it has no effect why do many scientists bother with this issue? Courant (Courant & Robbins, 1941), a famous applied mathematician, offers a clinical judgment: realists cling to their metaphysical assumption because it is a "psychological hardship" for them to accept theoretical constructs as fictions; they require a crutch of reality to satisfy their need to think in concrete terms.

Courant's conjecture can be considered relevant to the relative worth of psychological interpretations based upon "real" neurophysiological events (e.g., hypothalamic functioning) or "fictitious" processes (e.g., cognitions, habits) related to environmental factors, both past and present (e.g., amount of training). Do neurophysiological explanations of psychological events (e.g., auditory attention as a function of neurological events in the cochlear nerve and the auditory cortex) provide a depth of understanding that is unmatched by purely environmental-behavioral conceptions (e.g., auditory attention as a function of the pattern of stimulation)? Or, on the contrary, are these two kinds of knowledge fundamentally equivalent? To answer these questions one must analyze: (1) the epistemological status of psychophysiological and environmental-behavioral concepts and (2) the meaning of reductionism.

Physiological Versus Black-Box Theories

Many psychologists concerned with neurophysiological bases of behavior feel their task is different from the black-box theorist who seeks to formulate deductive theories that employ abstract theoretical constructs to bridge the gap between environmental manipulations and the behavior of organisms. Believing that they are dealing with the "real causes" of behavior, they feel that identifying the permanent physiological structures involved in behavior, and ascertaining their mode of functioning, is sufficient. Deductivism, as a means of explanation, seems to play at best an insignificant role in the theoretical construction. They see as being different the efforts of the behavior theorist, who formulates abstract theoretical constructs defined in terms of environmental manipulations (e.g., drives, organization, mental structures, association) that account for the behavioral laws observed.

The difference between the two approaches is usually highlighted at colloquia. The biopsychologists begin with a minimal introduction that identifies the behavior (e.g., the maintenance of bodily temperature) and the physiological structures involved, and with an enthusiastic description of the experimental equipment. Then a series of slides, always at least one too many, are flashed on the screen that illustrate the empirical relationships between the behavior and the functioning of the physiological structures. Since the facts speak for themselves, conclusions are kept to a minimum. Facts, facts, and more facts are the order of the hour.

In contrast, the colloquia of the behavioral psychologists usually include a lengthy introduction containing a modest statement of the profound significance of the research topic, an extolment of the theory that guided the research, and a disparagement of "superficial" competing formulations. Next comes a "justifiably" extended explication of a new experimental design that veritably controls all extraneous variables, followed by a few slides reporting data. A final conclusion involves a quaint combination of offensive and defensive remarks about the theoretical and empirical aspects of the talk, a bit of philosophy of science, and optimism about future research and theoretical developments. Although facts are reported the speculation-fact ratio is often embarrassingly high.

Perhaps the caricatures are excessive, but they drive home the point that the efforts of biopsychologists are usually much less abstract than those of the behavioral theorist. This difference may result from a selection process that attracts abstract thinkers to behavioral psychology, or from the demands for different thinking styles in each field, or, most likely, from a combination of both factors. The significant issue is whether each field obtains distinctive kinds of knowledge or is just that each encourages different research strategies and theoretical practices.

Hypothetical Constructs Versus Intervening Variables

MacCorquodale and Meehl (1948) sought to distingish between physiological and purely behavioral theories by contrasting two types of theoretical constructs, hypothetical constructs and intervening variables. The former "involve the hypothesization of an *entity, process,* or *event* which is not itself observed . . . [while the latter] do not involve such hypothesization." These writers demand "of a theory . . . that those elements which are hypothetical . . . have some probability of being in correspondence with the actual events underlying the behavior phenomenon . . ."

To appreciate the implications of their suggestion one must decide whether the proposed hypothesization of an *entity, process,* or *event* is intrinsic to the deductive capacity of the formulation or merely an unessential, speculative by-product. To answer this question consider the example MacCorquodale and Meehl chose to buttress their distinction; they refer to some of Clark Hull's theoretical articles and state:

> We suspect that Professor Hull himself was motivated to write these articles because he considered that the hypothetical events represented in his diagrams may have actually *occurred* and that the occurrence of these events represents the underlying truth about the learning phenomena he dealt with (1948, p. 104–5).

Although it may be clinically justified to assume that Hull had conceptions of physiological mechanisms coordinated to some of his theoretical constructs, the meaning of these constructs—operational, empirical, and theoretical (pages 87–94)—are not tied to the personal cogitation of the theorist. The deductive capacity of these theoretical constructs when embedded in their theoretical structures is not formally changed one whit by the theorists' "physiologizing." Consider the confusion that would result if it were. At the time Hull was speculating about physiological processes coordinated to his theoretical constructs, Spence, who played the role of a junior partner in the Hull-Spence theoretical enterprise, was denying that these constructs had any physiological implications. Should the concept of *habit* and other concepts that Hull thought might be related to physiological events have two or possibly more interpretations, not depending on their stated meanings but instead on the intuitive physiological conceptions of particular individuals? Or consider the other side of the coin: an intervening variable, a theoretical construct designed to summarize environmental-behavioral relationships, is found to be coordinated to some specific neurological process. Should that be a source of embarrassment because of the presumed nonphysiological character of the intervening variable? Of course not! It would be a fortunate case of serendipity that would enlarge the empirical scope of the theory involving that intervening variable. In sum, unnecessary confusion can result by impregnating the theoretical constructs with the physiological intuitions a theorist may be entertaining.

The distinction between hypothetical constructs and intervening variables achieves its greatest importance when referring to theoretical formulations that are, or are not, *clearly* embedded in physiological processes. Examples are the many etiological theories of schizophrenia that seek to explain genetic involvement (Heston, 1970). One such formulation (Stein & Wise, 1971) hypothesizes that a genetically determined metabolic disorder produces a chemical compound (6-hydroxydopamine or a closely related substance) that damages the reinforcement system, which in turn produces two behavioral consequences: (1) a disruption of the continuity of goal-directed behavior and (2) a reduced capacity to experience pleasure. These two behavioral consequences, it is suggested, resemble two major symptoms of schizophrenia: (1) diminished capacity to maintain goal-directed behavior, especially in regard to continuity of thought processes, and (2) anhedonia, a deficiency in experiencing pleasure. Such a theory with its primary assumption of a malfunctioning of the reinforcement process has definite psychophysiological implications for the effect of certain biochemical interventions upon the functioning of the reward centers in the hypothalamus. Repeated injections of 6-hydroxydopamine in rats reduced by 60 percent the rate of bar pressing reinforced by electrical stimulation to the hypothalamic rewards centers. The negative effect exerted by 6-hydroxydopamine on the reinforcement mechanism can be counteracted by the tranquilizing drug chlorpromazine, which is effective in eliminating some schizophrenic symptoms. The rate of bar pressing is restored to normal levels when chlorpromazine is injected into rats previously treated with 6-hydroxydopamine.

The intent of this discussion is not to justify the use of rats for research on schizophrenia nor to examine the validity of the Stein-Wise model (which has only been briefly sketched) but instead to differentiate between those physiological conjectures that function as integral components of a theory and those that do not. A purely behavioral theory of schizophrenia could be formulated that assumes a dysfunctioning of the reinforcement process. The Stein-Wise model does something more. It not only postulates that schizophrenia results from a genetically determined dysfunctioning of the reinforcement process, but it also specifies a physiological locus (hypothalamus) and a biochemical basis (6-hydroxydopamine or a closely related substance). If these assumptions were proven false, the guts of the theory (how much more physiological can one get!) would be destroyed. What benefits accrue from specific physiological postulates if they increase the probabilities of being wrong? A theory of schizophrenia that restricted itself solely to the behavioral aspects of reinforcement would not be embarrassed to find that genetic involvement is not mediated by a metabolic disturbance, that the reinforcement process is not localized in the hypothalamus, and that 6-hydroxydopamine, or a related substance, is not involved.

Presumed Advantages of Physiological Hypotheses

Three possible reasons could be given for proposing physiological hypotheses of behavior as integral assumptions within a theory. One, consistent with the commonly held belief of many biopsychologists, is that the real causes of schizophrenia are physiological in nature, and consequently, a theory that truly explains schizophrenia must be expressed in terms of physiological processes. The trouble with such an assumption is that it opens up a hornet's nest of metaphysical problems associated with the concept of *real causality*. If some can argue that the real cause of behavior occurs at the physiological level, others, with equal justification, can claim that "true explanations" reside in physiochemical or even atomic and subatomic interpretations. In addition, the concept of a true explanation might also exert a suffocating effect on research and theorizing by inhibiting further efforts toward a deeper understanding, a point made by Orville Wright in 1903: "But if we all worked on the assumption that what is accepted as true is really true, there would be little hope of advance" (Wright, 1953, p. 314).

The second justification for proposing physiological hypotheses as an integral part of a behavioral theory is that it increases the empirical content of the theory. Risking disproof by framing one's psychological theory in physiological terms enables one to reap a greater theoretical bounty. In addition to deducing consequences of environmental manipulations, psychophysiological relationships can also be explained. And by so doing, the theory holds greater promise for precise theoretical predictions as well as behavioral control. If schizophrenia were caused by a dysfunction in the reinforcement mechanism, knowing its physiological locus and biochemical features would improve the chances of modifying the disordered behavior.

Although a greater empirical content can result from physiological hypotheses, such a consequence need not follow. The crucial factor is the empirical realm to which a purely behavioral theory and a biopsychological conception is relevant. If a biopsychological theory interprets the known environmental-behavioral relationships as well as additional physiological events, then the biopsychological formulation obviously has the advantage of greater empirical breadth. However, a purely behavioral theory designed to explain environmental influences might be capable of interpreting facts outside the realm of a biopsychological theory. Suppose a physiological model of schizophrenia could explain all schizophrenic behavior (e.g., anhedonia, odd verbal and cognitive behavior, hallucinations) in terms of underlying neurological and biochemical events. In addition, it would suggest effective treatments that would eliminate schizophrenic behavior. Such a formulation, however, would not identify the environmental factors (e.g., low socioeconomic conditions, unfavorable interpersonal relationships) that encourage schizophrenia in those who are genetically vulnerable (Meehl, 1962). Although identifying the environmental inputs that influence the onset of schizophrenia would be greatly facilitated by knowledge of underlying physiological processes, such knowledge is not automatically included in biopsychological formulations. Consequently, the claim that physiological theories *always* possess a superior explanatory capacity as compared to purely behavioral formulations must be rejected.

The third argument to favor a physiological over a black-box conception is based upon strategic considerations. Looking underneath the skin for causal factors has a greater likelihood of achieving success. One "knows," unless one is a mystic, that behavior is a consequence of processes and events within the organism; something there *must* be related to the psychological phenomena that one seeks to understand. The events outside the skin are so vast, and so difficult to control and to synthesize into some coherent explanatory system, that the chances of successful theorizing are unpromising.

Black-box theories have been dominant in most areas of psychology: social, learning, memory, to name a few. All of these areas have been plagued by persistent and unresolvable theoretical disputes (e.g., attitudinal consistency, incremental versus one trial learning, the number of memory stores). One of the main reasons that these major theoretical disputes go unresolved[3] is that black-box theories do not provide sufficient constraints to allow for resolutions of theoretical disputes. The environmental operations are too far removed from the underlying biological mechanisms that are responsible for behavior. As a consequence numerous theoretical options are available to handle embarrassing data. The result is that the core assumptions of black-box theories are able to survive regardless of what results are obtained, thus effectively preventing one theory from achieving dominance over its competitors. In contrast, physiological theories that identify the operation of permanent structures or biochemical reactions as being responsible for given forms of behavior have relatively fewer options in defending their truth value when their predictions fail. One can always express reservations about the experimental procedures employed, but when repeated attempts fail to provide any evidence in favor of the hypothesized physiological involvement, one is forced to abandon one's conjectures. When, however, positive evidence is obtained, one becomes confident that the theoretical assumptions are generally correct, even though many unanswered questions remain.

The main support for the methodological conclusion that theoretical controversies are more easily resolved with physiological as compared to black-box theories is not based upon logical considerations but instead upon historical evidence. Black-box theories, in the past, have been notoriously unsuccessful in resolving their theoretical disputes. But reservations about the implications of this historical evidence can nevertheless be expressed. Past failures need not prevent future successes. Black-box theories could become more sophisticated and precise thus enabling theoretical resolutions to become possible. In addition, it should be recognized that even if the methodological advantages of physiological theories are acknowledged, it does not follow that they

3. Several important methodological issues, which will be analyzed later (pages 142–151), are involved in evaluating the relative merits of competing theories and the survival of one over others.

need to be formulated at the beginning of all research programs. It may be strategically desirable to gather systematic environmental-behavioral relationships to guide one's future physiological hypotheses. That is, ignoring physiological processes while environmental-behavioral relationships are being gathered may prove to be the most direct approach to a physiological understanding of behavior. One could point to the history of sensory psychology where psychophysical relationships proved useful in developing psychophysiological theories.

Realistic Versus Black-Box Theories

Some would disagree with the above analysis by arguing that physiological theories offer a qualitatively different kind of knowledge than that provided by black-box conceptions. This latter position (e.g., Harré, 1970) would maintain that a nonrealistic theory organized in a hypothetic-deductive fashion is, epistemologically speaking, not equivalent to a "realistic" theory that attributes phenomena to the operation of permanent structures (e.g., hypothalamus, auditory cortex, blood chemistry). Instead of assuming, as purely abstract deductive theories do, that logical order reflects natural order, the realist position maintains that empirical events are truly explained only when the operation of the permanent structures responsible for the phenomena are described. This position suffers from an ambiguity in the meaning of "permanent structure" and from inconsistencies stemming from the presumed qualitative difference between structural and deductive explanations.

The realist position, in its strong form, suggests that a true explanation depends on knowing how a "real" structure operates to produce a given phenomenon. If one considers, for example, the theoretical concept of gene it becomes difficult to know exactly when the requirement of a permanent structure is met: some bodily entity, a mechanism within the reproductive system, a germ cell, the chromosome, the DNA molecule? Before the DNA molecule was decided upon as the unit of heredity, accurate deductive predictions were made about a variety of genetic phenomena (e.g., human eye color). The fundamental change that did occur as the gene acquired a more permanent form was an enlargement in the empirical realm of genetic theory as well as a potential increase in its ability to control genetic phenomena. But these changes are quantitative, not qualitative. A common misconception is that knowledge of the operation of a permanent structure, like the DNA molecule, removes the need for deductive logic in explaining events. Since the structure causes an event no other explanation is required. However, the discovery of the DNA molecule raises a host of questions concerning the internal functioning of the molecule as well as its interaction with other biological structures and processes. In answering these questions theoretical speculations are required and their truth value is determined by how well their deductions coincide with empirical findings.

To bring this discussion closer to psychology, consider the consequences of the technical breakthrough that enabled the electrical activity of a single neuron to be recorded. Although this development permitted one to observe the operation of a fundamental permanent structure, the need for abstract theorizing actually increased in order to explain how behavior was influenced by the interaction among independent neurons. Regardless of how deep one penetrates into the physiological substrata of behavior, abstract theoretical problems will always remain. Contemporary physics, with its persistent search for subatomic particles that can never be directly observed, supports this expectation.

The lack of a functional difference between realistic and black-box theories is highlighted when total ignorance reigns about the identity or functioning of a structure responsible for a set of phenomena. In such a case, according to the realist position an iconic model should be invented that speculates about the structure responsible for a given event. Is anything gained by this methodological prescription except the suggestion that ultimately it would be wise to look for the psysiological correlates of behavior? The prescription can backfire when, in the absence of any firm notions of the relevant structure, a rash of unfounded speculations are encouraged that may carry an aura of respectability

and a source of persuasion, but nothing else. These kinds of conjectures have been derisively treated as attempts to change the
meaning of the C.N.S. (central nervous system) to the *Conceptual
Nervous System*. Iconic models, however, can serve some beneficial functions. They can facilitate theoretical efforts by concretiz-
ing abstract relationships. They can guide future research when
technical developments enable the direct investigation of the operation of the hypothesized structure. They can also encourage
the psychological theorist to employ available physiological evidence to guide and restrict his speculations. But these functions
do not create any qualitative difference between an iconic model
and a pure black-box conception. There is always the possibility
that a theoretical construct within a black-box conception can be
coordinated to a physiological structure even though the theorist
had no such intention.

The key question in this debate is what determines the truth
value of iconic models prior to their success, or failure, to be
coordinated to a permanent structure. The answer would seem to
be their deductive capacity. If they can interpret empirical events,
their truth value is enhanced. If they are unsuccessful, modification or rejection of the model is in order. If later events prove
that the structural speculations are justified, then the iconic model
would have a greater explanatory capacity than an equivalent
black-box theory. If, however, the structural speculations fail to
gain any empirical support, but the explanatory capacity of the
iconic model in regard to environmental-behavior relationships is
supported, then the basic model would be retained while the
structural speculations would be discarded. Thus, the conclusion
is that physiological theories, either with clearly measurable
physiological implications or purely speculative ones, are epistemologically similar to black-box conceptions because both employ the same litmus test of truth value, viz., their capacity to
generate empirically supported deductions.

The conclusion that physiological and black-box theories are
epistemologically similar does not mean that they do not differ
strategically. Historical evidence, as noted, suggests that when
physiological operations are involved theoretical controversies are

more easily resolved than when the competing conceptions contain only abstract constructs. The strategic advantage of physiological theories that are based upon physiological operations do not necessarily, if at all, extend to physiological speculations. To merely assume that some phenomena result from structures within the body does not automatically remedy the excessive lack of constraints that characterize black-box conceptions. Some precision is required to benefit from physiological assumptions. Although successful strategies cannot be spelled out either in advance or in detail, one useful rule of thumb is that if physiological hypotheses are to pay off by increasing the precision of psychological theorizing, then they must be coordinated to experimental operations that either intervene in bodily function or measure the ongoing activity of a given structure. The technological revolution in biopsychology has drastically diminished the justification for speculating in general about physiological functioning in the absence of any experimental intervention.

Empirical and Theoretical Reductionism

Now that epistemological and strategic considerations have been considered in regard to the comparison between physiological and black-box theories, the concept of reductionism can be analyzed. Like all important methodological concepts, *reductionism* suffers from a multiplicity of meanings. As a first approximation let me describe reductionism as used in psychology as the attempt to interpret psychological phenomena in terms of underlying physiological processes. This possible kind of interpretation can be accomplished in several different ways: (1) relating behavior directly to physiological variables, (2) adopting a model of behavior based on physiological evidence, or (3) coordinating a behavior theory to a physiological theory.

The most common type of psychophysiological interpretation occurs when behavior is related to some physiological characteristic of an organism. Some examples are: intellectual retardation as a function of phenylketonuria (a disorder that is transmitted as a simple recessive genetic characteristic involving a disturbance in protein metabolism and that can be alleviated by appropriate diet), rate of bar pressing as a function of reinforcement site in the hypothalamus, language behavior as a function of the size and site of cortical damage, and behavior of the heroin addict as a function of methadone treatment. Nonetheless, these simple psychophysiological laws can be considered as empirical relationships in which the dependent variable, behavior, is related to an independent variable representing some aspect of physiological functioning. As already argued, the epistemological characteristics of such laws are no different from those in which behavior is found to be a function of environmental stimulation (e.g., visual acuity as a function of level of illumination) or of past behavior (e.g., criminal behavior as a function of criminal record). They differ only in the characteristics of the independent variable (physiological, environmental, or behavioral).

Another way of interpreting behavior within a physiological framework is to use physiological knowledge and speculations as ideas for formulating behavioral assumptions: the characteristics of the theoretical assumptions are suggested by physiological processes. An example is the attempt to formulate hypotheses about cognitive development with the assistance of facts and conjectures about neurological development (H. H. Kendler & Kendler, 1975). The "physiologizing," strictly speaking, is not part of the theory of cognitive development; it represents an independent model that is not directly involved in the explanatory capacity of the theory (Lachman, 1960). The question that has been raised about such formulations is whether the physiological speculations are useful in the formulation of fruitful hypotheses and in making the theories more precise. The tentative answer offered is that their usefulness is proportional to their ability to initiate physiological investigations.

The final manner in which psychology is interpreted in terms of physiology is that of theoretical reductionisms: a theory of behavior is *subsumed* under a theory of physiology, and as a result, the physiological theory becomes capable of explaining psychological phenomena. Although the fundamental notion of theoretical reductionism from behavior to physiology appears simple, a careful scrutiny of the problem suggests otherwise. The first point, previously made, is that complete predictability does not necessarily occur when successful theoretical reductionism takes place. A physiological theory of schizophrenia, which would designate all the physiological processes involved in the disorder, would not necessarily identify all the environmental determiners even though such a task would be made much simpler. A similar situation would prevail for a theory of color vision that would give a complete physiological interpretation of color vision without accounting for the totality of empirical relationships between light waves and color sensations.

Subsumed can have another meaning, a much more demanding one. A theory of behavior is subsumed under a theory of physiology when each term of the psychological theory is *coordinated* with one of the physiological theory. If this is accomplished, as in the previously given examples of schizophrenia, then the physiological theory can completely predict the psychological phenomena, e.g., the relationship between interpersonal stress and schizophrenia. By coordinating the physiological constructs with the psychological constructs one bridges the gap between physiological and psychological knowledge.

Theoretical reductionism, in which the terms of a physiological and a psychological theory are coordinated, is presently more in the realm of science fiction than that of reality. To accomplish reductionism of this sort requires highly formalized theories of both physiology and behavior. Perhaps the closest psychophysiologists have come to this standard is in the area of sensory physiology where psychological phenomena (e.g., Mach Bands) have been coordinated to neurological processes (e.g., lateral inhibition). But even such successes fall short of the formal elegance demanded by theoretical reductionism although these efforts nevertheless do encourage the belief that the goal of theoretical reductionism between psychology and physiology is within striking distance for some sensory phenomena.

Although one can specify the criteria of theoretical reductionism, one cannot guarantee that reducing psychology to physiology can be accomplished. Kaplan vigorously expresses this viewpoint when answering the question of whether psychology is reducible to physiology (or chemistry or physics):

> An affirmative answer . . . as a matter of doctrine, seems to be . . . both unwarranted and scientifically useless. . . . As a methodological presupposition . . . it provides a valuable perspective in which the behavioral scientist can see continuing possibilities for turning to his own use the findings of other sciences. But the significance of such possibilities appears only as they are actualized; otherwise their affirmation expresses only a hope. . . . It may well be that the psychologist can derive his whole discipline from neurology, biochemistry, and the rest; it is not destructive skepticism but productive pragmatism to say, "I'd like to see him do it!" (1964, pp. 124–25).

Such a position might be considered inconsistent with the doctrine of a unity of sciences in which it is assumed that the various disciplines can be arranged hierarchically (e.g., physics, chemistry, biology, psychology) to reflect the potential theoretical reduction of any discipline to a more basic one. This assumption implies a determinism across disciplines[4] by accepting the notion that a less basic discipline (e.g., psychology) can in principle be explained by a more basic discipline (e.g., biology). By refusing to acknowledge the inevitability of theoretical reductionism from psychology to physiology, does not one concede the possible operation of some emergent process that precludes theoretical reductionism? Not necessarily. Unsuccessful attempts at theoretical reduction to physiology need not result only from unpredictable emergent qualities of psychological events. It could result from imperfect knowledge of psychology or physiology or from inadequate mathematical tools with which to perform the theoretical reduction. In the absence of a successful reduction it is difficult to conceive how the question of reductionism from psychology to physiology can be resolved conclusively; we cannot in principle deny the possibility of reductionism, but neither can we

4. One can reject this assumption without abandoning determinism. One can adopt an antireductionist position that assumes each discipline possesses emergent properties that cannot be predicted from a "lower" discipline while still accepting strict determinism for events *within* a discipline.

be certain that it is possible. Theoretical reductionism appears to be an admirable operating assumption but not necessarily a valid one.

Arguments have been advanced that insist that emergent psychological properties preclude the theoretical reduction of psychology to physiology. One such argument emerged from Brentano's phenomenological distinction between intentional and nonintentional acts. Turner summarizes the problem this way:

> [An intentional act] is a mental activity culminating in a decision which at the behavioral level is the occasion for some behavior selected from a set of behavioral options. In the language of intention, then, this activity underlies the motive for the particular decision. But the actual behavior reflecting the particular decision requires a different type of description, and as such, is reducible to physicalistic terms. On the other hand, the phrase "wanting to go to the movies" designates an intentional act in which the wanting is *about* going to the movies but which itself is not an objectively describable act. The two languages are quite different. One is mentalistic and intentional, the other is physicalistic and nonintentional, with neither a logical nor empirical bridge between the two. If one now wishes to maintain that psychology should concern itself with motivational explanation in the intentional language, and this would distinguish it logically from the physical sciences, then, to be sure, the idea of reduction would be incompatible with our understanding of psychology and physiology (1965, p. 347). .

Turner later argues, and I agree, that one is not required to accept the insulation of intentions as mental events from publicly observable physical events, behavioral or physiological. Intentions can be treated as theoretical constructs inferred from environmental-behavioral relationships, e.g., individual A develops an *intention* to attend the movies every Saturday night. Or *intention* can be treated as a dispositional concept inferred from behavior, e.g., individual B has an *intention* to go to the movies because he asks the question, "Are you interested in going to the movies tonight?" They can also be treated as physiological processes if it were possible to coordinate specific, for example, cortical events with introspective reports. This line of analysis suggests that the so-called mental *intention* can possibly be treated either as a motivational construct or a physiological construct. Within this context the reduction of the concept of *intention,* as an inferred phenomenological event, becomes a reasonable possibility. The previous point that psychology as a behavioral science can be reduced to physiology can be extended to the relationship between phenomenology on the one hand and behavioral psychology and/or physiology on the other. Such reductions are within the realm of the possible, although one cannot guarantee that they will necessarily occur. And it is important to recognize that the kind of reduction of *intention* that is being discussed is concerned with explaining phenomena in a deductive sense, not in describing its experiential characteristics. This point returns us to the previous analysis of *knowing* and *having,* the former being concerned with *causes,* the latter with *experience.*

A pragmatic and fruitful way of viewing the problem of emergent properties of psychological phenomena is to recognize that it is fundamentally a theoretical issue rather than a purely empirical one (Nagel, 1961). Assume that a particular psychological theory postulates emergent perceptual or cognitive properties that cannot be derived from physiological theory. One should not fault the theory because of its reductionistic "failure." An evaluation should be based upon its explanatory capacity. But no matter how successful the theory may be, one cannot conclude that its emergent behavioral assumption, which is not deducible from physiological knowledge, is necessarily "true." The possibility always remains that a subsequent formulation might achieve a reductionistic breakthrough by successfully deducing the totality of psychological laws from physiological assumptions. Although at present behavioral psychology need not fear being entirely consumed by physiological psychology, one must recognize that in principle this is always a possibility. Consequently, a wise methodological strategy to pursue is to ignore a priori claims that psychology is an emergent discipline or that it will ultimately be subsumed under physiology. This does not imply that either alternative cannot be adopted as a reasonable strategy as long as the question of the ultimate success of physiological reduction is left open.[5]

The Evaluation of Deductive Theories

Of all problems associated with deductive explanations none is more complex than that of judging the "truth value" of a theory. Philosophers and scientists have continually debated this issue and at the present moment there is no reason to believe they will ever achieve a consensus. Psychologists, in my estimation, have an easier task than philosophers in dealing with this problem because their needs are less demanding. Instead of having to cope with the subtle details of formulating specific epistemological principles for judging theories, the needs of the psychologist can be met by establishing general guidelines that will assist in the evaluation.

To begin our discussion of assessing theories that seek deductive validation, it will be best to describe in bold strokes three different conceptions of developmental changes in science: *traditional, subjective,* and *historical.* Each conception implies a different perspective for evaluating deductive theories.

The Traditional View

The traditional interpretation emerges from the commonsense conception of science that the accumulation of scientific knowledge proceeds in a progressive, linear fashion. All knowledge is a direct outgrowth of previous knowledge. When theoretical disagreements arise a crucial experiment is designed that is acknowledged by all to represent a fair test of the competing formulations. The crucial experiment yields unambiguous results as to which theory is right and which is wrong. In the finest tradition of Hollywood movies the two rival theorists accept the empirical verdict and compliment each other for their unswerving devotion

5. Problems of reducing psychology to physiology and emergentism are returned to in the final chapter, which discusses future trends in psychology.

to the search for truth. This scenario is repeated whenever theoretical disagreements occur, and as a result, science inevitably moves forward with a continual increase in empirical knowledge and theoretical understanding.

The main difficulty with the traditional conception of the growth of knowledge is that it fails to fit the facts of history. Sometimes competing theorists cannot agree upon an appropriate crucial experiment. Other times crucial experiments turn out not to be crucial because ad hoc interpretations allow a theory to incorporate unanticipated results. In addition, the history of science provides numerous incidents where significant evidence, reliably demonstrated, was ignored for long periods of time simply because it did not fit into prevailing theoretical conceptions.

The Subjective View

The most compelling argument against the traditional conception of scientific theory is contained in Thomas Kuhn's *The Structure of Scientific Revolutions* (1962). The preparation of this book was encouraged by James Conant when he was president of Harvard University. He believed that we needed "a widespread understanding of science in this country, for only thus can science be assimilated into our secular pattern" (Conant, 1947). Consequently, undergraduate education should involve some training in science, even for those who were not science majors. Conant persuaded Thomas Kuhn, then a doctoral student in the field of theoretical physics, to accept the responsibility for teaching a history of science course to the nonscientist. When preparing the course Kuhn was surprised to discover that scientific development and practices were radically different from what he was led to expect from his long-standing avocational interest in the philosophy of science. Instead of finding that scientific progress was based on the accumulation of individual discoveries and theoretical refinements, Kuhn perceived a repetitive pattern in the history of science consisting of two markedly different enterprises: *normal science* and *revolution.*

Normal science refers to the accumulation of knowledge

within a widely adopted global orientation, labeled by Kuhn as a *paradigm.* Indicating that the paradigm is incapable of any complete formulation, Kuhn suggested that it consists of a "strong network of commitments—conceptual, theoretical, instrumental, and methodological and quasi-metaphysical." Paradigms serve as "the source of the methods, problem-field, and standard of solution accepted by any mature scientific community at any given time." Normal science, according to Kuhn, consists of empirical and theoretical efforts within the paradigm that gather additional relevant information and improve the match between theoretical prediction and data.

A paradigm possesses two related social functions. First, it attracts to its fold a group of adherents; second, it provides them with a number of unanswered questions that keeps them busy experimenting and theorizing (and, of course, publishing). The paradigm provides an intellectual structure that integrates important facts but at the same time generates numerous research opportunities. Therefore Kuhn describes normal science as a "mopping-up" activity.

In the course of this "mopping-up" activity anomalous results occur that cannot simply be incorporated into the prevailing paradigm. Thus the stage begins to be set for the second stage of historical development—the *revolution*—during which time a prevailing paradigm is overthrown by a new one. Revolutions are not achieved by a simple and rapid shift in consensual agreement about which theory is valid. That is, a prevailing paradigm does not collapse in the face of embarrassing data thereby paving the way for the adoption of a new, more adequate paradigm. What actually happens in a revolution is that the facts embarrassing to an existing paradigm are discovered. The empirical area of the anomaly is then extensively investigated, and modifications in the paradigm are suggested in the hope of preserving its validity. Typically these modifications are not completely successful, but nevertheless the existing, though inadequate, paradigm survives. The adherents of the existing paradigm learn to live with or, perhaps more properly speaking, to ignore the inconsistent results. However, the anomalous results do inspire some young investigators, whose emotional attachments to the prevailing paradigm are neither deep nor enduring, to formulate a competing paradigm that can absorb the anomalous data. The struggle between the old and new paradigms requires many years to resolve, and its final resolution is more a result of the mortality of man than of any set of data or logical analyses. The older paradigm typically is not relinquished by those who were trained and who worked within it. They refuse to understand the new paradigm and argue against its validity. The younger people recognize the "superiority" of the new paradigm, adopt its standards and conceptions, and investigate the unanswered questions it generates. With time the control of the science passes from the hands of the older investigators with their "outmoded" paradigm to the younger scientists with their "superior" one. A stage of normal science sets in and prevails until a new set of anomalous data are discovered. Then the era of a revolution begins again.

According to the Kuhnian analysis science is not a cumulative discipline as is suggested by the traditional conception; scientific revolutions are "non-cumulative developmental episodes in which an older paradigm is replaced in whole or in part by an incompatible new one" (Kuhn, 1962, p. 91). In other words the new paradigm does not emerge from the old.

This historical analysis, at first glance, seems to characterize much of the history of psychology. One can cite the paradigmatic shifts from structuralism to behaviorism, from stimulus-response to cognitive psychology, from cognitive dissonance theory to attribution theory, and so on. In each case a shift takes place in a methodological orientation that involves changes in the investigatory procedures, problem areas, and even in the criteria of proof.

In spite of its apparent relevance to psychology Kuhn's hypothesis about the alternating historical sequence of normal science and revolution may not be applicable. Kuhn's historical model emerged primarily from his analysis of the development of physics from the time of Copernicus. One can argue that psychology has yet to reach a comparable stage of evolution. Properly speaking, psychology is in a *pre*paradigmatic stage because collective agreement has yet to be achieved about the nature of its proper methods and its significant problems. Physics, at one time, was at a preparadigmatic stage in which different conceptions of the fundamental methods of investigation competed for collective acceptance. The natural-science method finally won out, and today one can refer to a single discipline of physics in which essential agreement reigns about significant problems, methods of investigation, and concept of truth. This does not mean that those physicists who are interested in the philosophical underpinnings of their discipline are in total concurrence. What it does mean is that such philosophical disagreements that do exist are not so profound as to affect the day-to-day activities of physicists. One could not infer the philosophical commitments a physicist held about his discipline, assuming he held any, from the examination of his professional activities. In contrast, the professional behavior of a psychologist is highly related to his methodological commitments. By examining the professional behavior of the structuralist, the behaviorist, the psychoanalyst, and the humanistic psychologist, one could infer their epistemological conception of psychology.

It is quite possible, as has been suggested in discussing the subject matter and data base of psychology (Chapter 2), that a paradigmatic stage of development is beyond the reach of psychology because of its concern with intrinsically different kinds of phenomena. Although it is reasonable to hope that the facts of behavior, phenomenal experience, and physiological events will someday be deductively integrated, no a priori reason exists to insure success. Another obstacle to achieving the paradigmatic stage of historical development is the one presently being discussed—the adoption of a common criterion of truth. Again there is no reason to believe that psychologists will ever achieve consensual agreement.

In essence what is being suggested is that the historical forces within psychology differ radically from those that were operative in physics, and therefore the transition from a preparadigmatic to a paradigmatic stage of development will never be made. One obvious difference is that the high level of predictability achieved by early theories of mechanics and astronomy, which psychological theories have been unable to match, encouraged the domination of natural-science methodology by crushing methodological orientations that eschewed predictability as a significant component of the criterion of truth. A look at contemporary psychology would suggest that even if psychology had achieved the predictive successes of early physics, pressures would still be operating against a natural-science approach that relies on understanding of the sort that deductive explanation achieves. Psychology plays many roles in modern society and meets a variety of individual needs: a behavioral science that strives to operate within a natural-science framework, a source of moral precepts, a guide-to-living, a key to understanding human experience, a source of entertainment, and a sophisticated form of commonsense. Even if natural-science psychology were more successful, the desires of many psychologists and many segments of society who seek answers to "psychological" questions that a natural-science approach ignores or dismisses would remain unsatisfied. Thus psychology is predestined, within a Kuhnian frame of reference, to remain in a preparadigmatic stage because society demands more of psychology than a natural-science approach can deliver.

If the prepadadigmatic-paradigmatic historical sequence is to be applied to psychology it must be limited to that segment that seeks to operate according to natural-science principles. If this is done it still remains unclear, partly due to the ambiguities inherent in the concept of paradigm[6] whether psychology is at the preparadigmatic stage or whether some harder areas (e.g., sensory physiology or theories of perception, learning, and memory) have progressed to the paradigmatic stage. We need not be too concerned with whether certain fields of natural-science psychology fulfill the requirements of a paradigmatic shift as conceptualized by Kuhn. Some similarity seems obvious. The goal of this present analysis is not to pin down the exact meaning of Kuhn's historical analysis but instead to clarify the process by

6. Kuhn (1974) confesses that the popularity of the paradigm concept results in part from its vagueness, which allows readers to interpret its meaning according to their own biases.

which deductive theories are evaluated. And it is within this context that Kuhn, along with other philosophers of science (Hanson, 1958; Polyani, 1958) who have emphasized subjective factors in science, has offered an important and influential suggestion.

Kuhn's views, which have changed over the years as a result of intense criticism (e.g., Lakatos & Musgrave, 1970) and his own efforts toward precision (Kuhn, 1970), can be expressed either in a strong or weak fashion. The strong position, which emphasizes the view that all facts are theory laden, is expressed in Kuhn's (1962) own words: "The competition between paradigms is not the sort of battle that can be resolved by proofs" (p. 147) but is more like a "conversion experience" (p. 150). In essence, this subjective view of paradigmatic choice[7] argues a relativist position that the superiority of one paradigm over a competing one is fundamentally a matter of personal taste. The weak form of Kuhn's position is that personal taste enters into a controversy between paradigms but does not exclusively determine its resolution. Some rational, objective evaluative procedures are invoked when choosing between competing paradigms.

The subjective view is presently identified with the strong interpretation of Kuhn's position. In essence, this position assumes that competing paradigms are incommensurable in that one cannot translate the meaningful content of one paradigm into the language of the other. As a result, the relative superiority of one paradigm over the other cannot be ascertained except by a purely subjective judgment.

If the concept of a paradigm is used broadly to cover general methodological orientations such as structuralism and behaviorism as well as specific theoretical conceptions such as the inter-

7. It must be emphasized that I am not equating Kuhn's position with a subjective method of evaluating deductive explanations although Kuhn's first edition of *The Structure of Scientific Revolutions* (1962) did strongly imply this attitude and was most instrumental in encouraging such a view among many psychologists. For the record it should be noted that Kuhn (1970) has retreated from such a relativist position by acknowledging paradigmatic-independent facts and the validity of the notion of scientific progress.

ference and duplex (short- and long-term storage systems) theories of memory, then the kinds of paradigms being compared must be considered in evaluating the subjective view. Although the subjective view may be relevant for comparing the general methodological orientations of structuralism and behaviorism, it may be inappropriate for judging the merits of interference and duplex theories of memory. As the last chapter suggested, no compelling logic or evidence can be offered to support the contention that psychology *must* be the science of the mind (structuralism) or of behavior (behaviorism). In the final analysis it becomes a matter of personal choice as to which volitional decision will be adopted. This does not deny the possibility of reconciling a mind-oriented with a behavior-oriented psychology; it merely asserts that a decision between the two orientations may have to be made before the potentials of such a possible resolution can be judged.

The appropriateness of the subjective view of theoretical differences, such as those that distinguish between the interference and duplex theories of memory, appears less compelling than it does for the structuralism versus behaviorism issue. Although interference and duplex theories of forgetting have tended to focus on different empirical problems (e.g., retroactive inhibition studies versus free recall) and even to harbor somewhat different conceptions of proof (pp. 358–370), a fundamental overlap of empirical interest nevertheless exists. This common empirical interest can form the basis for judging the relative merits of the worth and validity of the competing conceptions. This conclusion can best be explicated by considering the historical view of judging deductively formulated theories.

The Historical View

The traditional and subjective views of evaluating competing theoretical conceptions employ different procedures for reaching a verdict. The former offers a simple decision rule that can be applied uniformly by all scientists. Within a historical framework a particular theory is dissected and an unequivocal decision is reached as to whether it is congruent with the available data. If it is, the theory is verified; if not, it is falsified. The essential ingredients of the traditional view are deliberation followed by a clear verdict that compels consensual agreement among the community of scientists.

The subjective view is completely at odds with the traditional conception. A paradigm consisting of both methodological commitments and a set of theoretical assumptions is viewed within a historical context. The decision to accept or reject is not constrained by any publicly adopted rules of evaluation; the choice of one paradigm over a rival does *not* occur "by deliberation and interpretation" (Kuhn, 1962, p. 121). All facts are paradigm-dependent and therefore cannot function as critical information for evaluating competing conceptions.

The historical view, now under scrutiny, differs from both the traditional and subjective conceptions but contains important ingredients of each. In line with the subjective view, it denies that at any stage of development a specific theory or general paradigm can be analyzed and evaluated according to a set of uniform rules that will yield a verdict acceptable to all scientists. Consistent with the traditional view, it accepts the notion of paradigm-neutral data that allow for deliberation and argumentation about the relative merits of competing conceptions. Competing paradigms are commensurable, according to the historical view, and the acceptance of one paradigm can be defended on the basis of explicit standards. Yet, in contrast to the traditional conception, the historical view does not suggest that only one set of explicit standards are available that all members of the scientific community will or must adopt.

Emphasizing the historical dimension for evaluating a paradigm is certainly not a novel notion. Many philosophers and psychologists have insisted that only this kind of analysis can yield a deep understanding of a paradigm. But acknowledging the significance of viewing a paradigm within a historical context will function as an empty slogan unless criteria are suggested to judge paradigmatic achievements.

Lakatos (1970a, 1970b) has suggested a frame of reference

with which to judge competing paradigms. He takes his cue from a paraphrase of Kant's famous dictum, "Philosophy of science without history of science is empty; history of science without philosophy of science is blind."

According to Lakatos the proper unit for historical analysis of scientific development is a *research program,* not a theory. A research program contains an infinite number of specific theories with a common cluster of core assumptions and a heuristic for selecting research problems. For example, the neobehavioristic (Hull-Spence) research program contained core assumptions such as the fundamental unit of behavior (stimulus-response association), two basic theoretical processes (habit and drive), drive energizes habit structures, each drive has its own distinctive cue (drive stimulus), total drive is a function of both physiological needs and incentive conditions, behavior is guided by anticipatory goal responses (r_g's), and the facts of conditioning are a fruitful source for formulating general principles of behavior.[8] The core assumptions of cognitive psychology are more difficult to identify because of the influences from diverse historical traditions—mentalism, perception, linguistics, computer science, and Tolman's (1936) theory of animal learning. From my vantage point, cognitive psychology possesses core assumptions such as organisms acquire internal representations (information) of the physical world that can be transformed; transformations occur in stages (levels); problem solving involves different plans (strategies) for employing available information; performance is a joint function of principles of cognition and action; and phenomenology, perception, and memory are fruitful sources of general principles of behavior. And finally an important heuristic in achieving an understanding of a psychological event is to represent it in a flow diagram.

In a similar vein, core assumptions can be identified for

8. This list of core assumptions is neither meant to be exhaustive nor definitive. There is no simple rule to identify core assumptions or to distinguish them from peripheral postulates. A historical analysis will presumably identify a set of notions that are adopted by a variety of specific theories that spring from a common research program.

operant-conditioning approach, attribution theory, social-learning theory, and other current research programs. The important consideration at present is not the explication of the core assumptions of various research programs but the justification of considering the research program as the basic unit of historical development. Why should not specific theories such as Hull's (1943) *Principles of Behavior* or Tolman's (1936) *Purposive Behavior in Animals and Men* or information-processing models of memory be considered the proper subject of methodological analysis? The reason is that such formulations possess a unique explanatory capacity of their own, but at the same time they are historically related to subsequent theories. The reason for this is that a theory can never be falsified by any experimental evidence. As already noted, tests of theories always involve ancillary assumptions about the appropriateness of the empirical procedures used. Results contrary to theoretical expectations can be attributed to the inappropriateness of the ancillary assumption rather than to any fundamental inadequacy of the theoretical assumption. An example of this is the controversy surrounding the interpretation of an experiment (Campione, 1970) designed to test the dual-stage theory of developmental changes in discrimination-shift behavior (H. H. Kendler, & Kendler, 1972). The results obtained failed to reveal any developmental trends and thus were interpreted to be at odds with the dual-stage theory that "predicted" ontogenetic changes. Proponents of the theory (H. H. Kendler, Kendler, & Ward, 1972) argued, however, that improper experimental procedures were used because special training techniques were instituted for slow learners, most of whom were from the youngest age group. They maintained that the dual-stage theory demanded that the subjects of different age groups receive essentially similar training, and thus the special procedures employed violated an assumption of the theory the experiment sought to test. Of course this dispute can be, and was, put to further empirical test (H.H. Kendler, Kendler, & Ward, 1972), but the important point for our discussion is that the theorist always has the option in the face of "embarrassing" data to reject the ancillary assumptions of the experiment.

The theorist has another defensive maneuver in the face of embarrassing evidence. He can make ad hoc modifications in his theory to accommodate the embarrassing data. An unlimited number of codifications become possible because a theory consisting of a set of logically independent postulates, can only be tested globally. The theorist, therefore, when attempting to accommodate inconsistent data, has numerous options ranging from changing any one of several assumptions to modifying the postulated relationships among them. Strictly speaking, one might argue that these theoretical changes do not modify a theory but in reality abandon it. Theories that generate different deductions are different theories. Although different from the viewpoint of their explanatory capacity, the two theories are obviously related historically, the newer one emerging from the older one. In the historical sense the two successive theories are components of what Lakatos considers a research program—a set of core assumptions that yield a variety of related theories generated in an attempt to interpret an expanding set of data.

Partly as the result of the traditional conception of historical development in science, a negative attitude in some quarters prevails toward defense tactics of preserving a research program by either rejecting ancillary assumptions or instituting ad hoc theoretical modifications. Rather than admit that his theory has been disproved by negative evidence, the theorist who rejects ancillary assumptions or reformulates his conception is considered to be indulging in some sort of skullduggery. He maintains his "theory" by invoking escape clauses. Since this can go on indefinitely he really is not abiding by the rules of the game of science. Bluntly, he is cheating. Another view is possible; the tenacious theorist who refuses to admit defeat is serving an important function in science. If a research program were abandoned at its first exposure to embarrassing data, we would never know if it could have been salvaged by appropriate revisions. Few, if any, scientists would disagree with the notion that some tinkering with a theory is appropriate when initially confronted with anomalous evidence. But how much tinkering is permissible? What decision rule can be formulated to indicate that further revisions will be a waste of time and effort? When can the theorist and the entire scientific community decide that a research program should be abandoned?

Implicit in these questions are two related issues: (1) the evaluation of a research program and (2) the decision to abandon it. Lakatos (1970a, 1970b) has suggested that a research program can be judged in terms of its historical development, particularly in terms of whether it is *progressive* or *degenerating*. Consider the specific case of an anomalous result that cannot be integrated within a particular theory of a given research program. A progressive change would occur when an ad hoc modification of the theory not only copes with the anomalous result but also predicts the occurrence of a novel event. In contrast, a research program is degenerating if an ad hoc modification does nothing more than accommodate the anomaly. Thus a progressive program is one in which modifications in the theoretical structure are accompanied by an expansion in its explanatory capacity while a degenerating program is one that repeatedly adds ad hoc theoretical assumptions in order to cope with embarrassing evidence.

However, the evaluation of the historical development is more complex than has just been suggested. Progressive changes can occur when dealing with some anomalous results but not with others. As a result, a simple verdict of "progressive" or "degenerating" may be hard to arrive at when evaluating a particular research program at a given time in its history. In addition, a research program is not evaluated in isolation. It is evaluated in comparison to competing programs. When compared to degenerating programs a particular research program that achieves modest progressive successes may be strongly supported but may be largely ignored when pitted *against* a competitor that is achieving dramatic progress. Finally, it must be emphasized that the characteristic that Lakatos selects to define progressive—the prediction of novel events—need not be accepted as an ultimate criterion. One might argue that theoretical precision is more important than empirical generality. There is nothing intrinsic in the scientific enterprise to suggest that one is more important than the other, and consequently, one cannot demand that progressive and degenerating be defined either in terms of predicting novel events or theoretical precision, or some optimal combination of both. I, for one, in viewing the history of psychology and noting the narrowness of many rigorously stated theories (e.g., mathematical models of learning), believe that it may be more strategic to value empirical generality over rigorous mathematical precision. But the opposite view is certainly reasonable. Nothing can match the confidence in a theory when its successful predictions are rigorously stated. It will not help to debate this issue because both theoretical precision and empirical generality are goals of deductive theorizing. The major strategic issue is whether one of the goals should be valued more at different stages of theoretical development.

Now that a frame of reference for evaluating competing research programs has been sketched out, we can return to the question of when a research program should be abandoned because it is hopelessly degenerated. The key to answering such a question is contained in the realization that an infinite number of ad hoc modifications can be made in a degenerating research program. One's estimate that additional ad hoc modifications will not salvage a degenerating research program must fall short of certainty. This does not mean that a theorist should blindly persist in his attempts to transform a degenerating formulation into a progressive one. He can reasonably reach a point when he concludes: "Enough is enough. There is no sense in continuing to patch up my formulation. It is likely that it is fundamentally wrong."

The decision that a research program should be abandoned will be reached at different times by different researchers. No psychologist should be surprised to discover that adherents, as compared to critics, of a particular research program would be more reluctant to conclude that it should be abandoned. Nor should psychologists experience difficulty in understanding that the tendency to persist in trying to salvage a research program will vary among its adherents because such a decision results more from psychological than logical factors. If we accept the notion that a scientist's behavior will be guided by his personality characteristics, then we can expect the stubborn scientist, assuming he is intellectually resourceful, to persevere more than the pliant one.

The fact that agreement will not prevail concerning the decision to abandon a research program does not place any real obstacle in the path of scientific progress. Each choice, persist or abandon, serves a useful function. The first will provide information about the fruitfulness of a previously untried revision. As previously indicated, a possibility always remains that a research program can be turned around from a degenerating to a progressive one. The choice to abandon indicates that a former adherent has reached the considered judgment that his research program is hopelessly degenerated, and therefore the scientific community is advised to expend no further effort to salvage it.

The preceding analysis sounds strikingly subjective, no different in quality than one that belittles the role of objective evidence in judging the relative merits of competing theories. Such a view misses the fundamental point of my analysis. One must distinguish between two positions: (1) all data are theory laden, and hence competing research programs are incommensurable and (2) data need not be contaminated by theoretical preconceptions and therefore research programs can be compared although difference in opinion can prevail about the appropriate criteria to be employed. In the first case objective evaluations are impossible while in the second they are within the realm of the possible.

The employment of the historical framework does not guarantee that those who are acquainted with research programs currently attempting to interpret the same set of phenomena will arrive at equivalent evaluations. Because subjective factors are involved, both in the selection of the criterion on which judgments will be based as well as in the decision about the future potential of the programs, differences of opinion will likely occur. But these differences in opinion can, by sound and diligent scholarship, be traced back to the making of subjective decisions and the rationale for their adoption.

This point becomes clearer when the historical frame of ref-

erence is contrasted with the traditional and subjective conceptions. The traditional framework suggests that a clearcut evaluation of competing theories is always possible and thus encourages
unrealistic expectations. When the results of an experiment that
is considered critical fail to produce consensus about its theoretical implications, the "traditional" scientist is confused by, and incapable of coping constructively with, the unresolved dispute. He
persists in perceiving the theoretical controversy in the false light
of an unrealistic epistemological framework. As a consequence,
endless, and in most ways fruitless, debates are generated about
the specifications of a truly critical experiment, the one valid form
of a given theory, and the unswerving demands of science. Confusion, not clarification, is the final outcome of a traditional epistemological analysis.

A subjective analysis of a theoretical dispute also will not
achieve any fundamental clarification although it may not be as
hampered by the pursuit of false issues as is a traditional analysis.
But it will overlook issues that could clarify the dispute instead
of treating the controversy simply as an expression of personal
taste. The important point is that if one equates scientific understanding with deductive explanation, then there is a basis for ex-
pecting that an epistemological analysis will clarify the issues at
stake among different research programs instead of denying such
a possibility. In essence, the subjective view denies the possibility
of a rational understanding because it is based upon a nihilistic
epistemology.

I do not wish to belittle the difficulties inherent in an historical analysis. The scholarship it demands is of a much higher degree than that required by the traditional and subjective analysis.
This level of scholarship, however, can be approached if one does
not fall victim to the expectations of agreement demanded by the
traditional view and the anticipation of disagreement encouraged
by the subjective view.

No simple recipe can be offered that will ensure a constructive and reasonable historical analysis. What is required, aside
from profundity and respect for research programs other than
one's own (qualities that may be in short supply) is an accurate

scoreboard of what the data are as well as knowledge of the logical consequences of the competing theoretical positions. This does not mean that if either is ambiguous a constructive analysis is precluded. It is not ambiguity that interferes with a historical analysis but rather the inability or the refusal to recognize it. Once it is identified its implications for the future of the research program can be analyzed and evaluated. By understanding the present one is in a better position to plan for the future.

On Understanding: Part Two

5

1. Interpretive consistency is a form of understanding that offers a coherent view of a set of empirical events. It differs from deductive explanation in that the precision of its logical organization falls short of yielding empirical predictions capable of being falsified. Subjective judgments play a significant role in determining whether given interpretations have met the criterion of consistency. Interpretive consistency meets the needs of human science but fails to meet the standards of natural science.

2. Managing the occurrence of a given phenomenon produces a form of understanding known as behavioral control. Operant methodology, which has been highly successful in controlling certain forms of behavior, operates on a probabilistic, not strictly deterministic, basis. The search for techniques of behavioral control generates a research strategy that, unlike the strategy employed by deductive theorists, focuses on the influence of powerful variables and on the development of rigorous experimental procedures that eliminate the effects of extraneous variables. Such a strategy may be particularly effective at this stage in the history of psychology.

3. Intuitive knowing is a form of understanding resulting from a subjective feeling of comprehension. The psychological factors producing intuitive knowing must be distinguished from its epistemological status as an independent form of scientific understanding. Intuitive knowing frequently anticipates deductive explanation but by itself fails to meet the standards of understanding demanded in the natural

sciences. Intuitive knowing is employed as a criterion of understanding more frequently than psychologists like to admit, especially when dealing with complex topics that involve both psychological and philosophical components (e.g., "the image of man").

4. The inability of psychologists to agree upon a basic mode of understanding has encouraged the suggestion that juridical methods be applied to the resolution of scientific controversies. The idea that scientific truth can be adjudicated is rejected although judicial procedure may have relevance to the application of scientific knowledge.

DEDUCTIVE EXPLANATION AND UNDERSTANDING

According to many tough-minded scientists, or at least those who believe they are, all that needs to be said about understanding has already been said. Scientific understanding, as represented by deductive explanation, is the only valid kind of understanding. All other forms generate deceptions.

The trouble with this conclusion is that it dismisses significant attempts at comprehension both within and outside of science. The human mind is capable of achieving understanding through other means than deductive explanation. In an effort to comprehend the current scene in psychology, attention must now be directed toward those other forms of comprehension that psychologists employ to arrive at their conception of truth.

INTERPRETIVE CONSISTENCY

A set of propositions is logically consistent when no contradiction can be derived from it. In this sense a deductive model of explanation demands consistency. It must provide a coherent view of a set of events; it cannot allow for inconsistent implications as would be the case for a theory of aggression that asserted that man is the only member of the animal kingdom who murders for the sake of killing while simultaneously predicting that members of other species also behave similarly.

Consistency, in the logical sense, must be distinguished from truth, in the empirical sense. A mathematical system, for example, could be logically consistent but have no truth value because it is not coordinated to events in the empirical world. But more significant for our present concern is the case of formulations that have apparent empirical relevance but whose empirical implications cannot be rigorously tested. That is, some psychological interpretations are formulated in such a manner, not necessarily deliberately, as to protect them from possible falsification. In spite of this, the formulation provides an apparently consistent interpretation of a particular empirical realm. This is not to say that the conception can be expressed in a strict logical form. Instead, it is limited to informal conceptions expressed in common language that give the impression of hanging together. The most notable examples of interpretive consistency in the absence of demonstrable empirical validity are various psychoanalytic interpretations of personality development.

If Freudian theory, for example, were judged by the demands of a deductive model of explanation, it would be found wanting. Nagel summarizes his methodological analysis of Freudian theory by concluding that "as a body of doctrine for which factual validity can be reasonably claimed, I can only echo the Scottish verdict: Not proven" (1959, p. 55). It would be difficult to disagree with such a conclusion *if one insists* that factual validity can only be achieved by a formulation that meets the demands of a deductive model of explanation. Freudian theory falls short of this requirement because it lacks any precision in its deductive capacity; any and all kinds of behavior appear consistent with it. One reason for this is that Freudian theory is filled with processes and mechanisms (e.g., id versus superego) that operate antagonistically. Because their mode of functioning is not precisely stated, a Freudian theorist, with a modicum of ingenuity, has license to offer a consistent interpretation of any form of behavior occurring under any set of conditions. If the pleasure principle proves inadequate to explain a given form of behavior, the death wish can be invoked. In addition, the same antecedent condition can predict all possible outcomes. A man's unresolved Oedipus complex can explain such widely diverse behaviors as homosexuality, marrying a woman who resembles his mother, marrying a woman who is totally unlike his mother, not marrying, or avoiding all sexual contacts.

Postulating opposed processes by itself does not necessarily produce laxness in predictability. Antagonistic processes operate, for example, in motivational theories of hunger, which postulate excitatory and inhibitory centers in the hypothalamus (Stellar, 1954; Teitelbaum, 1966) that, when operative, have the effect of encouraging or discouraging eating. Because these centers are assumed to have different modes of control, one could manipulate antecedent conditions in order to predict consequent behavior. Freudian theory is incapable of doing this. No objective criteria are available to determine the relative strengths of the antagonistic processes and their mode of interaction. As a result rigorous predictions about future behavior cannot be made, but consistent interpretations of past behavior can be proposed. Rabbi David Small, a fictional detective, expresses the same idea when questioning the explanatory ability of psychologists:

> In my experience . . . [being a psychologist] does not necessarily confer expertise in understanding the motives of men, only some skill in designing explanations of their behavior, which may or may not be true and which can't be proved one way or another (Kemelman, 1976, p. 64).

Popper's emphasis on the principle of falsifiability in order to demarcate empirical science from other kinds of systematic assertions (e.g., metaphysics, pseudosciences) appears particularly relevant to an evaluation of Freudian theory. As already noted, single bits of evidence cannot falsify a theory. All tests of theories involve ancillary assumptions that presumably specify those investigatory procedures that are appropriate for testing the theory. If the results obtained are inconsistent with the theory, the fault may lie with the ancillary assumptions, not the theoretical principles. Or the theoretical principles may be considered defective while the ancillary assumptions are accepted as valid. In either case, the presumably embarrassing evidence encourages modifications in the research program such as in a clearer specification of the ancillary assumptions or in the revision of the theoretical postulates, both of which lead to further empirical testing. Thus even though the theory itself may not be falsified in the strict sense of the word, alteration in the research program is demanded in light of evidence. And, as a consequence, a continuing dialogue is encouraged between the research program and empirical evidence.

Freudian theory fails to meet this relaxed standard of falsifiability, which requires a continuing interaction between theory and data. The theory is so loosely organized and ambiguously stated that it is incapable of generating unequivocal empirical predictions either of experimental results or clinical evidence. Consequently, in the hands of a Freudian the theory is easy to "confirm" but impossible to refute. Because of this deficiency Popper draws a shocking conclusion: psychoanalytic theory does not differ from the pseudosciences of astrology and phrenology. Such a conclusion would no doubt offend Freudians, and perhaps even some astrologists and phrenologists. What must be understood however is that such conclusion does not equate the quality of the content of Freudian theory with that of astrology and phrenology. The only implication of Popper's analysis is that the epistemological forms of these various conceptions—psychoanalytic theory, astrology, phrenology—are equivalent in the sense that they are all incapable of being falsified. One could accept such a conclusion while simultaneously maintaining that Freud's contribution to the *science* that searches for deductive explanations of psychology was profound. In spite of the inadequacies of his theoretical formulations, Freud was instrumental in contributing important orienting attitudes and keen empirical insights that exerted salutary effects on the development of psychology as an empirical science, e.g., a deterministic orientation for all forms of behavior, recognition of unconscious processes (motives of which the behaving individual is unaware), prevalence of conflict behavior, and a variety of defense mechanisms to reduce or avoid aversive feelings and events (Kendler, 1974). The implication of this analysis is that although a particular formulation is on the wrong side of the tracks in regard to the criterion of falsifiability, it does not follow that it is completely irrelevant and useless to an empirical science that seeks deductive explanation. A formulation that cannot be falsified can develop into a falsifiable formulation or inspire the creation of one.

Since there appeared to be a natural affinity between Freudian theory of personality and the experimental psychology of learning because each emphasizes the role of past experience in their interpretation of behavior, the hope was harbored that psychoanalytic concepts could be resystematized into a coherent order that would meet the requirements of deductive explanation. Although research was done to illustrate experimental analogues of Freudian mechanisms of behavior (e.g., fixation, regression), and surveys were conducted to exemplify developmental aspects of psychoanalytic theory (e.g., infantile sexuality, dreams as wish-fulfillments), no real progress was made in improving the deductive capacity of the formulation. In one survey of objective studies of psychoanalytic concepts, a pessimistic conclusion was expressed about the chances of Freudian theory being remolded into a deductive form:

> Other social and psychological sciences must gain as many hypotheses and intuitions as possible from psychoanalysis but . . . further analysis of psychoanalytic concepts by nonpsychoanalytic techniques may be relatively fruitless so long as those concepts rest in the theoretical framework of psychoanalysis (Sears, 1943, p. 143).

This conclusion has stood the test of time. Little has been accomplished in increasing the falsifiable potential of Freudian theory.[1] Instead the course of historical events has underlined the

---

1. This conclusion has been challenged. Silverman (1976) insists that his research could have yielded results inconsistent with psychoanalytic theory. Meehl (1970) has suggested some Freudian hypotheses that are falsifiable. Both positions are certainly defensible because, as noted pre-

hopelessness of such endeavors. Freudian theory has inspired a variety of competing theories, similar in epistemological form but drastically different in content. Both Adler and Jung rebelled against Freud's emphasis on sex. Adler assumed that the fundamental driving force in human behavior was a self-assertive drive, not the sex-oriented libido of Freud. Jung adhered to the concept of the libido but did not restrict it to sexual pleasure. The libido underwent changes with age: in infancy it is directed toward nourishment; in childhood toward play; after puberty toward sexuality; and later in life toward spiritual values. Although all these formulations can provide an apparently reasonable and consistent interpretation of human behavior, their relative merits cannot be judged in any objective fashion by empirical means.

Natural Science Versus Human Science

Why has this kind of theorizing arisen in psychology and what can be done about it? In answer to the first question the distinction between two fundamentally different conceptions of *science* should be noted (Berlyne, 1975). In one conception, prevalent in America and common in hard science and experimental psychology courses, is the conventional view that science is a method of controlled empirical inquiry designed to interpret and predict events. To draw warranted conclusions from such inquiries one must meet the demands of deductive explanation. Another conception of science, more common in Europe, is much broader and looser in that it refers to systematic scholarship that offers coherent interpretations of phenomena.

The looser sense of science can take many different forms

---

viously, a formulation that fails to meet the standards of falsifiability can be modified to one that can. In estimating this possibility one must not only consider the adequacy of Silverman's (1976) research program and the potential of Meehl's (1970) suggestions but also the willingness and capacity of some segment of the psychoanalytic community to do at least some of the research and theorizing needed to make the psychoanalytic research program meet the standards of falsifiability.

and is responsible for the application of the term *science* to a variety of disciplines including history, law, literary criticism, and even religion (e.g., Patai, 1971). One reasonable interpretation of this looser sense of science is that it refers to a qualitatively different discipline than the hard sciences. An important exponent of such a view was Giambattista Vico (1668–1744), a Neapolitan philosopher of history, social theorist, and jurist. Rather than denigrate the level of understanding that history offers in comparison to physics, Vico (Gardiner, 1967) took the position that an historian can achieve a more profound and intimate understanding of his subject matter than can a physical scientist. Vico denied that the scientific method used to study the physical sciences was the only valid method of scientific inquiry and insisted that there are different kinds of sciences, i.e., history requires a method that is distinct from physics. One important feature of this difference is the kind of understanding that can be achieved by these two disciplines. Because the physicist is external to the inanimate subject matter he studies, he cannot achieve the personal understanding that is ultimately available to the historian. The historian, a human studying human events, is capable of empathizing with those who made history and therefore can achieve an intimate acquaintance with his subject matter that is denied the physical scientist.

If this is true then one would like to know the exact details of the methods used to achieve understanding of the "human" sciences such as history and the "litmus test" by which one distinguishes between true and false interpretations. No critical test akin to deductive "validation" through empirical tests is offered. Only important interpretative safeguards are suggested. The historian must assume a proper perspective when viewing past events. He cannot project his own consciousness or the standards of conduct, values, and motivations of his society onto historical personages. In some fashion he must reconstruct the psychology and sociology of past eras and interpret historical events within that "valid" framework.

Vico also viewed history in a highly integrative fashion, in terms of both ahistorical and historical features. A society cannot be properly understood if it is treated as a set of isolated systems: legal, ethical, artistic, political, and so on. The entire society forms a coherent pattern in which all component systems exert a reciprocal influence. In a similar vein Vico argued that societal evolution develops in a strictly deterministic fashion. He proposed an interesting cyclical hypothesis to account for the historical evolution of societies. In brief he postulated that societies develop through several stages, from loosely federated groups of patriarchal families to larger integrated oligarchies. Human reason ultimately dominates, and democratic ideals and values are expressed. Enlightened social, legal, and political institutions are created, but they contain the seeds of their own destruction. The questioning attitudes that democracy encourages become focused on the values of democracy itself. As a result the social institutions are corrupted and become weaker, and finally the society undergoes decay as a function of internal dissolution and/or external conquest. Primitive conditions return and the historical cycle begins anew.

Vico's ideas were more or less ignored until the nineteenth century and not fully appreciated until recent times. His notions anticipated many important social philosophers and theorists, including Karl Marx. My concern is more with their epistemological structure than their theoretical content, and from this perspective, the central issue revolves about the method of ascertaining the validity of conceptions such as Vico's. No doubt the cyclical conception of societal evolution can be faulted because of its failure to jibe with certain historical "facts," perhaps those associated with the development of India and China. I cannot help but feel that in the hands of an ingenious theorizer the argument could be offered that apparent inconsistencies revealed upon close examination really do not invalidate Vico's formulation because they either result from improper interpretations or ignore potential theoretical modifications.

Are not such "theoretical defense mechanisms" equivalent to those used for formulations that explicitly adopt the deductive model of explanation? Does not the historical framework suggested by Lakatos (1970a) in his proposed analysis of progressive and degenerating aspects of theories essentially endorse those defense tactics designed to maintain the validity and integrity of a theory? I think not. The crucial difference is that Lakatos's frame of reference demands that *specific* implications of a formulation be falsifiable, a demand not met by conceptions such as Vico's. A case in point is the Marxist economic interpretation of history. Popper described Marxism (and also Freudian theory) as a "myth" because it was detached from the empirical world in that its implications were beyond falsification. If one examines the history of Marxist principles, with the endless exegetical discussions and disputes concerning their meaning and validity, and the perfect survival rate of the conception in the hands of its adherents, one is likely to conclude that Marxism as a theory of history and economics is fundamentally different from the theories in physics, like those of Newton and Einstein. The difference, it must be underlined, is not in terms of axiomatic elegance but in deductive consequences.

One possible reason for the difference between the predictive capacities of physical theories and historical conceptions of social change is that the latter are not always governed by lawlike regularities. Physical systems, especially when placed under the scrutiny of experimental analysis, are insulated from unpredictable outside influences. This is not true for the historical development of a society. Unpredictable events can shape the future course of a society. For example, scientific breakthroughs, which triggered the industrial revolution and the atomic age, are themselves essentially unpredictable. How can social change be predicted if a major cause of it cannot?

Another factor that operates against predictability of social change is the accidental interaction among independent systems. Take the case of the person who runs out of his house to prevent a stray dog from digging up his lawn and breaks his leg when he slips on a banana peel dropped out of a garbage pail by an inexperienced replacement of the regular garbageman who was called to jury duty. In order to predict the accident one would have had to anticipate, among other events, the coincidence of the activities of the stray dog, the jury duty of the regular garbageman, and the sloppiness of his replacement. Do not important historical events have the same unpredictability? Was the disastrous involvement of the United States in Vietnam equally unpredictable? Was it not the result of the coincidence of numerous unrelated events such as the assassination of President Kennedy, the "macho" personality of President Johnson, and the naiveté of Secretary McNamara's faith that systems analysis and computer technology could predict the behavior of the Vietnamese?

The questions posed identify a clash between two competing "in principle" arguments. One suggests that the power of the scientific method can be applied successfully to any natural occurrence while the other maintains that limits to predictability operate. Consistent with previously expressed reservations of "in principle" arguments, sides in this controversy will not be taken. This does not mean that the problem should be ignored. It should be realized that successful predictions of events become more difficult as the number of operating variables increase and as the interactions among them become more complex. Predicting the time it will take a leaf to fall when in a windstorm is a much more difficult task than when it is in a vacuum. Regardless of "in principle" arguments it would be reasonable to expect that social theories have a greater difficulty of meeting demanding standards of deductive explanation than do physical theories.

Whatever explanatory limits may be placed upon theories that seek to account for societal evolution, it must be understood that they do not necessarily apply to all historical changes. In my previous discussion of the change in the incidence of peptic ulcers in men and women during the last 100 years (page 115), it was noted that deductions from an informally stated theory met the standards of falsifiability. A much more interesting and significant example of a historical theory, and one that has special relevance to psychology both in form and content, is Darwin's theory of natural selection. Perhaps the future will prove, if it has not already been demonstrated, that theoretical psychologists, such as Hull (1943) and Lewin (1935), made a strategic error when they sought conceptual guidance from the physical theories of Newton and Galileo rather than from Darwin.

Darwinian Theory: A Historical Theory
with Deductive Capacity

Darwin's theory of evolution has been criticized as a gigantic tautology (the fittest survive because they are the fittest) and faulted because it can explain but not predict. Both views are incorrect because the formulation does have the capacity to predict future events. This point was overlooked, even by Darwin himself, probably because the retrospective aspect of the theory had such profound implications that its predictive capacity was ignored. For the prevailing view that the variety of animal and plant species represents the unalterable work of God, Darwin substituted the conception that species evolve over time by virtue of environmental pressures that favor the survival of one life form over another. Another probable reason for disregarding the predictive capacity of natural selection theory is that the biological mechanism responsible for variations within a species was unknown. With the advent of genetic theory this gap was filled, and consequently, the deductive capacity of natural selection theory increased enormously. But the significant point is that Darwinian theory in its original form provides the basis for prediction of future events. One can cite experimental evidence that is consistent with the predictive capacity of the original formulation.

One such example is the well-known case of two varieties of the peppered moth in England that appeared to have different survival rates in different environments. One form of the peppered moth is light colored with dark spots scattered irregularly over the body and wings. The other form, due to the presence of the melanin pigment, is much darker. On trees covered with lichens the light varieties of the peppered moth are effectively camouflaged, but the darker forms stand out and consequently are more subject to predation from birds. The opposite relationship prevails in industrial areas where tree trunks are darkened from soot; the light-colored forms are more visible. In short, the lighter form has greater selective advantage in nonindustrial areas while the darker forms have the advantage in the industrial areas.

One would therefore predict that due to the protective coloration the survival rate of light and dark peppered moths would vary in industrial and nonindustrial regions. This hypothesis was tested by releasing an equal number of light and dark moths in each environment and after a given amount of time recapturing as many as possible. In line with the expectations a greater percentage of the dark forms were recaptured in industrial areas while the opposite occurred in the nonindustrial areas (Baker & Allen, 1971).

One can also cite evidence that extends beyond a given generation to support natural selection theory. A mixture of grass and clover was planted in a field, which was later divided into halves by erecting a fence. For a three-year period one side was cut a few times during the summer for hay while the other side was heavily grazed by cattle. Plants from each side of the fence were then dug up and transplanted in an experimental garden. After a period of growth under uniform conditions it was found that the grasses and clover from the ungrazed half produced plants that for the most part were erect and vigorous while the high proportion of plants from the grazed side were short and rambling. From natural selection theory one would have predicted this outcome: in the ungrazed field natural selection favored the tall plants, which because of their height would compete successfully for sunlight with the short, rambling forms, but in the grazed half the opposite relationship would prevail because low and small plants had a greater chance of not being consumed by the cattle (Baker & Allen, 1971).

Neo-Darwinism, the theory of natural selection supplemented by modern genetic formulations, has a greater explanatory capacity than is suggested by the kind of experimental evidence just cited. For example, it predicts experimental data that express the operation of sexual selection, a concept that was original with Darwin but was unrelated to any specific mechanism of hereditary transmission. If sexual mating is encouraged by some physical characteristic then the genetic basis of the characteristic will increase over successive generations. Female fruit flies, for example, mate more readily with red-eyed males than with white-eyed ones. Consequently, in a controlled laboratory population in which the percentage of red- and white-eye genes are known, one would predict that the proportion of red-eye genes will increase in successive generations, a prediction that has been confirmed (Baker & Allen, 1971).

One can also point to the guidance provided by natural selection theory in unraveling the mystery surrounding the distribution of the sickle-cell gene responsible for sickle-cell anemia, a usually fatal disorder in which the red blood cells become sickle shaped when deprived of oxygen. It was discovered that both parents, usually black, of children suffering from sickle-cell anemia possessed the "sickle-cell trait"; only some of their red blood cells became sickle shaped when deprived of oxygen. Children born to such parents exhibit the basic Mendelian proportions of 25 percent normals (nonsicklers), 50 percent with the sickle-cell trait, and 25 percent with sickle-cell anemia, who usually die in early life. One would expect, according to principles of natural selection, that the sickle-cell gene would decrease in successive generations because most of the offspring who inherit this gene from each parent would fail to reproduce. The sickle-cell gene has decreased among American blacks with its rate of occurrence, as expected, becoming less for successive generations (with more effective genetic counseling the decreasing rate could become larger). Environmental conditions, however, can influence gene frequencies as demonstrated by the distribution of the sickle-cell gene in certain parts of Africa where a high incidence of malaria is prevalent. The heterozygous person with a sickle-cell gene from one parent and a normal gene from the other possesses greater resistance to malaria than the homozygous individual who inherits a nonsickling gene from each parent. Whereas the frequency of the sickle-cell gene is approximately 5 percent among American blacks, it has been found to be as high as 45 percent in certain lowland sections of Africa along rivers that are infested with the malaria parasite (Dunn, 1965). Because the heterozygous individual with the sickle-cell trait is more resistant to malaria than is the homozygous nonsickling person, it can be predicted that the sickle-cell gene will be preserved at a higher proportion in malaria-infested regions than in other areas.

The final example of the predictive capacity of natural selection theory will involve science fiction. One of the most compelling arguments in favor of natural selection is its retrospective explanation of the absence of saltatory differences among species—"nature" has no gaps. Since the diversity of species is accounted for by random variation and natural selection, the difference between species, according to the theory, should not be extreme but rather gradual. The "gap" between large classes of organisms, such as reptiles and mammals, is occupied by transitional forms with characteristics of both, e.g., the duckbill platypus lays eggs like a reptile yet nurses its young like a mammal. Its body temperature also varies, not as much as that of a reptile but considerably more than that of a typical mammal like a dog.

The slight variations that natural selection predicts among neighboring species is dramatically illustrated by the differences among the Galapagos finches, who presumably descended from a single species that emigrated to the Galapagos from the mainland of South America. The ancestor species was probably a seed-eating ground finch, but as a result of individual variation and natural selection fourteen different kinds of finches developed (Lack, 1947)—some ground dwellers, others tree dwellers—each with a somewhat different diet thus reducing the competition for survival. The significant point is that the unique combination of "chance" individual variations and environmental diversity represented by a variety of ecological niches favored the development of novel forms of finches. Although natural selection theory could not predict the exact forms the new species would assume, the expectation was that their divergence would be gradual.

From this sort of analysis one would make the prediction that if another planet with life was discovered that operated on the same biological principles as does this planet, the speciation of that planet would differ markedly from ours. The random variation of offsprings combined with environmental pressures of natural selection on that planet would produce a unique constellation of variables, and as a consequence its life forms would diverge significantly from ours.

This extended discussion of natural selection theory was designed to demonstrate that Darwin's formulation achieved the standards of deductive explanation. One might disagree with such a claim by noting that: (1) natural selection theory was, and still is, incapable of predicting future evolutionary changes in species or the creation of new species, and (2) natural selection theory, as originally formulated by Darwin, achieved the status of a deductive theory only with the development of genetic theory.

Both of these criticisms are off the mark. Admittedly, Darwin's original formulation fell short of deductive elegance, but at all stages of its development it could be put to the empirical test, which in principle could yield embarrassing evidence. As already noted, the original formulation was testable in regard to the assumption concerning differential survival as a function of environmental pressures. For a theory to be empirically meaningful does not require that all its assumptions be directly testable. A theory is a global conception when it comes to prediction. If a formulation can yield some deductive consequences that are empirically testable, then it has explanatory capabilities.

Natural selection theory appears to be a classic example of a theory that has developed progressively. Genetic theory did not save the formulation but rather represents a consistent extension of it. In other words, the deductive possibilities of natural selection theory were not created by genetic theory but instead enlarged by it. Differential survival as a function of environmental adaptation (a key assumption in Darwin's theory) became subordinate, with the advent of genetic knowledge, to the differential reproduction of genetic material. Differential survival is mainly responsible for differential reproduction of genetic material, and thus selection becomes the mechanism by which systematic, inheritable changes occur during successive generations. And finally we can look to the future with some optimism (and trepidation) that increases in the knowledge of the chemistry and physics of genetic material will allow us to investigate directly the problems of evolutionary changes in species and even the creation of new species.

My excursion into natural selection theory was to demonstrate that theories designed to account for historical phenomena are capable of being formulated in a manner that yields deductive consequences. After contrasting Darwinism with Freudianism and Marxism I concluded that the empirical implications of the first met the standards of falsifiability while the latter two did not. Why was Darwinism successful in meeting such standards and achieving general acceptance in the scientific community while Freudianism and Marxism failed in comparison? An obvious answer is that Darwinism is fundamentally valid, in the deductive explanatory sense, while Freudianism and Marxism are not. Perhaps such an evaluation is the most appropriate response, but nevertheless, it may be incomplete.

Deductive Explanation and Interpretive
Consistency as Forms of Understanding

Without implying that Freudianism and Marxism contain the kernel truths that Darwinism possesses, the suggestion can be made that different orienting attitudes toward the nature of understanding influenced the development of these various conceptions. These differences could be a consequence of many factors including general methodological stances that prevailed in some segments of the behavioral and social sciences at the time as well as the intrinsic difficulties involved in isolating and controlling the relevant variables in these fields. In addition, a combined epistemological-psychological factor can be mentioned. This factor rests upon a division between two kinds of knowledge, one of which can be described as a *conception* while the other, the medium for deductive explanation, is designated as a *theory*. The psychological underpinnings of this distinction are expressed in the contrast between the pursuit of meaning and the search for causes.

A conception, in this methodological analysis, is an awareness of a general schema that governs the functioning of a given system. One example of a conception is Vico's analysis of the continuity in the rhythm of history as expressed in the rise and decline of human societies. Similarly, Oswald Spengler (1950) perceived the history of cultures as an expression of a cohesive force that creates a configuration in which all of its components—religion, art, economics, politics—reflect a specific quality of its people. Spengler assumed that cultures are self-contained systems and, as such, obey certain laws of historical development and decline. Arnold Toynbee (1946–57), in turn, examined twenty-one civilizations and adduced a particular pattern of development and decline that presumably characterized all societies. To this list can be added Marx's historical materialism, which attributed to economic processes the key role in historical development; and Freud's psychoanalytic theory, which postulated that psychosexual development underlies personality formation.

I maintain that all of these *conceptions* illuminate, in a profound sense, the phenomena they sought to clarify. This illumination of historical events, and I think it is appropriate to consider personality development within that context, was achieved by providing a cohesive formulation of events that had been for the most part ignored. In each case, from Vico to Freud, an explanatory vacuum was replaced by an imaginative interpretation that had the appearance of both consistency and validity. Although none of these interpretations met the standards required of a deductive explanation, they nevertheless provided some sense of understanding by identifying a problem considered by some to be pointless and by others to be inexplicable. Thus the rise and decline of societies, the economic force in social organization, and the psychological significance of dreams—all hidden by neglect or oversight—were brought forward and recognized as significant issues. In addition, *possible* interpretations were offered.

Darwin's theory of natural selection could be considered a conception in this context. He perceived the problem of variation of species in relation to environmental diversity and formulated a possible interpretation of the phenomenon. But his conception was transformed into a theory of natural selection that, as has been argued, meets the standards of a deductive explanatory system. Thus the fundamental difference between *conception* and *theory* is that the latter possesses a predictive component. The absence of this component does not justify dismissal of such conceptions as myths if we mean by such a designation purely a product of one's fancy. Conceptions further understanding both by directing attention to a significant phenomenon and by suggesting a possible interpretation. In this sense the term *conception* could not properly be applied to astrology or phrenology because neither deals with a significant empirical relationship. There is no evidence to justify the belief that the position of the stars or the shape of a person's skull is related to his behavior. *Misconception* would be a more appropriate characterization.

In spite of identifying significant empirical relationships, Freudian theory could not generate unambiguous predictions about *specific* empirical events. It did suggest in a general way that children engage in erotic behavior, an observation that has been supported by empirical evidence (e.g., Sears, 1943). But the psychosexual theory of personality development implied more to infantile sexuality than simple self-initiated genital activity. The fundamental concern of the theory revolved about concepts such as stages (oral, anal, and genital) of psychosexual development, Oedipus, Electra, and castration complexes, and penis envy. The empirical consequences flowing from the theoretical relationships among these concepts appear to be beyond falsification. Failure, for example, to obtain evidence of penis envy may be due to the operation of some unconscious process that suppresses any observable consequence of the mechanism. Regardless of the evidence it is always possible to argue, as devout Freudians do, that penis envy does in fact operate.

The significant question is why so many formulations in the so-called "human sciences" (social and behavioral) assume the empirically unassailable position that is characteristic of psychoanalytic theories. The answer would seem to lie in the function such formulations serve in satisfying the need for understanding. Some psychologists pursue meaning while others search for causes. Meaning in this sense is expressed by a consistent interpretation (i.e., a conception) that provides a compelling sense of understanding whereas the identification of cause is achieved by a successful deductive theory. The two are not mutually exclusive when an "objective" deductive theory offers a "subjective" compelling sense of understanding. However, in the absence of a successful deductive theory a consistent interpretation can provide a satisfying sense of understanding. And what is more important, even when a deductive theory is available some psychologists will find the meaning offered by a consistent interpretation more appealing than a causal interpretation.

Vico was explicit in affirming that the criterion of understanding human events was different from those employed to interpret physical phenomena. He suggested that the difference revolved about the position of the interpreter in relation to the events he seeks to understand; the physical scientist is detached while the scientific investigator of human affairs, such as the historian, is involved. The kind of understanding is different because the behavioral scientist can draw upon his own personal experience in comprehending human events. As noted, Vico argued that the intimate acquaintance a historian can have with his subject matter enables him to achieve a deeper understanding than what a physical scientist can possibly achieve.

Numerous social and behavioral scientists have argued along the lines of Vico in maintaining that understanding human events involves a different process than comprehending natural phenomena. More often than not this claim for a distinctive method in the human sciences is made in the absence of any description of what that special method is.

Criteria of Interpretive Consistency

There are obviously numerous forms of understanding human events aside from deductive explanations. The line of argument being pursued here is that one general "method" of comprehension, known as *interpretive consistency,* is different from deductive explanation but is nevertheless capable of providing a compelling sense of understanding. It may very well be that the "rules" underlying this kind of understanding cannot be clearly explicated because, unlike the method of deductive explanation, interpretive consistency is not evaluated by a set of explicit judgments that yields a consensual agreement about its truth value. In the absence of any precise set of regulations to judge *interpretive consistency* the most one can do in describing this kind of understanding is to characterize its procedures. One possible starting point is Vico's suggestion that historical events become comprehensible when placed in the context of the experiencing individuals. This orientation is related to the notion of *verstehen,* a concept that has been suggested by numerous social theorists as representing the method of achieving understanding of human events (Abel, 1948). In essence, *verstehen* is a cognitive operation that the human scientist performs in order to understand human behavior. He accomplishes this by attempting to share another person's state of mind—a task, the success of which is difficult, and sometimes impossible, to judge as my discussion of "shared experience" suggests (page 64).

Consider this simple case of achieving *verstehen* (Abel, 1948). During a freezing spell in early spring a man observes his neighbor rise from his desk by a window and walk to the woodshed where he starts chopping wood. After completing the task the neighbor carries the wood into his house and places it in the fireplace where he lights it. He then returns to his desk and resumes his daily writing chores.

The explanation of the neighbor's behavior appears obvious; he felt chilly and lit a fire to warm up. This interpretation is arrived at by filling in a psychological gap between two events that the observer thinks are important, the dropping temperature and the heat produced by fire. The psychological gap is filled by the observer postulating that if he had been in his neighbor's shoes he would have started a fire. According to this analysis, *verstehen* is achieved when we perceive a person's action as consistent with what we would have done under similar circumstances.

Although plausible, the interpretation of the neighbor's behavior may not be correct. Perhaps he likes the cold temperature in his study but lights the fire to show off his fireplace to an anticipated visitor, or perhaps he is suffering financial difficulties and unconsciously hopes that the fire will "accidentally" produce a conflagration that will enable him to collect some insurance money.

Conceivably these alternative hypotheses could be tested in a deductive fashion by gathering additional information—e.g., the neighbor's own explanation for lighting the fire, the arrival of any visitors, the neighbor's financial condition, his behavior in similar situations in the future. The point however is that the initial explanation is so compelling that other interpretations and further evidence are not sought. In other words, *verstehen* provides a phenomenologically satisfying interpretation that rings "true" and resists rejection.

It is necessary to distinguish between the cognitive operation of *verstehen* and the content and quality of the interpretation that produces *verstehen*. Certainly the interpretation of the neighbor's behavior in no way approaches the complexity and profundity of the explanations offered by Vico, Spengler, Toynbee, and Freud. The point here however is that a similarity prevails in regard to how the understanding is achieved; an event is understood by fitting it into the observer's explanatory framework. This framework can vary from a naive, but *consistent*, intuitive conception of the sort that generated the explanation of the neighbor's behavior to a sophisticated theoretical Freudian paradigm. Between these extremes is Vico's historical position, which postulates that the actions of historical figures are understood by reconstructing their consciousness.

The use of an explanatory framework to interpret phenomena obviously does not distinguish understanding achieved by interpretive consistency from deductive explanations. Theories, regardless of what criteria are employed to evaluate them, provide conceptual frameworks that influence the interpretation of events. The fundamental difference between understanding achieved by interpretive consistency and deductive explanation is the criteria adopted for evaluating proposed interpretations. In the case of the anecdote of the neighbor's behavior and Vico's conception of the human sciences, the criteria for understanding are clearly different from those used for deductive explanation. Vico explicitly makes this point, and consequently if one acknowledges his distinction, no confusion need arise as to the general procedure that is to be employed to evaluate whether a given theoretical proposal is seeking deductive explanation or interpretive consistency. This is not to say that a simple "litmus test" can be applied to an interpretation to determine whether it meets either standard. Some ambiguity exists, but the important factor is that the two kinds of interpretations are sufficiently different so that no confusion between the two need occur *if* the theorist explicitly states what his explanatory goals are.

I am reminded of a conversation with a distinguished historian who in response to my query about how he judged historical explanations responded simply "Aesthetics!" He elaborated by indicating that one interpretation was favored over another if it created a sense of understanding that was deeper, fuller, and more coherent than the other. This sense of understanding was not equivalent to a deductive explanation because he thought that a search for such understanding in history was a highly romantic and unrealistic enterprise for a variety of reasons including the incompleteness of historical data, the fallibility of most historical sources, and the inability to devise a satisfactory deductive test of a theory. In addition, he was willing to argue that a purely deductive explanation, even if it were possible, could fall short of a satisfactory level of understanding by failing to offer a "meaningful" interpretation.

The meaning of "meaningful" in this sense may be clarified by shifting our attention to early developments in mathematical-learning theory. Two similar mathematical representations of simple learning processes were offered by Bush and Mosteller (1951) and Estes (1950), each possessing essentially the same deductive consequences. They differed however in that Estes's theory was supplemented by a "meaningful" interpretation of why the mathematical processes operated as they did. He suggested that learning occurred in a manner consistent with Guthrie's brand of stimulus-response associationism (Hilgard & Bower, 1975). According to Estes's formulation the experimental situation consisted of a population of stimulus elements, which were sampled on successive trials. The sampled elements were attached to the correct response. Learning was complete when all the stimulus elements were associated with the correct response.

If the predictive consequences of the two mathematical models are the same, then one could argue that the supplementary interpretation provided by the stimulus-sampling notion was superfluous. But viewing theories within a historical perspective would suggest that factors other than their deductive capacities can play a role in their development. The stimulus-sampling interpretation of learning has instrumental value; it provides the theorist with an analogy for interpreting a variety of phenomena within a common theoretical framework. Thus the supplementary interpretation aids the theorist in his attempt to expand the empirical domain of his formulation. In this function the stimulus-sampling notion operates as a tool of thought for seeing similarities not revealed by the mathematical representation.

At this point it will be advantageous to back off from specific points and regain the appropriate perspective for viewing the fundamental methodological issue. The line of analysis being pursued is that a difference exists between interpretive consistency and deductive explanation. This difference is fairly obvious when the criteria of the two are clearly distinguished as is the case for Vico, who postulates different forms of understanding (*verstehen* versus deductive explanation) for the human and physical sciences. The distinction becomes much hazier when an explicit difference is denied as is the case when a theorist claims that the standards of deductive explanation are met but the implications of his conception, upon examination, prove to be immune to falsification. It should be clear from previous discussions that the argument is not that deductive explanations cannot be achieved in the human and biological sciences but instead that other kinds of understandings are possible. One major task in comprehending psychological knowledge is to identify the criteria of understanding that is sought. Although many psychoanalytic theorists would argue that their conceptions are of the natural-science variety, a historical analysis of the claim suggests otherwise. This historical failure does not deny that psychoanalytic explanations can be intellectually convincing.

> Over and above all of the other virtues of (Freud's) theory stands this one—it tries to envisage a full-bodied individual living partly in the world of reality and partly in the world of make-believe,

beset by conflicts and inner contradictions, yet capable of rational thought and action, moved by forces of which he has little knowledge and by aspirations which are beyond his reach, by turn confused and clearheaded, frustrated and satisfied, hopeful and despairing, selfish and altruistic; in short, a complex human being. For many people, this picture of man has an essential validity (Hall & Lindzey, 1957, p. 72).

And once this "picture" is judged valid it becomes immune to falsification.[2]

The concept of interpretive consistency, if it is to be fully understood, must await more complete psychological analysis. It represents a cognitive knowing that is achieved by a coherent interpretation. Quite obviously individual differences play an important role; what is "aesthetic," or encourages *"verstehen,"* or produces a *consistent interpretation* for one person will not necessarily be equally effective for another. For this reason the level of consensual agreement that is attainable in deductive explanations will not be approached by understanding achieved through interpretive consistency. The fact, however, that a particular consistent interpretation is not widely accepted in no way denies the reality of its psychological validity for those who adopt it.

One reason for adopting interpretive consistency as a criterion for understanding in preference to deductive explanation is that the demands of the human sciences are different from those of the natural sciences. These demands can be met by suggesting, as Vico did, a conception of understanding that differs from that of the natural sciences. It would be possible to argue that although deductive explanation is the deepest kind of understanding that can be achieved, meeting such standards is an impossibility for many phenomena in the behavioral sciences. To be specific, no true deductive explanation can ever be confirmed, or even approached, for certain kinds of phenomena such as Richard Nixon's

2. A reaction to Freudian theory that one hears at cocktail parties, is that Freud did not create a new science of man but instead a new picture of man. This statement, translated into the present nomenclature, would read: "Freud did not create a new theory of man but instead a new conception of man."

behavior in the Watergate Affair or the true causes of the Vietnam War. The only realistic and rational approach to such phenomena, one can argue, is to realize the impossibility of achieving deductive explanation but at the same time to be guided by the ideals of such interpretations. That is, one can formulate a consistent interpretation based upon psychological and/or historical theories that have yielded predictions about other phenomena susceptible to deductive confirmation.

So we see that understanding via interpretive consistency can be arrived at by opposite routes; from the conviction that different rules for understanding must be invoked in the human sciences to the belief that deductive explanations are incapable of being achieved but possible to approach.

One other psychological factor should be mentioned for the ready acceptance of interpretive consistency as an index of understanding. Attempts at understanding phenomena frequently begin by identifying a variable or process that is assumed to be *the* causal agent. This tendency is exemplified by commonsense interpretations of the sort that are expressed in oversimplified maxims such as "Practice makes perfect" and "Spare the rod and spoil the child." Practice and punishment are potent psychological variables but neither can bear the entire explanatory burden for even the simplest type of behavior. Whether the practice is being reinforced and what the organism's reaction to noxious stimulation is must also be considered. Although the elaborate and profoundly influential formulations of Marx and Freud are not comparable to these maxims in form or content, they nevertheless exaggerate the importance of a single factor (e.g., economics, sex). This overemphasis can be considered a natural by-product of human thought. When analyzing multivariable phenomena people tend to overestimate the influence of certain variables to the exclusion of others. This tendency toward oversimplification encourages the adoption of interpretive consistency as a mode of understanding. By ignoring or minimizing the influence of factors other than the one originally focused on, the theorist is forced to spin out an interpretive web that maintains the priority of the favored variable while simultaneously protecting the entire formulation from deductive embarrassment.

The Relative Value of Interpretive Consistency
and Deductive Explanation

The reader could easily get the impression that an invidious
comparison has been made between the understanding that is
achieved by *deductive explanation* and that which results from
interpretive consistency. The major thrust of this analysis has
been to identify two qualitatively different kinds of understanding. This is not to say that a particular formulation cannot shift
over time from one kind to the other, from deductive explanation
to interpretive consistency or vice versa. Nor does it imply that it
will always be easy to establish a clear demarcation line between
these two kinds of understanding. My suggestion is that the possibility of formulating a falsifiable implication distinguishes deductive explanation from interpretive consistency. No doubt some
differences of opinion can occur in deciding on which side of the
demarcation line a particular formulation falls. It seems that epistemological analysis is inevitably burdened by fuzzy boundary
lines between significant distinctions. Nevertheless, the distinctions between the two forms of understanding can still serve a
useful purpose in the epistemological clarification of different
theoretical formulations.

My major defense against the accusation that an invidious
comparison has been made is that the distinction need not be considered within a judgmental perspective. Those who seek predictability will choose to operate within a deductive explanatory
framework. But it must be recognized that the ultimate achievement of satisfactory deductive explanations cannot be guaranteed
for all phenomena. Failures could result either from the limitations of the human intellect or from the intrinsic indeterminism
of given phenomena.[3] In either case the most that can be hoped

3. There is no way of proving indeterminism. The ability to predict
phenomena demonstrates a deterministic system. The absence of predictability however does not imply the absence of determinism. It can simply
reflect inadequate knowledge or a defective theory. The deterministic principle can be supported by successful theories, but it cannot be falsified by
unsuccessful formulations. In essence, determinism is not a thesis about the
nature of the world but instead a guiding research strategy.

for in understanding certain phenomena, ranging from political revolutions to the creative efforts of geniuses, is interpretive consistency. Consequently, interpretive consistency is, for some, a more valued form of understanding than is deductive explanation simply because it represents the form of comprehending "truly significant human events."

BEHAVIORAL CONTROL

One approach to understanding an event is to discover the factors that control its occurrence, i.e., behavior is understood when it is controlled. Some of those who achieve a sense of understanding by meeting the demands of interpretive consistency or deductive explanation cannot comprehend how anyone could presume to understand a phenomenon by controlling its occurrence. How can a trivial demonstration of control provide the same deep understanding conveyed by a conceptual superstructure that interprets a given fact as an expression of abstract principles? To be specific, how could the control of a phobic act, such as fear of snakes, be equated with the rich interpretation offered by Freudian theory? And finally, can anyone insist that we do not understand planetary motion because we cannot control it?

Two separate issues are embedded in this set of questions, one of conscious experience associated with a sense of understanding, the other of methodological preference for certain criteria of understanding. If a "sense of understanding" is viewed as a subjective state, then one cannot refute a psychologist's insistence that he understands behavior when it can be controlled in the absence of any theoretical interpretation. We cannot deny his subjective reality. If we shift gears and view the problem from a methodological perspective, then the selection of behavioral control as a criterion of understanding should become comprehensible. After considering the vast effort expended in psychological theorizing and the meager payoff in rigorous and successful conceptions, it becomes easy to comprehend how some psychologists would opt for control as a sign of understanding. The choice of behavior control becomes even clearer when it occurs in the American cultural setting that values a pragmatic view of science.

Behavioral control is commonly associated with effective training methods. The essence of this mode is expressed in John Watson's famous boast:

> Give me a dozen healthy infants, well formed, and my own specified world to bring them up in, and I'll guarantee to take any one at random and train him to become any type of specialist I might select—a doctor, lawyer, artist, merchant-chief, and yes, even beggar-man and thief, regardless of his talents, penchants, tendencies, abilities, vocations and race of his ancestors (Watson, 1926, p. 10).[4]

In reacting to this and other statements of Watson, Skinner (1959) noted that "polemics led [Watson] into extreme positions from which he never escaped," a tendency that Skinner, himself, has exhibited. Skinner and some of his colleagues have, at times, encouraged the belief that their behavioral management techniques are capable of strict deterministic control of behavior comparable in power to Watson's claim. Their confidence and optimism were encouraged by their successes in "shaping" the behav-

4. The purpose of citing this quotation is to illustrate, clearly and dramatically, an example of behavioral control. It must be mentioned, however, that this quote is taken out of context, its usual fate. The quotation is frequently employed to discredit Watson in particular and behaviorism in general. The sentence that follows, which is usually ignored, states, "I am going beyond my facts and I admit it, but so have the advocates of the contrary and they have been doing it for many thousands of years." A tolerant interpretation of Watson's remarks is that he was attempting to counteract the extreme position that genetic factors solely determined a person's behavior by an extreme environmentalism that was as equally justified (or unjustified).

Environmentalism is not a logical by-product of methodological behaviorism. Methodological behaviorism espouses a public, objective approach in psychology, making no substantive assumptions about the manner in which genetic and environmental factors influence behavior. The interest of early behaviorists in environmental control of behavior was not an expression of a methodological commitment, but instead a reflection of influential philosophical and sociological forces in American psychology (Kendler, 1979).

ior of rats and pigeons during operant conditioning and learning of complex tricks (e.g., pigeons playing Ping-Pong). It became a matter of faith among some operant conditioners that shaping, if properly and persistently applied, could fashion behavior in any desired form. Those who were wedded to this notion did not fully appreciate that the successes achieved were to some extent a function of the tasks selected and the narrow range of organisms used.

A ceiling on the effectiveness of shaping techniques became apparent when the Brelands (Breland & Breland, 1961) attempted to shape raccoons to drop coins in a piggy bank for a behavioral display in a municipal zoo. The subjects tended to rub the coins together and dip them in the slot in a manner that raccoons use to wash food. The instinctive pattern of behavior prevented the shaping procedure from achieving the desired goal.

Many other instances can be cited to demonstrate that operant methods of controlling behavior developed in the laboratory have definite limits. At one time hopes were harbored that myna birds could be taught to communicate in English, but such naive aspirations were abandoned when it was realized that emitting appropriate sounds did not qualify as learning a language. Shaping techniques were also thought to hold the key for curing schizophrenics and autistic children. Such high hopes were dashed when it became apparent that operant methodology was not as effective in changing psychotic to normal behavior as it was for training pigeons to play Ping-Pong. (Pigeon Ping-Pong, in truth, was a pale imitation of human Ping-Pong. The impact of the demonstration rested not on how well pigeons played the game but only that they could play it at all.) Operant conditioners have backed off from their early hopes of curing psychotic behavior, justifying their efforts by the claim that psychotic patients in behavior management programs "make fewer demands on the staff and yet display as much dignity and happiness as their pathology permits." (Skinner, 1969).

The failures of operant methodology to control certain forms of behavior do not invalidate the principle that regulating response-reinforcement contingencies is an effective method of managing behavior. They merely show that such a method of controlling behavior is not sufficient by itself. Other factors must be considered, particularly the genetic predispositions and physiological capacities required for certain forms of behavior.

If the control of behavior by operant methods is viewed within the context of the entire range of phenomena to which it has been applied, then the conclusion must be drawn that the shaping technique is not a strictly deterministic mode of controlling behavior. Failures can and do occur. The chances of success vary with the organism and the task. Information about the success rate of behavior modification techniques suggests that operant conditioning methodology represents a probabilistic mode of controlling behavior. Complete success in eliminating undesirable forms of behavior, ranging from a phobia to compulsive smoking, is never achieved. The most that can be said for these operant methods is that they have a certain probability of success.

Theoretical and Practical Orientations in Controlling Behavior

An interesting methodological conflict, which has important implications for the control of behavior, has occurred in the psychology of learning between traditional theorists who employ abstract concepts (Hull, 1943; Spence, 1956; Tolman, 1932) and those who accept control of behavior as their primary goal. Proponents of traditional theories of learning tested their deductive powers on the performance of groups. Their strategy was to formulate basic principles that applied to all organisms and leave to later the discovery of idiosyncratic factors that influence individual performance. Such general formulations could therefore only offer probabilistic information for those who sought to employ the theory for the purpose of controlling individual behavior. This, as noted, does not distinguish the knowledge underlying deductive theories from the information used by operant conditioners. Yet, principles of operant conditioning proved far more effective for controlling behavior than did deductive theories. Why? The answer seems to lie in the differences in strategy employed by those who were formulating deductive theories (e.g., Hull) and those who were concerned with controlling behavior (e.g., Skinner).

Traditional deductive theorists and control-oriented operant conditioners perceived the relationship between experimental operations and behavior differently. Both the theorist and the operant conditioner manipulated experimental conditions, but the theorist's actions were governed by the nature of his theoretical constructs while those of the operant conditioner were determined by the behavior of his subject. The theorist tended to accept the control exerted by his experimental manipulations especially when deductions coincided with expectations. In contrast, the behavior-controllers persistently attempted to improve upon the control exerted by environmental manipulations. This encouraged the operant conditioner to focus on individual behavior while the theorist was concerned only with group averages.

This primary concern with individual behavior underlies the operant conditioner's rejection of traditional statistical evaluations. If one aspires to understand behavior, one must deal, the argument goes, with the form in which it occurs (individual behavior) and not as some abstraction (a group average). Resorting to statistical evaluation is an admission of ignorance about factors that control behavior and an expression of despair that effective management can never be achieved. Rather than succumb to this pessimism one can actively seek to identify the conditions that control the behavior of individual organisms. The search for understanding then becomes the search for control.

Although the argument in favor of investigating individual behavior appears reasonable, even though one may not fully agree with it, the interesting question remains as to the relationship that prevails between individual and group data. Sidman offers a clear-cut, but puzzling answer: "The two types of data represent, in a real sense, different subject matters" (1960, p. 53). Others have worked primarily with individual data without adopting this extreme view. Ebbinghaus, for example, studied only his own behavior with the purpose of uncovering general principles of human memory. His goal was no different from modern memory theorists who utilize between-group experimental designs. One can also refer to the efforts of psychophysicists who test individual subjects repeatedly. Similar designs are also being used in information-processing studies (e.g., Sternberg, 1969) and experiments on the effects of meditation (e.g., Wallace & Benson, 1972), and again one finds no implication that such data need be set apart from group averages. One can also note that the between-subjects design is not completely foreign to the house organ of operant conditioners, the *Journal of the Experimental Analysis of Behavior,* even though it is relatively rare, much below the percentage that appears in traditional APA and Psychonomic Society's journals (Hilgard & Bower, 1975). Finally it should be mentioned that some operant conditioners have become enticed by theoretical issues (Honig, 1962; Terrace, 1968), particularly those surrounding discrimination learning. Although they employ operant conditioning methods and their basic data consists of cumulative records, they are nevertheless able to make contact with theories based upon evidence from between-group studies involving discrete trials (Spence, 1936, 1937). Obviously in this context one cannot conclude that two kinds of data, group and individual, are fundamentally different.

Nor can one maintain the sharp distinction between the two when viewed from the observational level. Average results are simply a mathematical combination of individual events. The two are related in the sense that from knowledge of statistical averages combined with measures of variability it becomes possible to infer the observational basis of individual behavior. Thus from both theoretical and observational perspectives a strict segregation between group and individual data, as suggested by Sidman, appears unwarranted.

There is another way of looking at the difference between group and individual data that is in terms of strategy. A detached view of psychology very often leads to the conclusion that different experimental practices (e.g., free responding versus separate trials in conditioning) are equally justified in the sense that none is logically demanded. Although true, this conclusion does not mean that each alternative will be equally fruitful. Research practices, themselves, are experimental in nature because the kind and quality of knowledge they will yield cannot be completely anticipated. One can, nevertheless, argue that some practices will be more fruitful than others in generating important information. It is within this context that Sidman's distinction gains its best defense.

The history of behavioral psychology suggests that its phenomena are forbiddingly complex. One could argue that the inability of the discipline to achieve a widely accepted theoretical interpretation of any broad area of behavior from learning to perception or from personality to social behavior results from the indefinite number of causal agents that operate in the simplest experimental task. The difficulty of achieving interpretations that cross situational boundaries without losing explanatory precision simply results from the tremendous changes in causal patterns from one situation to the next.

The fundamental tactic in arriving at a broad interpretation of behavior may be in coping effectively with the complexity of the pattern of causal agents that operate in various experimental designs. The strength of the operant approach may be in its capacity to simplify the causal patterns of behavior more effectively than other orientations. This, it can be argued, is accomplished in two ways: (1) by exerting more effective control than others over experimental procedures thus reducing the effects of extraneous variables and (2) by identifying crucial processes in behavior that are relevant to a wide range of situations.

In regard to the first, a comparison between the experimental practices of operant conditioners and traditional learning theorists tends to support the view that the former group exerted much tighter control (D'Amato, 1970). Being primarily concerned with arranging satisfactory tests of their model, traditional learning theorists, such as Hull, Spence, and Tolman, frequently ignored ways of improving the precision with which stimulus patterns were presented and responses measured. They employed much cruder equipment—puzzle boxes, multiunit mazes, T-mazes, discrimination-learning apparatus than did operant conditioners.

Of course, this difference could be considered the consequence of Skinner's early fascination with gadgetry (Skinner, 1976), which was expressed in its final form in the sophisticated electronic technology of the operant-conditioning laboratory. But, it should be remembered, skilled technicians were available also to learning theorists. It is mainly that the problems operant conditioners thought essential in their pursuit of behavioral control encouraged the use of highly sophisticated equipment. Another aspect of the looser control exerted by theorists is the relatively brief time their subjects were confronted with an experimental task, usually no more than a few trials a day extended over a period of a week or so. These brief encounters were in marked contrast to the intensive experimental experience of operant subjects, lengthy daily experimental sessions spanning weeks and even months.

Admittedly, it is difficult to draw a firm historical conclusion about the exact cause of the difference in experimental practices between learning theorists and operant conditioners. It could be that the aim of exerting tight control over behavior influenced the empirical methodology of operant conditioning in the direction of its goal. It could be argued that the tight experimental control emanated primarily from the identification of the potent variable of response-reinforcement contingencies that made attempts at behavior management effective. Whatever the reasons, the important point is that operant conditioning outstripped theoretical orientations in its ability to control behavior, even though it has fallen short of the strict deterministic management to which it aspired.

The conclusion of this analysis is that individual behavior and group behavior, expressed in cumulative records and mean performance, do not represent qualitatively distinct sets of events but instead consequences of different orienting attitudes. These consequences can be compared and the conclusion can be drawn that one sort of data (e.g., individual cumulative records) is more significant than others and that the strategy of behavioral control is superior to that of formulating deductive theories. Such an argument returns us to the problem of defining significance, a task that demands specifying the aims of a research program. This circularity, however, can be broken by considering two questions: (1) what is the relative success of different response measures (e.g., cumulative records, average group performance) in achieving the goals for which they were selected (e.g., behavioral control, theoretical interpretation)? and (2) how useful is a particular response measure for the goals of other research programs? My impression of the evidence is that cumulative records, on both counts, would receive a higher score than average group performance. This does not mean that a science of behavior employing only cumulative response curves would be complete. Far from it. Cumulative records certainly do not represent all of behavior.

Operant conditioners initially ignored acquisition processes in conditioning. By using every trick of shaping, operant conditioners got their subjects to behave as rapidly as possible at asymptotic ("steady state") performance levels. Acquisition, therefore was perceived as an uninteresting problem, representing an obstacle to be overcome in order to get at the critical problem of achieving steady-state performance. In addition cumulative records have not proved to be particularly effective in unravelling the mysteries of many research areas (e.g., cognitive processes, social behavior). But these shortcomings must be judged in terms of the present state of knowledge in psychology and not some future ideal. In this context the significance of the operant research strategy with its emphasis on the behavior of individuals in the form of cumulative response records cannot be overestimated. From animal training to child rearing to educational technology to behavior modification to psychopharmacology, operant methods have contributed important procedures for effective behavior management. And the fundamental reason for its success, in the last analysis, may be that the search for effective methods of behavioral control is a particularly effective strategy in behavioral psychology. The overwhelming number of causal agents that operate even in the simplest situation makes the problem of theory construction grotesquely difficult. When concerned with controlling behavior one learns very quickly whether one is on the right track. The feedback is rapid, especially when compared with the complicated validation procedures associated with theorizing. One can argue, at least at this stage of its history, that striving for behavioral control may be the optimal strategy for the complicated science of psychology.

INTUITIVE KNOWING

Comprehension by intuitive knowing is strikingly different from the understanding achieved by deductive explanation, interpretive consistency, and behavioral control. Whereas the claims of understanding produced by deductive explanation, interpretive consistency, and behavioral control can be examined by others, intuitive knowing is purely a personal experience. It represents "pure understanding" in the absence of any knowledge.

In essence, intuitive knowing is a subjective psychological phenomenon in which an individual experiences insightful apprehension or comprehension of an event. There is no reason to believe either that different individuals achieve such insightful experiences in the same way or that their intuitive revelations have common phenomenal characteristics. In fact, the subsequent discussion will suggest the opposite.

Some psychologists, although admitting that the subjective phenomenon of intuitive knowing occurs, would nevertheless consider it irrelevant to an analysis of science. Science, for them, is essentially a discipline that was created in order to avoid drawing conclusions based on subjective judgments. Warranted conclusions are justified only when the evidence and logic supporting them are open to public purview. Intuitive knowing is locked in an individual's mind and therefore does not qualify as a scientific conclusion. This concept should be discarded.

Such a view is unrealistic, especially when applied to psychology. It ignores an apparently significant cognitive phenomenon that may be central to methodological issues and controversies. More importantly, the blunt rejection of intuitive knowing as a form of understanding is based on the naive belief that science always operates with a simple set of objective standards.

Even if intuitive knowing were rejected as an appropriate scientific mode of comprehension it would still be of interest for the role it presumably plays in achieving more acceptable forms of understanding. One of the many examples that can be cited to illustrate the role of intuitive knowing in theorizing is Einstein's description of his own efforts that led to the theory of relativity:

> During all those years there was a feeling of direction, of going straight toward something concrete. It is, of course, very hard to express that feeling in words; but it was decidedly the case, and clearly to be distinguished from later considerations about the rational form of the solution (Wertheimer, 1945, p. 184).

In a general sense Einstein acknowledged an intuitive knowing of a theoretical solution prior to his being able to formulate a rational explanation. This understanding encouraged him to pursue the problem to its successful solution. Numerous other examples of intuitive knowing in the absence of an explicit rational proof can be mentioned. Already reported was Poincaré's (page 82) conviction that his sudden solution to a logical problem was correct even though he had no time to check the proof. On a more personal note, examples of intuitive knowing from my own experience can be described. After struggling unsuccessfully for two days in an attempt to design a "critical" test of two competing interpretations of a latent-learning study (Spence & Lippit, 1946), I had a dream from which I awoke with the realization that I had the key to the design of the experiment even though the details had yet to be worked out. The next morning the experiment was planned and later executed (Kendler & Mencher, 1948). On another occasion, I recall treating a young soldier of twenty who was depressed and remorseful. He had just suffered a death in the family similar to one I had experienced as an adolescent. His reactions resembled mine. I intuitively "knew" how he felt and my empathic reaction seemed to facilitate the treatment. He began to realize that the unfortunate event itself was the cause of his difficulty and was not a result of any personal inadequacy.

Psychological Versus Epistemological
Analysis of Intuitive Knowing

Four examples of intuitive knowing have been offered. The first three represent a phenomenological experience that preceded problem solving: the formulation of a theory, a logical proof, and an experimental design. The intuitive knowing in all of these examples is not to be confused with the successful problem solving itself. In all three cases the intuitive knowing fell short of problem solving in the objective sense of providing a rational solution. But in each case the intuitive knowing represents a subjective preawareness of an objective solution. In more analytical terms, within a phenomenological frame of reference the preawareness seemed to possess a cognitive and motivational component, with the former anticipating the solution and the latter encouraging its achievement.

My interest in the phenomenological aspects of intuitive knowing is tangential to the central issue of its status as an *independent* form of scientific comprehension. I am not really interested in the argument that intuitive knowing is a necessary link in arriving at scientific comprehension. That is an empirical problem that properly belongs to the psychology of creative thinking. Intuitive knowing as a means to an end is a problem for psychology; intuitive knowing as an end in itself is a problem for epistemology.

The fourth example of intuitive knowing occurred as an empathic reaction to a patient's problem. Empathy, the "projection" of one's experience into another's consciousness, illustrates some of the epistemological problems associated with intuitive knowing as a form of understanding. Some psychotherapists seek to empathize with patients because of the conviction that such identification is either essential to, or helpful for, effective treatment. The belief also prevails that the ability to empathize with others underlies moral development; the golden rule, "Do unto others as you would have them do unto you," cannot be obeyed unless one has the capacity to empathize with other human beings. Great literature, some would suggest, is created when the author enables one to empathize with his characters and thereby share their experiences while simultaneously learning about oneself. Dostoievski and Bellow, for me, are particularly effective in this respect.

My impression is that the intuitive knowing experienced when reading literature is comparable to the experience of a clinician when he empathizes with a patient. The relationship between the two kinds of experience posed an interesting puzzle for me when I was trying to decide whether to take an undergraduate major in psychology. I was at that time enrolled in an introductory psychology course that had as its text John F. Dashiell's *Fundamentals of Objective Psychology*. I was surprised and pleased with the book because the intimate relationship between psychological principles and experimental evidence was a new and intriguing concept to me. All in all, psychology in 1938 appeared less vague and more objective than other so-called social sciences, and from my viewpoint, more appealing. This impression, however, was badly shaken when I attended a symposium in which most of the psychology department participated. The topic was "Human Nature," and without exception, each psychologist, to clarify his or her position, quoted a passage from some great novel or poem. This was confusing because I expected that their arguments would be buttressed by experimental evidence. If literature was to be employed to interpret psychological principles perhaps my interest in psychology would be better served by majoring in English? But that alternative had an apparent drawback because at that time the leading lights of the English department were offering psychoanalytic interpretations of literature!

In restrospect, that symposium was not as confusing as it initially appeared. If one accepts the position that different modes of understanding are possible, it should not be too surprising to discover that more than one kind can be employed especially for different occasions. Although one may be committed to explain the maze behavior of rats by deductive explanation, one could easily shift to the mode of intuitive knowing when confronted with the imposing task of interpreting human nature. An interesting sidelight to this issue is contained in Skinner's autobiography when he discusses his own search for understanding:

> I had apparently failed as a writer but was it not possible that literature had failed me as a method? One might enjoy Proust's reminiscences and share the emotional torment of Dostoevski's characters but did Proust or Dostoevski really *understand?* (1976, p. 291).

The toughest-minded psychologist of all times, at least in the opinion of some, once entertained the possibility that literature provided the key for understanding human behavior!

Criterion of Intuitive Knowing

Perhaps the most significant question concerning the concept of intuitive knowing is the criterion to be employed for determining whether understanding has been achieved. The fundamental question in this regard is whether intersubjective agreement should be sought or whether a radical subjectivism is sufficient. One example of an extreme subjective position is characterized by the self-acknowledged sensitive clinician who has complete confidence in his ability to intuitively understand his patients. Because his experiences are so compelling, he sees no need to support them by additional evidence. If the intuitions of others are at variance with his own, then they must be defective. Although such arrogance may be difficult to stomach, we should not lose sight of the fact that in other fields, such as aesthetics, it is generally acknowledged that some individuals possess exceptional aesthetic sensitivities, superior to most others. Why cannot the same relationship prevail in intuitively knowing another person, in sensing his inner world of experience? The reasons for the expert's greater sensitivity may be difficult to identify, but its existence, for many, is nevertheless obvious.

The above argument has two components that require separate treatment. One concerns the possibility that individuals vary in their capacity for intuitive understanding, which in a clinical situation may take the form of successfully empathizing with the patient. The second involves the evidence that is demanded to demonstrate that such understanding has been achieved. The answer to the first question should not generate any disagreement because it would seem obvious that individuals do differ in their capacity to achieve insight into a variety of intellectual and psychological problems. The second question gets to the key epistemological issue about which there is much fundamental disagreement in contemporary psychology—the criterion of intuitive knowing.

Intuitive Knowing in Art and Science

Although the similarity in the inner experiences underlying aesthetic sensitivity in literature and empathic identification in clinical psychology has been noted, this similarity does not demand, or even suggest, that the two experiences be evaluated in the same way. Aesthetic sensitivities can be questioned and rejected, but they cannot be denied. For example, the judgment that a particular work of pop art is beautiful can be considered to border on the absurd, but one cannot deny that an observer is perceiving beauty when he insists he is. "Beauty is in the eye of the beholder."

Even when the evaluation of beauty is limited to those who are acknowledged to be experts, either as critics or as artists, complete agreement about what works of art possess aesthetic value will not be forthcoming. And when comparisons are made in the aesthetic judgments of "experts" from different eras, the disagreements become even more marked; works of art that are considered to reflect the essence of beauty in one era are repulsive or deathly dull to another. Many of El Greco's contemporaries who were considered to be his equal or superior are presently neglected. Such historical differences cannot be attributed to progress either in the form of the increased creativity of artists or in the sensitivity of critics. The notion that modern music is more beautiful than classical or baroque or that artistic criticism is continuously improving would be vigorously challenged. A more reasonable conclusion is that the concept of artistic progress, in a sense comparable to scientific progress, is inappropriate. Art does not progress but rather it is expressed in constantly changing forms. This does not mean that technical procedures (e.g., quality of clay or paints) cannot improve (or deteriorate) or that within a given time span (e.g., the Renaissance or Elizabethan) an outburst of artistic creativity cannot take place. Ultimately, what it does mean is that beauty is intuited, not measured by rational procedures.

This conclusion is easily misinterpreted. It does not deny the possibility that aesthetics can be investigated in an objective fashion. One could strive to discover characteristics of art objects and observers that yield aesthetic reactions. If such an effort produced an adequate theory, that theory would explain aesthetic reactions but would not measure beauty in the same way that a scale measures weight. The reason is that the weight of an object is independent of the observer—its beauty is not.

The changing tastes in art do not necessarily support a completely relativistic view of aesthetic value and the implication that by appropriate training a person could be made to perceive beauty in any object. One possibility is that the innate structure of our receptors and nervous system places some limit on the range of objects to which we can have aesthetic reactions. Leonard Bernstein expresses, somewhat dramatically, the same notion about the tonal foundations of beautiful music:

> My words are poor, my diagrams even poorer, but this is one thing I intuitively know to be true, and I will put my hand in the fire for it, that whatever that creative mystery is . . . it cannot exist or come to be unless it is inextricably rooted in the rich earth of our innate response in the deep unconscious regions where the universals of tonality . . . reside (1976, p. 417).

Like Chomsky, on whom his arguments are based, Bernstein tends to ignore environmental influences. Although innate factors influence aesthetic reactions, they do not dictate completely the nature of beauty. Within the range of potentially beautiful objects great individual differences will occur making it necessary to consider the properties of both the object and observer when formulating a theory of aesthetics. The significant point is that a valid psychological theory of aesthetics is possible, but such a theory should not be confused with an independent and absolute scale of beauty.

The thesis that the aesthetic value of an object can be apprehended but not verified does not imply that aesthetic judgments are necessarily impulsive. Intuitive reactions need not occur in a flash; they can occur gradually, the understanding becoming deeper and enlarged. They need not be mystical and inexpressible; they can be a product of lengthy contemplation. The difficulty in characterizing *intuition* is due to the problems inherent in phenomenological descriptions (pages 39–64). These difficulties become disturbing only when viewed within a scientific framework that seeks precision, reliability, and validity.

Philosophers have dealt with the problems of aesthetics since the time of Plato, and even though they have sought an answer to the question, "What is beauty?" they do not feel that they have failed by not achieving a universally acceptable answer. Their discipline is fundamentally undisciplined in the sense of demanding precise criteria to judge conflicting answers to a common question. But this need not be perceived as a limitation. Although the question of "What is beauty" has not been answered in a manner acceptable to all, the philosophical considerations have provided an interesting history of ideas and generated a variety of questions (e.g., the relationship between aesthetics and morality) that would not at first glance appear to be related to the problem of aesthetics. And if the past indicates the future we can anticipate that the present unresolved controversies in the philosophy of aesthetics will continue to be debated, new questions will will be raised, and further disagreements will be generated.

The person who seeks a "valid" interpretation of beauty within the complete flow of world history is confronted with apparent chaos. This condition need not be considered to be defective or unfortunate. Regardless of whether beauty is understood in any formal objective sense, one should recognize that the time, effort, and money that people expend in their pursuit of artistic enjoyment is highly worthwhile; it is one of the most gratifying aspects of life. One could also speculate that if other areas of life were as successful in meeting the needs of people as is art, our present societies would be more attractive. And finally, one could raise the issue of whether artistic enjoyment might not be diminished if we had a better understanding of the psychology of aesthetics; perhaps destroying the mystery in the apprehension of beauty would lessen the enjoyment.

The analysis of aesthetic sensitivity as a form of intuitive knowing highlights problems with this form of understanding in psychology. Aesthetic sensitivity possesses an intrinsic subjectivity that cannot be overcome. Although one can offer a rational defense of one's aesthetic taste, or even an empirical theory to explain it, one cannot assert its truth. However, in psychology intuitive knowing can acquire truth value by becoming a component in an empirical relationship. For example, the ability to empathize, which is presently being considered as a form of intuitive knowing, can be investigated to determine whether it influences the outcome of psychotherapy. Because empathy itself represents a presumed accurate projection of one's own consciousness (e.g., that of the therapist) onto another (e.g., the patient)—an event locked into the consciousness of two individuals—it becomes necessary to relate these intrasubjective states to publicly observed events. A number of studies have attempted to use a variety of objective measures to infer empathy (e.g., rating transcripts of psychotherapeutic sessions, psychological tests, introspective reports) and evaluate psychotherapy. In general, the results suggest that *"the therapist's empathy . . . facilitates the patient's gain from psychotherapy"* (Luborsky, Chandler, Auerbach, Cohen, & Bachrach, 1971, p. 153).[5]

Intuitive knowing can also be incorporated into a natural-

5. It is not the intent of this analysis to get embroiled in the empirical problem of the effectiveness of psychotherapy and the role that empathy plays. My concern is with the concept of intuitive knowing as a source of understanding and as an empirical variable in psychological investigations. The analysis of the concept of empathy serves that purpose.

science orientation that seeks deductive explanation. The history of the Gestalt principle of prägnanz, or *good form*, illustrates this development. The perceptual principle of prägnanz states that stimulus elements that compose a *good form* tend to be perceived together. For example Figure 5.1A is perceived as a pattern consisting of a half circle intersected by a straight line, as in B, and not as one containing the components of C.

But what is a *good form?* Although the definition of *good form* is admittedly "vague" (Koffka, 1935), *good form* itself was considered easy to intuit. Gestalt psychologists were willing to accept this kind of understanding because of the confidence they placed in the capacity of phenomenological analysis to reveal theoretical principles of perception. Identifying good and poor examples of *good form* demonstrated to them that the concept was valid. But this kind of understanding did not satisfy some American psychologists who were sympathetic to Gestalt conceptions but not to the subjective quality of their theoretical principles. They reformulated the law of *good form* into an objective statement: patterns with *good form* are redundant, i.e., they contain surplus information.

Figure 5.2 illustrates the relationship between redundancy and form quality. Both patterns have been drawn on graph paper within an area of 100 small squares, 10 rows by 10 columns. Predicting the shape of the form by knowledge of its parts is an easier task for pattern A than for pattern B. This can be demonstrated by instructing subjects, prior to their perceiving the entire figure, to "move," beginning with the upper left-hand corner, square by square across the page guessing before the next square is uncovered whether it is black or white. Subjects will have a higher percentage of correct hits with pattern A than with pattern B. Guessing would be required at the beginning for both patterns, but one would very rapidly learn to guess correctly for the upper three rows of A because they are all white. The upper-left black square of the rectangle would be guessed incorrectly, but soon the errors would disappear as the subject perceived the entire pattern. Pattern B would generate significantly more errors because of its irregular contours and unsymmetrical shape. Fig-

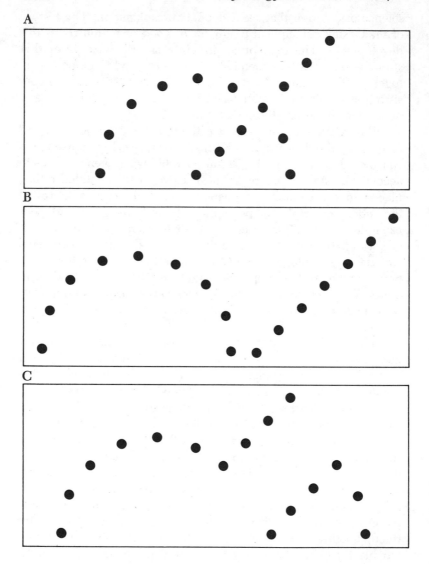

Figure 5.1   A stimulus pattern (A) illustrating the principles of good form. You tend to perceive this pattern as made up of the components in B, not those in C.

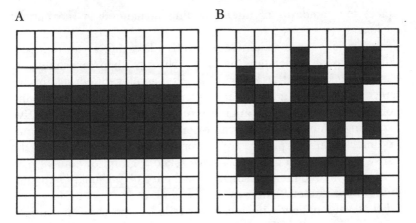

Figure 5.2   Which form has a higher amount of "goodness"? As the text explains, form A is more redundant and hence is a "better" figure.

ure A is redundant, e.g., if you know the upper half you can predict the lower half. In essence, *good forms* are redundant because the whole can be predicted from a few parts while poor forms are unpredictable. This principle can be represented mathematically (Attneave, 1954; Garner, 1962). My concern, however, is with the development of the meaning of the concept of *good form* (prägnanz). Initially it was based upon intuitive knowing, but later it could be described by objectively defined constructs. This represents another example of intuitive knowing anticipating future developments in a natural-science oriented psychology.

Intuitive Knowing and Understanding

Intuitive knowing has been viewed both as an interesting psychological phenomenon and as a form of understanding. In the former case it has been noted that the phenomenon occurs both in art and science and is capable of being empirically analyzed. In the latter case it has been suggested that intuitive knowing frequently anticipates deductive explanation but by itself fails to meet the standards of understanding demanded in the natural sciences.

There is more reliance on intuitive knowing as an independent form of understanding in psychology than is usually acknowledged. Intuitive knowing is often employed, consciously or unconsciously, as an ancillary, alternative, or fundamental kind of understanding. As an ancillary form of understanding intuitive knowing can be regarded as an essential component within a multidimensional interpretive framework. One example of this is the answers given to a question I once asked a group of clinical psychologists: "Would you consider a theory of personality to provide a satisfactory sense of understanding if it accurately predicted your patient's behavior but failed to provide any insight into his inner life?" To a woman they all answered, "No!" Some believed that a deductive theory was incomplete if the proposed theoretical processes failed to characterize the inner life of patients. Others thought that a deductive theory and a phenomenological theory could be independent, each serving a separate need.

Intuitive Knowing as a Fundamental Mode of Understanding

Intuitive knowing as a fundamental mode of understanding is rarely discussed among psychologists in an open and frank manner. It plays a much more important role than most psychologists are willing to admit. The position is implicit in the oft-repeated phrase, "Psychology is an art." One possible interpretation of this statement is that the effective psychologist possesses a special knack of knowing others, just as the esteemed art or literary critic with his highly developed aesthetic sensibilities knows what is good art. Each deals with profoundly human experiences that, from the viewpoint of the experiencing psychologist or critic, are basically ineffable. Each must communicate these experiences as best as possible. This can be achieved by adopting communicative criteria that are reasonable rather than invent ones that are unattainable. Thus we must identify those individuals with exceptional capacities for intuitive knowing and trust their judgments, even though in some cases we can entertain reservations. And as already noted, within communities of like-minded critics and psychologists, certain individuals attain a position of authority so that their judgments serve as the criterion for that group. In essence, their judgments are considered valid although the means by which the conclusions are reached remain unclear.

The proponents of intuitive knowing as *the* sole criterion of understanding can offer two lines of argument to defend their position. One is that intuitive knowing is employed in science and logic as a criterion of understanding. For example, it has recently been suggested (Kolata, 1976) that contemporary mathematics is confronted with a crisis because extremely lengthy and complex proofs, which are becoming more common, are too involved to be properly understood. Chernoff (1976), a mathematician, denies that this is the case. He admits that computational errors and logical blunders can be made in "monster proofs," but for the most part they can be assimilated by mathematicians without confusion and difficulty. His position is as follows:

> The point is simply this: a human mathematician does not attain an understanding of a proof merely by checking that all the individual steps have been strung together according to the rules. On the contrary, such detailed mechanical plodding is neither necessary nor sufficient. What is crucial is to see through the technicalities to grasp the underlying ideas and intuitions, which often can be expressed concisely and even pictorially. Once the gestalt is perceived, the competent technician can fill in as much formal detail as needed (1976, p. 276).

The basic point expressed here is that intuitive knowing possesses a psychological primacy in achieving understanding. If it can play this role in mathematics why cannot it play the same role in psychology?

The second line of argument to support the use of intuitive knowing as the criterion of understanding is analogous to the one offered in support of interpretive consistency. There are some significant phenomena that cannot be interpreted by natural-science methodology. Why not employ intuitive knowing in attempting to understand them rather than accept the notion that they are incomprehensible? Intuitive knowing is effective in dealing with problems of everyday life. Why not exploit it in formulating comprehensive psychological theories, especially those concerned with understanding the human condition? Psychologists, if they really are serious about interpreting the full range of human experience and behavior, must resort to methods of understanding appropriate to their task.

Intuitive Knowing and the Image of Man

Intuitive knowing appears to be at the roots of the claim that an understanding of human psychology must be based upon an adequate "image of man" (Chein, 1972; Rychlak, 1968). Without a proper conception of humans, it is claimed, research findings will unavoidably be incomplete and misleading. Equating humans with machines will inevitably distort human psychology. Pavlov committed this fatal error when he stated:

> Man is, of course, a system—roughly speaking, a machine—like every other system in nature subject to the unescapable and uniform laws of all nature; but the human system, in the horizon of our contemporary scientific view, is unique in being most highly self-regulatory. Among the products of man's hands, we are already familiar with machines which regulate themselves in various ways. From this standpoint, the method of investigating the system of man is precisely the same as that of any other system: decomposition into parts, study of the significance of each part, study of the connexions of the parts, study of the relations with the environment, and finally the interpretation on this basis of its general workings and administration, if this be within the capacity of man (1941, p. 144).

The conception of *man as a machine* appears in a variety of forms all of which are equally objectionable to those who insist that such interpretations strip humans of their intrinsic humanity and thus distort the image of man. The opposition to machinelike conceptions of human behavior should not be confused with disagreements concerning the relative merits of analytic or holistic approaches. One might fault Pavlov for his emphasis on analysis but nevertheless agree with the essence of his remarks that humans can be best conceptualized as some kind of mechanism. Such disagreements really revolve about the kind of machine that best represents human psychology. The machine models can vary from slot machines to electronic computers. The psychological models that these machine models suggest cover the range from single-unit stimulus-response theories, which assume environmental inputs determine behavioral outputs, to the information-processing conceptions, which postulate numerous mediating mechanisms that transform incoming information into an organized body of knowledge that guides subsequent behavior. All these formulations, favored by a majority of experimental psychologists, it is argued, ignore the "identity" of human subjects, that unique quality of human self-awareness that cannot reside in any machine or subhuman animal. In attempting to explicate what "identity" means, Rychlak asserts that,

> . . . subject behavior has to be conceptualized identically with experimenter behavior (as they are both human beings, etc.). Hence if the experimenter is capable of formulating hypotheses, designing experimental tests of these suggestions, and then evaluating the outcome of such efforts according to an arbitrary level of statistical significance, so too can we think of the subject as formulating hypotheses, designing tests of what direction he wants the course of his life to take, and then judging the outcome of his self-induced efforts to make things end up where he would like them to be, based on what he favors as a worthwhile eventuality (1976, p. 221).

One interpretation of the above is that the experimenter, aware of his own *identity*, or what some might prefer to label *self* or *ego*, fails to attribute the same experience to his subject. This inner experience of a *self-identity* possesses a reality for the experimenter, and to ignore it for the subject creates a false "image of man."

A person's identity has several meanings. One extreme would

be to equate it with an attribute of a person's inner experience, such as his self-image, with the additional assumption that it possesses an existence independent of outer behavior. Interpreting identity within this context, at least for me, achieves a reasonable level of intersubjective agreement required to pursue the implications of the maxim that an appropriate "image of man" is a prerequisite for understanding human psychology. Thus if the concept of identity is essential in the psychological analysis of humans, this means that an adequate theory of behavior will never be developed as long as conscious experience is ignored as a set of core observations. According to this argument, methodological behaviorism, which asserts that behavior can be investigated and explained without direct examination of mental states, is doomed to failure. This predicted failure would apply to the efforts of the methodological behaviorist who acknowledges the significance of inner experience and attempts to create a theoretical model of the mind to represent its influence on behavior (page 35). It would also apply to the methodological behaviorist who decides that the methods and subject matter of phenomenology and behavioral science are separate and distinct, neither being superior to the other, just different (page 67). In sum, one *must* incorporate the direct observations of inner experiences into any satisfactory account of human psychology. In addition, these inner observations must include that component of inner experience that represents the *identity* of an individual. Both of these conclusions, one methodological, the other substantive, have emerged from an intuitive conviction that they are correct. It would be impossible to prove by explicit logical means at this stage in psychology's history, that methodological behaviorism is doomed to total failure or that a combined phenomenological-behavioral approach that does not involve a concept of identity will prove inadequate. It must be recognized that the claim made here is not the modest one that it may be more strategic to incorporate inner experience in one's approach to psychology or that the concept of identity will prove to be fruitful. Instead what is being stated is that one intuitively knows that both of these alternatives are *valid*.

Self-fulfillment. The concept of *identity* or *ego* or *self* can be interpreted in a much more idealistic or mystical fashion. It can refer to the intrinsic potential of a person, the kind of individual he really is and should be. This kind of conception, which is common within certain religious traditions, is captured in the following tale, from Hasidic Jewish lore:

> Before his death, Rabbi Zusya said, "In the coming world, they will not ask me: 'Why were you not Moses?' They will ask me: 'Why were you not Zusya?' " (Howe, 1976, p. 642).

Religions usually specify what it means to be fulfilled. If one fully accepts religious authority then one cannot question its capacity to describe the meaning of self-fulfillment and to determine when it has been achieved. Is it possible to ascertain self-fulfillment in the absence of such authority? Maslow thought so. His concept of self-fulfillment was based on the hypothesis that humans possess a hierarchy of inborn needs, the highest of which is self-actualization: "The desire to become more and more what one is, to become everything that one is capable of becoming" (1954, p. 92).

Maslow offered empirical evidence to buttress his conception of self-actualization. He provided examples (e.g., Beethoven, Lincoln, Einstein, Eleanor Roosevelt) of historical as well as contemporary personalities who had achieved creative fulfillment of their potentialities. In addition he listed experiential characteristics of self-actualizers. One is a peak experience, during which time a person is completely integrated and fuses into one with the world; is at the height of his or her powers; lives only in the present; and becomes free of inhibitions, sincere, emancipated from the thoughts of the past and the future. Peak experiences are not situationally defined; they can occur during moments of artistic creativity, simple reflection, or when giving birth.

The key question is whether the concept of self-actualization was demanded by empirical considerations or instead has infiltrated humanistic psychological theories because of ethical considerations. In answering this question it becomes important to recognize that the concept of self-fulfillment antedates psychology. It emerges from the powerful philosophical tradition of humanism that is not committed to a faith in an Almighty but nevertheless insists that humans are spiritual beings whose behavior cannot be reduced to the demands of the flesh.

This general humanistic conception, as well as the specific one proposed by Maslow, contains two basic assumptions, each with a different epistemological characteristic. The first is that human motivation cannot be reduced to animal motivation. The second is that humans seek to realize their own intrinsic potential that represents their true self.

The first position is in line with much evidence of species-specific behavior. Since the behavior of all species differs in some way from each other it should come as no surprise to discover that some of the motives of homo sapiens are distinguishable from those of other animal species. These motivational differences presumably could be expressed in theoretical formulations with determinate empirical consequences. Thus it should be possible to establish points of contact between humanistic motivational theories and more traditional ones. Theoretical differences among such conceptions could be evaluated by the deductive mode of achieving understanding.

When it comes to the assumption that humans possess a motive for seeking self-fulfillment, the chances of a theoretical resolution occurring between humanistic and natural-science formulations appear dim. The apparent incompatibility does not stem from the basic notion that individual humans have different potentialities. This widely accepted idea is a key assumption in the model of aptitude testing. Individuals have many potentialities (aptitudes) that are, or fail to be, realized depending upon environmental pressures and opportunities. Self-fulfillment is based upon essentially the same notion although the nature of the potentialities are neither as precisely defined nor as easily measured as conventional aptitudes. Self-fulfillment represents a broader, more complex concept referring not only to specific talents but also to personal and social values. Presumably, if deemed desirable, humanistic psychologists could develop quantitative measures of these potentialities.

The critical epistemological issue associated with the concept of self-fulfillment concerns the criteria employed to identify those potentialities that would be self-actualizing. Conventional aptitude testing does not have such a problem. A person has many aptitudes, but none is more truly representative of the individual than is another. They vary only in their probability of being realized. A vocational guidance counselor may encourage his client to reach his potential in regard to one aptitude in preference to others because of practical, economic, or social reasons but not because that particular potentiality reflects "what one is."

To make the issue of the criteria of self-fulfillment more concrete, let us consider the case of Eleanor Roosevelt who, according to Maslow, achieved self-actualization. Would she have been considered self-actualized if she had divorced Franklin Roosevelt because of his marital infidelities, become a Republican, and espoused laissez-faire capitalism as the only way to help the poor and disadvantaged? Or would have Presidents Kennedy and Johnson been self-actualized if they had avoided getting their country involved in the Vietnam War? And finally the interesting question can be posed as to whether Woody Allen, a self-admitted anhedonic and widely acclaimed humorist and movie director, is self-actualized.

The thrust of these questions is obvious. Is self-fulfillment a phenomenon that is basically empirical in nature or does it depend on value judgments? How would it be possible to resolve a dispute between psychologists who differed as to whether a particular person (e.g., Jimmy Carter, Henry Kissinger) was self-actualized? In answering these questions it is useful to look at the concept of self-fulfillment as employed by political theorists.

According to the Marxist view, self-fulfillment can only be achieved in a socialistic society. The institution of private property with its encouragement of competition and acquisition of material goods prevents members of a capitalistic society from reaching their human potential. Hitler argued that Aryans could achieve self-realization only in a Nazi society. With the same line of argument, but with obviously different ethical commitments and political outcomes, others insist that only in a political democracy can humans realize their potentialities. Within the context of political theory it would appear that the interpretation of self-fulfillment depends on preferences for different forms of political and economic organizations. In psychology, the concept of self-fulfillment has also been impregnated with value judgments. Although apparently concerned with empirical issues in his analysis of human motivation, Maslow was in fact making moral judgments when formulating his concept of self-actualization.

The issues in this kind of debate about the behavioral and experiential characteristics that define self-fulfillment are complex. They will be treated in Chapter 7. For the time being I have adopted the position that one cannot by empirical means *alone* demonstrate that certain kinds of behavior and experiences constitute the true or real potential of humans. Our empirical knowledge suggests that humans have a wide (not limitless) variety of potentialities and that environmental circumstances will determine which ones will be achieved. The choice of any criterion of self-fulfillment always involves a value judgment.[6]

How can one justify the value judgments that lie at the core of the concept of self-fulfillment? Maslow suggests that empirical evidence dictates his view; all individuals have a motive to actualize themselves and will succeed if their more basic drives are satisfied. Our analysis leads to a different conclusion. Moral values for Maslow appear to be self-evident truths arrived at by intuitive knowing. The empirical evidence (examples of self-actualized people and experiential qualities of a peak experience) Maslow offers is selected to rationalize his moral preferences.

The conclusion that the "image of man" as conceived by humanistic psychology is based upon intuitive knowing and is not solely an empirically based concept does not in any way attenuate its social significance. An "image of man" in the sense of characterizing the potential of human beings, plays a central role in the organization and functioning of any society because it identifies "good" and "bad" behavior. All societies require some conception of the "image of man" to support their legal and ethical systems.

6. This does not mean that all conceptions of self-fulfillment are equally achievable or ethically equivalent.

The significant question is whether it is the responsibility or obligation of psychologists to offer such conceptions when they are not demanded by empirical evidence.

The above analysis of the "image of man" is not offered as a criticism of intuitive knowing as a form of understanding. Intuitive knowing is beyond criticism if considered as the ultimate type of understanding. The implication of the analysis is that those who employ intuitive knowing to arrive at conclusions should not confuse it with other forms of understanding. In this regard, one must recognize that when intuitive knowing is defended as a legitimate mode of understanding it must stand alone. To defend the choice of intuitive knowing by insisting that it has some built-in validity because it frequently anticipates deductive explanations would be self-defeating. The difficulty with such a line of argument is that at times intuitive knowing fails to coincide with the requirements of deductive explanation although these failures are usually not publicized by those who expound the virtues of intuition. Most persons, at some time in their lives, intuitively "knew" that the earth was flat or that heavier objects fall in space more rapidly than lighter ones. And some theorists will confess that, at one time or another, they have formulated models they "knew" to be intuitively true only to discover later that their faith in intuition was misplaced.

One, of course, can take the position that intuitive knowing is the mode of understanding for problems that cannot be resolved by deductive explanation, such as the nature of the "image of man." This position creates an inconsistency because if one accepted the goal of understanding via deductive explanation, then one would argue that the "image of man" should be contained in a psychological theory that can explain psychological events. In other words, it is the purpose of psychological theory to discover the "image of man" rather than simply proclaim it.

At this point we return once again to the evaluation of humanistic theories of personality, such as Maslow's. Do they deductively integrate some or all of the facts of personality, or do they provide an intuitively appealing picture coupled with moral guidance?

Intuitive Knowing Versus Interpretive Consistency

Before closing this section on intuitive knowing further clarification is required of the distinction between it and interpretive consistency. The distinguishing characteristic of the latter is that the interpretation is complex, consisting of a pattern of assumptions that are rationally interlinked, as is the case for Freudian and Marxist theories. Intuitive knowing, in contrast, is less systematic, relying more on understanding through apprehension than rationalistic means. Another way of expressing this is to state that the understanding achieved by interpretive consistency depends on elaborate rational justification while understanding acquired by intuitive knowing is essentially impressionistic in nature. This does not mean, of course, that they do not share any common properties or that they are always mutually exclusive. Both are fundamentally subjective in the sense that they rely more on personal conviction than public acceptance. In a similar vein, both are more psychological in nature than is the understanding achieved through deductive explanation and behavioral control.

Interpretive consistency and intuitive knowing can be considered as separate stages in arriving at a broad interpretation that is not designed to meet the demands of deductive explanation. Interpretive consistency may represent a rationalization of intuitive knowing. Apprehending the significance of sex in personality development or of economic forces in history could be the first step in the formulation of Freudian and Marxist interpretations.

CONSENSUAL AGREEMENT AND MODES OF UNDERSTANDING

My major thesis is that psychologists employ different standards of understanding and that the frank admission of the criteria utilized would do much to clarify methodological and theoretical disputes that plague psychology. Rather than insist that one form of understanding is superior to others, it would be more useful to recognize that different forms of understanding can be employed and each can be defended for certain reasons and rejected for others.

The four forms of understanding that I have analyzed can be differentiated in terms of the public nature of criteria they employ. Deductive explanation and behavioral control emphasize public criteria that yield a higher level of consensual agreement than do interpretive consistency and intuitive knowing. This does not mean that consensual agreement is always forthcoming if deductive explanation or behavioral control is adopted as a criterion of understanding. There are many reasons that these forms of understanding cannot guarantee total agreement. First of all, the meaning of the term *consensual agreement* is not as clear as some would like to believe. Consensual agreement among whom? Everybody? Like it or not, scientists in general and psychologists in particular belong to an elitist community that demands of its members a degree of training and aptitude not shared by others. Even within the community of psychologists some are more qualified to judge the validity of a particular statement than others. The deductive explanation expressed in mathematical logic can only be evaluated by competent mathematicians. Statements about the control of brain waves can only be assessed by those who can read EEG records. Finally, there are observational and theoretical disagreements that require time, sometimes years or even generations, to be resolved or clarified. But in spite of these problems one should recognize that consensual agreement about the validity of statements is often within reach when deductive explanation or behavioral control is used as a criterion of understanding even though such statements may have to be modified in the future in the face of new evidence. For example, the statements that *the perception of Mach Bands is due to retinal inhibition* is a valid statement, as is also the proposition that *the resistance to experimental extinction in pigeons can be controlled by manipulating the schedule of reinforcements*. Even a psychologist who thought such statements were trivial, or at best peripheral to the major interests of human psychology, could, I believe, support the validity of such propositions if he or she were willing for a moment to adopt the criterion of deductive explanation or behavioral control. The same would not be true for statements such as *male homosexuality results from an unresolved Oedipus complex* or the *"image of man" is intrinsically good*. The emphasis on public criteria that characterizes deductive explanation and behavioral control is absent from interpretive consistency and intuitive knowing. As a result, consensual agreement seems impossible to achieve for those who employ interpretive consistency or intuitive knowing as a criterion of understanding. Consensual agreement is possible for a segment of those communities that share a common conceptual frame of reference. Psychologists who accept interpretive consistency as an appropriate form of understanding but do not subscribe to orthodox psychoanalytical theory would reject the validity of the hypothesis that male homosexuality is due to an unresolved Oedipus complex. Similarly, psychologists who adopt an intuitive-knowing frame of reference would not necessarily agree that the *"image of man" is intrinsically good*. It should be recognized that this failure to achieve consensual agreement as already noted, does not invalidate the criterion of understanding employed. It can be argued that consensual agreement is not the ultimate criterion of truth. In the human sciences the sensitivity of a single individual, like Sigmund Freud or Jean-Paul Sartre, may be more significant than the consensual agreement of thousands of experimental psychologists.

The point of the present discussion is not to resolve these issues simply because they cannot be resolved, only clarified. But the discussion does lead to an entirely different method of achieving consensual agreement about scientific conclusions. The basic notion is to apply the methods of judicial processes—the adversary system that operates in courts of law—to the resolution of scientific controversies. The exact procedures suggested differ over a wide range, from simple jury trials to cases before a Supreme Court. The issues considered appropriate for judicial resolution vary from the determination of valid conclusions to the proper application of research findings. The former topic, the determination of valid conclusions, is relevant to the issue of understanding because judicial verdicts could provide the basis for achieving stable beliefs concerning empirical and theoretical knowledge. For many, especially those who received a traditional education about the structure of science, the notion that judicial processes can reveal scientific truth represents not only an absurdity but a threat to the very foundation of science. If nothing else Galileo's experiences with a judicial system illustrate the incompatibility of legal and scientific procedures and values.

The trial of Galileo, which led to the verdict that the sun revolves around the earth, need not be considered as representative of all judicial-scientific courts. The verdict in Galileo's trial would have probably been different if the judges were qualified scientists instead of churchmen who believed that knowledge comes from God or at least from religious authority. It can also be argued that the judicial system of the sort that common and Roman law encourages bears an intrinsic similarity to the scientific method. I recall an attempt to disabuse introductory psychology students of common misconceptions about the nature of psychology. A warning was given that the course would be limited to "conclusions warranted by evidence and logic." A perceptive student noted that such a criterion had as much relevance to law as to science.

The most revolutionary justification for arriving at warranted scientific conclusions by judicial means is that the behavioral and social sciences demand it. This thesis is advanced by Levine (1974), who questions the adequacy of experimental methods and statistical inference to deal with significant social phenomena as they occur in a natural setting. A research project, for example, cannot employ random assignment when comparing the behaviors of "schizophrenics and the brain damaged, . . . the alienated with the unalienated, . . . achievement test scores of black and white children." With such interests a researcher is confronted with a choice between employing inadequate natural-science methods or developing "additional methods of approach that are in their own right rigorous but appropriate to the substantive problems with which they deal." Levine denies "that the model of the laboratory experiment is the best if not the only way of becoming certain of truth" and suggests that a "method based on legal proceedings . . . may be suitable for many of psychology's problems, in particular for field, clinical, and evaluative studies."

Levine should be given credit for offering an alternative to more traditional scientific methods of arriving at warranted conclusions. It is easy to criticize behavioristic methodologies for their failure to provide unequivocal information that can be used to solve significant social problems. It is also easy to state that other methods are required. But what methods? At least he has the courage to try to answer that question.

Levine's position, however, is based on two questionable premises. First, he equates natural-science methodology with laboratory experimentation. Second, he denies that laboratory phenomena in the behavioral sciences can reflect principles that govern naturally occurring events. The history of physics fails to jibe with these assumptions. Many warranted conclusions, emerging within a deductive explanatory framework, have been arrived at by the observations of natural events such as the motion of astronomical bodies. In addition, a productive interaction has frequently occurred between observations of natural events and the results of laboratory studies. The history of the biological sciences fails to justify an antithesis between laboratory and naturally occurring events. Darwinian theory of evolution and its subsequent impact on the experimental analysis of genetic determination underline the reciprocal relationship that can occur between laboratory phenomena and natural events. I would like to suggest that laboratory studies of individual differences and the related development of psychological tests have led to a fundamental understanding of individual differences in behavior in social situations such as in schools and industry. There seems to be no justification to limit the natural-science method to the laboratory.

The failure to generalize from laboratory studies to complex social situations may not represent any intrinsic limitation of the former but may instead be a consequence of any number of factors such as lack of ingenuity in designing laboratory studies, inadequate theorizing, unrealistic expectations, and a desire to solve social issues that do not lend themselves purely to empirical resolution. We must also realize that some real-life events are too complex for simple interpretations. Physicists cannot predict the exact course that a leaf will take when descending in a windstorm. Psychologists should not try to outperform physicists in their theoretical predictions. And like physicists as well as weathermen, physicians, and surgeons, psychologists must frequently couch their predictions in probability statements. Finally, there may be problems, and social psychologists have exhibited a penchant for getting involved in them, that cannot be resolved by empirical means. Solutions to many fundamental social issues that surround problems such as poverty, race relations, minorities, and others, will not emerge from empirical efforts alone.

I am not arguing that if we exclude unrealistic expectations and avoid empirically unresolvable problems that theories based on laboratory experiments will be able to make valid leaps to real-life situations. I doubt if that will happen. My intuition is that a closer reciprocal interaction between the laboratory and natural events, of the sort that has taken place between ethology and experimental comparative psychology, will be more productive. Social psychologists too rapidly climbed on the methodological bandwagon of small-group research believing that it would automatically yield the basic principles of social behavior. For many the behavior of the small group became an end in itself, an encapsulated world isolated from the real one. Small-group research generated many studies and much amusement but little concern with whether it was dealing with social processes that operated in the natural environment. Yet there is no reason to deny the possibility that laboratory studies can contribute *some* understanding of individual and social events occurring in the natural environment.

The core issue is whether truth can be adjudicated. In one sense it can, if we accept the notion that the decision of a science court will be legally binding on all. This would be one method of arriving at stable beliefs. Once and for all, it might be argued, such nagging problems as the nature of intelligence and language acquisition and the validity of cognitive dissonance theory could be put to rest. Are such hopes reasonable or realistic? The Supreme Court dictates the meaning of the United States Constitution but that does not truly guarantee agreement because dissident views are not squelched, and the possibility is always open to modify or change the decision by new arguments or by changing the membership of the court. Imagine what a Chomsky or a Skinner would do if the scientific court ruled against them. It is difficult to believe that they would modify their scientific judgment one whit. Judicial processes would be unsuccessful in countering the principles inherent in Galileo's statement: "In questions of science the authority of a thousand is not worth the humble reasoning of a single individual."

The distinction between employing a judicial-type system to arrive at scientific truth and adopting a particular social policy must be kept in mind. Levine fails to make this distinction perhaps because he does not believe that separation of facts from values is possible. However, my point is that the adversary system is not only counterscientific but also incapable of resolving theoretical controversy and establishing stable beliefs about psychological knowledge. In contrast, the adversary system may prove to be an effective procedure for applying scientific knowledge in a political democracy. Before this topic can be discussed it will be necessary to analyze the role of value in psychology, the subject matter of the next two chapters.

Psychology and Values: Epistemological Considerations

6

1. A methodological analysis of modern psychology demands a clarification of the relationships between empirical evidence and moral judgments.

2. Any single overall statement about the relationship between science and values (e.g., "science is value free," "science and values are inextricably intertwined") must be rejected because the relationship between the two is not the same for different scientific activities (e.g., data collecting, applying scientific knowledge).

3. The methodological position that moral principles are logically dissociated from empirical evidence has been challenged by the view that the social and behavioral sciences operate within the value orientation of their host society thus preventing the isolation of facts from the ethical preconceptions that determine their ultimate use. This position is analyzed in relation to the controversies surrounding sociobiology and intelligence testing. The conclusion is drawn that facts and values are logically dissociated but empirical evidence is relevant to choices among competing social policies that share common ethical goals.

EPISTEMOLOGY AND ETHICS

Epistemology is concerned with knowledge while ethics deals with morality. A popular philosophical opinion is that a sharp division exists between engendering knowledge and evaluating its moral implication. Consequently, the inclusion of the topic *psychology and values* in a book dedicated to the methodological analysis of psychology may appear inappropriate. Without necessarily denying the lack of a direct relationship between epistemology and ethics, the argument can be advanced that a methodological analysis of psychology would, of necessity, be incomplete if the topic of ethics were ignored. Problems of morality are frequently involved in the discovery and application of psychological knowledge. Many psychologists have chosen their profession because of their deep conviction that psychology can contribute to the building of a better society. For them, psychological knowledge is intimately related to ethical issues. The fundamental problem, which they cannot ignore, is the appropriate role that ethical decisions should play in the profession of psychology. Finally, ethics can properly be considered a part of psychology simply because moral behavior, like any other form of behavior, is subject to a psychological analysis. An understanding of modern psychology demands the clarification of the relationship between psychology and values.

THE ROLE OF VALUES IN SCIENCE

Two statements that have generated much confusion and mischief are "Science is value-free" and "Science and values cannot be dissociated." Each statement, in its own peculiar way, has distorted the role of psychology in society and thus has hampered psychology's contributions.

The global beliefs that *science is value-free* and *science and values are inextricably intertwined* tend to overlook the fact that scientific effort consists of a variety of activities, a few of which are selecting research problems, forming hypotheses, collecting data, determining the nature of an empirical law, interpreting the theoretical significance of data, applying knowledge to solve a practical problem. For example, the attempt to reduce ethnic and racial antagonisms is usually based upon the value judgments that such social conflicts should be eliminated and that members of minorities should be treated fairly. The involvement of value judgments is appreciably less when dealing solely with a factual problem, e.g., investigating ontogenetic changes in clustering. However, it must be recognized that even when such apparently "neutral" problems are investigated, values are involved because science itself possesses a value system of its own. One obvious value is that of honesty. Science is a social effort that demands of its practitioners accurate reporting of data. In science it is not a matter of honesty being the *best* policy, it is the *only* policy. Science would inevitably collapse if dishonesty were rampant. This demand for veracity does not imply, as noted in the previous discussion of *understanding*, that biases in favor of one theory over another should not occur. In fact, one can suggest that persistence in exploring the full potentialities of theoretical positions is a value implicit in the scientific method in its search for truth. I am, however, not interested in a complete listing of all the values that are inherent in the scientific method, an effort that would inevitably generate marked disagreements.[1] The significant question is whether any value is intrinsic. If so, the notion that science is value-free must be rejected. To justify this conclusion it is sufficient to identify the essential value of honesty in science. I do not know of any disagreement with the principle that it is morally wrong for a scientist to fake or distort data, or even to treat evidence in a cavalier fashion. This does not mean that all scientists abide by this mandate of honesty. Nor does it mean that dishonesty will always be punished or even detected, or that when it occurs it will lead to a permanent distortion of scientific knowledge. In the long run, dishonest reports are cor-

1. For example, no disagreements would prevail among scientists about their rights to question reigning theoretical assumptions, but at the same time many would dispute the rights of all scientists to have free access to scientific information when defense secrets are involved.

rected in the light of further research. What the value of honesty does mean is that for an overwhelming majority of scientists honesty is a moral imperative that effectively controls their behavior when reporting results.

In essence, in science honesty is good and dishonesty is bad. But what is good and what is bad? This question lends itself to two possible interpretations. What are the criteria that we employ when we characterize some behavior as good or bad? What are the psychological reasons that some behaviors are "good" while others are "bad"? The first question merely asks for an operational definition while the second seeks a theoretical explanation. For the present my concern is with the first query because I am trying to understand what is meant by a value so that I can comprehend its relations to fact. The second question will be analyzed later when attention shifts to the analysis of the relationships that might prevail between values and facts.

Some would argue that ethical terms, such as *good, valuable,* or *desirable,* are indefinable. I interpret such a position to mean that goodness, for example, is a rock-bottom experience that cannot be analyzed into more basic experiences. However, for my purposes, a behavioral analysis of ethical terms in preference to a phenomenological one has advantages in identifying what is considered to be *good* and *bad,* or *better* and *worse.* From this point of reference *goodness* represents a choice and judgment. Honesty, for example, is chosen in preference to dishonesty because it is judged to be good while dishonesty is judged to be bad. When discussing ethical values within this framework, the operational meaning is expressed by choice behavior and its linguistic justification. Admittedly, this simple definition of a value judgment is not very satisfying because it neither illuminates nor is sufficiently restrictive. But the purpose of an operational definition is not to clarify but rather to identify (page 88). The fact that my definition of a value applies equally well to the trivial preference for chocolate to vanilla ice cream as it does to the profound choice between good and evil should not be disconcerting because a sharp dividing line may not exist between a value and a preference; they merely vary in importance.

Now that the nature of value judgment has been identified or, perhaps more properly speaking, approximated, we can proceed to the crucial issue of the relationships between facts and values. In the analysis of this problem it is important to distinguish between the logical and psychological aspects of the relationship. In the case of the former the issue is whether facts logically demand the adoption of certain values. In other words, are facts simply descriptive or prescriptive? The second relationship, the psychological, treats ethical commitments as a form of behavior that can be empirically investigated to determine why they were adopted and what their consequences are for the individual and society. Although the two issues are distinct we will discover that their subtle interactions often make it difficult to maintain their independence.

THE LOGICAL DISSOCIATION BETWEEN VALUES AND FACTS

Passmore (1953), in attempting to answer the general question, "Can the social sciences be value-free?" suggests that facts and values can and should be dissociated. In explicating his position he considers a problem of social policy, "Ought we to abolish class distinction?" Let us assume that in attempting to answer this question data are obtained that indicate that the abolition of class distinctions decreases servility and diminishes cultural variety. Although agreeing about the validity of the empirical evidence, two individuals could reasonably disagree about the social policy that should be adopted, i.e., whether to retain or eliminate class distinctions. "Our policy is determined in the light of facts, but is not deduced from them" (Passmore, 1953, p. 675). In short, a particular social policy does not follow logically from the data. The only moral justification for adopting a policy of preserving or abolishing class distinctions, after considering the evidence, is the acceptance of an ethical principle that values cultural diversity more than social equality or vice versa. Within such a moral framework one could argue logically for the preservation or for the abolition of class distinctions. But the core of that logical argument resides in the moral premise rather than in the empirical evidence. By being morally committed to a principle that values cultural diversity or abhors servility, one could support a social policy concerning the abolition of class distinctions. Without the moral premise the empirical evidence is purely descriptive; it does not prescribe social policy concerning class distinctions.

The argument that moral principles are logically dissociated from facts, as expressed by Passmore, is vulnerable to several objections. First, the empirical problem raised—pitting cultural diversity against social equality—is a trivial one that does not represent crucial human events involving life and death, freedom and slavery, happiness and despair that demand consideration of the factual basis of values. Second, the detached view that is encouraged in deciding between cultural diversity and equality is illusory. All science, but especially social science, proceeds within a social context in which pure objectivity cannot operate. The attempt to invoke a detached, impartial view is essentially a political act designed to achieve certain social goals while simultaneously thwarting others. Third, the empirical study of human behavior will reveal a source of moral values. Knowledge of human behavior essentially endorses a moral viewpoint. Fourth, regardless of attempts to analyze the nature of moral discourse, the central issue for mankind is to learn to act rightly. No matter how persuasive an analysis of metaethics may be, if it does not provide a practical ethics to govern behavior it will have failed. Although these four arguments against the position that values cannot be deduced from facts are epistemologically interrelated, they nevertheless represent distinct positions that can best be analyzed separately.

Moral Values and Significant Human Events

There is no question that the values assigned to cultural diversity and servility appear insignificant when compared to more important values associated with human existence, e.g., life, liberty, and the pursuit of happiness. One can argue that a social policy that endorses death, imprisonment, and denies the right to achieve happiness is morally repugnant. The social consequences of such policies, as in Nazi Germany, are so abhorrent that one need not condemn them by reference to any higher moral authority or principle. However, a more careful analysis suggests otherwise. No matter how repugnant Nazi atrocities were, their moral rejection is not fundamentally *factual*. Taking a life need not be considered morally wrong. Many individuals who found Nazism morally abhorrent would nevertheless condone a person's right to commit suicide, especially when succumbing to a painful terminal illness. Some would also condone killing in a war that they thought justified, as was the case for most Americans in World War II. Imprisonment would also be morally acceptable if it were employed against a person who if free would probably commit a felony. Nor would it be morally objectionable to deprive a sadist of any opportunity to seek "happiness" by satisfying his motive. The point is that facts of murder, imprisonment, and denial of the pursuit of happiness do not logically lead to their moral rejection. One must recognize that the abhorrence of Nazi atrocities is not an expression of a *true* moral judgment but, instead, what is considered to be a *sound* moral judgment. One could describe the ethical principles that one has adopted and then recognize that they are incompatible with Nazism. This leads to the sound moral judgment that Nazism should be opposed because it is morally repugnant. Just as was the case for deciding either to abolish or to retain class distinctions, the facts themselves do not lead logically to a moral imperative. The moral position one adopts, whether one deals with "trivial" or "significant" facts, has its origins in the ethical framework within which the facts are judged.

Values and Political Preconceptions

It can be argued that the example offered by Passmore (1953), suggesting the possibility of a detached choice between social equality and cultural diversity, essentially distorts the nature of the options. It suggests a rational choice between two simple alternatives where in fact the choice is really complex because two different political and economic systems are at stake. Although many members of the middle class perceive the option of cultural diversity as particularly attractive due to their fondness for a variety of ethnic and artistic traditions, they nevertheless would be reluctant to admit that they harbor undemocratic attitudes that condone servility. The manner in which Passmore presents the choice effectively hides the fundamental conflict that is at stake— a choice between an economically democratic society and an exploitative one in which some members are forced to behave like servants, if not slaves. In fact, the suggestion that cultural diversity has to be purchased at the price of individual servility is a factual distortion. It may be true for a capitalist economy but certainly not for a socialist society in which ethnic cultural integrity and social democracy go hand in hand. Although the facts do not demand the adoption of the goal of ethnic diversity or social equality, facts associated with the social, economic, and political organization of a country will determine whether such a choice needs to be made. Thus this argument would suggest that Passmore's general conclusion that facts and values can be completely dissociated is misleading because it ignores the nature of the society in which ethical decisions are made.

Although Passmore's hypothetical example of the choice between ethnic diversity and social equality was useful in introducing the epistemological problem of the relationship between facts and values it now becomes necessary when analyzing political influences to deal with real problems that permit the discussion of specific factual and ethical issues. Two such problems, both of which have generated intense emotional debates, are sociobiology and intelligence testing.

Ethical Issues in Sociobiology

The appearance of *Sociobiology: The New Synthesis* by the zoologist Edward O. Wilson (1975) touched off a storm of debate by suggesting that many significant forms of human social behavior have genetic roots rather than being shaped totally by environmental factors. Wilson supported his speculations about the genetic determination of human social behavior with evidence obtained from animal and insect societies. For example, altruistic behavior is exhibited by "soldier" termites who, in response to ants that attack their colony, will explode themselves and spray poison over the invaders. From such evidence it is suggested that genetic factors, admittedly to a lesser degree, also operate in human social behavior. For example, the self-sacrificing behavior of mothers toward their children may not be simply an expression of effective moral training but, instead, of genetic influences that have helped our species to survive.

One might think that the suggestion that human social behavior is to some extent genetically determined would surprise and offend no one. However nature-nurture debates have a history of arousing strong emotional reactions due in part to past participants offering an oversimplified view of genetic and environmental contributions to complex forms of behavior. Gaylord G. Simpson, the distinguished evolutionist, offers an appropriate warning:

> Much of the critical discussion of sociobiology . . . has been another form of the nature-nurture debate, a discussion that has proved futile and indeed meaningless because that is not a legitimate either-or question. Man is not born a tabula rasa, nor is born a programmed automaton. When the argument approaches that extreme polarization, it is sensible to say, "A plague o'both your houses" (1977, p. 774).

It is one thing to argue that human social behavior is rigidly and inevitably controlled by genetic factors but quite another thing to state that genetic factors predispose humans to acquire certain social behaviors in preference to others. In the former case the argument is based upon the assumption that humans are "programmed automatons" while in the latter case the suggestion is that genetic and environmental factors interact. It is not my purpose to debate the issue as to which of these two positions Wilson adopts although some would insist that it is the latter (e.g., Wade, 1976). Neither will it be my concern to judge whether Wilson and other sociobiologists have misused animal analogies in interpreting human social behavior although my impression is that they have. *My sole concern is with the ethical implications of empirical laws that demonstrate that genetic factors influence behavior.*

If one accepts the position that facts and values are dissociated, then one can conclude that the implication of a genetic predisposition does not *logically* lead to the adoption of a particular value. In primitive societies men tended to engage in strenuous activities that involved lengthy periods of travel (e.g., hunting) while women usually indulged in less physically taxing endeavors such as preparing food and caring for the young (Murdock, 1937). This division of labor would have survival value for the group because important jobs (e.g., fighting, hunting, nursing) are assigned to those possessing aptitude for them. It does not, however, follow logically that such a division is morally justified unless one accepts the survival of the group as the ultimate value. And even if one did accept such a moral position it could be argued that a division of labor based *strictly* on gender would be counterproductive because some women, especially if they received appropriate training, would be more effective at some strenuous activities than some men. Today in a modern industrial society the justification for assigning jobs on the basis of sex, even when one adopts survival as a moral imperative, becomes less warranted. Most professional, business, and political positions do not require physical strength; society's future is served better by considering women along with men for its most important tasks. And even when specifying the requirements for a job that requires strength, such as a ditchdigger or stevedore, sex need not be considered even though the probability would be greater that a larger proportion of men than women would meet the desired standards.

The preceding analysis, it should be recognized, does not so much encourage the elimination or preservation of sex discrimination as argue that the biological facts associated with being male and female do not logically lead to any moral position regarding the social treatment of the sexes. And this conclusion applies with equal force to situations in which survival of the individual or the society would be enhanced if sexual discrimination was practiced. History is filled with incidents in which individuals (e.g., early Christian martyrs) or groups (e.g., the Jews at Masada) decided that some moral values were more important than survival itself.

Political Involvement in Science

The argument against the position that facts and values are logically independent is that it fails to represent the realities of science. According to the Sociobiology Study Group, a group of scientists who vehemently criticized Wilson's *Sociobiology*, scientific knowledge and political preconceptions are intertwined:

> Our central point is that sociobiology—like all science—proceeds in a social context: "pure objectivity" is as much a myth for sociobiologists as for science reporters. All attitudes toward sociobiology—ours as much as any—reflect certain political preconceptions which need to be made explicit. The weaker the restraint of fact, and the closer the subject to immediate human concern, the greater the influence of these preconceptions (Alper et al., 1976, pp. 424–27).

Although strongly and sharply stated the position nevertheless contains many ambiguities, not the least of which is the implication that political preconceptions are *inevitably* involved in scientific efforts. The argument is reminiscent of the discussion surrounding the issue of "immaculate perceptions" in scientific observations: whether pure "objectivity" can be achieved or whether theoretical preconceptions determine what is observed (pages 48–64).

There is no doubt that political preconceptions can be involved in the interpretation of factual data. One case in point is that of Trofim Lysenko, the Russian agronomist, who claimed that by changing the environment of the seeds of spring wheat it was possible to impart to them the genetic characteristics of winter wheat. He interpreted his findings as supporting the doctrine of inheritance of acquired characteristics, which had been discredited by modern geneticists. Lysenko argued that his theoretical interpretation was consistent with Marxism, and in this view he received support from Stalin and the Soviet Central Committee. Only after the death of Stalin were Soviet scientists able to publicly reject his genetic theory and its presumed tie to Marxian orthodoxy.

American geneticists have also been influenced by political preconceptions. Charles B. Davenport in 1917 drew erroneous conclusions about human race crossings from data obtained with hens (Provine, 1973). It had been discovered that crossing Leghorns, who had been bred to lay eggs but not to brood, with Brahmas, who had been bred to lay eggs and brood and hatch them before laying more, resulted in offspring that lacked the advantages of each strain. The hybrid were neither good layers nor brooders, thus failing to serve the needs of chicken farmers with or without artificial incubators.

Davenport assumed that natural selection encouraged the development of genetic traits that were harmoniously adjusted both with each other and to the environment. Crossbreeding, reasoned Davenport from the evidence obtained with Leghorns and Brahmas, created the danger of disharmony among genetic characteristics such as might occur when a member of a human race with large stature had a child with one from a race with small stature. A disharmonious relationship might occur between the inherited stature and size of the circulatory system of the offspring; the circulatory system might be too large to fit into a small stature. Davenport suggested that similar unfortunate results might occur from crossbreeding between blacks and whites. "One often sees in mulattos an ambition and push combined with intellectual inadequacy which makes the unhappy hybrid dissatisfied with his lot and a nuisance to others." He concluded: "Miscegenation commonly spells disharmony of physical, mental and temperamental qualities and this means also disharmony with environment. A hybridized people are a badly put together people and a restless, ineffective people" (quoted in Provine, 1973, p. 791). Although Davenport was careful to avoid labeling any race as inferior to another, other genticists of that era supported legislation against interbreeding between white and blacks to prevent the degradation of the population.

In viewing these two examples of the political influence on the science of genetics, it would be wise to avoid, or at least de-emphasize, the murky problem of explaining the scientist's behavior. Did Lysenko and/or Davenport and their co-workers deliberately try to deceive their audience, or were they merely "unconscious" victims of a dominant political atmosphere that induced them to perceive and interpret evidence in a biased fashion? I know of no simple litmus test that could discriminate between those two possibilities. For the present discussion it is not necessary to attempt such a difficult clinical judgment. The point at issue is whether political preconceptions can determine scientific conclusions, and the evidence suggests an affirmative answer. In fact, Provine's analysis, which traces the history of geneticists' attitudes toward the biological consequences of racial interbreeding, reveals an interesting sequence of events.

> Geneticists in England and the United States clearly reversed their published remarks on the effects of race crossing between 1930 and 1950. The reversal occurred in two steps. First came the change in the 1930's from a condemnation of wide race crosses to an agnostic view. The second change, from the agnostic view to the belief that wide race crossings were at worst biologically harmless, took place during and shortly after World War II. (1973, p. 796).

These "reversals," however, "occurred in the light of a little new compelling data from studies of actual human crossings." According to Provine, the major reason that caused geneticists to change their minds,

> was the revulsion of educated people in the United States and England to Nazi race doctrines and their use in justifying extermination of Jews. Few geneticists wanted to argue, as had the Nazis, that biology showed race crossings was harmful. Instead, having witnessed the horrible toll, geneticists naturally wanted to argue that biology showed race crossings was at worst harmless.

No racist nation could misuse that conclusion. And geneticists did revise their biology to fit their feelings of revulsion (ibid., p. 796).

From his historical analysis, Provine concludes:

It is necessary and natural that changing social attitudes will influence areas of biology where little is known and the conclusions are possibly socially explosive. The real danger is not that biology changes with society, but that the public expects biology to provide the objective truth apart from social influences. Geneticists and the public should realize that the science of genetics is often closely intertwined with social attitudes and political considerations (ibid., p. 796).

Provine's conclusions are consistent with those of the Sociobiology Study Group, but the reasons for the agreement are not spelled out. Is it because political biases cannot be unravelled from empirical knowledge? The position that political beliefs cannot be separated from empirical evidence is difficult to defend against the fact that some scientists refused to succumb to political and other pressures. Several leading Russian geneticists stuck to the traditional view that acquired characteristics cannot be inherited. Similarly, in spite of dominant biases in the United States against black and white interbreeding, several American geneticists questioned the data upon which this social prejudice was based (Provine, 1973). Were these protests of the Russian and American geneticists merely an expression of competing political philosophies, or were they determined by the demands of scientific traditions in evaluating evidence? The latter interpretation appears appropriate. Lysenko's opponents were not necessarily anticommunists; they disagreed, apparently justifiably, with his interpretation of his data while failing to perceive any incompatibility between Marxism and traditional genetic theory. In a similar vein, several American geneticists took reasonable exception to the kind of evidence that was offered about the ill effects of race crossings. Some even recognized the difficulty of drawing conclusions from data or race crossings for social policy; if racial crossings had some possible negative biological or psychological effect would that justify legal sanctions against racial interbreeding? Adherence to democratic ideals, in which individuals are free to choose their own mate, can be considered to be more valuable than minimizing possible negative consequences of racial inter-breeding.

The line of argument that scientists are incapable of resisting accepted social dogma collapses when attention is focused on the great leaps forward in the history of science. Although the Roman Catholic Church in 1616 denounced the Copernican system as dangerous to their faith, Galileo published a book for the layman that supported its validity while simultaneously questioning the Ptolemaic system, which the church embraced. Charles Darwin allowed the weight of evidence to change his preconceptions about the origin of species. Darwin had studied for the ministry, and while on the *Beagle* expedition he wrote notes in his diary that were in line with a creationist interpretation (Ghiselin, 1969). But as we know from history the data he collected forced him to adopt an evolutionary theory. Although all scientists may not be able to resist political or religious preconceptions, some obviously can. If this is so, one must reject the view that "pure objectivity" is a myth. Certainly scientists possess preconceptions—theoretical, political, religious—but these "subjective" factors do not always operate in an all-powerful fashion in the final determination of empirical evidence and its theoretical interpretation.

The evidence offered to support the position that preconceptions in the form of political and religious influences can be resisted also suggests that political biases can be unravelled from empirical knowledge. Again it is important to note that the argument is not that these influences do not have an effect upon the course of science but instead that their influences can be minimized and overcome by the force of data and reason. If that be the case then the position that powerful political or religious preconceptions prevent the dissociation of facts from values must also be rejected.

The preceding analysis, which maintains that facts and values are not logically related, fails to answer the question as to why some scientists insist that they are. Is this insistence simply a confusion about the intrinsic properties of the scientific endeavor, or does it represent a philosophical position that is extrinsic to the scientific effort itself? Although the answer to this question depends on clinical judgment, and therefore one must be very cautious in one's interpretation, it does appear that the latter factor plays the dominant role for many scientists in current controversies surrounding the implications of genetic influences on human behavior. One can distinguish between those researchers who frankly wish to politicize the issue from those who attempt to separate the empirical evidence from social policy. For example, Richard Lewontin, one of the leaders of the Sociobiology Study Group, states: "Nothing we can know about the genetics of human behavior can have any implications for human society" (quoted in Wade, 1976). This statement is consistent with the epistemological position supported by the analysis that facts and values can be dissociated. Nevertheless Lewontin's position diverges from that neutral stance by adding an empirical generalization to the epistemological assumption. Inevitably human genetic research will be used for some political goal or as Lewontin states: "The process (of doing research in human genetics) has social impact because the announcement that research is being done is a political act" (ibid.). In essence, he argues that research in human genetics "is bound to produce a pseudo science that will inevitably be misused" (ibid.). Such research, as in Wilson's *Sociobiology,* "represents an effort to cloak in modern terminology the age-old political doctrine that the main features of human social existence are biologically determined" (Alper et al., 1976).

Several assumptions underlie this argument: (1) research on human genetics will be misinterpreted and/or distorted; (2) the misinterpretation and/or distortion will produce undesirable effects; and (3) the evidence, whether misinterpreted or distorted, plays an influential role in political decision-making.

In evaluating this analysis consider the effect of different social philosophies "based on" evolutionary theory, which assumes a higher reproduction rate of fit as compared to unfit organisms. Most people are familiar with the employment of evolutionary theory to justify social practices (social Darwinism) that would be morally repugnant to most present-day Americans. In the nineteenth century men of wealth and political power argued against child labor laws, public education, compulsory safety regulations in factories and mines, and other social welfare legislation because such laws went "against nature" as implied by evolutionary theory. Society, like the jungle, was perceived as an arena in which individuals competed against each other to survive and reproduce. Only if complete freedom was permitted could natural laws operate. Welfare legislation encouraged the survival of the less fit.

Evolutionism, however, was employed not only to justify the status quo but also social reform. Karl Marx wanted to dedicate the first volume of *Das Kapital* to Darwin. He and other social reformers interpreted Darwin's theory as indicating that social organizations were constantly undergoing change and that therefore political governments and economic processes were alterable. The forces of history would lead to progressive changes in social organizations that would serve the needs of the people to survive and reproduce.

Let us assume that a particular scientist is a firm believer in either laissez faire capitalism or Marxism. If he accepts the notion that facts and values can be dissociated, he could not conclude, as a scientist, that evolutionary theory supports his political position or that of his opponent. However, extrascientific considerations could encourage him to assume a stance at odds with his belief as a scientist that evolutionary theory has no logical implication for social policy. He could conclude that his metaethical analysis that facts and ethics are logically independent is too subtle to be appreciated by laypersons and even some scientists. His political opponents in the scientific community would surely misuse evolutionary theory to support their political position to the detriment of his own. His only defense is to retaliate by demonstrating that evolutionary theory can be interpreted to support his own political doctrine. To himself he might admit that his roles as a scientist and a politically active citizen are in conflict; but he might also believe that for the good of society, as well as for the welfare of science, it becomes necessary for scientists to accommodate to the demands of political action by discarding their metaethical conclusion.

The difficulty with this rationalization is that scientists with opposed political convictions can argue in the same manner to support their thesis. As a result the scientific evidence becomes unnecessary baggage in the political dispute. The scientific evidence, as shown with evolutionary theory, can be used to support any political doctrine and social policy. The likely result of this kind of debate in which scientific evidence is slanted to support competing political philosophies is that the public will learn to look with suspicion on the social-policy recommendations of scientists. Similar consequences will result when politically active scientists assume the methodological stance that scientific knowledge is inextricably intertwined with ethical judgments. Thus when scientists assign political implications to scientific evidence, regardless of their methodological positions concerning the logical relationship between facts and ethics, the evidence of necessity will be unconvincing because contradictory interpretations will be offered simultaneously.

My analysis supports the position that facts and values can be decoupled while simultaneously noting that scientists differ in their desire to politicize the relationship between empirical evidence and social policy. Those who are interested in the depoliticization process are committed to the idea that there are objective laws of nature independent of political beliefs. Politically oriented scientists need not necessarily deny this assumption, but they could insist that scientific evidence must be viewed within a political framework to guarantee the attainment of proper social goals.

A Methodological Analysis of Problems Associated with the Investigation of Racial Differences in Intelligence

This analysis of some of the reactions to sociobiology highlights the major issues associated with the relationships among facts, values, and politics. But many subtle points remain. To further clarify the general problem and deal with remaining issues, it will be useful to analyze a perennial and painful problem in psychology—racial differences in intelligence. In treating this topic it is necessary to discuss: (1) the meaning of intelligence, (2) the meaning of race, (3) the ethical justification for investigating racial differences in behavior, (4) the ethical implications of obtained racial differences in behavior, and (5) an appropriate framework for judging research on racial differences.

The Meaning of Intelligence

Two views have dominated in the attempt to specify the meaning of intelligence. The one that both has historical precedent and approximates commonsense interpretations is that intelligence, which might be tentatively conceptualized as the power to understand and reason, is some innate physiological entity that presides over intellectual functioning. This view dates back to Aristotle, who assumed that humans had many souls, each with a different function. The lowest soul, shared by all living things, supervised vegetative functions. The highest soul, intellect, possessed only by humans, controlled reason.

In contrast to the position that intelligence is some innate entity hidden in a deep recess of the body is the interpretation that intelligence is an attribute of behavior. According to this view, the first step in understanding intelligence, its causes as well as its behavioral consequences, would be to develop some measure of it. Once such a measure is fashioned, it can be further refined and improved.

The second approach has proved to be more practical. Although it appears reasonable to assume that some neurological entity, obviously the brain, controls intellectual functioning, it is not completely clear what particular patterns of neural anatomy and biochemical functions are involved. In addition, it must be recognized that whatever neurophysiological unit serves as the seat of intelligence, it does not operate in a static manner. The brain itself can be modified by a variety of external inputs ranging from the quality of nourishment to different forms of environmental stimulation. One must also realize that any search for the neurophysiological substrata of intelligence would have to be guided by some behavioral evidence. Any anatomical site or neural process that did not influence commonly acknowledged forms of intellectual behavior would automatically be suspect as the "seat" of intelligence. In sum, the notion that there are "real" neurophysiological substrates of intelligence is reasonable, but the direct search for such processes when psychologists first became interested in intelligence testing in all likelihood would have been unproductive.

Measures of Intelligence. An early attempt to construct a "mental test" was made by James McKeen Cattell in 1890. He gave a series of ten tests to undergraduates at Columbia University. The tests were designed mainly to test their sensory and motor skills: reaction time for sound, dynamometric pressure, estimation of 10-second interval, and others (Tuddenham, 1962). The selection of such tests could be defended by assuming that the more sensitive and responsive a person is the greater would be his mental ability. Is this assumption justified? The criterion employed to answer this question holds the key to understanding the meaning of intelligence in contemporary psychology.

Cattell's test encouraged others to develop similar measures. Many psychologists of that era were convinced that as a consequence of Cattell's effort a significant breakthrough was taking place in the measurement of mental abilities. However, their optimism was short-lived. The tests were found wanting when evaluated by the newly developed Pearson correlation method. These tests were found not to be correlated with behavior that could be called "intelligent." For example, Cattell's test was uncorrelated with college grades although the grades in different courses were correlated among themselves. How could a valid test of mental ability be unrelated to behavior that is presumed to be an expression of intellectual abilities? Failure to offer a satisfactory answer to this and related questions resulted in a disenchantment with these tests. By 1905 when Alfred Binet and his collaborator, Theodore Simon, produced their test of intelligence, interest in the Cattell-type test was practically dead.

It is important to recognize a fundamental difference between the efforts of Cattell and those of Binet and Simon. The assumption that mental ability was a function of sensitivity and responsiveness served as the sole guideline for Cattell in constructing his test. No apparent consideration was given to the problem of whether scores on such a test would be correlated with any intellectual form of behavior. Binet and Simon, in contrast, set out to construct a test that would be correlated with academic success. They were given the specific assignment by the French Minister of Public Instruction to identify those children who could not profit from regular academic training. With this clear goal in mind and the ingenuity to formulate a dimension of intelligence in the form of a mental age scale, Binet and Simon were able to identify students whose academic potential was limited. It was not a perfect or foolproof test in that errors could be made either in the assessment of an individual's academic potential or in the administration of the test and interpretation of the results. Nevertheless, it was far superior to any other technique for evaluating children's ability to be educated. In addition, later versions and modifications of the Binet test proved to be extremely useful in selecting individuals for a variety of industrial, commercial, and military positions.

It must be recognized that however effective one might consider intelligence tests to be in measuring academic ability, it does not follow that one can demand such tests be adopted as the best or true measure of intelligence. As already noted, intelligence tests measure certain attributes of behavior, and one can always argue that those attributes selected may be inappropriate or incomplete. The problem is not unlike that of selecting indices for defining the economic concept of *gross national product*, which is not a problem of discovering the "real" index but instead one of inventing a convenient and useful measure for representing a nation's productivity. The ultimate justification for a particular index is the contribution it makes to the gathering of a significant body of knowledge. But no matter how systematic and extensive these empirical laws may be one can always insist that some significant aspect of "productivity" is ignored. For example, one could insist that a crucial element in the gross national product is the variety of social services offered, and any index that ignores that feature will provide a distorted view of the economy. Similarly, one can argue that because schools tend to encourage conformity, linking intelligence to academic performance will inevitably generate measures of intelligence that ignore intellectual creativity.

These objections can be countered by the argument that the initial operational definition of a concept, such as *gross national product* or *intelligence,* need not be considered so frozen as to preclude further modification. The concepts can be expanded to include an additional attribute (e.g., creativity). Or one could investigate how that particular attribute (e.g., creativity) is related to the original concept (e.g., IQ). The history of intelligence testing illustrates a continued concern with understanding the nature of intelligence test scores as well as repeated attempts to develop a "better" measure of intelligence. Factor analysis, the statistical technique that breaks down complex behavioral patterns into basic components, demonstrates that a common factor is involved in responding to a widely diverse set of intelligence test items thus supporting the notion that there is such a behavioral characteristic as general intelligence. More recently, a greater interest has been expressed in the relationship between traditional tests of intelligence and theoretical interpretations of intellectual development. But, in the final analysis, many would argue that the greatest justification for the traditional intelligence test to be viewed as a "real," or more properly a reasonable, test of intelligence is the substantial correlations intelligence test scores have with criteria of educational and occupational achievement.

As already suggested, one can reject, for a variety of reasons, the notion that the concept of intelligence can be equated with scores obtained on traditional intelligence tests. One of many arguments is that of Medawar, an English Nobel Laureate in the field of medicine, who insists that it is impossible to attach a single-number valuation to intelligence because of its intrinsic complexity. Among the elements of intelligence are,

> speed and span of *grasp* (of understanding), the ability to see implications and conversely to discern non sequiturs and other

fallacies, the ability to discern analogies and formal parallels between outwardly dissimilar phenomena or thought structures, and much else besides. One number will not do for all of these . . . (Medawar, 1977, p. 13).

To support his argument Medawar notes the confusions generated by numerous attempts to attach single-number valuations to complex concepts in other sciences. One such example involved the quality of soil in terms of its agricultural worth. A single-number valuation could not incorporate the variety of attributes that played a significant role: porosity, particle size and shape, water content and hygroscopy, hydrogen-iron concentration, and material flora.

Medawar's argument may appear telling but it is really not very compelling. Psychologists are not as simple-minded as Medawar, and many other biological and physical scientists, would like to believe they are. Most psychologists, since Binet, share the view that a single number fails to convey a complete description of a person's intelligence. Factor analysis has revealed specific factors (e.g., verbal, spatial, numerical, memory) in addition to a general factor. The Wechsler Adult Intelligence Scale (Matarazzo, 1972) distinguished between verbal and performance intelligence, as well as components within each. Although a multinumber valuation of intelligence possesses certain advantages over single-number valuation, it does not follow that the latter is useless. As already noted, single-number valuations of general intelligence are useful predictors of academic and vocational achievement. And it should be recognized that a more sophisticated multinumber valuation has emerged from the original pragmatic decision to characterize intelligence with a single number.

Any decision to employ the traditional IQ test as a research instrument to investigate racial differences in intelligence is not binding for psychologists in particular and society in general. It is reasonable, although not necessarily compelling, to argue that the traditional intelligence test possesses too many limitations (e.g., excessive linkage to academic success, lack of theoretical rationale) to be used as a measuring instrument in investigating the socially explosive issue of possible racial difference in intelligence. The interesting question is whether such a position implies any entailed decision. In the refusal to accept the traditional intelligence test as a valid measure and in the absence of offering an alternative measuring instrument that meets standards of reliability and validity, is it not incumbent upon such a person to remain mute in regard to the nature of the possible relationship between race and intelligence? It would seem odd, at least to me, for any individual who essentially argues that the empirical question cannot be properly invesigated to insist that there are, or are not, real differences in intelligence among races.

The Meaning of Race

Just as it is possible to reject IQ tests as measures of intelligence one can also refuse to employ racial distinctions in research by arguing that the concept of race is too vague to be used in scientific research. Races are not clearly definable biological entities, and hence an inevitable distortion will be created by treating them as such.

The charge that the concept of race is too ill-defined to serve any useful research function can be countered. Such a position perhaps is an expression of a desire for race to mean what common sense would like it to mean rather than what the facts demand it to mean. No satisfactory definition of race can be forthcoming if one makes an a priori demand that the division between races should be absolutely sharp, i.e., races should be "pure." Humans from all parts of the world are interfertile, and throughout the course of history much interbreeding has occurred among different subgroups that previously had been reproductively isolated. Consequently, the concept of race cannot be defined in terms of characteristics of individuals but must instead be defined by genetically determined attributes (e.g., morphological, serological) attributes of subpopulations. By accepting such an operational definition we will then be able to assimilate the fact that members of the same *race* are not genetically identical but can vary markedly among themselves. In addition, and most important, with such a definition the similarities among members of the same race can be ascertained and the difference between races can be measured.

The Ethical Justification for Investigating Racial Differences in Behavior

Is it proper for scientists to investigate possible racial differences in behavior, especially those involving highly valued assets such as intelligence, when the results could be socially disruptive and offensive to individual groups? Do not scientists have an ethical obligation to abstain from such investigations? There is no answer, certainly not a simple one, to these questions. The questions, however, can be clarified by discussing certain issues.

Although many scientists would like to believe that a "true" democracy would afford them complete freedom to investigate any problem, some restrictions are always imposed. Democratic societies, as well as professional organizations, have a right, as well as a duty, to impose limitations on research that threatens the well-being of its members. It would be difficult to persuade a majority of the scientific community that their rights are being threatened if an individual researcher is denied the privilege of inflicting pain and suffering on human subjects in order to study sadomasochistic behavior. Obviously no sharp boundary exists, socially and professionally, between acceptable research and unacceptable research. This point is testified to by the controversy that surrounded the ethical justification of the Milgram study (Milgram, 1963) in which subjects were instructed to administer shocks to other humans. Although no shocks were actually administered, the subjects thought they were, and many, during the course of the experiment suffered intense emotional reactions. Was such research ethically justified? Some psychologists thought not.

Investigating racial differences in intelligence between races or among distinctive social groups can be considered socially destructive. When I was in Israel for an academic year during the mid-1970s I heard numerous rumors that the government was discouraging research that was focussed on the differences in intelligence test scores and academic performance of Ashkenazi Jews on the one hand, and Sephardic and Oriental Jews on the other. Ashkenazi Jews are European Jews, or their descendents, who emigrated to Israel mainly from Poland, Russia, and Germany. Sephardic Jews are descendents of those Jews who were expelled from Spain in 1492 and dispersed themselves mainly throughout the Mediterranean basin. Oriental Jews, in turn, are presumably descendents of those Jews who stayed in the general vicinity of the Holy Land after the destruction of the second Temple in 70 A.D. Although the dividing line is not always sharp, especially between the Sephardim and Orientals, several different criteria including surnames, language spoken, and country of origin can be employed for classifying Israeli Jews into these categories.

Ashkenazis are disproportionately represented in the professions, the upper socioeconomic class, and in higher education. Could this be a consequence of differences in IQ? When I informally posed this question to a number of Israeli psychologists the response was affirmative, but the explanation of the cause of the difference varied. Some attributed it to environmental factors; the cultural heritage of European Jews with their greater emphasis and achievements in education gave them an advantage over Sephardic and Oriental Jews. Others suggested that it was genetic; although they were all Jews the migration of the Jews throughout history had produced distinctive breeding populations. It is interesting to note that the controversy about differences in intelligence between different groups of Jews was investigated in Brooklyn, New York (Gross, 1967) where a community of Orthodox Ashkenazis and Sephardim lived. A 17-point difference in the IQ's of the two groups was found, and a controversy was created as to whether the difference in favor of the Ashkenazis was due to possible environmental or genetic differences (Jensen, 1973).

It seems eminently reasonable for a garrison state like Israel to avoid supporting research that might prove socially divisive and thus endanger its chances of survival. In order to resist the threatened destruction by its enemies, it is necessary for Israel to maintain a harmonious relationship among its different social groups, at least to the extent that its members cooperate among themselves when serving in the armed forces. To obtain evidence that would encourage feelings of inferiority among the Sephardic and Oriental Jews might make them less effective citizens and soldiers.

The significant point here is that it does not follow that science, with its need for freedom of inquiry, is necessarily threatened by the failure of a government to support certain kinds of research. Governments, as well as the scientific community itself, can impose restrictions based upon countervailing values such as human welfare and society's survival. Admittedly, the scientific effort can be threatened if such terms as *human welfare* and *society's survival* are used loosely by a government that seeks to prevent the gathering and dissemination of information that is embarrassing to its reputation. It is presumed that in a political democracy with a free press such political shenanigans will ultimately be revealed to the government's disadvantage at the next election.

More important than the question of government support is the issue of whether a government has a right to ban certain kinds of research. Again the existence of countervailing values of the freedom of scientific inquiry must be recognized. Research that is potentially dangerous to the health of a community or damaging to the environment would appear to be legitimate targets for governmental restrictions. But in such cases it is not the question (e.g., the nature of certain chemical reactions) being investigated that is rejected but instead the hazardous method by which it is being studied. If less dangerous procedures were invented the question could then be pursued.

Cannot it be argued that some problems should be prohibited from being studied? If a government decides not to support research on racial differences in intelligence because of potential social disruptions does not the government have the obligation to ban such research? If the research is going to be socially disruptive, does it matter who supports it? Although some might find this argument attractive the distinction between the government's policies of refusing to finance a research project and legally banning it should be recognized.

A government has an obvious right to order its priorities in the kinds of research it desires to support. But that right, in a political democracy, does not provide them with any consequent privilege to impose restrictions on the freedom of scientists to pursue problems that they believe are important. Although many psychologists in Israel and the United States entertain moral qualms about investigating racial differences in intelligence and/or believe it to be a theoretically insignificant issue, they nevertheless would object strenuously to any governmental restrictions. Such a governmental decree would be perceived as a direct threat to freedom of inquiry.

Many arguments can be offered in opposition to any ban of research that might demonstrate that races do indeed differ in certain characteristics. In general, the position can be taken that whatever benefits might accrue in reducing racial tension would be offset by the damage done to a free society in general and the scientific enterprise in particular. On a more analytical level, the justification of the government for banning the investigation of certain problems because of their social implications would be denied by the premise that facts and values can be dissociated thus making it impossible for any factual evidence to invalidate a moral principle. No matter what findings were obtained about racial differences in intelligence they could not invalidate the moral principle of equal treatment for all before the law. In addition, those psychologists who might have moral qualms about engaging in such research could nevertheless be sufficiently tolerant to entertain the possibility that some who do can be above moral reproach. While black-white differences in intelligence were sometimes investigated to justify racial prejudice in the form of unequal social treatment (Kamin, 1974), such motivation need not be involved.

It is of interest to note that Arthur Jensen's concern with black-white differences in intelligence emerged as a result of an initial conviction "that the much higher incidence of [intellectual] retardation among children of low SES [socioeconomic status],

and particularly among minority children, was the fault of IQ
tests and also, possibly, of the schools" (1974, p. 224). The results
he obtained in pursuing this hypothesis encouraged him to reject
it. But even though he ultimately adopted the hypothesis that genetic factors were responsible for some of the difference between
the IQ scores of blacks and whites, he did not employ such data,
as did other psychologists and politicians, to justify school segregation or other forms of differential treatment:

> It is unjust to allow the mere fact of an individual's racial or social
> background to affect the treatment accorded him. All persons
> rightfully must be regarded on the basis of their individual qual-
> ities and merits, and all social, educational, and economic institu-
> tions must have built into them the mechanisms for insuring and
> maximizing the treatment of persons according to their individual
> behavior (Jensen, 1969, p. 78).

The implications of this discussion of the ethical issues surrounding the research topic of racial differences in intelligence is
that moral questions cannot be avoided. At the same time a single
moral position cannot be recommended or expected. And it should
be realized that moral questions are involved in all choices between different scientific activities *though we are not always consciously aware of them.* An experimental psychologist who chooses
to investigate the different kinds of memory stores rather than
employ his talents to improve educational practices is making a
moral judgment that the former activity is more important than is
the second. The clinical psychologist also makes a moral decision
when he employs unproven therapeutic techniques in preference
to discovering whether they are truly effective.

However, when the psychologist, or other scientist, gets embroiled in a highly controversial issue that many believe possesses
numerous social implications (e.g., racial differences in intelligence, the employment of a neutron bomb) he rapidly becomes
aware that he is confronted with a moral dilemma. Whatever actions he takes he is almost certain to be accused of moral delinquency or moral cowardice.

What guidelines can be offered to the scientist who contemplates becoming involved in socially controversial questions? An assiduous commitment to the ideal of scientific integrity, critical thinking, and a great deal of courage should stand him in good stead. But it must be recognized that specific actions do not flow automatically from the adherence to the ideals of scientific integrity and the ability to think critically. Two scientists, of equal integrity and ability might choose entirely different moral, empirical, and theoretical positions in regard to a socially controversial issue. Except for the moral issue, the situation is not unlike that of the two scientists who disagree about the interpretation of a common phenomenon. Their theoretical differences encourage them to investigate different facets of the same general phenomenon. The resolution of the controversy, if deductive explanation (pages 142–151) is sought, and assuming that the competing interpretations are empirically meaningful, will be achieved only in a historical context. The moral position adds an additional ingredient, which can and does cloud the empirical and theoretical issues for some investigators but need not for all.

The Ethical Implications of Racial Differences in Behavior

In the case of the debate surrounding racial differences in intelligence there appear to be two main sources of confusion generated by moral and related political considerations. One has already been alluded to previously—the conflation of factual statements with moral judgments. A common misconception is that if racial differences were found they would indicate the existence of racial inferiority and ipso facto be incompatible with democratic principles. As a result many people, especially psychologists involved with social issues, harbor the hope that all races are equal in regard to psychological abilities. Their hope, consciously or unconsciously, becomes a hypothesis that they defend vigorously. There is nothing wrong in defending such a hypothesis as long as it is recognized that it need not be true and that the functioning of a democratic society does not depend upon it. Admittedly, if the hypothesis were found to be true, fewer social problems would be created than if it were proved to be false.

If one fully appreciated the influences of genetic variations, it would come as no surprise that races *could* differ in psychological abilities. Natural selection, in addition to the effects of mutation and selective migration, can exert powerful effects on the biological structure of members of different breeding populations that were equivalent in intelligence at one time; but because of natural selection, which might encourage a higher reproductive rate of brighter members of one race, genetic differences could ultimately develop. One could argue that the wide variations in the environments of the breeding populations of the world combined with the markedly different cultural traditions associated with mate selection and differential reproduction rates of different segments of society would make racial differences more likely than not. But in the final analysis, this is an empirical problem that requires evidence, not prejudgments.

The possible occurrence of racial differences raises the threat that the concept of racial superiority will be invoked thus encouraging the fear of support for racial segregation, persecution, and even genocide. These worries cannot be ignored but they are not necessarily warranted. Racial differences and racial superiority are not equivalent terms, and the former neither implies the latter nor does it imply any form of differential social treatment. Consider cases in which races differ in regard to certain biological attributes. Oriental infants, for example, are more sensitive to alcoholic ingestion than are Caucasians (Wolff, 1972). Can it be argued, therefore, assuming that alcoholism is considered to be a liability, that Orientals, with a lower rate of alcoholism, are superior to Caucasians because their chances of being victimized by alcoholism are less? The notion of Oriental racial superiority would be immediately rejected because a reduced susceptibility to alcoholism would not be accepted as an index of racial superiority. If one desired to use the term "superior" the only conclusion one could draw was that Orientals are superior to Caucasians in resisting alcoholism, and the evidence cited indicates that this superiority is to some extent an expression of genetic factors.

Consider, for the moment, the assumption that genetic factors are related to performance in athletic events. A person who is tall, can leap high, and has good vision has a much better chance of becoming a successful basketball player than one who is short, a poor jumper, and near-sighted. Various racial groups differ in their body size and proportions, bone density, and visual acuity. Is it reasonable to assume that members of different racial groups have different probabilities of excelling in certain sports because of genetic factors? For example, is it beyond belief that blacks have a greater chance of becoming outstanding basketball players than Japanese? Blacks tend to be taller and have better vision. In contrast, the more compact build of Japanese may be responsible for their superior performance in gymnastics. Simple principles of physics dictate that a person who has long legs and a short torso will have more difficulty in developing outstanding skills in gymnastics than one with a more compact build resulting in a lower center of gravity.

Because racial differences is such a touchy topic, I am forced to qualify my comments in order to guard against the polite accusation of being an extreme biological determinist and the insulting charge of being a racist.[2] Social motives and environmental

2. *Racist* is a pejorative term the meaning of which has expanded in recent years. Initially it referred to a person who harbored prejudice against members of certain races (or breeding populations such as Jews) and encouraged the social policy of differential treatment. Two examples of racism practiced against blacks were school segregation and refusal to permit them to be employed in major league baseball. Today it is not an uncommon practice to be labeled a racist if one either investigates racial differences in behavior or suggests that such differences might exist even while explicitly affirming that it is nevertheless morally repugnant to practice social discrimination on the basis of race. Andrew Young, the former United States Ambassador to the United Nations, added a new dimension of racism. A racist is a person who cannot empathize with members of another race. Such a subjective definition obviously makes it difficult to identify a racist. I would suspect that everybody to some degree, including Andrew Young, is a racist according to this definition. It is difficult, if not impossible, for many to understand how it feels to be a member of an ethnic group, like the Armenians and Jews, who were victims of genocide. How does it feel to know that at some other time in another place one would have been slaughtered simply because of his ethnic origins? I would also suspect that many ethnic minorities are insensitive to the phenomenological experiences associated with being a WASP (white Anglo-Saxon Protestant). A WASP friend of mine, raised in an ethnic neighborhood in New York City, bitterly com-

variables are not being ruled out as significant factors influencing athletic achievements. One can argue that basketball is a recreation that is particularly suited to the concrete playgrounds of the black ghettos. And the large number of black superstars in basketball has encouraged black youths to excel in this sport. But to acknowledge the influence of environmental factors in no way denies the important role genetic factors can play. The "either-or" orientation inevitably produces distortion and confusion; a complete account of any behavior must include both genetic and environmental variables.

The main point is that there may be racial differences in behavior and such differences may have a significant genetic component. Therefore for a *given* form of behavior it can be stated that one race outperforms or is superior to another. But there is no evidence to support the contention that one race is superior in all forms of behavior. Consequently it is factually wrong, and if one accepts a democratic ethic, morally repugnant, to employ the concept of racial superiority. And finally, the obvious point bears repeating that any known obtained racial difference in behavior represents a divergence between the two distributions. Thus for any given attribute of behavior, racial membership could not be used by itself as a selective index for predicting a specific level of performance.

An Appropriate Framework for Judging Research on Racial Differences

One way of viewing the controversy about racial differences in intelligence is to consider it as a dispute between two competing research programs (page 144)—one hypothesizing a genetic involvement, the other suggesting a purely environmental inter-

---

plained that as a child his schoolmates did not understand him. Unfortunately, the term racist today is widely employed as a weapon to intimidate political opponents. Because the term possesses so many different meanings, it is not clear what moral crime, if any, the victim of the accusation committed.

pretation. This approach would encourage the detachment of ethical issues from empirical ones. But there is no way to force a scientist to decouple political considerations from factual ones. As a result, within the scientific community the continuing debate about political implications of scientific evidence remains irresolvable simply because different rules for accepting evidence and drawing conclusions are employed. But the political implications of scientific evidence extend beyond the scientific community. In a political democracy the problems will be disposed of by political institutions and processes, not by the actions of scientists. The only reasonable expectation a scientist can hope for is to receive a fair hearing about his scientific interpretation and political position. From my vantage point I would argue that the social and moral issues are more effectively handled within a democratic system when they are distinguished from the scientific ones. In an attempt to demonstrate this view, consider the problem of racial differences in intelligence within the framework of competing research programs.

As previously noted, to actively deal with this issue one must accept the notion that the concepts of *intelligence* and *race* can be both meaningful and reliably measured. One can decide to reject either or both assumptions and thus reject the results of empirical studies that employ these concepts as presently measured. It is assumed that this scientifically conservative stance requires that one remain mute about the true relationship between race and intelligence. If, however, one accepts these measures, not necessarily as final ones but instead as reasonable indices of intelligence and race that will likely be improved upon in the future, then certain methodological precautions must be appreciated.

First, a major methodological booby trap must be recognized. One cannot naively assume that a critical experiment can be designed, the results of which will lead to the unequivocal conclusion that there is, or there is not, some genetic involvement in the obtained difference of approximately 15 points in the mean IQ of whites and blacks (Shuey, 1966). It has been previously argued (page 145) that even under ideal conditions, such as mature theories and precise experimental methods, crucial experiments are not possible. Data from experiments that are presumed to be critical of a theory can be either incorporated into the theory by ad hoc assumptions or rejected by ad hoc arguments that insist the study failed to meet the empirical specifications of the theory.[3]

In the case of the competing research programs postulating a genetic or purely environmental interpretation of black-white differences in intelligence, the ideal of a critical-type experiment is far removed from any reasonable approximation because of our ignorance about several crucial factors: a full understanding of possible environmental influences in IQ, a measure of an environment's level of intellectual stimulation, a satisfactory theory of intelligence, knowing precisely the genetic determinants of intelligence, and so on. As a result of a lack of sophistication the interpretations of any research finding are indecisive in regard to the fundamental issue that is being debated. If this be true, two questions immediately come to mind: "How can one make judgments about the validity of the competing theories?" and "What is the sense of doing such research if individual studies cannot yield unambiguous results?"

In regard to the first question, it does seem reasonable to assume that either the genetic-involvement or environmental-disadvantage theory is valid or, as some might prefer to state, has a greater verisimilitude. In order to make a decision in regard to the competing theories, different participants in the controversy have employed different criteria to support their judgments.

3. Jensen (1975) in his efforts to argue that genetic factors should be considered as a possible cause of some of the difference in IQ scores between whites and blacks points out the difficulty of proving a genetic link. He notes that there is no definitive proof that the mean difference between the heights of Pygmies and Watusis is genetic in origin. These two groups live in markedly different environments, consume different diets, and practice different social customs. The presumption is that genetic factors are involved because of the magnitude of the difference in the average height relative to the standard deviation within each group plus the fact that height is a physical trait with high heritability. But this presumption is not equivalent to "proof" because it would be possible to maintain that some unexplored environmental factor is responsible for the obtained difference.

The Box-Score Method. One procedure employed to evaluate competing formulations is the "box-score" method, named after the system used in sporting events, like baseball, to determine which team outperforms the other (e.g., scores more runs) and therefore is victorious. The box-score method applied to the controversy surrounding racial difference in IQ would involve listing all relevant studies and determining which position, the environmental disadvantage or genetic hypothesis, was favored by more studies. Even if it were possible to determine reliably whether a given study supported one of the two competing theories, the box-score method would have the grave defect of treating all studies as equally well designed and equally informative. Some studies throw more light upon a given question than do others and this difference cannot, and should not, be ignored. Some findings have been replicated while others have not. A comparison of positive results of competing research problems may reflect no more than the relative number of investigators committed to each position or to the intensity of their motivation. It would be a pathetic commentary on the science of psychology if truth were determined by the box-score method.[4]

The Fatal-Flaw Method. Another procedure, the opposite of the box-score method, can be described as the "fatal-flaw" orientation. Instead of considering all studies of equal weight, it rejects all investigations that fail to control all possible variables. That is, it demands that only those studies that are truly crucial be considered in judging competing formulations. An example of the fatal-flaw orientation is Leon Kamin's controversial *The Science and Politics of IQ,* which draws the conclusion that "there exists

4. It is a frankly embarrassing commentary on psychology to discuss the box-score method as a possible procedure for evaluating theoretical disputes. Fundamentally it appears so antithetical to the rational spirit of science, which demands an integrative analysis of all data. But the box-score method requires mention because psychologists do employ it. At papers and lectures I have heard psychologists support one theoretical position over another because the results of a majority of studies favor it. Textbooks frequently report box scores in tabular form, listing all relevant studies and the theoretical position each favors. The theory that has the most supportive data wins!

no data which would lead a prudent man to accept the hypothesis that IQ scores are in any degree heritable" (1974, p. 1). One reviewer argues that Kamin's conclusion that IQ differences have no genetic basis rests on a questionable strategy: "He evidently assembled a checklist of 'fatal flaws' and applied it to each study as an isolated event" (Scarr-Salapatek, 1976, p. 99). Because no experimental design is capable of controlling all possible variables that might be considered relevant by each of the competing theories, then it becomes possible by the fatal-flaw method to reject any empirical result by arguing it is a consequence of some uncontrolled variable. If the fatal-flaw method is applied to each competing research program, the conclusion will be encouraged that the theoretical issue at stake (Do human breeding populations differ in terms of their mean intelligence?) is not presently, or in the future, resolvable. However, if the fatal-flaw method is applied asymmetrically it becomes a convenient weapon to dismiss an opponent's research program.

Kamin argues that IQ tests have served as instruments to oppress the poor by attributing their economic deprivation to "fixed biological causes." Kamin's aim in writing his book (1974) was "not only to contribute to the scientific knowledge, but also to influence policy makers, and, perhaps, some scientists who do not recognize that their science and their policies are not clearly separable." This latter statement is ambiguous because it fails to distinguish between the belief that in regard to the IQ controversy politics and science have not been kept separate or that they cannot be kept separate. In any case, assuming a political stance encourages the use of the fatal-flaw method because it facilitates rejection of evidence that is perceived as contrary to one's political commitments.

The Historical Method. Although the box-score and fatal-flaw methods offer a definitive verdict, the verdict itself is suspect because of the limitations of the rational foundations of the methods. In contrast, the historical method of evaluating competing research programs does not offer a definitive rule by which one research program can be considered superior to another, but it does offer a rational procedure for reaching a judgment about the relative merits of competing formulations. The historical method (Lakatos, 1970a, 1970b), as applied to the specific issue of racial differences in IQ and the larger problem of the genetic and environmental components in intelligence test scores, would suggest that the competing formulations be analyzed with two trends in mind: progressive and degenerating (page 147). Progressive implies advancement in knowledge either in the form of predicting new discoveries, particularly of a novel nature, or in improving the deductive precision of the theoretical model. A degenerating course, in contrast, is characterized by a failure to yield new facts coupled with a proliferation of ad hoc assumptions for interpreting recalcitrant findings.[5]

The historical method itself is not necessarily committed to a specific or to a single criterion. What the method does imply is that whatever criterion is employed should be made explicit. It should be noted that even though the goals of theoretical precision and empirical breadth might point a research program in different directions the two objectives are not necessarily incompatible. Actually, theoretical precision can encourage the discovery of novel facts.

It is particularly important when employing the historical method as the basis for comparing competing research programs to critically assess proposed explanations of anomalous results. Although research programs have the potential to have their assumptions modified, or even to have new ones added, the theorist who is trying to incorporate recalcitrant data has an obligation to practice some restraints. Consider the previously mentioned study (Gross, 1967) that found a 17-point difference between the IQs of Brooklyn-born boys who were descendents of Ashkenazi and Sephardic Jews. The family environment of the two groups were carefully examined to discover the source of this discrepancy.

5. P. Urbach has employed Lakatos's frame of reference in evaluating competing genetic and environmental interpretations of intelligence. His article published in the *British Journal of the Philosophy of Science*, 1974, 25, 99–135, 235–59 is entitled "Progress and Degeneration in the IQ Debate."

Only one significant factor could be found—parental attitudes toward making money. Three times as many Sephardic mothers stated that they wanted their sons to be "wealthy" while twice as many Ashkenazi mothers said that earnings were "unimportant." Havighurst (1970) who accepts the very reasonable notion that the education of socially disadvantaged children would profit from the knowledge and the utilization of kinds of rewards and punishments that operate in minority subcultures, interprets the difference in the intelligence of the two groups of Jews as the consequence of differing parental attitudes toward making money. Although this hypothesis presently cannot be rejected, the question should be entertained as to whether similar environmental influences have been or can be demonstrated to produce such large IQ differences. It is absurdly simple to invent an environmental hypothesis to account for any difference in IQs between distinct social groups because they inevitably have different experiences. It should, however, be incumbent upon those who advance ad hoc conjectures to ask themselves: what evidence is available and what study can be done to support my speculation?

Social Policy and Empirical Finding

The epistemological principle under examination here is that facts and values are logically dissociated. Consequently if genetic differences were found between different breeding populations or ethnic groups the findings would have no *direct* implications for social policy.

This principle was ignored during the days of enforced segregation of black and white students in the public schools of many southern states. White supremacists, including some psychologists, argued that the obtained difference in mean IQ of whites and blacks was genetic in origin and therefore justified school segregation. Those who rebutted their position by arguing that the difference was environmental in origin fell into a dialectical trap. By implication their argument placed the issue of school segregation on the basis of race into the arena of fact when it properly belongs to the field of morality. Accepting a democratic ethic makes it morally repugnant to treat individuals differently solely on the basis of their racial or ethnic membership. All individuals in a democratic society, regardless of any physical differences, are entitled to be treated with an equality of concern. Those who in past decades argued that racial segregation was unjustified because the racial differences in IQ were due to environmental influences would be placed in an embarrassing position of endorsing segregation if it were later discovered that the difference had a genetic basis.

One could also argue against the views of the racial segregationist by pointing out a logical flaw in the argument. If a difference in IQ justifies segregation, then racial segregation is unjustified because the difference in IQ between the means of the races is less than the differences within races. Consequently, a strict adherence to IQ standards for admission into different schools would automatically destroy racial segregation. This is, however, a logical, not a moral, refutation of the segregationist's position.

Segregating students into special classes or schools need not be considered morally repugnant. It is one thing to assign a student to a remedial class because he does poorly on an academic aptitude test; it is quite another matter to force him to go to a special school because of his racial or ethnic heritage. The former in no way conflicts with the ethics of a social democracy because the individual is being treated the same as everybody else with low academic aptitudes. In addition, the segregation on the basis of aptitude is implemented for the welfare of the individual concerned although an unfortunate social stigma may be attached to his limitations. The important point is that such a child is not being forced to bear that stigma unfairly because of ethnic or racial considerations.[6]

6. There appears to be a profound psychological difference at least for the social observer, if not for the victim, between a person being maltreated because of his racial or religious background as compared to being abused because of some political transgression or quirk of fate. It seemed to have been morally more obnoxious for a black to be victimized politically in South Africa than in Idi Amin's Uganda. In the case of South Africa the

Psychological Aspects. If any possible difference in IQs between races has no logical implication for social policy why does
the issue have such an emotional impact? There are many reasons, too many to identify and discuss for our purposes. One that
has already been mentioned is that many people, scientists among
them, frequently from both extremes of the political spectrum, do
not recognize or cannot accept the logical separation of facts from
social policy. For them any difference in intelligence among races
or ethnic groups would encourage or justify differential treatment
of members of each group. Thus the question of racial differences
in intelligence is not a factual problem but a political issue and, as
such, generates much emotion.

If we shift from a logical to a psychological framework we
have to recognize that the behavioral attribute of intelligence cannot be viewed by many in the relatively detached manner that
physical and or other psychological characteristics are considered,
e.g., eye color, height, musical and clerical aptitudes, and athletic
abilities. It is psychologically easier to have a handicap of 15 in
golf than to have a handicap of 15 IQ points (although one golf
buff I know would gladly exchange IQ points for a reduction in
his golf handicap). For the individual who is a member of a racial
or ethnic group that scores lower on intelligence tests, the emotional reactions can be intense. The lower mean score carries a
stigma of inferiority, and when this is combined with inferior living standards including such vital factors as housing, medical
care, and educational facilities, an angry resentment, understand-
ably, becomes a common reaction. As long as one is operating
within a psychological framework, it should be realized that these
reactions of inferiority and animus are socially determined, not a
necessary by-product of racially linked genetic factors. Whether

---

suffering of the black results from something over which he has no control
while in the case of Uganda, assuming the victim was not a member of a
persecuted tribe, the punishment, even though unjustified, could in principle
have been avoided if the victim had behaved differently. Perhaps that is
why the genocide of the Armenians and European Jews appears to be more
of a heinous crime than government-inspired murders of political prisoners
even though the consequence for the victim is the same.

there is or is not a racially linked genetic factor in hereditary differences among humans, people with lower intelligence would be disgruntled if their living conditions were shockingly different from those with greater aptitude. There is no doubt that social problems are exacerbated when obvious cues associated with race and ethnic groups are involved, but the basic point is that social difficulties produced by racial differences in IQ scores are to some extent socially determined. In other words, the hierarchy of social prestige and rewards associated with IQ scores is not necessarily unmodifiable; it is amenable to change so that the diverse talents of different groups are recognized, esteemed, and rewarded. For example, if the discrepancy between the employment rates of black and white youth were minimized or eliminated, presumed differences in intelligence would probably not be as explosive an issue as it is today.

Because of individual differences we are all inferior, but we need not get upset by it. Einstein was an inferior violinist. William James wanted to be a painter but was convinced he lacked talent. Many distinguished professors are professors because they could not make it as concert pianists or professional athletes or standup comedians. Consider the popular sport of basketball. Many successful college players are unsuccessful in pursuing a professional career. Strictly speaking, most of them are probably inferior basketball players in comparison to those who succeed, and no doubt some of those who fail suffer from a sense of inferiority. And it may very well be that these feelings of inadequacy are more prevalent among white than black players. This speculation is suggested from the fact that 70 percent of basketball players in the elitist National Basketball Association are blacks, a proportion that far exceeds the 11 percent that blacks represent in the general population. Although there is no definitive proof that the greater probability of blacks to excel at basketball is genetically determined, the hypothesis nevertheless remains plausible. Such a hypothesis does not generate as much emotion as one that assumes a genetic base for racial differences in intelligence. But it should be recognized that if the observed racial difference in the proportion of professional-grade basketball players among blacks and whites is genetically determined, then a higher proportion of whites may suffer a sense of inferiority in regard to their basketball ability.

In sum, feelings of inferiority are an expression of the human condition. They can in principle be generated by genetic factors that are involved with behavioral differences among races and ethnic groups. Their destructive effects upon individuals can be minimized or eliminated by social engineering that values diversity and minimizes suffering. The major empirical point here is that in light of available evidence the formulation of genetic[7] hypotheses to account for some behavioral differences among races or ethnic groups is reasonable.

Some psychologists, and many laypersons, insist that genetically rooted differences in behavior are impossible. By assuming this stance they are accepting a factual statement as valid, e.g., all racial and ethnic groups have equal native intelligence. From this it follows that all racial and ethnic groups (e.g., blacks, Chicanos) should be proportionally represented in the professions and other positions demanding high intelligence. The absence of this proportional representation implies that some form of discrimination is operating. Since this discrimination is justified neither by the distribution of talent nor by democratic principles of fair treatment, some rectification of the unbalanced representation of minority groups[8] in prestigious positions should and must take

7. Interactionist is a more accurate term because genetic hypotheses that attempt to account for racial differences in behavior typically assume that environmental factors also can account for some of the difference (Jensen, 1977).

8. Minority status is not only dependent on the proportion a particular racial, ethnic, or sexual group represents in the total population, but also upon whether the group is underrepresented in the professions and political positions and appointments. Consequently, blacks, Chicanos, and American Indians are considered minorities in regard to admission policies for college and professional schools, whereas Jews are not. Orientals who tend to be overrepresented in medical schools and somewhat underrepresented in law schools are sometimes considered minorities and at other times not. Females, who strictly speaking, represent a majority of the population, are treated in affirmative action programs as members of a "minority."

place. In addition to this plea for social fairness, one can also argue that a balanced representation of racial and ethnic groups "is a basic requirement for a democratic republic. Security of person and property requires that each community have its share of lawyers, teachers, doctors, and professional experts" (Garcia, 1978).

One method of achieving balanced representation of "each community" is to employ an admission program into professional schools that will produce racial, ethnic, and sexual representation in different professions approximately proportional to their numbers in the population. Those in favor of such a plan frequently employ such terms as *goals* and *timetables* to indicate that some method that favorably weights minority membership should be employed to increase the representation of members of that group. The exact proportion, as well as the target date to achieve it, is somewhat elastic, but the purpose is clear that systems that do not encourage the admission of minority groups are to be changed to those that do. Some critics, as well as some defenders, of the proposal to have balanced representation have employed the blunter, more precise term *quota* to designate the goal of the proposed admission policy—an exact proportion of a certain minority must be admitted.

One procedure used to achieve balanced representation entitles members of the minority group to receive special consideration for admission by being permitted to meet standards lower than those for "majority" students. When this is done the problem of separating questions of facts from those of values becomes very subtle. For the most part values and facts have been conflated by both proponents and critics of affirmative action programs. Although policy questions associated with these programs will ultimately be answered by judicial, legislative, and administrative actions, psychologists can play a helpful role in making these political decisions. A useful starting point for describing this role will be a review and analysis of the well-publicized Bakke case.

The Bakke Case. Allen Bakke, a white applicant to the medical school of the University of California, Davis, was rejected both in 1973 and 1974 even though he would have been admitted on the strength of his qualifications if he were black. (Bakke scored in the 90th percentile in the medical college admission test while the mean of the admitted minority students was below the 50th percentile.) Sixteen of 100 places in the first-year class had been set aside for disadvantaged students. The term *disadvantaged* was not defined by economic criteria, it was based on race and ethnic background.

The California Supreme Court ruled that this special admission plan was unlawful since Bakke had been discriminated against because of his race, in violation of the constitutional guarantee of the Fourteenth Amendment that no state should "deny to any person within its jurisdiction the equal protection of the laws." It should be noted that this ruling was not against the special admission plan for minorities itself but was instead against the manner in which it was formulated. If minority status did not have a racial criterion the special admission policy would have been legal. If, for example, minority status was defined in terms of economic level, then the program would have been perceived by the court as constitutional. However, the university, in appealing the court's decision, noted that the entire purpose of their affirmative action program would be defeated. If an economic criterion was employed less affluent whites would be substituted for more affluent whites (thus creating a somewhat different moral and legal issue). As a result of defining disadvantaged status in economic terms, the University of California argued that significant minority representation of blacks in medical school education would not be achieved.

The United States Supreme Court, during 1978, in a set of split (5 to 4) and hair-splitting decisions ruled that Bakke was rejected from the medical school at the University of California, Davis, on unconstitutional grounds and insisted he be admitted into the next class. The court decided that setting aside a precise number of places for racial minorities is unacceptable. The Supreme Court of the United States, in these two decisions, agreed with the ruling of the California Supreme Court. A sharp area of disagreement occurred in the United States Supreme Court ruling that race could be considered as one of several factors in the university's admission policy, whereas the California Supreme Court had ruled that race could not be a selective factor. The five United States Supreme Court Justices did not agree as to how race should be used as a selective admission factor. Three different goals were mentioned in the various decisions: to redress past discriminations, to increase the number of minority physicians, and to attain a diverse student body.

My intent is not to get involved in the legal and political debate surrounding the rulings in the Bakke case, rather it is to disentangle ethical and empirical components from arguments about affirmative action programs. One of the central assumptions of many who defend affirmative action programs is that in order to redress past discriminations it becomes necessary to do away with "undemocratic" selection procedures that operate against members of minorities. The argument advanced is that some minority students, such as blacks, are disadvantaged in that they have not shared in the past benefits received by majority students. Consequently, the special admission policy, which allows race to be a selective factor, compensates for past inequalities and thereby establishes a truly fair competition among applicants.

An analogy of a foot race has been used to highlight the issues in special admission policies. Proponents of affirmative action argue that the use of aptitude tests operates as a handicap against blacks because the tests do not take into consideration the socially imposed disadvantages of blacks. Without a special admission policy the blacks would be starting in the competition to get into medical and other schools behind majority applicants. Because aptitude tests do not consider blacks' disadvantaged status they are biased and essentially undemocratic.

Three Interpretations of a Democratic Ethic as Applied to Test Bias. In an attempt to analyze the meaning of *test bias,* Hunter and Schmidt (1976) concluded that the meaning depends upon the ethical position one associates with democracy. A psychological test could be unbiased according to one ethical position but biased in reference to another. To demonstrate this, Hunt and Schmidt distinguish among three distinct ethical positions that would be supported by some faction as being consistent with democratic ethics. These three positions—*unqualified individualism, quotas, qualified individualism*—are useful for our analysis of the relationship between facts and values as raised in the Bakke case.

The ethical position, characterized as *unqualified individualism,* is the one that many associate with the traditional democratic value of judging individuals as individuals and not as members of any groups: racial, ethnic, religious, or sexual. Thus, admission into professional school or advancement to a better job should be determined by information that would be correlated with potential success. The persons selected would always be those with the highest predicted performance. According to this ethical position there are two ways in which an institution like a medical school or business organization could behave immorally. First, it may knowingly use an invalid predictor in preference to a valid one—appearance may be employed in preference to a score obtained on a valid aptitude test. Second, it may knowingly fail to employ all relevant knowledge for predicting success. For example, it may not use race, sex, or ethnic group membership when these distinctions have been demonstrated to be valid predictors of future performance in addition to other useful measures. Although many tend to resist the notion, in certain situations it may be possible to make a better prediction of future success knowing whether an applicant is black or white, or male or female. This possibility would have to be determined by empirical evidence.

The ethical position, described as the *quota system,* postulates that society should be divided up into certain well-defined groups, such as black, white, Chicano, etc., and that each group has a right to receive its fair share of society's rewards. There are many different ways that this system can be implemented both in terms of the manner in which society is to be sliced into different segments (race, sex, ethnic background, etc.) as well as what rewards are to be divided (e.g., governmental positions, admissions into colleges and professional schools, etc.). In terms of the former problem certain "minorities," such as blacks, women, and Chicanos, have been most vocal in demanding their rights, but it should be recognized that other minorities can and will argue that they have an equal claim to the rewards of society. Religious, sex, and age groups are but a few of the infinite number of segments into which society could be divided. These groups most probably will not be mutually exclusive, which creates problems as to how the overlapping memberships (e.g., black *and* female) will be dealt with when the system is implemented. In terms of the second problem, the division of social rewards among different groups, numerous alternatives are possible. Should the quota system be limited to governmental jobs? Elected positions? Corporations and private universities? Small businesses? Any kind of quota system would be confronted with innumerable problems, not least of which would be the opposition of groups who favor a quota system but believe that they are not properly represented. These problems, which represent serious and difficult issues, do not in any a priori manner invalidate a quota system as an ethical guide to social organization. One should recall that great difficulty was experienced, and much time was needed, in designing the variety of political procedures used in present-day democratic societies. If a quota system is deemed appropriate some acceptable arrangement can probably be developed.

Qualified individualism, in contrast to *unqualified individualism,* highlights an important ethical consideration. Should a person's race, religion, ethnic background, or sex enter into consideration for selection for a position even if it improves the prediction of success? Qualified individualism says "No"; unqualified individualism says "Yes." The justification for qualified individualism is that it is ethically abhorrent to deny a person his complete individuality even when knowledge of his group affiliations will increase the power to predict his or her behavior.

Let us consider two cases to highlight the distinction between unqualified and qualified individualism. Several decades ago it was common practice for departments of psychology to discriminate against women applicants to graduate school. In support of this policy the argument was advanced that women were poorer risks for obtaining a doctorate and pursuing a professional career with vigor because it was assumed that they would abandon their careers at the first chance of marriage and raising a family. If, in fact, women were poorer risks, it still would be immoral for a supporter of qualified individualism to select a male applicant with slightly less promising aptitude scores·than a female applicant even though the former would, considering all factors, possess a greater probability of completing his graduate education and vigorously pursuing a professional career. A proponent of unqualified individualism, while selecting the male applicant, could acknowledge that social forces, including prejudices, were responsible for making women poorer risks. He could nevertheless justify his selection by stating his only interest is in picking the best prospect.

Another example that is useful to consider is the high school track coach who must choose between a white or black sprinter who are running equally well. The coach must consider not only their present performance but also their future potential because they have yet to achieve their best times. Because blacks have a greater probability of excelling in the sprints, it is common practice among high school coaches to select blacks for sprinters and encourage white runners to specialize in longer distances. This example again illustrates the basic ethical conflict between advocates of unqualified and qualified individualism, with the former opting for the black and the latter being unable to make any decision in the absence of further information.

The three positions described do not exhaust all possible ethical stands concerning the appropriate moral treatment of members of different social groups. However they are sufficient to illustrate some of the methodological issues associated with ethical decisions. First of all, it must be recognized that these three ethical positions can be justified in their own right as moral imperatives, or they can be defended in terms of some higher moral commitment. In the case of the former each of the three positions can be adopted because of its intrinsic ethical righteousness that provides a moral authority of its own. Or each can be defended as a moral derivative of a specific abstract ethical principle. For example, a person who believes that the guiding moral principle in social organization should be the achievement of the greatest good for the greatest number of citizens could reach the logical conclusion that selecting individuals in the most effective manner possible would be consistent with his fundamental conviction. A person who adopted the quota system might arrive at his position by a commitment to the ethical concept of social fairness: members of a socially identifiable group should not perceive themselves as deprived or inferior. The position of qualified individualism, it could be argued, is derived logically from a more abstract democratic commitment to social equality *independent* of race, religion, ethnic group, or sex.

If any one of these three positions is accepted as an ethical imperative, it becomes impervious to any rational analysis that could yield a verdict against it. Hunter and Schmidt (1976), who bring to bear statistical analyses in their methodological dissection of ethical stands associated with *test bias,* conclude that the disputes among the different positions cannot be "objectively resolved." To support their conclusion they admit that they were unable to reach agreement about what ethical position should be adopted: "Each person must choose as he sees fit."

If, however, the three orientations are perceived neither as ethical imperatives nor as logical implications from competing moral principles, but instead as positions derivable from an agreed-upon higher value (such as an acceptance of a democratic ethic), then objective procedures *might* be useful in deciding which position should be adopted. The first question that should be posed is whether only one of the three positions (unqualified individualism, quotas, or qualified individualism) is logically derivable from a commonly accepted higher moral principle. For example, according to the principle that fairness or justice is the ultimate moral value, and assuming these concepts are clear, it might be demonstrated logically that one of the three ethical positions discussed is fairer or more just than the others. Therefore, a controversy among three individuals, each favoring a different ethical stand, could be resolved by their adopting a higher moral value that is demonstrated to be logically consistent with one of the three competing ethical stands.

Another possibility for rationally resolving an ethical conflict would be to answer an empirical question that is embedded in the controversy. For example, two individuals might both favor the general ethic that society should be organized around the utilitarian principle of the greatest good for the greatest number of people, but nevertheless disagree as to whether unqualified individualism or the quota system best meets these specifications. For them there is no logical resolution of their disagreement—only an empirical one. The proponent of unqualified individualism would argue that his position will produce the most talented person for each position, and therefore society will be most effectively served. In the case of medical service the patient will receive the best possible care because the physicians will be the most competent that society can provide. The advocate of quotas might question these assumptions by denying that the medical competence of the practicing physician will be different if quotas are employed. He might even advance the argument that medical service would actually be improved by instituting a quota system. Psychotherapy for some minority members may be more effective when carried out by therapists of the same ethnic group. Consequently, if members of minority groups are underrepresented in psychiatry and clinical psychology, then the effectiveness of such treatment for minority members would be less than if quotas were employed.

If evidence were obtained on the quality of medical practitioners admitted on the basis of a quota system for minorities, and the effectiveness of psychotherapy when the therapist shares minority status with his patient was demonstrated, then it could be decided which principle, unqualified individualism or quotas, yields the greatest utility. By agreeing upon the basic moral commitment, empirical evidence can demonstrate which subsidiary moral beliefs produce consequences that are in line with the values of the ethical imperative. In the present example, which only touches upon a few of many complex empirical issues, the results need not favor only one of the two competing ethical positions.

For example, if it were discovered that students who are admitted on the basis of minority status with lower aptitude scores become inferior surgeons but better psychotherapists, then the advocates of unqualified individualism and quotas, who share the common moral imperative of utilitarianism, would be forced to adjust their position in light of the evidence. Both would favor a quota system for potential psychiatrists but not for potential surgeons.

Psychology and Values: Psychological Considerations

7

1. The claim that a moral basis for behavior can be derived from empirical evidence is examined. The argument is made that when psychologists attempt to establish an ethical imperative on the basis of psychological data they are essentially offering themselves, or the discipline of psychology, as a moral authority. The conclusion is drawn that psychology is unable to offer an unqualified authority upon which to base an ethical system to govern human behavior.

2. Practical considerations demand that society develop an effective moral code. The major point here is that ethical beliefs can be founded on, but not determined by, psychology. Psychology can provide information about the empirical consequences of a social policy but cannot serve as an authority for its adoption or rejection. For that, political processes are needed.

3. Psychology can play a useful social role in evaluating the empirical consequences of different social policies thereby helping political institutions to make appropriate decisions. To do this effectively psychologists must function as detached scientists and not involved advocates.

HUMAN BEHAVIOR AS A SOURCE
OF MORAL ABSOLUTES

By accepting the ethical principle that the status of truth is denied to moral absolutes, one can easily fall victim to the belief that all moral choices are ultimately arbitrary, that is, capricious or without reason. Such a conclusion is at odds with our contention that factual evidence is relevant to choices among competing social programs (e.g., negative income tax versus direct welfare payments) that share common ethical goals (e.g., the elimination of suffering and the encouragement of economic independence). Admittedly, the kind of research that would be required to evaluate the empirical consequences of a negative income tax versus direct welfare payments would be exceedingly complex, and no doubt debate would rage about the correct interpretation of any results. In addition, opinions would differ as to whether each program was fairly represented by the experimental operations employed as well as to the appropriateness of the criteria used to measure "suffering" and "economic independence." However difficult such research may be, and however many empirical issues may remain unresolved, the important point is that research can illuminate some of the empirical consequences of each program and thereby provide information concerning which program comes closer to desired ethical outcomes. In essence then, relevant facts *can* determine moral choices when subsidiary moral principles are involved (e.g., "poor people should be given minimal financial assistance while being motivated to improve their plight" versus "the basic economic needs of all persons should be satisfied") and when agreement prevails about moral absolutes (e.g., the elimination of suffering and the encouragement of economic independence).

The conclusion that factual evidence is relevant to certain moral choices might encourage one to reconsider the premise that moral absolutes cannot be deduced from or confirmed by empirical evidence. Is it not possible that some set of facts could justify a standard of morality by which ethical imperatives could be judged? The argument can be advanced that an empirically based universal standard of morality has not been found because we have been misguided in our search. We have sought a universal standard of morality in some divine authority or governmental decree whereas it actually resides within human behavior itself. By examining human behavior it should be possible to extract an empirically based standard of morality. Consider this possibility in relation to the problem of moral development.

Without becoming committed to any particular interpretation of moral development (e.g., Kohlberg, 1973) or to any assumption concerning the relationship between moral thought and moral action, it appears reasonable, in light of available evidence, to conclude that developmental differences can be used to evaluate moral beliefs and behavior. It should be possible to construct a test of morality similar in design to that of the intelligence test. An individual's moral quotient could be determined in a fashion analagous to his intelligence quotient. In addition to serving as a measure of a person's intelligence, an intelligence test can also serve as a measure of a problem's difficulty. A higher mental age is required to solve the problem "In what way are a tree and a fly alike?" than the problem "In what way are a pear and a peach alike?" Therefore the first problem is more difficult than the second. In the same manner ethical principles can be evaluated by the level of development that is required for their adoption. In essence, the suggestion is being offered that the age standard method that Binet applied to the measurement of intelligence can also be employed to measure morality. This suggestion raises the question of whether the moral age required to comprehend an ethical imperative cannot provide the empirical basis for favoring one ethical imperative over another. For example, the moral imperative of "Do unto others as you would have them do unto you" demands a higher level of moral development than does the moral commitment of "Obey the law." Does it not follow that the former principle is superior to the latter? If it is agreed that the first is better than the second, we would have an empirical base to justify an ethical imperative.

In order to pinpoint the crucial epistemological issue of whether a factual basis can be discovered for ethical imperatives, I will assume, for the moment, that it would be possible to develop a scale of moral development that would transcend cultural differences. It would therefore be possible to evaluate different societies, as well as religions, in terms of the level of moral development they have achieved and to which they aspire. According to one line of reasoning then I have in my possession psychological facts that demonstrate that some moral imperatives are superior to others.

Although it is true that a scale of moral development could be employed to evaluate ethical imperatives in terms of their "maturity," it does not necessarily follow that the more mature principle is *better* than the less mature one. For example, in evaluating intellectual functioning it is one thing to conclude that formulating a theory of relativity requires more intelligence than tuning a piano or repairing a defective plumbing system, but is quite another thing to say that the former is better for society than are the latter. Many people believe that highly developed intellectual functioning has been a curse on society, producing more harm than good. Humankind would be happier, they feel, if high level brainpower had less influence in our society, e.g., the ordeal of Vietnam may have been avoided if academics had not been so influential in government. In sum, more intellect does not mean *better* intellect.

A similar argument can be advanced against the position that the level of moral development is a valid indicator of moral supremacy. No matter how mature one must be to behave according to the golden rule, *"Do unto others as you would have them do unto you,"* it does not follow that such an ethical principle is intrinsically better than the less mature moral exhortation, *"An eye for an eye, and a tooth for a tooth."* Good and bad, or better and worse, are rock-bottom decisions; no amount of facts can dictate that the former moral principle is intrinsically better than the latter.

The rejection of moral development as the ultimate litmus test for moral imperatives does not mean that a standard of moral development cannot be used in analyzing ethical controversies. The conflict between the Western democracies and Nazi Germany involved fundamental moral differences that made the conflagration of World War II unavoidable. One could argue, properly, I believe, that the collision was not simply an expression of a cultural relativism that produced different moral codes, which in the final analysis were simply an expression of arbitrary moral choices. The Nazi's morality can be described in psychological terms as pathological and immature, a description that can justify its rejection. But such a rejection is not based upon a compelling logic that demands its rejection in the same sense that one rejects the conclusion that two plus two are five.

Employing moral development as a frame of reference for evaluating ethical imperatives is similar to Maslow's efforts to discover "moral principles common to the entire human species, which can be scientifically confirmed" (Goble, 1971, p. 91). Instead of using moral development as a criterion for judging ethical imperatives, Maslow resorts to his own theory of motivation, which postulates a hierarchy of inborn needs the highest of which is the need for self-actualization.[1]

Maslow suggests that by examining self-actualizing people it becomes possible to discover a scientifically valid ethical system. His rationale for this argument is that self-actualizing individuals are the healthiest, having achieved the highest level of human potential:

> You can find the values by which mankind must live, and for which man has always sought, by digging into the best people in depth. I believe . . . that I can find ultimate values which are right for mankind by observing the best of mankind. . . . If under the best conditions and in the best specimens I simply stand aside and describe in a scientific way what these human values are, I find values that are the old values of truth, goodness, and beauty and some additional ones as well—for instance, gaiety, justice, and joy (1961, pp. 5–6).

---

1. See pages 205–209 for a discussion of self-actualization in the context of intuitive knowing as a form of understanding.

The link between the empirical evidence and the "right" set of values is not as direct as some would like to believe. In fact, it is suggested that Maslow's argument represents a simple tautology. Maslow selects self-actualizers who share his own personal value system. He labels them as the "best," and therefore their ethical commitments—his own, basically—become the "ultimate values which are right for mankind."

As noted previously (page 207), the concept of self-actualization is impregnated with value judgments. According to Plato, people would realize their potentialities by conforming to the ideal model of the human soul. Thomas Aquinas suggested that human fulfillment could be secured by the practice of virtue and by allegiance to the church and its sacraments. Johann Fichte (1762–1814), a German idealist, provides an interesting and instructive example of the potentials of a concept such as self-actualization. While retaining the concept of self-realization Fichte radically changed its meaning. Initially self-realization was to be achieved by the acceptance of an austere moral code, then by accepting the will of God, and finally by identifying with the will of German nationalism, the latter formulation anticipating the extreme national chauvinism of Nazism. And today, the Red Brigade justifies its ruthless terrorism (e.g., "Kill a cop and go home for dinner") by appealing to the need for self-fulfillment. Reforming present states, they argue, either in the direction of liberal capitalism or democratic socialism, will not be sufficient for developing a state dedicated to personal self-realization. Present states must be abolished, destroyed before that goal can be achieved (Sheehan, 1979).

This analysis suggests that Maslow deluded himself into believing that his proposed ethical system was demanded by psychological facts in contrast to other systems that depend on some outside authority such as the church or the state. In truth, he was only substituting the authority of the psychologist—in this case, himself—for that of God or government. The difficulty with Maslow's position, it must be underlined, is not with the values Maslow chose to adopt, because psychologists, like other people, are entitled to choose values they consider best. The fault is with the manner in which Maslow chose to justify his value system. By insisting that his value system is demanded by psychological facts and is a consequence of a purely scientific analysis, Maslow misled himself as well as his audience.

What should be realized is that when psychologists attempt to support a moral position by empirical evidence, they really are offering themselves, or the discipline of psychology, as a moral authority. If one is inclined to believe in God, it becomes easy to accept God as a source of moral authority. There is no confusion as to whether God has the "right" to speak with authority. Such is not the case for the psychologist, no matter how eminently clever he may be in persuading the public that his proposed set of ethical imperatives emerge from psychological evidence, the truth of the matter is that his ethics express his own personal qualified he may feel to play the same role. Regardless of how preference. Psychologists and other behavior scientists will never agree as to what constitutes a valid set of ethical imperatives simply because of the logical impossibility of crossing the gap between facts and values.

If this analysis is correct, it becomes incumbent upon behavior scientists to speak to the public about moral issues with great care and a strong sense of responsibility. Many years ago Kurt Lewin advised Jewish parents to provide their children with cultural and religious training so that they could effectively adjust to their Jewishness and cope with any expression of anti-Semitism that they might encounter. For many, this seemed to be a reasonable recommendation especially when empirical evidence was offered to support it. But a closer analysis suggests that Lewin should have been more precise in his recommendation, particularly because he was expressing his own personal values. Even accepting the evidence, which some would not, that religiously trained Jewish children are better adjusted than those who are not, one should make a distinction between the psychological recommendation that "Jewish children *ought* to receive religious training" and "Jewish children *should* receive religious training *if* personal adjustment is considered a more important value than one's moral view of organized religion." The significant point is that psychologists must be careful not to use the reputation of their profession for the purpose of advocating their own personal values. It would also be helpful if the public could feel confident that when psychologists discuss ethical problems they would abide by rigorous standards of accuracy in reporting relevant empirical findings. The public has, with reason, become skeptical about claims of psychologists who argue for the adoption of particular value systems. And the more psychologists persist in these attempts the more cynical society will become about the entire enterprise of psychology.

PRACTICAL AND CRITICAL ETHICS

The preceding discussion of psychology and values can be faulted for not coming to grips with the most important problem of ethics: providing guidance to help individuals act properly. Without a moral code to steer people in the right direction, society will inevitably collapse under the pressures of the conflicting needs, desires, and passions of its members. One can also suggest that the absence of an ethical commitment is destructive to the individual himself, regardless of the demands of society. Some psychologists (e.g., Frank, 1972; Maslow, 1964) have argued that valuelessness—the lack of a sense of what is right and wrong, what is desirable and undesirable—represents the major psychological disturbance of our time. At one extreme, it generates a social malaise that alienates individuals from their society while at the other extreme it creates an irrational violence that seeks to destroy the entire society. Without purpose individuals become demoralized and society drifts aimlessly, incapable of coping effectively with its current problems while being unable to plan for its future.

My concern here is not with the empirical justification of the above generalizations but rather to clarify the distinction between practical and critical ethics. Great moral philosophers from Aristotle on considered the problems of ethics to be of a practical concern because they were concerned with distinguishing right from wrong. Contemporary moral philosophers, particularly British and North American, have assumed a detached critical stance of concern not with identifying right from wrong but instead with analyzing the nature of moral arguments. This critical approach has led to the conclusion that science in general, and psychology in particular, can offer no unqualified authority upon which to base an ethical system. If this critical conclusion is combined with the reasonable acknowledgment that ethical commitments profoundly influence individual behavior and the functioning of an entire society, then psychologists are caught on the horns of a disturbing dilemma; ethical commitments are psychologically important, but moral truth is alien to the science of psychology.

In the face of such a dilemma what can the psychologist do? One possibility is that he can encourage individuals to adopt ethical imperatives on the basis of faith in sources outside of psychology. Such an action, it must be recognized, is consistent with the critical conclusion but is certainly not demanded by it. Because psychology cannot offer valid ethical imperatives and yet moral guidance is needed, it does not logically follow that psychologists should encourage individuals to seek values through religious faith or political fervor. Another possibility, on pragmatic grounds, is to renounce the critical conclusion that psychology cannot recommend the ethical imperatives that humanity needs; any critical conclusion, no matter how impeccable the logic may be, that counters the fundamental needs of humans and their society must be rejected. An additional alternative is to finesse the disturbing dilemma by failing to recognize it. By uncritically insisting that psychology offers special insights into moral truth, one can serve the public interest while simultaneously enhancing one's own sense of social responsibility and self-righteousness.

Those who demand intellectual rigorousness need not abandon the field of ethics to those who do not. But they do have to contemplate the disturbing thought that their methodological stance creates a moral vacuum that could be employed to justify even nihilism. Since no moral imperative is valid all moral positions can be denied. Once this conclusion is accepted an opening wedge is created, which might lead to the stark conclu-

sion that prevailing political institutions are unjustified and therefore should be destroyed. Unfortunately, one need only point to
the spread of violence and destructiveness of the past decades,
and the nihilistic rationalizations of it, to justify one's worst fears
about possible side-effects that are created when science fails to
offer any ethical code to govern human behavior.

How can this dreary consequence of the denial of the validity
of moral principles be coped with? As noted, one could agree
with the epistemological conclusions but for pragmatic reasons
decide not to abide by it. The world does not offer any ultimate
morality but it needs one, and therefore it must be created by
some act of faith in religion, political philosophy, or psychology.
A more realistic choice, and intellectually more justified, is to
recognize that moral imperatives are not to be found in nature;
our demands for the ultimate values of life must go unheeded.
For some, the ethical plight of humanity demonstrates that life is
absurd; for others, it highlights the animalistic origins of homo
sapiens. In either case, there is no escape from this moral predicament; we can only hope to adjust to it. If one takes seriously
the consequences of this critical analysis, then self-deception is
not a viable alternative; a rational solution remains the only
possibility.

The Role of Empirical Evidence in Moral Decisions

If there is no authority for moral values, and the moral values influence the behavior of individuals and the functioning of society,
then humans must create their own values if they wish to control
their own destiny. It is not that the facts of psychology *demand*
that individuals adopt a set of values and certainly not that they
adopt a specific ethical system. But it should be recognized that
individual and social behavior are different when moral codes are
operating than when they are not. For example, psychopathic
personalities without a concept of justice, cheat, deceive, and in
general exploit their fellow humans. In sharp contrast are individuals whose behavior is guided by moral principles. Similarly, the

social effects of economic poverty depend upon the ethical values of its victims. The destructive consequences are less when the commitments to moral standards are strong (Lewis, 1966).

The empirical consequences of moral beliefs do not provide any simple objective index of their acceptability. But such information can be important to individuals for approving or rejecting them. In some cases, the empirical consequences of certain moral principles encourages their universal adoption. Toilet training, although not generally recognized, poses a moral issue. Ought parents toilet train their children? Should not the parent have the freedom to decide whether a child should control his biological functioning? Should not the child have the final say? These issues are not debated simply because rejecting toilet training as a moral responsibility produces consequences that are aversive to society, parents, and children themselves. As a consequence, toilet training is acceptable not because it is morally right or valid but instead because it produces a state of affairs, both individually and socially, that is more desirable than the condition that would result from failing to employ it.

In contrast, capital punishment, even assuming the available evidence about empirical consequences were clear, inevitably generates much debate and disagreement about its moral justification. There is little likelihood that uncontroversial evidence portraying its empirical consequences would generate universal agreement about its desirability as a social policy. If it were demonstrated that capital punishment deterred crimes such as murder (e.g., among "lifers" in prison or burglars), some would nevertheless oppose it because they argue that it erodes human compassion. Essentially, the argument would be that a lack of compassion toward others exerts a more deleterious effect on society than the total number of murders committed by "lifers" and burglars. Evidence, of course, could be obtained on these presumed deleterious side-effects, and such data may prove effective in changing attitudes toward capital punishment. But because there is no way of achieving a universally agreed upon trade-off function between the number of murders prevented and the deleterious side-effects of capital punishment, it would be naive to expect anything approaching a unanimous decision as to whether capital punishment should be adopted as a social policy. And it should also be recognized that new conditions could be created that would encourage many to change their positions. For example, many who had considered capital punishment to be morally repugnant changed their minds as a result of the rash of hijackings designed to trade hostages for imprisoned hijackers. Their reasoning is that capital punishment for terrorists would be effective in reducing hijacking and the concomitant woundings and killings of innocent hostages because hijacking for the purpose of freeing imprisoned terrorists would be unwarranted.

The major point here is that ethical beliefs can be founded on but not determined by psychology. Psychologists can provide information about the empirical consequences of a given social policy (e.g., capital punishment) but cannot serve as an authority for its adoption or rejection. In other words, the information psychology provides can help a person decide what policy to support but cannot demand which policy to support. The same empirical outcome could encourage one person to favor capital punishment and another person to oppose it. This analysis has two important implications.

First, in the absence of a supreme moral authority to justify ethical imperatives, difference of opinion will surely reign about what is right and wrong, and/or good and bad. If freedom of discussion prevails many general ethical systems and specific moral positions will be advanced. The former will include philosophical positions enunciating different ethical ideals (e.g., goodness, happiness, pleasure, utility, justice, individual self-realization, fairness, elimination of individual suffering) while the latter will involve specific moral stands about social policies (e.g., governmental support of abortion, affirmative action, building of a neutron bomb). This diversity of moral commitments appears inevitable as long as individuals are free to choose, and probably is inevitable even if they are not. In addition, it should be noted again that an individual's or an entire society's commitment to one system or position should not be viewed as permanent because new evidence may encourage a change of attitude.

Second, a rational resolution of basic differences in ethical principles and moral positions becomes possible. To achieve this goal one has to abandon the ideal of discovering an unambiguous answer to a moral conflict that will be accepted by all. If one limits the meaning of *rational* to the development of reasonable procedures that can be employed to make choices between competing social policies that express fundamental moral principles, then rational resolutions of moral conflicts are possible.

The entire American political system, including the executive, legislative and judicial branches, provides rational procedures to resolve ethical disputes. Sometimes arguments arise as to whether the rational procedures are being followed as is the case when one branch of government is accused of assuming the powers of another. But for the most part, the entire system has usually been able to solve its internal procedural problems and has provided a means of resolving ethical disputes such as that of segregation. The one notable exception is the moral issue of slavery, which required the Civil War for its resolution.

Some would argue (Roche, 1968) that the issue of slavery had to be resolved by war because it was solely a moral issue and therefore not strictly a juridical problem. Such a position is difficult to understand because a juridical issue was involved in the defining of the black slave as a "person" or "property." According to the Fifth Amendment no person "shall be deprived of life, liberty, or property without due process of law." If the black slave was property then slave-owners could not be deprived of their wealth. If the black slave was a person then he could not be deprived of his "life" and "liberty" and therefore could not remain as a slave.

In principle, the question of slavery could have been solved by political processes. This was prevented because commitments to moral positions on the slavery question were stronger than those related to maintaining the integrity of the federal government. In contrast, segregation, a significant moral issue, was resolved without war by the greater willingness of the population to abide by governmental decrees in 1954 than in 1861.

Political processes then can be considered as mechanisms for resolving moral controversies although it must be recognized that the moral position adopted by the society is not considered a moral imperative either in the sense that it is valid or that individuals must believe in it. The only demand is that individuals abide by it. At the same time one has the right to employ appropriate political procedures to overturn the moral decision that the political processes have generated. No moral decision is protected from change or ultimate rejection. For example, rulings of the Supreme Court have been rejected by subsequent rulings, congressional laws, and amendments to the Constitution.

What can the psychologist contribute to the resolution of moral conflicts in the political arena? My belief is that the contributions can be both substantial and helpful as long as psychologists avoid conflict of interests between their ideological commitments and scientific responsibilities. Obviously, psychologists, like everyone else, have political beliefs and ethical commitments. It would be naive to believe that they do not, and unfair to insist that they should not. The significant problem is whether their ideological positions can and should be kept separate from their scientific activities.

It seems quite clear that in some cases psychological evidence can be insulated from the influence of ideological commitments. One example of this is the actions of a psychologist (T. S. Kendler) who became involved in the legal issue resulting from the passage of a statute in Hawaii in 1943 that prohibited the study of foreign languages (other than English) before a child reached the age of ten or completed the fourth grade. The law also prohibited the teaching of a foreign language to a child under fifteen years of age who received a below-average grade in English composition. This act was based on the legislative finding that "the study and persistent use of foreign languages by children of average intelligence in their . . . early years definitely detract from their ability to understand and assimilate their normal studies in the English language . . . may and do, in many cases, cause serious emotional disturbances, conflicts and maladjustments" (T. S. Kendler, 1950, p. 505). The legal justification of the statute was that it sought to improve the education of the children and protect their welfare.

This law was considered by some to be directed against the efforts of ethnic groups, such as the Japanese, to maintain their cultural heritage by teaching their children the language and traditions of their ancestors. The law also threatened some forms of religious training that depended on knowledge of another language such as Hebrew or Latin. The Commission on Law and Socal Action of the American Jewish Congress decided to file a brief in the United States Supreme Court questioning the constitutionality of the Hawaiian statute and requested assistance from Tracy Kendler, then in their employ, to obtain information relevant to the presumed deleterious effects of learning and using a second language.

A review of the literature revealed several studies that were inconsistent with the legislative findings of the deleterious effects of second-language learning. Schiller (1934) found that Jewish children from homes in which Yiddish was the primary language performed on English verbal tests as well as did Jewish children from homes in which English was predominant. Symonds (1924) found the Chinese students were not harmed by attendance at foreign language schools. It was also pointed out that a study (Spoerl, 1943) that reported a superior adjustment of monoglot college students as compared to bilingual students need not be interpreted as demonstrating the detrimental effects of bilingualism; a more reasonable interpretation is that bilingualism and the greater degree of maladjustment are both consequences of environmental factors associated with second-generation American status. Thus the conclusion was drawn that the legislative findings that bilingualism produced maladjustment and educational retardation were empirically unfounded.

A cynic might very well question whether the above example demonstrates the possibility of separating ideological commitments from scientific efforts. After all, the psychologist in this example was merely doing the bidding of the American Jewish Congress who, because of their own interests, was concerned only with data that were opposed to the findings of the Hawaiian legislature. But this example was deliberately selected to make clear the scientific responsibilities of a psychologist who provides evidence relevant to social policy. Certainly it is legitimate for an organization such as an American Jewish Congress to defend its own social and political interests. In doing so, it possesses a clear right to hire scientists to provide information that can be used in its legal, political, and social activities. It is also legitimate for a scientist to accept a position in an organization that advocates certain social policies because no necessary conflict of interest *need* arise. If the organization insists that the scientist provide evidence that is not scientifically justified, then an obvious conflict would be created that would make it impossible for a scientist to maintain her integrity. But in this particular case the scientist could make a judgment, and her opinion could be exposed to the scrutiny of other scientists, as to whether the presumed deleterious effects of bilingualism were factually justified. Admittedly, the issue could be clarified by additional research that would isolate the important variables and yield more precise conclusions. But it is not incumbent on an organization, such as the American Jewish Congress, that espouses particular social policies to solve complex psychological problems. Nor is a psychologist working in their employ required to achieve a complete understanding of the empirical issues before drawing any scientific conclusion. The fundamental demand is that in evaluating the empirical issue a psychologist should not compromise her scientific standards. When a psychologist reports data to a court or a legislative hearing, she has the obligation to society, as well as a responsibility to her profession, not to offer testimony of a dubious scientific value.

In contrast one can consider the testimony of social scientists in the famous *Brown* v. *Board of Education* case in which the Supreme Court ruled that segregating students on the basis of race was unconstitutional. One bit of evidence offered was a survey of opinions of anthropologists, sociologists, and psychologists (Deutscher & Chein, 1948) as to the psychological consequences of enforced segregation. A large majority (90 percent) of those who responded to the poll believed that enforced segregation had a detrimental effect on black children even in cases where the educational facilities provided were equal to those provided white children. A slightly smaller percentage (83 percent) believed that school segregation had detrimental effects on white children.

Several problems are raised by such testimony. One is whether any evidence, empirical findings or expert testimony, is required. Some persons would consider that the problem of segregation is primarily an ethical issue, and therefore psychological data are not centrally relevant. This position argues that the basic assumption of a democratic society is that all members of society should be treated equally. Segregation obviously implies unequal treatment, which is immoral regardless of any empirical evidence.

Although this position is attractive in its simplicity and ethical sensitivity, it is unrealistic. First, segregation, in spite of the fact that the United States is a "democratic" society, was condoned by the Supreme Court with its "separate but equal" doctrine. Second, since the time of Louis Brandeis, who included social and economic data in his brief to defend the Oregon ten-hour per day work law for women, social science evidence has influenced judicial decision (T. S. Kendler, 1950). If the "separate but equal" doctrine were to be challenged it would appear strategic to offer data that would contradict its major assumption.

Once the argument shifts from the level of ethical imperatives to that of the empirical consequences of particular laws, one is forced to accept the verdict of the empirical evidence. If later evidence contradicts the initial data, it becomes incumbent upon those who justified the original policy to reverse their policy recommendations. To be specific, suppose that at some future time American social scientists change their political attitudes from their present "liberal" stance to a more "conservative" or "reactionary" position, or that the refractoriness of the problems of interracial tensions encourages them to respond to a new survey in support of the position that school segregation need not have detrimental psychological or social consequences. Such data would certainly be rejected as biased by those who initially offered survey data to demonstrate the harmful effects of school segregation. But can it not be argued that the original survey was biased because the results could have been influenced by the political and ethical commitments of social scientists? Could one have any

confidence in the conclusion that their responses to the questions
of the survey were independent of their political desires? Such an
accusation could be rebutted by arguing that it would have been
easy, as I suspect it would, to obtain empirical evidence that
school segregation exerted harmful effects, both to the education
of the children and to their personal and social adjustment. But
such a rebuttal essentially rebukes those who offer the results of
the survey. Why offer dubious evidence when rigorous scientific
standards could have been met. Is it not the responsibility of the
scientist to offer unbiased evidence? If he cannot he should re-
frain from testifying. If psychology is to play a significant role in
evaluating the empirical consequences of different social policies,
and thereby assist political institutions in executing their responsibilities, then its evidence must be trusted. Unless that confidence
is earned it will not be forthcoming, and the potential value of
psychology to society will have been lost.

Richard C. Atkinson, a psychologist who was recently Director of the National Science Foundation, strongly believes that
confidence is lacking in psychology's ability to offer unbiased scientific evidence. In an address to the American Psychological Association, he notes that:

> there are many reasons behind this country's current negative atti-
> tude toward the social sciences. But I want to emphasize that we,
> as social scientists, have contributed to this state of affairs. We
> have done so by not being careful enough in drawing a sharp dis-
> tinction between our role of scientists versus another role—that of
> political advocate and policy-maker. The psychologist's job as a
> scientist is to search for data, principles, and laws that enlarge
> our understanding of psychological phenomena. But too often, in
> reporting research findings, we become advocates for a particular
> public policy. There is no reason why psychologists should not
> advocate political viewpoints, but they should advocate them only
> as individual citizens. The psychologist's role as a scientist is to
> set forth the facts, and to set forth those facts in as value free a
> fashion as possible. It is the job of the citizens of this country and
> their elected representatives to use those facts in making policy
> decisions. Too often I have witnessed psychologists, speaking on
> education, child rearing, social institutions, and mental health,
> using what they claim is research evidence as a disguise for ad-

vocating a particular public policy. Psychologists and social scientists, more so than other scientists, need to carefully distinguish between providing scientific data and making policy. If a psychologist is fascinated by political power and the ability to shape public policy, he or she should run for elective office and not disguise political efforts by cloaking them in the framework of psychological research. I recognize that it is difficult, if not impossible, to present scientific findings in a value-free fashion. But every effort must be made to do so. Otherwise psychology will come to be regarded as a social force rather than a scientific discipline. If that should occur, psychology's potential for helping to solve society's problems will be lost.

Let me add a proviso to these remarks. Obviously psychologists must be prepared to offer their best judgment on policy issues, even when that judgment is based on data and theory of questionable validity. But in giving such advice, care must be taken to emphasize the limitations of the scientific evidence and to explain that there may be other tenable interpretations. Most disturbing to me is the psychologist who, on the basis of the flimsiest data, makes pronouncements as though they were backed by the full weight of science (1977, pp. 207–8).

Similar concern has been expressed about psychology's role in legal proceedings: "At present, it is still possible for the social psychologist to 'hoodwink a judge who is not overwise' without intending to do so; but successes of this kind are too costly for science to desire them" (Cahn, 1955, p. 166). Concern is also expressed for the law: "Recognizing as we do how sagacious Mr. Justice Holmes was to insist that the constitution be not tied to the wheels of any economic system whatsoever, we ought to keep it similarly uncommitted in relation to the other social sciences" (ibid., p. 167).

The Conflation of Ethical Decisions and Empirical Evidence

Two major factors encourage scientists to conflate ethical decisions and empirical data. One results from either failing to grasp the distinction or from refusing to acknowledge it, the other from rejecting it. Consider *action research* as an example that appears to represent the first kind of confusion.

Action research (Chein, Cook, & Harding, 1948) was encouraged by Kurt Lewin who attempted to combine the goal of understanding social behavior with the solution of practical problems. Examples of action research were attempts, begun several decades ago, to reduce interracial hostilities in public schools, housing developments, and recreational centers where blacks and whites intermingled. Such a goal obviously need not generate any conflict between scientific responsibilities and social and political involvements. Reducing interracial friction is both an interesting theoretical problem and a widely accepted moral goal in a democratic society.

An epistemological analysis of doing action research on reducing interracial hostilities indicates that two separate decisions are involved: (1) an ethical decision that reducing interracial hostilities is virtuous and (2) a scientific decision that empirical methods can be developed that will enable one to understand and control the phenomenon. In justifying this kind of research Chein, Cook, and Harding (1948) tend to fuse these two separate issues so that the reader is encouraged to believe that by doing so a scientific ideal is achieved that is denied to those who try to keep issues of ethics separate from those of facts.

> Such an approach [action research] to scientific endeavor, one which is aimed at the discovery of the determining conditions of events, is obviously ideal for the scientist whose life as a scientist is integrated with his life as a citizen, who wishes to pursue a scientific way of life and at the same time to devote his energies toward civic betterment.
>
> It is with these considerations in mind that one can, perhaps, best understand the field of action research. It is a field which developed to satisfy the needs of the socio-political individual who recognizes that, in science, he can find the most reliable guide to effective action, and the needs of the scientist who wants his labors to be of *maximal social utility* [italics mine] as well as theoretical significance (Chein, Cook, & Harding, 1948, pp. 43–44).

Although these authors acknowledge the influence subjective factors can exert on the collection and interpretation of data from action research, they do not appear to recognize that the meaning of *maximal social utility* can be influenced, even completely determined, by subjective factors. Perhaps this oversight is due, in part, to their belief that they comprehend the motivation of the scientist:

> The scientific way of life is governed by three broad classes of interacting motives: *curiosity,* the desire to know what is going on when one's back is turned, where one's vision cannot easily reach, or where a situation is too complex for clear viewing; *practicality,* the desire that the results of one's labor, search, and enquiry should be useful and significant, that they should "make a difference"; and *intrinsic orderliness,* the desire that the masses of accumulated data be reduced to a comprehensible order and that the complexities which have been unraveled in the satisfaction of one's curiosity be not again obscured by the imposition upon the data of an arbitrary order (ibid., 1948, p. 43).

Unless one insists in an a priori manner that this motivational pattern defines a "true" scientist it is most doubtful that it represents an accurate picture of all scientists simply because the motivations of scientists vary. Many scientists with whom I am acquainted appear to be motivated solely by sheer *curiosity;* practical applications do not even enter their minds. Others seem more concerned with collecting facts, the more the better.

Debating the issue of the motivational patterns of scientists is not my aim beyond questioning the validity of the above quotation. The significant point is that by postulating the "true" motivational pattern of scientists, action researchers are encouraged to believe that their practical concerns are purely an expression of scientific motives and by so doing they gloss over complex ethical issues. Are they truly functioning as scientists when they select the criterion of social utility or are they behaving as political advocates? If action research simply represents an attempt to employ scientific method to discover the most effective programs to implement a given social policy, then the problems of facts and ethical judgments are not conflated. If, however, action research implies a scientific mechanism by which valid ethical judgments can be identified, then the two distinct issues of facts and ethical decision have been confused.

There is obviously no way to achieve total agreement in the scientific community as to the proper method to treat questions of facts and ethics. There are those who will remain convinced that psychologists have the right, as well as the duty, to advocate social policies and ethical imperatives in the name of the science of psychology. There are others who will insist that a tough-minded epistemological analysis will fail to yield any scientific validation procedure that is able to identify ethical imperatives, and therefore when psychologists do make such claims they are misleading their audience. And there will be those who will knowingly or unknowingly ignore the problem. Although one can not demand that a given viewpoint about the relationship between values and facts be accepted by all psychologists, if for no other reason than the command will go unheeded, one can never-theless encourage psychologists, when commenting on public pol-icy, to make their own viewpoint very clear. By so doing they will be fulfilling their responsibilities to psychology and to so-ciety. It might be argued that the lay public will not be able to comprehend such a subtle philosophic issue, but if one accepts Atkinson's observation that some believe that psychology is being used falsely as an advocate for public policy, then it must be con-cluded that at least some segments of society believe that they do understand the problem. If one has faith both in democracy and the power of education, public discussion of the problem of the relationship between facts and values may produce a level of un-derstanding beyond what many would expect. I believe that so-ciety will resolve the issues raised in this chapter and hope that rational procedures will be employed.

PSYCHOLOGY AND SOCIAL PROBLEMS

The contributions of psychology to the solution of social problems have been commented upon but not treated in any detail. Two major kinds of contributions are possible: revealing the conse-quences of a given social policy and developing effective methods of moral training.

Assessing Social Policy

Assessing the results of a social policy can be accomplished either by evaluating the results of a given policy that is presently in force (e.g., busing) or by executing a pilot study to estimate the effects of a program that is being considered for adoption (e.g., negative-income tax). In either case, it must be remembered that the findings of such studies would be irrelevant to those who are committed to an unqualified and unchangeable ethical view about the policy under consideration (e.g., achieving school integration is an ethical imperative, all forms of welfare are bad). For those who maintain a pragmatic view, probably a large majority for most controversial social programs, the outcome of such research will influence their support for the social policy that is being evaluated. To meet the needs of society the final outcomes of such evaluative studies should probably include a host of behavioral measures reflecting those effects that some believe to be of prime importance. For example, in assessing the results of busing information should be obtained about the reduction of interracial strife, the effectiveness of education for black and white students, the financial costs, and so forth. It also should be noted that evaluative research could provide information (e.g., indentification of personalities and intellectual characteristics of children that are associated with positive outcomes of busing) that might suggest modifications of the busing program that would encourage greater public support.

Another example of evaluation research contributing to the possible amelioration of a social problem is the determination of the contributions of TV news coverage of violent crimes to subsequent crimes of a similar sort. The evidence is that contagious violence does occur (Berkowitz, 1970), but much more needs to be learned about its underlying mechanisms. As usual, there will be those who will insist that, whatever its consequences, no attempt should be made to censor TV news for the simple reason that freedom of news broadcasting is a more important value than reducing violent crime. But it is possible that even these reservations might dissipate in light of clarifying evidence. If we were able to fully grasp the true nature of the facts about contagious violence, TV networks might be willing to police themselves and refuse to show news episodes that might trigger violent behavior.

The idea that evaluation research could prove useful in solving problems of busing and contagious violence would be considered by some as the height of optimism, if not outright folly. Much research has been done on busing and contagious violence, and we are no nearer a satisfactory resolution of these issues than we were prior to the research. Such research, the argument goes, inevitably will produce ambiguous and conflicting results that will be incomprehensible to those who sincerely seek information relevant to forming an opinion about the issue. Although there is a factual basis to these accusations, they must be understood in the context in which evaluative research is conceived and conducted and the results disseminated. For the most part individual researchers have decided to investigate the problem within the limits of available resources. The communication of the results by the news media to society has frequently been misleading; accuracy has been sacrificed for dramatic effects. No serious effort has been made to educate the populace, as well as members of the government, as to the appropriate methods for interpreting evaluation research. What is obviously needed is a more systematic method for planning, executing, and disseminating the results of socially significant evaluation research. There are many institutional and organizational forms that such a systematic method could take, but it would be premature to offer any exact recommendation. Some warnings, however, are in order. If one accepts the notion that the evaluative research should approach the ideals of objectivity, then it is recommended that those who conduct the research not be wedded or opposed to the policy under investigation. This concern, for example, would rule out the governmental agency that is responsible for implementing a social policy from evaluating it. Just as the ombudsman is independent of the governmental apparatus that he is called upon to investigate so should researchers investigating the social policies be free of the influence of those who have a stake in the success or failure of that policy. Whether this requires that all evaluation research be done by nongovernmental organizations or whether it demands that several independent groups should research the same policy in order to guard against possible sources of bias is a problem that can be illuminated later.

The potential value of doing pilot research on social programs being considered for adoption would probably exceed by far the worth of evaluations of programs in operation. One of the inescapable consequences of technological advances and social changes in this complex modern society are unanticipated side effects, usually negative in nature. The automobile, for example, has led to air pollution, traffic fatalities, highway-scarred countryside, traffic jams, and an energy crisis. Would the automobile have been aborted if its negative side effects had been known at its conception? Probably not, but its development might have been planned more wisely. Social planning, based on data from pilot studies, could have minimized the terrible price society is currently paying for the combustion-engine automobile.

Social programs designed to eliminate society's ills have also produced negative side effects. Welfare programs designed to assist persons have at times encouraged excessive dependence and demoralization. Public housing programs have destroyed neighborhoods they were designed to help. Medicaid programs have produced scandalous overcharging, unanticipated taxing of physicians' services and hospital facilities, and skyrocketing costs.

Must we always remain in the dark about consequences of an innovative invention or social program? Need unwanted side effects be discovered only after they occur? Since science is a method for foretelling the future, can it not be employed to judge the effectiveness of programs that have yet to be tried? This notion is presently gaining favor and many psychologists and other behavioral scientists are actively engaged in evaluating social programs that are being considered for adoption. One example has been the attempt to predict the consequences of a negative-income tax. The basic notion of such a program is that the income tax system is extended downwards so that the families falling below a poverty level receive cash (negative taxes) to compensate for their lack of earnings. As the family income rises above the poverty level, as a result of a member getting a job, the tax payments do not necessarily stop. Instead they are reduced so that the total income will always increase when the family's earned income is augmented. Many programs at present automatically remove a family from welfare rolls if a member accepts a position even though the wage received is less than the total welfare payment. Under such conditions a person on welfare is reinforced for refusing a position. A negative-income-tax program, in contrast, encourages job acceptance because it leads to increased income.

But is it not possible that the income guaranteed by a negative-income-tax program reduces the motivation to find a job? Although a job will necessarily increase a family's total income perhaps the added money will not be sufficient to encourage a person to seek a job when he has the option of not working? One attempt to estimate whether a negative-income-tax plan would destroy the incentive to work was conducted in a number of cities in the New Jersey-Pennsylvania area (Elesh, Ladinsky, Lefcowitz, & Spilerman, 1971). Families on a negative-income-tax program were compared with an equivalent group with no supplementary income. The families on the program were free to do whatever they wanted with their payments. The major finding was that the earned income of the experimental and control groups was the same thus indicating that the negative-income-tax plan did not reduce the incentive to work. The only effect noticed was that the total hours worked by families of the experimental group were less than those of the control group, apparently because people in the negative-income-tax plan took a longer time to find a job to their liking.

An experiment like this does not answer all questions about the negative-income-tax program. In fact it must be recognized that one study, or even many, will not be able to answer *all* questions. One must be realistic about the contributions of applied social experimentation of the sort that has just been described. Inevitably, the amount of information will be limited. The underlying assumption of applied social experimentation is that a wiser decision can be made about social programs in the light of evidence, unavoidably incomplete, than in the absence of any data.

It may appear that a sharp break in the discussion has occurred—an involvement with social policy has suddenly been substituted for a concern with ethical issues. In reality, a logical transition has occurred between the discussion of practical ethics and an examination of applied social experimentation with its goal of evaluating present and future social programs. Essentially, social policies are an expression of practical ethics. The adoption of new social programs is supported and encouraged because their goals represent desired values, i.e., social consequences that are good or at least better than those that result from currently operating policies. The role that psychology can play in practical ethics is to reveal, in an impartial manner, the consequences of different social programs that are designed to achieve certain moral ends. However, to repeat an important point, the results of such research will only be considered relevant to the social issue if the efforts of the psychologists and other behavioral scientists have the trust and respect of the society. If their efforts are perceived as a form of advocacy of their own political and social values, then their findings will be, and should be, ignored. In the long run a backlash could occur that would confirm Atkinson's prediction: "To permit psychology to be misused as an advocate for public policy will lead inevitably to the demise of the field" (1977, p. 210).

For a variety of reasons it would be naive to consider applied social experimentation as a panacea for all of the social ills. Although many of the major problems confronting this society (e.g., poverty, deteriorating education, pollution, interracial strife, population control, drug abuse, job monotony, aging, criminality) could be better understood and maybe solved, or at least meliorated, by research, one must entertain the possibility that some problems may prove to be intractable to any kind of solution in the foreseeable future. But that in itself would be a positive contribution in that it would encourage a more realistic perception of the problem and perhaps even stimulate new approaches in adjusting to it.

It must also be recognized that a "multiethical" society such

as the United States will always have fundamental moral conflicts (e.g., abortion) among different groups; inevitably some
segments of society of the population will become offended by
and resent the solution that is adopted. However, even in this respect, research might suggest techniques that will be helpful in
reducing intergroup friction.

Some might fear that applied social experimentation will
threaten basic liberties. For example, research might indicate that
the most effective method of coping with terrorism would be to
sacrifice the liberty that guarantees protection "against unreasonable searches and seizures." However, to perceive the applied social experimentation as the source of the threat would be mistaken. Applied social experimentation provides knowledge; society
determines how it is to be used.

Moral Training

The final point in my discussion of the potential contributions of
psychology to the solution of ethical problems is a simple one, although of great theoretical and empirical complexity. If one accepts both the notion that a society can adopt ethical modes of
behavior and that individuals can be trained to behave in a manner consistent with those modes, then psychologists should be
able to develop effective methods of moral training. What form
these training techniques will assume must be left open-ended
particularly in regard to such fundamental issues as to whether
training in a school setting can be substituted for family training.
But it is certainly within the realm of the possible that educational procedures can be designed that will decrease the incidence
of moral delinquency expressed both in criminal and ruthless behavior. Again, the basic assumption here is that if psychologists
are provided with a clear conception of some final behavioral performance that society deems desirable, then techniques can be
developed to increase the probability of occurrence of the desired behavior. The only obstacle to such an optimistic expectation would be unmodifiable forms of unethical behavior that are

genetically determined. Although future research might demonstrate that such a pessimistic view is appropriate for some limited forms of criminal behavior, it seems inconceivable that it would apply to the entire spectrum of a socially defined range of immorality.

One point frequently overlooked in moral training is that certain goals may be more easily attained than others. One such example, which stems from a dispute in the history of ethics, is whether "happiness" constitutes a more appropriate ethical imperative than "the absence of suffering." Should a society be "engineered" so that its members will be happy or would it be a more reasonable goal to attempt to eliminate "suffering." Some psychologists would immediately dismiss such a question as meaningless because of the inability to define precisely such phenomenological states such as "happiness" and "suffering." This reaction could be considered excessively harsh and rigid because it should be possible to use such phenomenological descriptions when developing intersubjectively reliable behavioral measures of "happiness" and "suffering."

This problem is similar to the dispute that revolves about the concept of "mental health." Should it be defined as a list of positive behavioral characteristics, or is it more reasonable to define mental health as the absence of pathological reactions such as hallucinations, incapacitating anxiety, and persistent and inappropriate depression? Although a positive conception of mental health appears at first glance to represent a more desirable goal than the mere absence of pathological reactions, it soon becomes apparent that the positive conception of mental health is burdened with complex ethical issues associated with "goodness" and "desirability" plus an intrinsic inelasticity to cope with the profound behavioral variability among humans. Thus any positive conception of mental health might be impractical and perhaps even threatening to a conception of individual freedom that recognizes the immense diversity of human behavior. In the same vein, the human condition may make the romantic notion of happiness for all a naive hope rather than a realistic goal. Perhaps the "best" society a democracy can engineer (and it is more than likely that other forms of government would not do as well) would be one based upon the ethical goal of eliminating "suffering."

As a psychologist, I do not wish to be placed in the position of supporting or favoring a pessimistic view of the human potential. The only thrust of my argument is that psychology, when considering ethical behavior, cannot limit its sights exclusively to problems of moral training. The obvious point that all moral goals are not equally achievable must be recognized and its implications fully appreciated. By recognizing this point and its intrinsic relationship to the problem of ethical training, psychology will be in the best position to offer positive contributions to the solution of some of the most pressing ethical issues of our time.

The effectiveness of psychologists' contributions will depend upon their ability to disabuse themselves of the notion that they can dictate what is good and bad. Philip Handler (1980), when president of the National Academy of Sciences, warned that, "Scientists best serve public policy by living within the ethics of science, not those of politics." Psychologists must always be aware of the threat of a tyrannical morality to a democracy by those who are convinced that they alone know what is right—whether they be religious zealots, political fanatics, or theoretical psychologists.

Future Trends in Psychology

8

1. A fundamental disagreement prevails among psychologists about the nature of their discipline and the role it should play in society. These differences represent irreconcilable views that prevent psychology from operating as a unified science or profession.

2. In the coming years the following trends are expected to develop or continue: (a) Neurophysiological interpretations of behavior will increase in popularity because of recent biological and technological developments and also because of the increased disenchantment with "black-box" behavioral theories, which due to insufficient constraints do not provide for clear-cut resolutions of theoretical differences. This trend toward neurophysiological interpretations does not spell the demise of "black-box" formulations because they can provide a functional analysis of behavior that can guide neurophysiological research and theorizing. (b) In order to avoid doing research that yields trivial results psychologists will try to develop strategies that increase the probabilities of fruitful investigations (e.g., conduct research within a developmental or comparative framework). (c) The failure of experimental social psychology to yield major theoretical breakthrough has encouraged social research in natural settings. Although such research may not be theoretically more significant, it promises to have greater social utility. Of particular importance is evaluation research, which has the potential for providing appropriate information for the selection of effective social policies and programs. (d) Two controversies, holism versus atomism and rationalism versus empiricism, that have

persisted throughout the history of psychology will continue to occupy the center stage of psychological theorizing. Neither controversy lends itself to any simple resolution because each position in both conflicts represents an important research and theoretical strategy that has some merit. (e) Although the effectiveness of psychotherapy, "talk therapy," has frequently been questioned, its popularity will continue because it serves many personal needs ranging from offering the patients "psychological health" or "spiritual guidance" to providing them with an intrinsically interesting or entertaining experience. In the context of a national health program, psychotherapy has the greatest chance of receiving government support when it demonstrates its cost effectiveness in a medical setting. (f) The information-processing paradigm, although experiencing an unrivalled success in capturing the allegiance of a large proportion of experimental psychologists interested in learning, memory, perception, and thinking, is presently confronted with experimental and theoretical problems that do not lend themselves to any simple solutions. The absence of a cohesive theory has resulted in a proliferation of models that share, at best, a common language but no core assumptions. The explanatory capacity of information-processing models have frequently been overstated when theoretical conjectures are offered in the guise of substantive formulations. The use of the computer analogy to explain human behavior must continue to be considered a strategy the value of which has yet to be convincingly demonstrated. In essence, the information-processing paradigm is an experiment in theorizing, the results of which are not yet in.

THE PRESENT STATE OF PSYCHOLOGY

This examination of the epistemological structure of psychology has revealed a diversity of basic assumptions and ultimate goals. What does this methodological state portend for the future of psychology?

Although the question seemed eminently appropriate for the concluding chapter of a book that seeks to reveal the nature of psychology, an answer is not easily forthcoming. Pessimistic evaluations of its future by some discerning critics contrasted with enthusiastic promises of human salvation by some of its practitioners, plus claims of psychology's social value along with fears of its social consequences, all suggest that prediction of psychology's future is a complex and risky task. The task can be made easier by lowering one's sights from that of an aspiring oracle who strives to predict the exact shape that psychology will assume in years to come to that of a modest prognosticator who attempts to identify some of the directions that psychology will take. By adopting the more modest option, the task of previewing the future becomes manageable.

THE STATUS OF CONTEMPORARY PSYCHOLOGY

Most psychologists feel both secure and confident about the future of their discipline. Its growth has been phenomenal during the past decades, illustrated by the increase of the membership of the American Psychological Association (APA) from less than 1,000 in 1925 to well over 40,000 today. Concomitant growths have also occurred in the number of publications and journals, as well as in departments and schools that are offering doctorates in psychology. But hidden behind these figures are sources of dissension that seek to split psychology, at least into two, if not more, separate and independent disciplines. Many natural-science oriented psychologists became disenchanted with the APA following World War II because of what they perceived as an over-concern with professional issues at the expense of scientific affairs and standards of scholarship. As a result a new organization was formed in 1959, the Psychonomic Society, designed not to compete with the APA for its membership but rather to sever ties with most of the psychologists who belonged to APA. The aim of the Psychonomic Society was to limit its membership to those psychologists who demonstrated proven research skills of the sort that was consistent with a natural-science approach. The Psychonomic Society deliberately avoided matters of professional interests, limiting its concern mainly to the holding of annual meetings to encourage communication about empirical and theoretical matters in the behavioral sciences. Although initially most members of the Psychonomic Society held joint membership in the APA, the continued professionalization of that organization encouraged some older psychologists to terminate their APA membership and some younger ones to refuse to join.

The founders of the Psychonomic Society had no desire to abandon the name of psychology or its traditions. The most controversial step in founding the organization was the selection of the name *psychonomic* in preference to a title that would include the term *psychology*. They desired a name that would set them apart from the APA but at the same time would not deny their psychological heritage. If the name Society of Experimental Psychology, or some variation of it, were available, it would have been adopted. But that option was precluded by the existence of an honorary organization, the Society of Experimental Psychologists, organized by Edward B. Tichener in 1927.

Although the Psychonomic Society was perceived by many outsiders as an effort of ivory-tower psychologists to turn their backs on problems of society, the charge was unfounded. Experimental psychology from its beginning in the United States had an interest in applied fields such as psychological testing, education, advertising, industry, and medicine (McKinney, 1976). Many of the founders of the Psychonomic Society had been active in applied programs during World War II, particularly those associated with the selection and training of Air Force personnel. Although members of the Psychonomic Society might differ as to when it was strategic to apply methods and knowledge of psychology to the solution of practical problems, the traditions of natural science denied any unbridgeable chasm between pure and applied research. In fact, many "psychonomes" would argue that the distinction between pure and applied research is tenuous at best: Can the development of the transitor or a psychological test be simply classified as either an expression of pure or applied research?

One can point to several other conflicts that signified a fundamental divisiveness in contemporary psychology that were not, as some claimed, simply a contest for professional power or a disagreement about applied psychology. Departments of psychology, after struggling to achieve their academic independence, found themselves struggling to retain their integrity. Some notable failures occurred. At one distinguished university two departments had to be formed: a department of social relations, which attracted psychologists with a social-science bent, and a department of psychology, which primarily contained tradition-oriented experimental psychologists in the fields of sensation, perception, and learning. The department of social relations, consisting mainly of personality and social psychologists, as well as anthropologists and sociologists, felt it necessary to provide training in traditional experimental psychology but difficulties arose when some of the experimental psychologists and their students found it intolerable to be isolated from the methodological and historical moorings they coveted.

Throughout the country departments of psychology were attempting all sorts of maneuvers to reconcile the differing conceptions of graduate education appropriate for experimental, clinical, and social psychologists. In some cases the clinical programs were dropped or transferred to the schools of education. Many decided to avoid the conflicts by not having a clinical training program. One alternative offered was to give a doctorate in psychology (D.Psy.) that did not require a research thesis. All these academic machinations, expressions of a fundamental discord between clinical and experimental psychology, were not passively accepted by clinicians. Those who felt that their future was being controlled by psychologists who, at best, did not understand the needs of clinical psychology and, at worst, did not understand psychology established independent schools of psychology that were not affiliated with universities but nevertheless granted doctorate degrees.

More recently, physiological psychologists, many of whom prefer the designation of biopsychologists or neuroscientists, have revealed a new source of friction. They find that their ties to biology in particular, and to neurosciences in general, are much greater than to their nonphysiologically oriented colleagues. In a few cases independent departments of biopsychology have been established while in other cases special training programs in bio-psychology have been created that have encouraged the isolation of biopsychologists from other psychologists.

This ongoing tendency toward fission in psychology can be simply viewed as a consequence of the age of specialization that characterizes all sciences. From physics to biology there are fields of specialization that appear to have nothing in common with other areas. Although specialization (perhaps overspecialization) is a source of divisiveness in contemporary psychology it is not the main source of turmoil. The roots are deeper within the fundamental nature of psychology.

About a decade ago I delivered a talk (Kendler, 1970) entitled "The Unity of Psychology" to the Division of General Psychology of APA, whose members consider themselves to be involved with problems and issues that transcend the boundaries of the numerous fields of psychology. In this talk the diversity of volitional decisions that psychologists have made in choosing their subject matter and the mode of understanding was recognized but hope was expressed that the integrity of the field, in spite of the fundamental differences in orientation, could be achieved:

> The unity of psychology is not beyond the realm of possibility and consequently it cannot be considered to be completely unreal. Whether a unity is achieved or not will be dependent on the psychological community accepting a criterion of explanation that will permit a framework by which the relative merits of competing interpretations can be judged, not necessarily to provide a single unequivocal overall evaluation but instead to identify the assets and liabilities of each. It may seem naive to think that a common explanatory frame of reference can be agreed upon by such an already fragmented community but a look at the annals of more mature sciences testifies to the ability of historical processes to settle what initially appeared to be unresolvable controversies (ibid., pp. 45–46).

My methodological preferences then were exhibited by suggesting that, "the most likely candidate for a mutually acceptable explanatory frame of reference is one that requires a deductive component."

In retrospect I must confess to being naive and unrealistic. I harbored the optimistic belief that the natural-science method in psychology would ultimately achieve a level of success that would encourage the abandonment of competing methodological approaches. Methodological controversies had occurred during the early stages of physics, chemistry, and biology, but the natural-science methodology prevailed because of the successes it generated.

My optimism was unjustified for two reasons. Natural-science methodology was not as successful in discovering and integrating the facts of psychology as I had anticipated. Even if it were more successful the need for other methodological approaches (e.g., humanistic, literary) would remain. This point struck home recently when, in search of a paperback, I wandered over to a large drugstore in an airline terminal. The display was divided into seven major sections, one of which was psychology. I failed to recognize most of the books except those in the general areas of psychoanalysis and humanistic psychology. The titles suggested that these books possessed a variety of appeals: recipes for adjustment, acquaintance with other minds, knowledge of psychoanalysis and humanistic psychology, disclosures about abnormal behavior, descriptions of encounter groups, insights into moral beliefs, and fun and games. If natural-science psychology, with its demanding requirements for warranted conclusions, were more successful, some of these books would lose their appeal. Psychological games and simple recipes for living, regardless of their justification, are attractive to many people as is demonstrated by the persistent interest in astrology. These needs will be satisfied by authors who, because of conviction or profit, will continue to produce their wares in the absence of any critical natural-science standards to evaluate their efforts.

But returning to the more basic question, why has the progress of natural-science psychology been disappointing? Back in 1929, Boring, in concluding his famous book *A History of Experimental Psychology* "confesses to a certain disappointment . . . that experimental psychology had not accomplished more than it has in seventy years of life" (p. 659).[1] Fifty years later many distinguished experimentalists would still bemoan the lack of impressive progress and perhaps even affirm William James's characterization of psychology as a "nasty little subject."[2] Boring offered two explanations for the lack of progress in psychology. One was that psychology had no great men like Darwin, the other that psychology was too involved in philosophy: "Psychology ought to fare better when it completely surrenders its philosophical heritage, in fact as well as in voiced principle, and proceed, unimpeded by a divided soul, about its business" (1929, p. 661).

Neither reason is compelling. The absence of a genius may reflect the refractoriness of psychological problems to any broad-range theoretical solutions. In other words, psychology does not provide opportunities for gifted individuals to achieve genius status.[3] Perhaps the overconcern with methodological issues expresses the unique problems of psychology that are not shared by other disciplines. In addition, it can be argued that the methodological discussions have not been too excessive but instead too superficial.

In contrast to Boring's disappointments, Sigmund Koch's (1974) view of psychology is exhilaratingly depressed. He notes that John Stuart Mill in 1843 suggested that the "backward state" of the psychological sciences, which Mill labeled the "moral sciences," could "only be remedied by applying to them the methods of the physical sciences." Koch believes Mill's recommendations have been implemented over the past 100 years and "the Millian hypothesis has been fulsomely disconfirmed."

Koch backs up his conclusions with a variety of arguments.

1. Boring (1929) dates the beginning of experimental psychology to Gustav Fechner's publication of *Elemente der Psychophysik* in 1860.

2. Many psychologists mistakenly remember James's disparaging comment as that "nasty little science." When he completed *The Principles of Psychology* he informed his publisher that his book proved that there was no science of psychology (Watson, 1978).

3. Boring (1950) in his second edition of *A History of Experimental Psychology* abandoned his great-man theory of scientific progress; great men were not "*causes* of progress" but only "*agents.*"

Psychology cannot be considered a coherent field, either theoretically or substantively—a view that is, in some sense, in agreement with my own. Failure to achieve theoretical coherence is not particularly damning because, as Koch recognizes, contemporary physics also does not qualify as a coherent discipline.

Can psychology be considered a science? Koch, admitting that the term *science* has not yet been, and probably never will be, precisely explicated, nevertheless decides that physics obviously qualifies for that designation but psychology does not. He retreats somewhat from this latter conclusion by admitting that biopsychology approximates a science but then suggests that it properly belongs to biology and would benefit from such an affiliation. He ignores the contributions of psychology to the successes of biopsychology—the empirical laws that have provided direction to psychophysiological research and a sophisticated methodology, particularly in regard to measuring behavior. Only when nonpsychologists attempt to measure behavior do the achievements of psychologists become obvious. Consider the contributions of psychological methods to pharmacology in evaluating the influence of drugs on behavior and to ethology in clarifying such concepts as *sensitive period* and *imprinting*. Regardless of its future departmental affiliations, biopsychology will lose much if it ignores psychological measures of behavior as well as the laws that relate behavior to environmental events and past experience.

Koch's thesis is that one cannot create a field of science by edict as behaviorists have attempted. He accuses them of being more concerned with their commitment to science than to their subject matter. According to Koch this criticism is no less appropriate for information-processing models than it is for stimulus-response conceptions:

> The strategy now becomes that of turning to the revered natural sciences, especially the engineering disciplines, not merely for prefabricated methods but for prefabricated answers as well. We thus get the models based on computer simulation (in some of which the computer *is* the psychological subject) or on transpositions to the events generated by actual human subjects of a

variety of developments in applied mathematics, ranging from information theory to the theory of games. In this way does the *science* of psychology maintain consistency with its history; by headlong retreat from the psychological subject immediately upon the long delayed moment of reconfrontation (1974, p. 18).

Because the knowledge emanating from what I call here natural-science psychology is fundamentally spurious, according to Koch, it generates a degrading image of man. Those who expect that Koch's concern with the concept of the image of man, as discussed earlier (page 202), would lead him to be more sympathetic to humanistic psychology will be sadly disappointed.

Koch's initial contact with humanistic psychologists led him to characterize them as "a motley group with heterogeneous interests" that was "not a 'force' at all but, rather 'a large number of individuals who would have . . . difficulty communicating with each other and who stand for nothing focal, other than a feeling of disaffection from the emphasis of recent American psychology'" (ibid., p. 34). His final verdict for the human potential movement, which, properly speaking, can only be considered as a segment of humanistic psychology, is that "it challenges any conception of the person that would make life worth living, in a degree far in excess of behaviorism" (ibid., p. 37). Depth psychology fares no better; it is emphatically dismissed because of its obvious scientific inadequacies:

> The widely shared idea that psychoanalysis is a "science" which can cumulate and progress by a logic of verification similar to that of physics or even biology is absurd. As a result of all these generous efforts, a jungle of phony discourse has grown up in this area which would be unique in its capacity to obfuscate the enthusiasts who assent to it, were it not for the superior virtuosity of Marshal McLuhan, or perhaps certain Existential philosophers (ibid., p. 31).

Having shown to his own satisfaction the dismal condition of contemporary psychology, Koch raises the question of what should be done to improve the state of psychology. Suggesting remedies proves to be more difficult than offering criticisms.

Koch admits to being unable to "offer a constructive and merry coda." He thinks that, "We are . . . at a grave impasse in the history of scholarship—indeed, the history of intelligence. I am sanguine enough to believe it a temporary one. But I have no recipe for its removal" (ibid., p. 38). IIe does make one strong recommendation that the term *psychology* should be replaced with the phrase *the psychological studies.* This substitution would underline the fact that psychology is not a coherent discipline with one methodological approach: "The psychological studies, if they are really to address the historically constituted objectives of psychological thought, must range over an immense and disorderly spectrum of human activity and experience" (ibid., p. 26). To prepare for this examination Koch encourages a change in attitudes:

> We who are psychologists or humanists must become for a while not psychologists or humanists, but men. Let the teaching of the psychological studies and the humanities be a matter of men exploring the meanings of human experience, actions, and artifacts at their most value-charged reaches, among men. Let the teacher be wiser, more able than the student to discriminate finely and value precisely within important segments of human reality (ibid., p. 39).

It would be unfortunate, and unwise, to dismiss Koch's criticisms if for no other reason than that they articulate a disenchantment with psychology felt by many people, including psychologists and their students. Are such feelings justified? A simple "Yes" or "No" response is inappropriate because independent issues are involved, each demanding a qualified answer.

If a simple litmus test is not available to identify a true science it would appear both foolish and unproductive to pursue the question of whether Koch's negative verdict about psychology is correct. If one accepts the notion that the assignment of the designation *science* to a discipline is appropriate when progressive increase in a body of factual knowledge takes place with a concomitant integration of those facts, then the conclusion can be drawn that psychology would qualify as a science. My support of this thesis is no doubt influenced by my decision to write an introductory psychology text (Kendler, 1963, 1968, 1974) that was based upon the assumption that a scientific text was possible. Executing the task confirmed the initial judgment. The following research areas, certainly not all that could be mentioned, contain a body of facts that are integrated either in the form of deductive models of explanation or by systematic methods to control the phenomena's occurrence: visual and auditory sensitivity, color vision, visual space perception, size constancy, acquisition and extinction of classical condition responses, schedules of reinforcement in operant conditioning, reinforcement by brain stimulation, effects of punishment, "instinctive" behavior, organization and memory, developmental changes in human learning, language acquisition, functional fixedness, human aggression, individual differences and psychological testing, human sexuality, child rearing, behavior modification, genetic basis of behavior disorders, psychopharmacology, and attitude change.

If one examines these topics within a historical perspective, an appropriate conclusion would be that knowledge of the empirical relationships has increased and understanding has improved. In short, scientific progress has occurred. A person siding with Koch's position could refute this claim of scientific progress by arguing that criteria employed of scientific knowledge is too lenient, that the evidence cited emphasizes both the lack of coherence of psychology and the failure of psychology to deal with significant aspects of being human such as personal experience and artistic achievements.

According to Koch the analytic pattern that characterizes science requires:

> (a) the disembedding from a domain of phenomena of a small family of "variables" which demarcate important aspects of the domain's structure, when that domain is considered as an idealized, momentary static system; and (b) that this family of variables be such, by virtue of appropriate internal relations, that it can be ordered to a mathematical or formal system capable of correctly describing changes in selected aspects of the state of the system as a function of time and/or system changes describable as alterations of the "values" of specified variables (ibid., p. 23).

Koch notes that this description characterizes such "simple" physical systems as the laws of the pendulum and the motions of falling bodies, achievements that required "a prolonged development of ancillary knowledge, culminating in an act of genius . . ." My reading of Koch's two requirements of scientific status would exclude Darwin's formulation of his evolutionary theory. They would also exclude other parts of biology, particularly those that are in their early stages of development (e.g., brain chemistry). Koch's requirements appear too stringent; they emphasize characteristics of final goals of scientific knowledge while ignoring intermediate points.

Perhaps the key criticism directed at contemporary psychology by Koch is its failure to deal with subject matters that he considers to be related to the most distinctive and most highly valued aspects of human activity, i.e., conscious experience, particularly that associated with aesthetic creativity and appreciation. A natural science of phenomenology, as has been suggested (pages 94–99), *may* be unachievable simply because the observer and what he observes cannot be separated. If aesthetic creativity and appreciation must be understood in terms of human experience, and not in terms of a detached symbolic system that organizes the factual domain of aesthetic behavior, then perhaps Koch is asking too much of natural-science psychology. Saul Bellow, the distinguished American novelist and Nobel Laureate, offers an interesting commentary upon this issue. In his novel *Humboldt's Gift* he describes the desire of his protagonist, Charles Citrine, a writer, to understand the desires of others.

> To do this one had to remove all personal opinions, all interfering judgments; one should be neither for nor against this desire. In this way one might come gradually to feel what another soul was feeling. I had made this experiment with my own child Mary. For her last birthday she desired a bicycle, the ten-speed type. I wasn't convinced that she was old enough to have one. When we went to the shop it was by no means certain that I would buy it. Now what was her desire, and what did she experience? I wanted to know this, and tried to desire in the way that she desired. This was my kid, whom I loved, and it should have been elementary to find out what a soul in its fresh state craved with such inten-

sity. But I couldn't do this. I tried until I broke into a sweat, humiliated, disgraced by my failure. If I couldn't know this kid's desire could I know any human being? I tried it on a large number of people. And then, defeated, I asked where was I anyway? And what did I really know of anyone? The only desires I knew were my own and those of nonexistent people like Macbeth or Prospero. These I knew because the insight and language of genius made them clear (1975, p. 416).

The suggestion is clear. Maybe the humanities, literature in particular, can only reveal what Koch longs to discover, the significant experiences of being human. Although the potential success of a natural-science approach to phenomenological experience, not merely the causes and consequences of it, but rather a valid description of experience itself, cannot be ruled out, but neither can its success be guaranteed (pages 94–97). Bellow may be correct in concluding that only the language of the artistic genius can convey to a receptive audience an intuitively valid description of the experience of others.

Whatever the future may hold for experiential psychology, it would appear that the suggestion of substituting a department of psychological studies for the traditional department of psychology as it is now constituted, represents more of a hollow hope than a productive alternative. Even if one assumed that the intellectual interaction between humanists and psychologists would be beneficial to the latter, and perhaps even to the former, there is no guarantee that such benefits would result from institutionalizing a department of psychological studies. History has demonstrated that the intellectual stress and strain among psychologists, resulting from their different conceptions of "science" has often been sufficiently great to divide them into separate departments or even institutions. Forcing individuals from widely divergent disciplines to share a common department is no guarantee that presumed similarities will appear more apparent, attractive, and significant than the obvious differences. If there is any justification for a department of psychological studies, then it should be possible to devise a set of core courses that should be required for all its students, from those who are fascinated by Anthony Trollope's characterizations to those who seek to understand the interrelationships between linguistic abilities and problem solving during early childhood.

The obvious reservations expressed about the potential contributions of a department of psychological studies stems from the conclusion of my analysis that psychology is a multidisciplinary study with different subject matters and a variety of epistemological assumptions about what constitutes "truth." To attempt a reconciliation among these diverse orientations would be tantamount to conducting a game between a chess and a checker player without changing the rules of either game. It cannot be done. Recognizing and accepting the fundamental differences in contemporary psychology may be a wiser alternative than attempting to combine artistic and scientific traditions and "methods" that at best could yield a homogenized product without the positive attributes of either.

FUTURE TRENDS OF PSYCHOLOGY

An understanding of the past provides a glimpse into the future. By identifying significant historical trends and charting their courses, one can predict the directions that psychology will take in decades to come.

Neurophysiological Interpretations of Behavior

Methodological arguments have previously been advanced (pages 119–135) questioning the inevitability, and even the desirability, of neurophysiological interpretations of behavior and experience. These arguments have been challenged by two historical forces—the obvious dramatic improvements in research technology (e.g., monitoring the activities of individual neurons, techniques for measuring minute biochemical changes) and increases in biological knowledge both of which have stimulated biopsychological research and theorizing. Another reason, less obvious, for the increased popularity of the neurophysiological approach is the failure of "black-box" behavior theories—formulations that employ abstract intervening variables to bridge the gap between environmental manipulations and the behavior of the organism—to offer satisfactory accounts of the phenomena they sought to explain. The attempt to explain the psychology of learning by these blackbox theories offers an instructive case history that in many ways parallels attempts in other areas, such as cognition, perception, and motivation, to formulate intervening-variable type conceptions. These formulations of the learning process led to many heated controversies such as latent learning, incremental versus one-trial learning, contiguity versus reinforcement, and selective attention. These disputes proved unresolvable in the sense that the evidence did not clearly favor one formulation over the competing one as was the case for the Copernican and Ptolmaic conceptions, and the evolutionary and creationist conceptions. A common opinion, which I shared, about these unresolvable controversies in the psychology of learning was that the difficulties emanated from the ambiguity of the competing theories:

> It appeared to many, a decade ago, that certain theories notably those of Hull and Tolman, were engaged in mortal combat in the arena of hard data. Now that the dust has settled, it seems that the combatants were more often shadow boxing. Damage to the theoretical positions did occur but in many instances the wounds were self-inflicted. However, these theoretical disputes nevertheless did serve a purpose. They provided much interesting data; but more important, they revealed the stark inadequacies and limitations of existing learning theories (Kendler, 1959, p. 43).

The solution to this theoretical impasse seemed obvious. Learning theories had to be made more precise. This need for precision was expressed in mathematical models of the learning process employing stochastic processes (e.g., Estes, 1950). But it became apparent over the years that these mathematical representations, although they served as an effective antidote to the ambiguities indigenous to general learning theories (Hull, 1943; Tolman, 1932), were forced to sacrifice the generality of the formulations they were designed to replace. No mathematical model was proposed that effectively accounted for the diversity of conditioning phenomena, much less the data from more complex learning tasks. Specific models for specific phenomena became the order of the day, and it became abundantly clear that if black-box theorists desired precision the purchase price was generality. For most theorists the price was too high as evidenced by the gradual decrease of interest in these highly specialized models. At best, these models offered limited answers to narrow questions.[4]

In order to explain the failure of general learning theories to be specific and specific mathematical models to be general the structural characteristics of black-box theories must be examined. They contain three major components: a set of independent variables, a related network of theoretical constructs, and rules for theoretical derivations of the to-be-expected behavior. The actual control exerted on the subject's behavior resides primarily in the regulation of the independent variables such as the nature of the discriminanda, their temporal relationships, the nature and size of the incentive, the management of the subject's background and home environment, and so on. It is generally acknowledged that there are many fluctuating and steady conditions within both the environment and the subject that influence the behavior and over which the experimenter has little or no control or knowledge. Such a theoretical system can be aptly described as being empirically open in the sense that variables not accounted for by the theory exert important influences on behavior, i.e., a lot of "noise" affects the results. In addition, and perhaps of greater importance, is the capacity of black-box theories to accommodate embarrassing data by ad hoc modifications. There appear to be no end to the escape clauses that can be invoked by black-box theories to handle any phenomenon. This empirical openness and lack

---

4. Although failing to achieve a broad conception of the learning process, these mathematical models did exert a salutary effect on theoretical practices. In addition to making precise predictions, some encouraged an interest in trial-to-trial changes in the learning process that was largely ignored by general theories because of their primary concern with group differences.

of theoretical constraints place a definite limit on the explanatory capacity of general black-box theories.

To overcome the deficiencies of black-box formulations the influences of extraneous variables must be reduced and the theoretical constraints must be increased. Perhaps this can only occur by changing their very character—a shift of interest from environmental-behavioral relationships to neurophysiological-behavioral dependencies. A sensible assumption, if behavior is not assumed to be an emergent product of a vitalist force, is that the causal basis of behavior resides within the physiology of an organism. The excessive noise that is characteristic of black-box research can be reduced by manipulating neurophysiological variables, the effects of which are more easily assessed than are the influences of environmental variables. This shift of focus can also reduce the theoretical flexibility of such theories. It is much easier to obtain negative evidence against a hypothesis concerning the operation of some physiological process than it is to discover that a set of abstract theoretical processes are incapable of explaining a set of behavioral phenomena. One example is the current controversy as to whether the contingency or contiguity between the conditioned and unconditioned stimuli is responsible for the formation of classical conditioned responses. Perhaps only neurophysiological evidence can provide an answer (Mpitsos, Collins, & McClellan, 1978).

In sum, the thrust of this analysis is that black-box theories have a limited capacity to resolve the theoretical issues that they have generated. To enlarge this capacity requires that the theoretical issue be translated into a neurophysiological question.

In support of a neurophysiological strategy one can contrast the history of theories involving environmental-behavior dependencies with those that have been concerned with neurophysiological-behavior relationships. If one considers a progressive increase in knowledge as the hallmark of a scientific advance, then one would have to conclude that biopsychology has progressed more than has black-box psychology. An inordinate amount of "progress" occurring in black-box psychology results from the rejection of a research program from one empirical domain (e.g., conditioning) in favor of a research program from a new empirical domain (e.g., memory). The shift of interest is justified by the argument that the new empirical realm is more significant than the old one.[5]

In contrast, biopsychology does not push aside its empirical legacy. "Real" structures (e.g., cones, brain) cannot be as easily dispensed with as can the "fictitious" concepts (e.g., field, association) of environmental-behavioral psychology. Color-vision theory, when approached in a neurophysiological manner, cannot avoid coping with the activities of the cones in the retina, bipolar cells, cells in the lateral geniculate body, the visual pathways, and of course, the visual centers of the brain. They are here to stay, and their functioning must be included in any theoretical account of color vision.

Although it is easy to identify the deficiencies of black-box theories and offer a biopsychological orientation as a remedy, it is difficult, if not impossible, to suggest the manner in which the transition between the two approaches is to be implemented. As a general strategy one can recommend that neurophysiological hypotheses should be encouraged when practicable, with the full realization that the qualifying phrase, *when practicable,* is highly ambiguous. By examining some alternative tactics the meaning of this phrase can be clarified.

Reservations have already been expressed about broadly speculative conceptions that have been more involved with the conceptual nervous system than the central nervous system. A distinction should be made between those conceptions that encourage a false sense of understanding while exerting no impact on research and those that suggest fruitful hypotheses and research programs. Hebb (1949) represents a superior effort of this latter type. He formulated a broad-based conception that combined knowledge of both physiology and behavior. His ideas exerted both a direct impact on research (e.g., the effect of early experi-

5. A commentary on this kind of "progress" is expressed in the observation that one generation of natural scientists stands on the shoulders of the previous generation while behavioral scientists step on the backs of their predecessors.

ence on later learning, perceptual development) and theory (e.g., central processes and behavior). Although Hebb's formulation with its emphasis on *cell assemblies* influenced future conceptions, its impact was greater in terms of the questions raised than the answers offered. In contrast are the efforts of Ratliff (1965) who dealt with a much narrower range of phenomena (Mach bands) but offered precise neurological answers to specific perceptual questions that in some form will probably stand the test of time. No invidious comparison is implied because both efforts are important but for different reasons. What is being suggested is that in the present era some strategies possess greater potential than do others. The impressive recent developments in neurology, biochemistry, genetics, pharmacology, endocrinology, and related technology, encourage an intimate relationship between biology and psychology in both empirical research and theoretical construction. The knowledge of psychology and biology has reached a level that justifies conceptualizing problems, when possible, within a biopsychological perspective capable of immediately yielding researchable questions. This view does not eschew broad integrative biopsychological theories but instead argues that the best strategy to achieve such goals is from the "bottom up" instead of from the "top down." Starting from the top has tended to generate broad speculations that are incapable of deductively integrating available evidence from physiology and psychology. The tactic that appears to possess more promise is to proceed upward from low-level theories—initially formulate, as did Ratliff, biopsychological models for fairly circumscribed empirical realms that include both psychological and physiological events. The expectation and hope is that independent low-level models would merge into broader conceptions by creative theorizing.

Two important qualifications are now in order. First, it is not being suggested that every empirical issue in psychology should be approached within a biopsychological framework. What is being argued is that over the years a biological framework has become increasingly relevant to all of psychology—from sensory psychology at one extreme to social behavior at the other—and this trend will continue in the future for natural-science psychology. Today one cannot understand sensory processes without considering biological mechanisms, and the evidence suggests that the same condition will prevail, in the very near future, for other fields as well (e.g., perception, learning, behavior pathology). Although this trend does not demand that theoretical notions always be expressed within a biopsychological framework, it does imply that graduate psychology students receive fundamental training in neurophysiology, not necessarily to be prepared to do biopsychological research but instead to understand future developments in their own specialized fields.

Second, the expressed reservation about black-box theories should not be interpreted as an epistemological prohibition against such theorizing nor does it necessarily deprecate environmental-behavioral research or, for that matter, phenomenological analyses. Consider the history of theories of color vision. The theoretical problems of this research area were posed by a careful phenomenological analysis of human color experiences. Understanding of color vision was further enhanced by environmental-behavioral research in which psychophysical methods revealed numerous relationships between physical characteristics of light waves and attributes of color experience. In addition, environmental-behavioral research also discovered significant phenomena relevant to color vision theories, e.g., color mixing, negative afterimages, simultaneous contrast. The entire set of environmental-behavioral data, however, failed to provide any clear-cut verdict in favor of one of the two dominant theoretical orientations: the Young-Helmholz model or the Hering formulation. With the advent of single-neuron recordings and other technical advances the task of evaluating the competing research programs assumed a clearer perspective because the theoretical issues could be interpreted in terms of neuronal functioning at different levels of the visual pathways. The Young-Helmholtz theory appears relevant to receptor functioning (MacNichol, 1964) while the Hering formulation seems applicable to the functioning of bipolar cells and cells of the lateral geniculate body (De Valois, Abramov, & Jacobs, 1966; De Valois & Jacobs, 1968). Although the original theories, which guided much productive environmental-behavioral research, had to be reformulated, they nevertheless served as useful guideposts for further theoretical development. Phenomenological analyses and black-box theories, without question, serve important functions in the quest for a natural-science understanding of psychological events, but their value will be best appreciated if they are perceived not as final destinations but as significant landmarks along the way.

Two major arguments can be directed at the preceding analysis, which encourages a transition from environmental-behavioral to neurophysiological-behavioral formulations. The first is that this strategic recommendation expresses an unreasonable impatience. Use of the historical method to evaluate competing research programs demands that sufficient time be available for controversies to be solved. The decades that have passed since numerous black-box research programs have been locked in dispute have not been sufficient for a satisfactory resolution to take place. Perhaps their resolution will be forthcoming with the advent of newer mathematical systems that are developed for psychological data and of better experimental methodologies that will exert more powerful controls. In essence, this argument denies a limit to the explanatory powers of environmental-behavioral theories and encourages a persistence that for the most part has been absent in psychology with its penchant for novelty.

The second argument against the strategy of encouraging biopsychological formulations is that it promises more than it can deliver. The notion that all of the causal agents for behavior are within the skin does not reduce much of the noise that permeates black-box research. The human brain consists of approximately 10 billion neurons woven into an incredibly concentrated and intricate pattern. Six hundred million synapses exist within one cubic inch of brain tissue. Each cortical neuron, depending on its location, has from 6,000 to 60,000 synapses. The potential number of different combinations of individual brain cells involved in various activity patterns defies imagination. The number of different combinations possible among only *five* cells would far exceed a trillion. Is it not the height of optimism to believe that the mysteries of such a system can be unravelled? How can the human brain understand itself?

Although these rebuttals do not dissuade me from encouraging a neurophysiological strategy to achieve the goals of a natural-science psychology, they cannot be rejected and should not be ignored. The major reason for offering this methodological analysis is not to persuade psychologists, including students, about what to do but instead to make them aware of the alternatives before committing themselves to a particular strategic decision. Although there will be those who will opt for a black-box strategy, the historical trend toward an expansion of the empirical realm of biopsychology appears inevitable. The question is how rapidly will this trend accelerate and how successful will its efforts be?

The Fruitfulness of Developmental and Comparative Research

Nobody, in my experience, has ever denied that much of psychological research is trivial. That is to say nothing would have been lost if the research had not been done and that having been done it exerts no influence on psychology, now or in the future. With the explosion in the number of new psychological journals, the complaints increase about the amount of unnecessary research.

Although general agreement prevails about the high incidence of trivial studies, there is little consensus about the defining characteristics of such research. One can easily get the impression that the bottom-line meaning of triviality revolves about the paradigmatic commitments of the accuser. Research that one does, or that is conducted within the general orientation that one has adopted, is automatically significant. Everything else is trivial. A different attitude, which some would consider more enlightened and others would consider more biased, is that certain research areas yield significant evidence while others inevitably produce trivial results. At one extreme is the position that only socially significant research dealing with real problems of life is important and therefore most laboratory studies are trivial; their only justification is to meet the academic demands of "publish-or-perish." At the other extreme would be the view that socially significant problems are too complex and too value-ridden to be profitably investigated; tough-minded and tightly controlled investigations are needed to provide a solid empirical base on which a scientific psychology can be erected.

There are numerous other frames of references that are employed to distinguish trivial from significant research but none have gained universal or even majority acceptance. Yet the excess of trivial research appears real to most psychologists. Only a small proportion of papers are cited with any frequency, and an even smaller percent are attended to after the passage of a decade or more.

Is there any strategy that can be pursued that would reduce the incidence of trivial research? In answering such a question, it must first be realized that clear-cut criteria that identify significant investigations are impossible. The significance of any empirical study will depend upon a variety of influences that cannot be adequately assessed at the time the investigation is being planned. The results that will be obtained, the potential of the research program in which the study is embedded, the impact of subsequent studies to determine whether the original investigation was "properly" designed, the future importance of the general research area, and other factors will all have an influence on the potential significance of any set of findings. In addition, it must be recognized that some trivial research is unavoidable because some conjectures, reasonable at the time they are formulated, will not lead to any payoff. Trivial research is also encouraged by institutional pressure on individuals to do "scholarly work." And finally it must be acknowledged that psychology provides an abundance of research problems. New research paradigms, which tend to be generated at a rapid rate, each contain a host of problems that simply involve systematic variations of the major variables. Anybody who desires to do research, for any reason, will experience no difficulty in selecting a problem to investigate.

In spite of the intrinsic vagueness of the term *trivial,* and the operation of several forces that encourage insignificant research, an argument can be advanced that strategic guidelines are available to increase the probability of significant research outcomes.

Nature can provide guidance, admittedly imperfect, to encourage important investigations; any phenomenon that exhibits developmental or comparative significance holds promise of being important. This argument in favor of a developmental and/or comparative research strategy rests upon a simple assumption that the structure and functioning of organisms undergo important changes during their ontogeny and phylogeny. When behavior is related to these changes they tend to possess a built-in significance. The question "Why" directed at the obtained relationship will probably focus on a fruitful question.

Two examples in support of the significance of comparative and developmental research are Beach's (1947) research on the evolutionary changes in mammalian sexual behavior as a function of hormonal secretions and Money and Ehrhardt's (1972) developmental analysis of the sexual behavior of human hermaphrodites with the same genetic sex but different sex typings. Both studies provide empirical evidence that are a consequence of potent variables and as a result possess an importance that is not fully dependent on the interpretive framework in which they are embedded. If the hypotheses that Beach, and Money and Ehrhardt offered as interpretations of their findings were ultimately rejected, the findings, assuming their reliability, would still be significant. In contrast are the numerous findings that are wedded to a specific empirical procedure for their theoretical justification. When the realization occurs that the research effort is failing to live up to its expectations, the empirical findings are discarded to be remembered only as a historical anomaly. One such example, which began at the beginning of the twentieth century, was the use of multiunit maze learning of animals as a source of theoretical principles of learning. When maze learning was investigated in great detail, it was discovered that a large number of specific factors influenced the results (Woodworth, 1938). Some of the factors were: (1) anticipatory errors (an error, for example, a right turn, that anticipates the final correct response that leads to the goal); (2) position habits (some rats exhibit a preference for right or left turns presumably because of their anatomical structures); (3) centrifugal swing (when swing-

ing around a corner a rapidly running rat tends to hug the wall
to which he is brought close encouraging him to enter the alley,
correct or not, that the wall leads to). The consequence of all the
research on multiunit maze learning was that the large number of
specific factors obscured or distorted whatever basic principles
were operating. Multiunit learning was abandoned as a research
area for the psychology of learning.

The argument that a natural significance attaches to developmental and comparative research might be considered to be another form of the previous position in favor of a biopsychological
orientation. Biopsychology investigates the relationship between
behavior and neurophysiological events and in essence the same
relationship is involved in the developmental and comparative
approaches. Although this may be potentially true it does not
necessarily follow that problems in developmental and comparative psychology must always be conceptualized within a biopsychological framework. The Piagetian research program is a
striking example of a developmental approach that avoids getting
involved in specifying, or even speculating about, the neurophysiological substrate of behavior. Only an acknowledgement is
made to the involvement of maturational factors in ontogenetic
changes in cognitive development. One can express reservations
about the Piagetian research program; yet one would be hard put
to deny the significance of both the obtained ontogenetic changes
in cognitive functioning and the general theoretical proposal that
the sequence of cognitive stages is invariant.

Similarly one can point to phylogenetic differences in learning set data. Harlow (1949) extended traditional discrimination-
learning procedures to a series of successive problems each with a
different pair of discriminanda. With monkeys as subjects he
noted an astonishing change in learning proficiency from slow,
gradual learning during the initial problems to the rapid, practically one-trial learning after three hundred problems. The ability
to learn-how-to-learn (i.e., to establish learning sets) is influenced
by phylogenetic differences; primates are markedly superior to
carnivores who, in turn, exceed by far the performance of rodents
(Warren, 1965). Although, at present, no black-box theory of

learning sets has gained wide acceptance, the data themselves will, in all likelihood, retain their significance because of their "natural" importance. And it is likely that their significance will be enhanced as biopsychological procedures improve. The learning-set paradigm represents a sensitive tool to analyze the relationships between neurophysiological structures and problem-solving behavior.

Developmental and comparative research designs are obviously no guarantee that a particular investigation will be well executed or conceptually significant. The history of developmental psychology is filled with uninspired investigations in which convenient behavioral measures are related to chronological age. In absence of any theoretical context or compelling justification for employing the response measure, the resulting evidence usually proves insignificant. But at the same time it should be noted that even in the absence of any grand theoretical design, empirical relationships between age and behavior can be important. The efforts of Gesell and his co-workers (1940, 1946) have provided interesting information about ontogenetic changes in the human child that has proved useful both to parents who desire to know whether their child is progressing normally and to behavior scientists who seek to understand developmental processes.

The developmental method of analyzing behavior also provides a powerful tool for analyzing the complex nature-nurture interactions. Consider the problem of trying to tease out environmental and hereditary influences on gender-related cognitive functioning. Presumably females, on the average, exceed males in several language skills while males, in contrast, surpass females in a variety of visual-spatial tasks (Wittig & Petersen, 1979). Is this a result of genetic influences or sex typing? Such a question would be impossible to answer by comparing groups of adult men and women. But if the problem is approached within a developmental framework, it becomes possible to identify prenatal and postnatal genetic and environmental influences, and their interactions, that lead to the observed adult difference. And when the developmental analysis of one species is compared with other species for behavior patterns that are shared (e.g., gender-related sex behavior), the obtained information becomes even more enlightening in unraveling hereditary and environmental influences.

If the suggestion is correct that developmental and comparative research possesses a built-in significance, except when conducted in a mindless fashion, then one can expect an increase in popularity of these fields in the future. Of course it should be recognized that the notion that developmental and comparative research is specially important is not a novel idea. Fundamentally these research areas represent an offshoot of a Darwinian orientation because ontogenetic and phylogenetic differences in behavior typically possess functional significance. This is why both kinds of research were encouraged initially by the functionalists and later by the behaviorists. However, this analysis goes one step further than simply admitting the importance of developmental and comparative research. My point is that these areas possess a special theoretical significance in psychology. Neisser (1974) expressed this point when he bemoaned the fragmented state of the information-processing research program and suggested that a developmental orientation might help to integrate it.

Developmental psychology has been a rapidly expanding field in recent decades, due in part to the influence of Piaget but also to the demands of society in coping with problems intrinsically developmental in nature such as the education of the young and the care of the aged. These problems cannot be approached without an appreciation of the developmental processes that are involved.

Although comparative psychology has not expanded as rapidly as has developmental psychology, partly because of its intimate relationship to biopsychology with its great demands for technical skills, it nevertheless has achieved a more central importance in theoretical conceptions including that of human behavior. We are now more aware of the importance of species-specific behavior than we were decades ago and are more sophisticated about the relationship between human and infrahuman behavior. If we take a hint from biological research and the Darwinian framework, we can avoid either extreme position that insists there is no difference or no similarity between human and infrahuman behavior. Continuities and discontinuities will be found, and their extent will be determined by the specific kind of behavior that is being analyzed.

In conclusion, forces within psychology demand that special attention be paid to developmental and comparative psychology. These areas contain empirical relationships that express the operation of basic processes that will have to be incorporated into any natural-science theory aspiring to some degree of generality.

Evaluation Research

Psychological methodology has outstripped psychological knowledge. The arsenal of mathematical weapons and modes of measuring behavior appear more sophisticated than the information that these techniques have produced. The area of psychology that is perhaps most aptly described by this commentary is social psychology, the field frequently viewed as being in a "crisis state." Many social psychologists admit to being disenchanted because the hopes their discipline initially engendered have not even begun to be realized. Not only were social psychologists going to participate in the exciting intellectual task of discovering the reciprocal influences that take place between individuals and society, but they also would contribute knowledge that would help implement needed social change.

Several reasons could be (and some have been) cited for the failures of social psychology—the limited explanatory capacity of black-box theories, the conflation of facts and values, the intractability of social problems, the resistance to social change, and others. For the moment attention will be shifted to a strategic decision made by many social psychologists that may have contributed to their failure.

Psychology as a discipline, from its very inception, attached great importance to the experimental method as the appropriate, or at least the most fruitful, procedure to achieve understanding. One tends to forget that although Wilhelm Wundt (1832–1920), the father of the independent discipline of psychology, extolled the virtues of the experimental method to study conscious experience, he nevertheless thought it inappropriate for analyzing social phenomena such as religion and customs that were treated in his book *Völkerpsychologie* [Ethnic psychology].

American social psychologists, however, were unwilling to accept the verdict that laboratory research was incompatible with their subject matter. Kurt Lewin and his associates rejected this assumption by observing social interactions under controlled experimental conditions. One of the pioneering investigations was a laboratory study designed to investigate the influence of "democratic" and "authoritarian" leadership on group behavior. Groups of 10-year-old boys were encouraged to form clubs ostensibly for the purpose of making theatrical masks. In some groups the leader was coached to behave "democratically," to be friendly, and to encourage group discussion and decisions while in others the leader was to be "authoritarian" and to deliberately dictate the group's policies and actions. Although the productivity of the "democratic" groups was not consistently superior to that of the "authoritarian" groups, they were friendlier, more cooperative, and less hostile (Lewin, Lippitt, & White, 1939). In referring to this and similar laboratory experiments in social psychology, I concluded:

> Their major significance . . . was a ground-breaking demonstration of the feasibility of adjusting the "social environment" experimentally and measuring group behavior objectively. This was an important contribution; the advancement of any science has been highly correlated with the ability to investigate phenomena in a controlled experimental situation (Kendler, 1963, p. 55).

This conventional conclusion appeared beyond debate when written. But today the value of small-group experimental research is being seriously questioned. The editors, associate editors, and consulting editors of three major social psychological journals were requested "to name up to five empirical studies which had made a significant contribution to the field of social psychology. Significant was purposely left undefined to allow respondents to use their own definitions" (Diamond & Morton, 1978, p. 217).

Although the respondents did not exhibit a high degree of

agreement about which studies were "significant," they did agree about why "significant" studies were important; they opened up new research areas and encouraged further explorations. Asch's (1956) experimental analysis of conformity received the largest number of citations; it stimulated many studies designed to investigate the influence of specific variables—situational, personality, group, cultural—on the tendency of individuals to conform to group pressures.

The second most popular study was the Festinger and Carlsmith's (1959) forced-compliance experiment. According to the cognitive-dissonance model forcing a communicator to deliver a deceitful message creates a dissonance between his actions and his attitudes. The dissonance is assumed to be greater when the reward for compliance is small (one dollar) as compared to large (twenty dollars). In the latter case the communicator can rationalize his deception by the sizable reward gained, but he cannot admit to lying for a paltry sum of one dollar. Consequently, the prediction, which was confirmed, was that the subjects who comply for one dollar would reduce the dissonance by changing their attitude toward the "deceptive" message, convincing themselves that it possesses some truth.

The cognitive-dissonance research program dominated experimental social psychology for many years, stimulating hundreds of experiments. Many perceived the cognitive-dissonance conception as a powerful theory that proved the scientific maturity of social psychology. Gradually, however, intrinsic ambiguities within the theory became obvious, and debates began to rage about the appropriate interpretations of experimental results. When interpreting the results of a given experiment, marked disagreements occurred as to whether dissonance was truly created and if so, whether it was reduced. It appeared to some (Berkowitz, 1969) that the theory had developed into a gigantic tautology; a given behavior is a consequence of dissonance because dissonance causes the behavior. What were obviously needed were independent measures of dissonance arousal and dissonance reduction.

The basic ambiguity inherent in the concepts of dissonance arousal and dissonance reduction led to the degeneration of the cognitive-dissonance research program. Ad hoc interpretations of apparently inconsistent results were easy to concoct while increasing precision of the theoretical concepts failed to materialize. Competing formulations could do no better in accounting for the wealth of data generated by the cognitive-dissonance model. The general pattern of historical development of the cognitive-dissonance research program resembled that of black-box learning conceptions; exciting new theories stimulated much research, the results of which ultimately demonstrated the inadequacies of the formulation.

The important methodological conclusion is that the "significant" experimental social psychology studies (Diamond & Morton, 1978) achieved prominence not because they were part of a research program that represented a theoretical breakthrough but rather because they stimulated a great deal of research. But as already noted, the ability to generate additional research may not be sufficient justification for a theoretical effort. Should it not be demanded that some of these efforts pay off in explaining a set of experimental phenomena as well as in interpreting similar behavior in its natural setting?

The optimism that accompanied the entrance of social psychology into the laboratory, in restrospect, seems unjustified. The most that could be said for the significant social psychology experiments is that they called attention to, and provided tentative insights into, apparently important processes of social behavior, which is no mean achievement, but still far removed from the original goals. But in some cases, experimental social psychology, failed to do even this. One notable example is the research on an experimental task, known as the prisoner's dilemma, in which two participants have an opportunity to profit from cooperation or suffer losses from competition: "What was originally a provocative stimulus to looking at conflict and bargaining in real social life in a new way became a highly technical specialty in its own right, a 'scientific' game adrift from social reality" (Smith, 1976, p. 440).

The failure of experimental social psychology to achieve its anticipated goals has encouraged a reexamination of the empirical techniques of social psychology as well as the means by which the discipline can best serve the needs of society. In regard to the first issue the thesis has been advanced that social psychology is primarily a historical inquiry because basic social forces cannot be replicated in the laboratory. As noted previously, a tendency has prevailed in certain segments of psychology to treat *experimental* and *empirical* as synonymous. For a discipline to be scientific, the experimental method, according to some, must be the dominant mode of inquiry. This position flies in the face of the history of science; Darwin demonstrated the power of naturalistic observations when combined with creative thought. One could also cite the achievements of paleontology and geology, both of which greatly depend on historical analysis.

A methodological prescription is not being offered to the effect that the historical method is either the appropriate or the best method for social psychology. Evolutionary theory, as well as paleontology and historical geology, has been supplemented in significant ways by experimental efforts. It would be foolish to suggest that at all times one specific empirical method should be the only or the most fruitful method for social psychology. But it would not be foolish to consider the relative accomplishments of historical and experimental social psychology while attempting to estimate their future value, especially for the near term.

To be specific, consider for a moment, the potential contributions of the analysis of civil strife by the political scientist, Gurr (1970), with the efforts of laboratory research to verify cognitive dissonance theory. By collecting and analyzing data from a large number of sources of civil strife in 114 countries and formulating summary measures of the strife (e.g., pervasiveness, intensity, duration) as well as of the characteristics of the societies (e.g., economic development, type of political system, geocultural region), Gurr proposes a theory of civil strife that emphasizes the influence of relative deprivation:

> People become most intensely discontented when they cannot get what they think they deserve, not just what they want in the ideal sense; and when they feel that they are making inadequate progress toward their goal, not whether they have actually attained them or not. . . . Underlying the relative deprivation approach to civil strife is the frustration-aggression mechanism, apparently

a fundamental part of our psychological makeup. When we feel
thwarted in an attempt to get something we want, we are likely
to become angry, and when we become angry the most satisfying
inherent response is to strike out at the source of frustration
(1970, p. 596).

The model identifies the general patterns of social conditions
that cause civil strife and hypothesizes about the possible influences of minority—group status, political objectives, amount of
education, and other variables. If Gurr's model were subjected to
the same empirical barrage as was the cognitive-dissonance formulation, ambiguities would inevitably appear. The history of the
frustration-aggression hypothesis has repeatedly demonstrated the
need for additional clarification. Today many would argue that a
social-learning theory of aggression, which does not postulate
frustration to be a causal factor, handles available evidence more
effectively (e.g., Christy, Gelfand, & Hartmann, 1971). The concept of relative deprivation, like that of cognitive dissonance, is
also burdened with difficult measurement problems.

One can suggest, however, that Gurr's model—emerging directly from data from a natural setting—in contrast to the cognitive-dissonance model, can be applied more easily and effectively
to the solution of a pressing social problem. Although the problem of civil strife may not be any more fundamental to a general
theory of social psychology than is attitudinal consistency, it no
doubt represents a much more critical problem in contemporary
societies. If the explanatory limits that characterize black-box
learning theories apply with equal, or greater, force to theoretical
models in social psychology, perhaps the efforts of social psychologists should be tilted more in the direction of contributing
to the solution of social problems. At this stage in its history social
psychology may be more effective in evaluating social programs
than in formulating abstract theories of social behavior. And for
its own good, as well as that of society, social psychology would
be better off doing what it can do best. The era of unqualified
support of research programs generated solely by a scientist's curiosity is over. Governmental funding appears now to be guided
by the pragmatic value implicit in William James's blunt, but elo-

quent, dictum: "Truth is the cash value of an idea." Within this perspective, evaluation of social programs would represent a much higher priority than would formulations of abstract theories of social psychology that have extremely limited explanatory capacities and range of application.

The recommendations that emerge from this analysis are simple in their implications but complex in their implementation. Society has many problems that demand solutions. Social psychology possesses the technology to assist in this effort by virtue of its capacity to evaluate objectively the consequences of different social treatments. In order to achieve this potential it becomes necessary to reorient interest away from purely laboratory phenomena to natural-occurring events. This does not necessarily imply abandonment of the experimental for the historical method. The two methods can be combined as was done in the study that evaluated the negative income tax (page 294). The methods can also be combined by relating studies in the natural setting to those in the laboratory. However, one cannot assume that laboratory studies automatically reflect processes operating in real-life situations. Instead, such relationships must be demonstrated.

A naively romantic attitude that assumes research alone will provide the necessary information for society to choose among several competing social programs is doomed to disappointment. The previous analysis of ethical commitments in interpreting the values of a social program argues against such a simplistic notion. But the conclusion was drawn that evaluation research could make a major social contribution if value judgments were isolated from facts and research findings were communicated in an unbiased fashion.

Two Unending Controversies: Holism Versus Atomism and Rationalism Versus Empiricism

Up to now, in an attempt to identify fundamental historical trends that will shape the future of psychology, attention has been focused on substantive topics: biopsychology, developmental and comparative psychology, and evaluation research. This analysis will now be concerned with two methodological controversies that have their roots in the history of philosophy instead of in research methods in psychology. These two disputes have had pervasive influences in the history of psychology and have occupied, in one form or another, the center stage of important theoretical controversies. Undoubtedly they will persist because each position represents an important research and theoretical strategy. In addition, the disputes are frequently involved with metaphysical and ethical considerations, and as a result neither controversy lends itself to any simple resolution. To understand their future impact upon psychology requires clarification of the methodological issues involved in each debate.

Atomism Versus Holism

Without suggesting that the concepts of *atomism* and *holism* are each limited to a single meaning, one can say that the task of science includes both an atomistic and holistic component—to analyze a phenomenon, or set of phenomena, into a basic set of variables or elements (atomistic) and to synthesize such elements into a valid interpretation (holism). From this descriptive perspective these two components, atomistic and holistic, are neither incompatible nor mutually exclusive. Instead they are complementary because each serves an essential need of science.

Fundamental errors can be made with both analysis and synthesis. A phenomenon can be incorrectly analyzed into erroneous elements. William James accused the structuralists of committing such an error, "the psychologist's fallacy," when they reported discrete elements in conscious experience. These elements (or processes), he argued, were not originally in conscious experience but rather were put there by the structuralists's preconceptions about the nature of consciousness. Similarly, early behaviorists accepted the atomistic assumption that the conditioned response was the unit of complex behavior. Pavlov stated, and Watson accepted, the position "that the different kinds of habits based on training, education and discipline of any sort are nothing but a long chain of conditioned reflexes" (Pavlov, 1927, p. 395). This view was adopted more as a matter of wishful thinking than as a consequence of empirical evidence. It was based upon an oversimplified conception of conditioning and a lack of knowledge about complex behavior. Of course, analytic attempts need not be failures. The interpretation of Mach bands (Ratliff, 1965) in terms of retinal inhibition is one of the notable examples of success in psychology.

Two points should be stressed in evaluating the potential of an atomistic approach that seeks to analyze a given phenomenon into basic elements. First, success is not guaranteed. Analyzing conscious experience into basic processes proved to be a failure as a result both of apparently contradictory evidence and of methodological limitations of introspection. The theoretical analysis of complex behavior into individual conditioned responses failed because of its inability to explain complex forms of behavior such as memory for meaningful material that depended upon hierarchical forms of representation (e.g., Bower, 1970).

Although success is not guaranteed with an atomistic approach, neither is failure preordained. One can not conclusively rule out, even though it appears highly improbable, that some elementary model of phenomenology or conditioning could achieve success where its predecessors failed. In other words, specific analytical attempts fail but not the analytical method. Consequently, a wholesale and a priori rejection of an atomistic approach is unjustified. Holistic conceptions denying the relevance of an atomistic approach have surfaced in many forms in the history of biology and psychology, often justified by the methodological thesis that the analytical dissecting methods of physics and chemistry are inappropriate for the life sciences (e.g., Goldstein, 1939). The accomplishments of Crick and Watson, who analyzed genetic transmission into a code consisting of four basic chemicals, should give pause to anyone considering the adoption of a general antiatomistic approach in the life sciences.

Two general strategies can operate when attempting to synthesize the results of analysis. One is that the basic elements will be sufficient to explain the operation of the entire system, the other is that they will not. An example of the former, in which the analysis alone provides the grist for the synthesis, is Boyle's law: At a constant temperature the volume of a confined gas decreases in inverse proportion to the pressure exerted on it. In this law the component variables (temperature, volume, pressure) are sufficient to describe the entire system without reference to any holistic principle. The dark adaptation curve of the human eye illustrates another case in which the entire system functions in a manner that can be described as "the whole is the sum of its parts." The curve of dark adaptation, which represents the weakest light a subject can see after he has been in the dark for various periods of time, has two sections. In the first section, it drops steeply and levels off after five minutes. The second section drops almost as sharply at the beginning, then levels off and drops very slowly for more than thirty minutes. The two sections result from the different operating characteristics of rods and cones with the first section representing cone adaptation and the second, rod adaptation.

Sometimes the entire system does not appear to operate in terms of only its component parts, i.e., the operative characteristics of the component parts do not appear sufficient to explain the operation of the entire system. Perceptual phenomena are often cited as illustrating the inadequacy of an atomistic approach; what one perceives is not simply an aggregate of the component elements but instead the entire configuration determines how the parts will appear. Figure 8.1 is a pattern of four dots that is perceived not only as four dots but also as a square. Gestalt psychologists suggest that the perception of the square illustrates the maxim: "The whole is more than the sum of its parts"; the perception of the dots is altered as a function of the configuration into which they enter.

Analytical terminology can also be employed to describe the perceptual phenomena generated by Figure 8.1. The perception of Figure 8.1 is a function of the four dots and the relationships among them, i.e., the pattern of stimulation is analyzed into two components, the individual dots and their positions in relation to each other.

Figure 8.1

Is one description—the holistic or atomistic—preferable to the other? On a very fundamental level they are equivalent in that they both identify the same set of variables, the four dots and the interrelationships among them. However equivalent they may be, the two interpretations can have markedly different influences on methodological and theoretical decisions, even when the importance of analysis is recognized in a holistic approach or the importance of synthesis in an atomistic orientation. For example, Gestalt psychologists, who emphasized the significance of configurations in psychological events, made it clear that analysis should be encouraged, as long as the intrinsic principles of the whole were not ignored. Similarly structuralists and stimulus-response psychologists, who expounded the virtues of analysis, nevertheless stressed the need for synthesis and even employed holistic language that suggested that parts were altered when embedded in a configuration. Titchener, when considering the problems of how the basic processes of consciousness combine to form a unitary experience, concluded that the effects of interaction were significant; the elementary processes "flow together, mix together, overlapping, reinforcing, modifying or arresting one another, in obedience to certain psychological laws" (1899, p. 17). Similarly, Hull postulated that individual stimuli when presented together "interact . . . in such a way that each receptor discharge changes all the others to a greater or lesser extent . . . This type of action [afferent interaction] is particularly important because the mediation of the responses of the organisms to distinctive combinations or patterns of stimuli, rather than to the components of the patterns, is presumably dependent upon it" (1943, p. 385).

Regardless of how much emphasis each placed upon a holistic or atomistic approach, Gestalt psychologists, structuralists, and stimulus-response psychologists acknowledged that the two orientations are complementary. However, the question can be raised as to whether the sentiments expressed paid only lip service to a scientific ideal rather than made a commitment to cope with the intricacies of the atomistic or holistic task. Overemphasizing either an atomistic or holistic approach tends to discourage a theorist from dealing constructively with the problems of the other orientation (analysis or synthesis).

Gestalt psychologists seemed for the most part satisfied to demonstrate, as is the case for the perception of Figure 8.1, that the whole is something other than just the sum of its parts. The demonstration provided many with an intuitive understanding (page 188) that the holistic interpretation was sufficient; further analysis and research were not needed.

The eagerness to accept a holistic interpretation without expending any effort to analyze the problem is nicely illustrated in Köhler's (1938) research on transposition, the phenomenon in which an organism transfers a relational solution from one discrimination problem to a similar one. Chickens were trained to peck for food at the lighter of two gray cards. After the subjects had learned to consistently select the lighter gray they were tested with a new pair containing the previously correct gray and a still lighter one. If they had learned a specific habit to each of the gray cards during the initial discrimination, Köhler argued that "it would be quite incomprehensible" for the animals to choose the lightest gray because they had been previously rewarded for selecting the gray that was now the darker one. The results showed that a majority of choice (68 percent) was to the lightest gray thus justifying a holistic interpretation that the chickens had learned, not two separate habits, but instead a relationship (e.g., select the lighter one) between the two stimuli.

A stronger commitment to analysis than Köhler had would have encouraged certain questions. Why were 32 percent of the responses to the previously rewarded stimulus, the darker one? What would have occurred if the difference between the pair of gray cards was greater or lesser than that employed by Köhler? Is it truly impossible that a theory based upon the learning of individual habits could explain Köhler's findings? Spence (1937), an S-R psychologist and therefore committed to an analytical approach, entertained such questions and formulated an ingenious conditioning model to explain transposition. His model was based on the assumption that in Köhler's experiment *two specific habits had been acquired;* thus, his effort, if nothing else, contradicted Köhler's conclusion that transposition could not be interpreted in terms of a simple habit model. Spence's model did more in that it explained the influence of the difference between training and test stimuli. However Spence's conception proved inadequate to the task of interpreting all transposition data mainly because the phenomenon proved to be much more complex than the initial evidence suggested. The major point here is that the study of transposition, as a case history in science, demonstrates how the ready acceptance of a holistic position can discourage further analytic attempts.

One can also point out that an extreme atomistic approach can discourage holistic (relational) considerations. Even though Titchener acknowledged that basic sensory experiences could modify each other, he never attempted to work out the principles of synthesis. His obsession with analysis prevented him from coping with the possible interrelationships among basic sensory experiences. Similarly, Hull's use of afferent interaction to deal with perceptual interaction effects, of the sort that interested Gestalt psychologists, was at best a recognition of the problem, but it accomplished nothing in contributing to its solution. Like Titchener, Hull's strong atomistic orientation hampered him in coping with possible interaction effects.

Emergentism

A discussion of holism versus atomism cannot be completed without some reference to emergentism—the assumption that properties of wholes cannot be understood from properties of their component parts. Gestalt psychologists essentially adopted this position in their treatment of the phi-phenomenon. In Wertheimer's demonstration of apparent movement two lights were successively projected through two slits, one vertical and the other about 25 degrees from the vertical. When the time interval between the two lights was approximately 60 milliseconds, the subject perceived the light move from one position to the other. Because there was no physical movement it was concluded that the perceived movement emerged from the perceptual configuration. The phi-phenomenon was an illustration of the fundamental "formula" of Gestalt theory:

> There are wholes, the behavior of which is not determined by that of their individual elements but where the part-processes are themselves determined by the intrinsic nature of the whole (Wertheimer, 1938, p. 2).

This holistic interpretation cannot simply be justified by a discrepancy between psychological and physical measurement, i.e., apparent movement occurs in the absence of physical movement. Psychological and physical measurement need not be perfectly matched because they reflect the operation of two different systems.

Understanding the significance of the phi-phenomenon requires distinguishing between its negative and positive theoretical implications. Too often this is not done, and as a consequence,

evidence that is embarassing to one theoretical position is automatically assumed to be in support of another.

The data of the phi-phenomenon are inconsistent with the
structuralist hypothesis that perceptions are combinations of elementary sensations. If this were true how could movement be perceived in the phi-phenomenon when only stationarity is sensed?
Structuralism could not offer a satisfactory answer to this question
but that does not preclude a satisfactory analytical interpretation.
It should be remembered that the research strategy of structuralism was first to discover the basic elements (or processes) of consciousness, then formulate principles that govern the synthesis of
basic elements, and finally to relate the analysis of experience to
physiological events. This research program foundered on the first
task because of the inability to formulate phenomenological criteria for designating an element of experience to be basic. The
failure of structuralism to provide a satisfactory account of the
phi-phenomenon did not stem directly from a failure of synthesis
but instead from insurmountable methodological problems of a
descriptive phenomenology (page 45). Assuming that a satisfactory method of treating phenomenological data could be developed, the likelihood of a satisfactory atomistic account of the phi-
phenomenon cannot be ruled out. Certainly an analytical neurophysiological theory would be within the realm of the possible.

The holistic interpretation of the phi-phenomenon based upon
"the intrinsic nature of the whole" suffers from both incompleteness and vagueness. It essentially states that the phi-phenomenon
does not require any explanation because it is irreducible to any
analytical interpretation. Should not an explanation, especially if
a deductive criterion is adopted, say something more? The notion that the whole determines the functioning of its parts is at
best obscure and at worst mystical. What is meant by the statement that the whole determines the functioning of its parts? Are
not wholes always parts of larger wholes? Can you explain the
behavior of a husband without considering the activities of the
wife? And should not the behavior of the children be considered?
His own parents? The extended family? Society as a whole?
Neighboring societies? The international situation? This line of

reasoning leads to the conclusion that the world, or perhaps the entire universe, determines the behavior of a husband. Although some would consider this to be an unreasonable example to illustrate the limitations of the holistic approach, it should be noted that holists in the history of biology constantly expanded the size of the system they thought necessary to consider. Initially it was argued that the fundamental biological unit was not the cell but the organism as a whole. Then it was argued that the organism in relation to its surrounding environment was unanalyzable (Phillips, 1976). This inherent tendency in holism to enlarge the size of the unanalyzable system is at the basis of William James's conclusion that holism is an impossible orientation because, "everything would have to be known before anything is known!" Bertrand Russell takes a similar dim view: "If all knowledge was knowledge of the universe as a whole, there would be no knowledge."[6]

Holism, when it takes on an exaggerated opposition to atomism, can assume a mystical posture. This was done by Hans Driesch (1908) who, in order to account for the whole determining the functioning of its entire self, postulated the existence of a vital spirit that guided the development of embryos. An extreme holism that takes the position that a whole is irreducible backs itself into a corner where it is confronted with a choice between mysticism or self-denial. Either a mystical force like an entelechy must be postulated to control the activities of the entire configuration, or the whole must be analyzed into specific entities and interactions that determine its operation. When the holistic commitment is excessive the tendency is to adopt a mystical force that binds the whole into an unanalyzable configuration. Phillips (1976) suggests that this tendency has operated in some conceptions of humanistic psychology. Accepting Kurt Goldstein's *The Organism* (1939) as the precursor of humanistic psychology, Phillips believes that the conception of a human being as a "functional whole" is a reasonable orientation when interpreted as emphasizing interrelationships among various components of the

6. Both quotations are cited in Phillips (1976).

human organism. But, as exemplified in the following quotation, when such a view becomes exaggerated enough to deny the relevance of the atomistic approach of the natural sciences, the holistic position crosses the boundary of science, however vague it may be, and enters into the realm of transcendentalism:

> Our procedure is rooted in a more profound conviction: *this is a conviction that a state of greater perfection can never be understood from that of less perfection, and that only the converse is possible.* It is very feasible to isolate parts from the whole, but a perfect whole can never be composed by synthesizing it from less perfect parts (Goldstein, 1939, p. 515).

A Logical Consideration

Debates about holism and atomism tend to ignore an important logical problem. Can consciousness be reduced to a set of neural events? The answer is "No" and "Yes" depending upon what is meant by "reduced." One cannot explain the experience of *happiness* by deducing it *directly* from neurophysiological hypotheses. The conclusion of a valid deduction cannot contain an expression that does not appear in the premises (e.g., All animals are mortal, all humans are animals, therefore all humans are mortal). However if a theory of consciousness were coordinated to a theory of neurophysiological processes, then it would be possible to explain happiness as a consequence of neurophysiological events (e.g., Happiness is an experience that results from x neurophysiological condition, x neurophysiological conditions are present in individual A, therefore individual A is happy). Within this context radical atomists delude themselves by believing that consciousness can simply be reduced to a set of neural events while extreme holists deceive themselves by denying the possibility that conscious experience can be analyzed in terms of neural events.

Summary

My methodological critique of holism may appear to be more severe than my critique of atomism. However true that may be, it would be a mistake to conclude that I believe holism represents a greater danger than atomism or that in the history of psychology holism has done more damage. The major thesis advanced is that analysis and synthesis are complementary activities in science, and the emphasis on one to the exclusion of the other will misdirect theoretical efforts. A radical atomism can be blind to significant interaction effects while an unbridled holism can be convinced that analysis is an inappropriate procedure in the life sciences.

It is tempting after dealing with the complexities of the relationship between holism and atomism to conclude, as did Gestalt psychologists, that analysis can be fruitful as long as the organizational principles of the whole are not ignored. Such advice says much less than it appears to. At best, it encourages one to be brilliantly prescient, a recommendation which one cannot disagree with but might experience difficulty achieving. At worst, it deludes one into believing that there is a simple orderly procedure to cope with the complexities of the analytic-synthetic problems of science. There is not.

Rationalism Versus Empiricism

Just as it is futile to argue about whether holism or atomism is the appropriate orientation in psychology, so is it fruitless to debate whether rationalism or empiricism is the proper framework for all of psychology or for any specific research problem.

Rationalism and empiricism will be discussed from both epistemological and psychological perspectives. This does not imply that epistemology is independent of psychology because epistemology is a human enterprise subject to psychological analysis (Piaget, 1978). But these two domains can be treated separately if one makes the subtle distinction between the origin and acquisition of knowledge.

The epistemological viewpoint of empiricism assumes that knowledge is derived from observation while rationalism supposes reason alone can yield truths about the world. If one accepts the notion that scientific knowledge is based on observations, then empiricism is an essential component of the scientific enterprise. But is it the only one? Not if the observations of individual facts and empirical laws are viewed as isolated events unrelated to each other. These events by themselves do not provide a coherent picture of the world; that can only be achieved by rational means. In other words, rational theory is required to integrate and interpret empirical observations. Rationalism and empiricism therefore supplement each other. This view is neatly expressed by Giorgio de Santillana: "The true scientist has an empiricist conscience and a rationalist imagination" (cited in Williams, 1967).

The psychological meaning of rationalism and empiricism has to do with an organism's acquisition of knowledge. Is all of our knowledge a result of our experiences (learning), or are we born with innate ideas such as God exists or with a blueprint for a universal grammar? The concept of innate ideas can be interpreted in one of two ways. One, impossible to accept, is that a neonate possesses a full-blow notion of an Almighty or a detailed knowledge of a universal grammar appropriate for all languages. Its linguistic and cognitive limitations prevent us from seriously entertaining such a hypothesis. The other possible meaning, difficult to reject, is that the human organism is genetically preprogrammed to develop neurophysiological structures that are essential for the acquisition of certain knowledge and forms of behavior. Our possession of two eyes assists us in developing a veridical concept of three-dimensional space; the structure of our genitalia predisposes humans to certain forms of erotic behavior and certain ideas about sex; the structure and functioning of our brain enables us to form a concept of the number system and to respond to certain sequences of sounds as music; and so on. There is nothing that we do or think that in some way is not an expression of our neurophysiological heritage. The theoretical issue is not whether we have "innate ideas" in the sense of genetic preprogramming, but instead the nature of the influence of genetic preprogramming on a given form of behavior. There is no question that in the history of American psychology a greater emphasis has been placed on learning as contrasted with innate factors in explaining most forms of behavior. The most extreme anti-innate position was expressed by Watson in his boast that a child could be selected at random and trained to be any kind of a specialist (page 180). To a significant extent this overemphasis of the power of learning was an expression of the political commitment that genetic limitations need not obstruct the realization of equalitarian ideals. Watson ultimately rejected his extreme environmentalism, and later learning theorists acknowledged the significance of maturational limitations on the effectiveness of training. For example, the concept of *reading readiness* implies that regardless of how potent training procedures are, they are ineffective for the child who has not yet reached an appropriate maturational level. Although not usually recognized as such the concept expresses a rationalist position in the rationalist versus empiricist debate. Essentially it states that we are born with an innate notion about reading that begins to operate when a certain maturational level is reached.

Up to this point, my analysis of the rationalism versus empiricism conflict raises no significant epistemological or empirical issue. The scientific effort contains both an empirical and rational component. From the psychological point of view the controversy at best represents the degree of emphasis one should place on genetic and environmental influence. Differences of opinion concerning the relative importance of these factors or the interaction between them can ultimately be investigated empirically.

Thus it should be possible to limit the differences between rationalistic and empirically oriented conceptions to those that could be empirically resolved. One notable exception would occur if a rationalist strictly adhered to the epistemological tradition, insisting that a rational interpretation of a phenomenon, independent of empirical evidence, was sufficient. For the most part psychologists have explicitly rejected this position even though their efforts, at times, appear to be consistent with it. Chomsky (1975), perhaps the most distinguished spokesman for a rationalist position, insists that his own interpretation of language acquisition is as much subject to empirical test as is any empiricist (learning) conception. In principle, such a claim cannot be denied. However, in practice, an exaggerated commitment to one side of the rationalism-empiricism controversy, as is the case in the holism-atomism conflict, can create a climate of confusion that impedes resolutions of empirical questions.

Schlesinger (in press) argues that Chomsky unfairly demands more empirical evidence to support the empiricist position than he requires for his own rationalist assumptions. It is not the rationalist assumption that innate factors are involved in language acquisition that is the cause of the asymmetry, but instead Chomsky's implementation of this view that encourages his own position to be impregnable to empirical attack while simultaneously creating a "straw-man" interpretation of the empiricist (learning theory) approach. This is accomplished by insisting that in order to explain human language acquisition it becomes necessary to postulate innate "fixed and highly restricted schemata which come into operation under limited conditions of exposure to data" (Chomsky, 1975, p. 154). As a result, a system of grammatical rules that represents knowledge of language develops from these postulated "schemata." This claim is not expressed within any specific theory; it is still only "a program of research" (Chomsky, 1968, p. 70). The trouble with it, Schlesinger argues, is that it fails to yield any empirically refutable hypotheses. Chomsky argues in favor of a universal grammar citing as an example the fact that English-speaking children unerringly make use of structure-dependent grammatical rules that they have had no opportunity to learn. Because it is inconceivable to think that children are preprogramed to learn only English, these grammatical rules must be universal. But if a universal grammar is not known, it becomes impossible to know whether any given language departs from its principles. And even if a set of languages revealed a grammar common to all, would the discovery of another language that obeyed a discrepant principle deny the assumption of innate schemata? No, suggests Schlesinger. The meaning of the innate schemata would most likely be expanded so that the universal grammar would have an option to contain principle A or its opposite.

Chomsky's argument in favor of his position over the learning-theory approach can be characterized as "negative theorizing." The assumption that language is innate, according to Chomsky, can only be faulted by a satisfactory learning theory. In essence, Chomsky's position is that rationalism is validated by the failures of empiricism. Whatever the inadequacies of learning theories, and however unsuccessful they may or will be, their failures do not confirm a rationalist position. Only a rationalist *theory* can accomplish that. Schlesinger (in press) stresses this point in his conclusion that, "Rationalism . . . becomes the last refuge for those too tired to search any further."

The methodological asymmetry between the demands of a rationalist and empiricist approach is greatest in relation to the demand for supporting evidence. A rationalist psychological theory tends to fall back on a rationalistic epistemological position in order to support its position. In contrast, the empiricist approach by its very nature encourages the search for supporting empirical evidence although, admittedly, decades ago learning theorists seemed to interpret language acquisition more in terms of theoretical analogies than independent empirical evidence. But now, primarily as a function of Chomsky's challenges, more fruitful empirical methodologies have been developed that have forced psycholinguists, even those trained in a rationalist tradition, to buttress their theoretical notions with relevant evidence. And now that the empirical realm of language acquisition is expanding (Schlesinger, in press), Chomsky's extreme rationalist position is withering in the face of evidence that suggests the importance of experience in language acquisition.

It is instructive to note that Schlesinger does not adopt the extreme learning-theory approach that encouraged Chomsky's original rationalistic position. Instead, he assumes an interactionist position that encourages a program that would include three areas of research:

A. Linguistic research with the aim of discovering generalizations about the principles underlying human language (putative linguistic universals).
B. Psychological research aiming at the discovery of other cognitive domains in which principles revealed in A operate.

C. Psychological research in which explanations are constructed and tested of how the principles revealed in A develop through interaction with the environment (ibid.).

The purpose of this discussion is neither to become involved in the empirical issues of the rationalist-empiricist debate concerning language acquisition nor to defend Schlesinger's conception of a fruitful research program. The major point is that all psychological activities are to some extent a function of complex interactions between genetic preprogramming and environmental influences. Because no simple or single answer is possible to this general problem, the rationalist-empiricist controversy will inevitably persist. In order to prevent the debate from engulfing us in confusion it becomes imperative to recognize the distinction between its epistemological and empirical meanings and to become aware of the possible methodological asymmetries that certain positions, either rationalist or empiricist, can promote. Although the present discussion of psycholinguistics noted the asymmetries that a rationalist position can encourage, the reverse can operate within an extreme environmentalism (page 252). In regard to epistemology the greatest confusion will be created by those who in self-delusion believe that they are operating as empiricists but in reality are functioning as full-blown rationalists. In regard to empiricism clarity will be enhanced by those who espouse the significance of innate or environmental processes without denying, or overlooking, the effect of complementary genetic or environmental factors.

Psychotherapy

One of the great mysteries in psychology is the popularity of psychotherapy, "talk therapy," which aims to modify a person's behavior and experience by communication techniques. For the most part, available evidence fails to demonstrate convincingly the effectiveness of various forms of psychotherapy. Yet the supply of patients, and even therapists, appears inexhaustible. In a recent advanced undergraduate class half of my students were involved in some form of psychotherapy, either as a patient or in a co-counselor relationship in which a pair of students exchange roles as counselor and client.

Why is psychotherapy so popular? If a certain form of behavior is widely practiced some form of reinforcement is apparently operating. The absence of overwhelming evidence for psychotherapy's effectiveness does not deny the possibility that the patient is being reinforced in some manner for his participation.

Over the years I have asked both patients and therapists about their evaluations of psychotherapy as a result of their personal experiences. The following anecdotes highlight both the difficulties of judging the effectiveness of psychotherapy and the variety of incentives that might be operating.

Many years ago at a cocktail party I met a man in his mid-forties who was married to an heiress and therefore able to pursue his personal interest in psychoanalysis. In our conversation he mentioned that he had been in analysis for the past twelve years. Surprised, and without any forethought, I exclaimed, "Any improvement?" He responded matter-of-factly, "Oh, no, but I would hate to think what I would be like if not for my analysis!"

Recently, in response to my query as to how a psychotherapist knew whether her counseling was effective for her patients, mostly male university students, the answer given was that prior to the counselling most of the students were virgins, afterwards none were. (The striking nature of the data left me so speechless that I forgot to ask what specific therapeutic procedure was employed.)

A successful and widely respected artist, on a well-known talk show, readily admitted that his analysis had not modified his neurotic behavior, but he was nevertheless convinced that it unleashed his creative potential.

A distinguished psychologist concluded that his own psychoanalysis did not do any more for him than a good friend could have done. His analyst retorted that it was interesting to note that his famous patient did not have a good friend.

Finally, Woody Allen, in one of his early recordings of a night club performance, questioned whether the fees to his psychoanalyst should be listed on his income tax as a medical expense or a religious contribution. It can also be asked whether, for some patients, psychotherapy should be considered a recreational expense?

The issue raised by these anecdotes is whether psychotherapy, in many cases, is truly a means to the end of achieving "psychological health" or is an end in itself. To be specific, one does not take an antibiotic, have a hernia repaired, or receive treatment to recover from alcoholism for the same reason that one goes to church, reads a book, or forms a friendship. The treatment itself is not an integral part of living but instead is a means by which one can live one's life in a desired fashion.

Back (1972) suggests that experiential groups (personal growth groups, T-groups, sensitivity training groups, etc.) frequently serve as ends, not just means. He speculates that their popularity is due to certain social forces unique to the United States; Europeans have not been attracted to experiential groups in any degree approaching that of the Americans. Back believes experiential groups are popular in the United States because of a combination of the mobility, affluence, and secularization of the society. The mobility of American society frustrates many persons' need for close personal relationships. Affluence provides money and time to seek satisfactions that money by itself fails to bring. The secularization of American society fails to provide the opportunities for strong emotional and mystical experiences that normally occur in a ritualistic setting. Furthermore, experiential groups can be fun and can lead to fun relationships. And if the person who wants to participate cannot accept a hedonistic interpretation of experiential groups, he can always justify them in terms of the need for personal growth.

The same characterization can be applied to many cases of one-on-one psychotherapy even to the extent of facilitating the formation of close personal relationships with the therapist and a community of others who undergo psychotherapy. Another factor, which may be the most important, is that psychotherapy clarifies the human condition. For many people Freud offered a picture with an "essential validity" (page 175). However persuasive Freud's conception is one should realize some people will be more drawn to other conceptions of the human condition such as those offered by Jung, Erikson, Maslow, Perls, or Werner Erhard. Therapists have offered a variety of pictures of the human condition varying in complexity, depth, and ethical commitments, and they all have found some audience that consider their interpretation to possess an "essential validity." The wide popularity of psychotherapy may be due in part to the search of many for a compelling picture of the human condition that they have been unsuccessful in finding outside of the therapeutic situation.

Albee (1977) suggests that historical forces have elevated the position of the psychotherapist to one of major social importance in American society. The early growth of capitalism demanded changes in human motivation involving both a repression and control of pleasure seeking, and a positive evaluation of hard work, thrift, long-range goals, plus a tough-minded rationalism. These changes are still operative in upwardly mobile groups in the United States and in less well-developed societies that are making the transition from an agrarian-village to an industrial-urban society.

This motivational pattern, similar to the Protestant ethic of Max Weber (1904–5, 1958), has been attenuated in large sections of the American middle-class. Albee suggests that this is due, in part, to the economic needs of the capitalistic system, which requires impulse buying and self-gratification to consume the excessive amount of manufactured goods that are not really needed. Several generations of people have already been raised in this consumer-oriented society who believe that it is "all right to yield to impulse, to buy without guilt, and to consume without shame" (Albee, 1977).

> With the deterioration of the Protestant ethic has also come a deterioration in rationalism and science as well as faith in traditional religious beliefs. Fifty years ago most people put their faith either in religion or in science as the best source of explaining away their existential anxieties and uncertainties. With both of these systems now in jeopardy, people are desperate for new answers to the eternal existential questions. As a result, we are

witnessing the rise of the psychotherapist as the new shaman, explanation giver, and guru. Psychology flourishes as the new myth system (ibid., p. 151).

An exponent of psychotherapy could readily acknowledge that Albee is a keen observer of the social scene and accept the validity of the distinction between psychotherapy as a method of healing and as an oracle for answers to eternal existential questions and still conclude, "So what?" If psychotherapy serves two important functions, so much the better! The popularity of psychotherapy demonstrates its capacity to satisfy these two needs (some would argue they are really one). But even those who accept the distinction and question the healing effectiveness of psychotherapy as well as the propriety of providing spiritual guidance would find it difficult to restrict the practice of psychotherapy. To deny a person's freedom to receive psychotherapy as a form of spiritual guidance might prove to be more difficult than to restrict his opportunity to receive it as a form of treatment. In the former case the right to a religious freedom is fundamental in American society, and from the political perspective the right to seek spiritual guidance from a psychotherapist is as justified as receiving it from a priest, minister, or rabbi. In the case of psychotherapy as a means of healing one can suggest that psychotherapists should be able to provide evidence to their patients that their techniques can be effective. But even this demand could be considered excessive because of a variety of factors not the least of which is the absence of any clear-cut, universally accepted criterion of mental health.

Psychotherapy can be perceived in another context, that of a social need rather than that of an individual choice. Sooner or later, the United States, like other Western democracies, will institute some form of a national health program. Many professional psychologists will argue that a national health program should include psychotherapeutic assistance to those who need it. But since the cost of this program is to be shared by the entire population, questions will be raised about the effectiveness of psychotherapy as practiced by psychiatrists, psychologists, and other professionals, as well as by untrained amateurs such as those who do co-counselling. Questions will also be raised about whether society should foot the bill for a "demoralized" individual's search for "spiritual guidance." Should a government get directly involved in a person's search for spiritual values with the threat it poses to the separation of religion and government? Or is "spiritual guidance" a "right" of an individual as is physical health and therefore should be included in any national health program? Even if the response to the second question is affirmative, the question will be raised as to what kind of guidance should be offered: the "Protestant ethic," human growth potential, a simple hedonism, or some other form?

The questions posed have obvious ethical components, but they also involve empirical issues that demand clarification. The efficacy of psychotherapy has been subjected to empirical evaluation for decades. The results have not been convincing, one way or the other. Some would even maintain that the problem is too complex for available techniques, an admission that would be self-defeating if one favored the inclusion of psychotherapy in a national health program.

The failure of past research to offer a definitive evaluation of psychotherapy may reflect the effects of an inappropriate research strategy. Initially the global questions of "Is psychotherapy effective?" or "Which kind of psychotherapy is best?" were asked. With time, more specific issues have been raised as to the effects of different variables (e.g., empathic ability of therapist, similarity between therapist and patient) and outcome measures (e.g., phenomenological reports, job performance) without regard to the particular form of psychotherapy that is being practiced. The increasing sophistication of research techniques plus a stronger demand from a tax-conscious society for a cost-effectiveness evaluation of governmental programs brings the expectation that future research on psychotherapy will be more informative than it has been in the past.

Two fundamental research topics, outcome measures and cost-effectiveness, promise to attract the attention of investigators in the future. These issues are highlighted by the results of a recent survey that sought to evaluate the outcome of psychotherapy and counseling (Smith & Glass, 1977). The conclusion drawn was that, "On the average the typical therapy client is better off than 75 percent of untreated individuals." Different types of therapy did not have much of an effect. Four major outcome measures were employed: fear-anxiety reduction, self-esteem, adjustment, and school/work achievement. Although these measures were not strictly comparable, the findings gave "a credible impression that fear and self-esteem are more susceptible to change in therapy than are the relatively more serious behaviors grouped under the categories 'adjustment' and 'achievement.'" Some psychologists would disagree as to what constitutes the "more serious" outcome measures, but the important point is that the results suggest the interesting notion that psychotherapy is more effective in changing the mental state of a patient, as measured by personality inventories (e.g., sobriety, disruptive behavior, job performance), than in changing overt behavior. This finding raises many interesting questions surrounding the relationship between "subjective" and "objective" outcomes. Is it possible that only the verbal descriptions of one's inner experience are being modified in psychotherapy, not the inner experience itself? Would not neurophysiological measures be helpful in trying to answer such a question? Investigating the relationships among the various outcome measures is an essential step in the evaluation of psychotherapy.

Even if the general implications of Smith and Glass's conclusions are accepted, the demonstration of psychotherapy's effectiveness is not sufficient evidence for it to be included in a national health program. Is it cost-effective? Gallo (1978) raises an interesting point when considering this question. Estimating that the average patient in the Smith and Glass study spent $510 for psychotherapy, a figure that would be considered a discount in New York and Los Angeles areas, Gallo remarks:

> Unfortunately, all we know in this case is the cost. We certainly do not know how the patients' adjustment would have been affected had they chosen to spend their $510 on a trip to Hawaii, dancing lessons, a new wardrobe, plastic surgery, or a sail boat. There are no data on alternative courses of action (1978, p. 516).

Gallo's position may appear extreme because it suggests that research to discover the cost-effectiveness of psychotherapy could be never-ending. If a trip to Hawaii is not as effective as psychotherapy, how about Bora-Bora? However demanding Gallo may appear the significant point is that when evaluating any therapeutic techniques the consequences of other alternatives must be considered. And the less effective a treatment is, the more likely it is that other alternatives will be examined.

If psychotherapy proves more effective than competing procedures, then the question will be raised as to how it can be most economically employed. What level of training, if any, is required? Are some individuals because of their personality capable of being good therapists with a minimal training? Cannot much of the need for psychotherapy be satisfied by teachers, ministers, nurses, friends, and self-help programs? These questions may appear unfair, imposing excessive demands upon psychology that exceed those directed at other professions, like medicine. Although this objection may possess some validity it should be recognized that the effectiveness of psychotherapy does not approach that of many medical procedures. However unfair one may feel such demands are, they nevertheless will be made, and psychologists will be well advised to be prepared for them.

Some problems of measuring the cost effectiveness of psychotherapy in a national health program may be solved by considering psychotherapy within the context of physical, not psychological health (Olbrisch, 1977). A number of studies have demonstrated the effectiveness of psychotherapy in hospital settings and the economic savings resulting from it. Patients undergoing heart surgery appear to be greatly benefited from relaxation therapy. A variety of surgical patients ranging from children undergoing tonsillectomies to women anticipating gynecological operations have been helped by psychotherapy. Some objective outcome measures that have been used in judging the effectiveness of psychotherapy are the number of days required for postoperative care before discharge, the amount of pain medication required, the incidence of postoperative psychosis, and the amount of vomiting in the recovery room. In some of these studies, it must be noted, successful psychotherapy was carried out by nurses and anesthesiologists.

The evidence (Olbrisch, 1977) that psychotherapy can meet the criterion of cost effectiveness in a hospital setting suggests an expansion of psychological services in the health sciences. Psychological, or what some would prefer to call behavioral, medicine could be widely practiced, depending upon the development of new procedures and their empirical validation.

The question has been raised whether a cost-conscious society will be willing to pay for psychological services that clearly do not pass some stringent criterion of cost effectiveness. This query was directed at psychotherapy that was mainly concerned with spiritual guidance and achieving "inner serenity" in the absence of significant behavior change. However, at the same time, the suggested effectiveness of psychotherapeutic procedures in surgical cases raises the question not of whether national health service can afford a psychological program but whether it can afford not to have one.

A major problem in a national health program would be created by individuals who overutilize services and facilities without any apparent medical disability. This would add to excessive costs while simultaneously diminishing the effectiveness of the entire program (Cummings, 1977). The early identification of these overutilizers and their effective treatment would be an enormous contribution to a national health program. Similarly, solving problems created by such prevalent disorders as alcoholism and hypertension would also reduce the drain on limited resources and thereby help elevate the level of service. All of these problems, and others of equal importance, have not escaped the attention of psychologists. Challenges imposed by a national health program may initiate research programs that will yield more effective techniques of coping with these problems than have occurred in the past. A national health program will confront psychologists with an opportunity to convince society, and perhaps even themselves, that they have an important role to play in the health sciences.

The Information-Processing Paradigm

If we use Kuhn's concept of paradigm loosely, and some (Masterman, 1970) would insist that it has never been used in any other way, we can discuss a recent movement in psychology as a single force although in reality it possesses much less unity than other popular paradigms of the past, e.g., Freudian psychoanalysis, Hull-Spence neobehaviorism, or cognitive dissonance theory. Since the historical process that produced the information-processing paradigm has yet to be completed it becomes difficult, if not impossible, to project its force and direction into psychology's future. Historical analysis should not begin until history is completed. At the same time any discussion of future trends in psychology would be incomplete if reference to the information-processing paradigm were not made. Having observed the rise and fall of several paradigms in psychology from 1938 on, I am impressed with the unrivalled success of the information-processing orientation in capturing the minds and hearts of such a large percentage of investigators in the general research area that used to be referred to as learning, memory, and problem solving.

The information-processing paradigm emerged from a concern with cognitive psychology, the domain of which is primarily man's higher mental processes (Lachman, Lachman, & Butterfield, 1978). Many historical forces operated to initiate and sustain the revolution in which the information-processing paradigm overthrew, in the sense of capturing a greater following, two dominant behavioristic orientations: operant behaviorism, which was initiated by Skinner, and neobehaviorism, which owes its methodological and theoretical stance mainly to Hull and Spence.

Neobehaviorism had reached its apogee of popularity during the 1950s and soon thereafter it became apparent to many, including its proponents, that Hull's optimistic notion of achieving a general theory based upon principles of conditioning, would not be realized. Spence, in particular, acknowledged that theories of animal learning would not suffice to explain human behavior, repeatedly emphasizing that the boundary conditions of his discrimination learning theory (1936) excluded articulate human organisms. In addition, when suggesting how a neobehavioristic orientation could handle human perception and cognition, Spence (1950) explicitly acknowledged the necessity for postulating processes not required for the interpretation of infrahuman behavior. This acknowledgement, in no way, undermined the strategy of formulating a theory of animal behavior based upon principles of conditioning. The absence of inconsistency was based upon both strategic and theoretical considerations. If one cannot formulate a satisfactory theory of the behavior of a rat how could one possibly hope to explain human behavior? Because of evolutionary considerations would not a theory of human behavior be assisted by knowledge of animal behavior? Should not the formulation of a theory of rat behavior provide methodological insights into the construction of a conception of a human behavior? Although one need not consider that affirmative answers are demanded, it is difficult to conclude that such answers are unreasonable.

Within the neobehaviorist's camp attempts were made to combine assumptions from conditioning theory with new principles and extend them to cognitive behavior (e.g., Osgood, 1957; H. H. Kendler & Kendler, 1962). In certain ways these attempts, which were characterized as mediational stimulus-response models, represented a transition from association theory to information-processing formulations since they postulated theoretical processes (e.g., the transformation of incoming stimuli into symbolic representations) that intervened between stimulus (input) and response (output) and served as mechanisms for rational, intelligent behavior. But for the most part this evolutionary change in neobehaviorism to account for human cognitive behavior was ignored, discounted, or flatly rejected by those who adopted the information-processing paradigm. Members of revolutionary movements in psychology tend to be sustained more by what they believe is wrong in a competing formulation rather than what they have proved to be right in their own formulation. This need for a revolutionary identity clearly distinct from all other movements led many of those committed to an information-processing approach to ignore differences among behaviorisms and to treat the entire behaviorist orientation as being equivalent to operant behaviorism, the form most opposed to their own views.

Of the various efforts to identify the historical ancestry of the information-processing paradigm, the efforts of Lachman, Lachman, and Butterfield (1978) appear the most successful although they too exhibit the tendency to conflate operant behaviorism with neobehaviorism. They cite six major influences on the development of the information-processing paradigm: neobehaviorism, verbal learning, human engineering, communication engineering, computer science, and linguistics. In each case the information-processing paradigm adopted some of the positions of its intellectual ancestors while rejecting others. For example, in discussing the influence of neobehaviorism, Lachman, Lachman, and Butterfield conclude that the information-processing paradigm adopted their positive attitudes toward nomothetic explanation, empiricism, laboratory experimentation, and operationism to describe empirical investigations, but rejected neobehaviorism's commitment to an all-encompassing theory, explanation by extrapolation, animal experimentation, a primary concern with learning, the concept of conditioned associations, an adherence to logical positivism, and an antimentalism. This simple listing highlights the complexity of the historical background of the information-processing viewpoint by emphasizing the diversity of its origins as well as the intricacies of the influences that flow from each intellectual ancestor. Because of this historical complexity and because of the rejection of the ideal of an overall global theory, the information-processing paradigm was not as integrated as its predecessors, thus allowing for modifications of strategic decisions and theoretical assumptions in light of their effects. In contrast, operant behaviorism and neobehaviorism were locked into positions that were difficult to abandon regardless of the consequences.

A price was paid for the great flexibility of the information-processing paradigm. The absence of a clear-cut theoretical goal to encompass a circumscribed empirical realm plus the ease with which the information-processing conception could be applied to practically all forms of behavior led to a gigantic mushrooming of research findings that lacked any general coherence aside from the terminology that was employed to report and interpret them. To this diversity of content has been added a range of explanatory standards that varies from rigorous mathematical deduction to intuitive interpretations represented solely by a flow chart.

The core concepts of the information-processing model have also tended to become reified. When these concepts are used to describe a phenomenon a belief is encouraged that an explanation has been offered where in fact only a pretheoretical model has been suggested. These models are theoretical trial balloons that tentatively interpret available evidence and guide future research. Pretheoretical models are a common gambit in psychological theorizing and serve an essential purpose. However, there are dangers, as the history of psychology testifies, when they are judged to be more than a "pilot study" in theorizing. Hull (1935), for example, offered a pretheoretical model that illustrated how novel combinations of stimulus-response associations *could* explain reasoning in animals. *Could* is not, however, synonymous with *would*. Hull perceived Maier's finding (1929) that rats could reason as a challenge to his stimulus-response associationism. He met this challenge by offering a persuasive associationistic interpretation. His overconcern with theory at the expense of data backfired. The phenomenon of reasoning was not as simple as Maier originally reported or as Hull thought (T. S. Kendler, & Kendler, 1967). What appeared to Hull, and his many adherents, as an incorporation of the facts of reasoning into a stimulus-response theory proved to be an ingenious pretheoretical model but nothing more.

The general strategy of forming pretheoretical models to superimpose on a relatively unexplored empirical area cannot properly be criticized. Theoretical conjectures are the life blood of a science. But a problem *can* be created by such a strategy when the model is perceived more as a valid interpretation than as an interesting speculation. Because the information-processing paradigm has such theoretical flexibility and empirical breadth, as well as a rich and persuasive terminology, the border between intuitive understanding and deductive explanation can, and has (Kendler, 1978), become badly blurred. This blurring has been encouraged by the greater devotion of some adherents of the information-processing paradigm to model building than to collecting relevant facts.

The explanatory capacities of information-processing conceptions based upon the operation of computers have been a special target for criticism. These models essentially liken human cognitive operations to functions in computer programs. One of the most vociferous critics of computer simulation of human cognition is Joseph Weizenbaum (1976), a distinguished computer scientist. Two of his major criticisms are (1) the operation of a computer is a poor base from which to infer the intellectual functioning of humans, and (2) the claims of computer models to explain human behavior are inflated.

The first criticism essentially states that humans and computers should not be viewed as members of the same genus since different principles govern their functioning. This kind of criticism is equivalent to the reservations expressed about interpreting the operation of the central nervous system as a telephone switchboard. Misconceptions, the argument goes, will inevitably spring from an inappropriate analogy. This criticism in no way questions the general value of computers as research tools and the specific contribution that can be made by translating a complex theory model into a computer program in order to discover the theoretical implications of the model. The thrust of the criticism is that humans and computers are constructed differently and therefore operate on different principles.

This criticism is rejected by computer enthusiasts who argue that the analogy is justified, at least tentatively, because both the computer program and the human thought process essentially are expressions of a set of symbol manipulating rules. If we discover that the output of a computer program matches that of a human in a problem-solving task can we not conclude that both are employing the same set of rules? The answer is obviously "No," but at the same time the possibility that it could be true in a given case cannot be rejected. The problem is not unlike that of discovering whether two individuals arriving in New York from Boston reached their destination in the same way. Both could have come by car but they need not have.

The question of whether the same set of rules underlie the similarity between the output of a computer program and human performance in a cognitive task is obviously an empirical and theoretical problem that cannot be solved by a priori arguments, no matter how persuasive they may appear. In considering this task certain problems need be recognized.

First, the concept of *matching outputs* is not as clear as it initially appears. One of the early simulations of human cognition attempted to model human proofs of theorems in symbolic logic (Newell & Simon, 1961). Although some success was achieved in matching the introspective reports of subjects with that of the computer output, obvious discrepancies occurred between the language of the subject, which was idiomatic English (e.g., "I'm looking at the idea of reversing these two things now") and the telegraphic, logical communication of the computer (e.g., Goal 6: Apply R3 to L1). In addition, the computer sometimes provided more information than the human subject and at other times less. If matching computer outputs to human performance serves as the litmus test to evaluate the computer simulation how are these discrepancies to be evaluated? What is the dividing line between a successful and unsuccessful match? This question can be bypassed by those who seek to understand human cognition by computer simulation because their only concern is to identify the best simulation of a given cognitive task and to improve upon it in the future. But if one adopts a questioning attitude about the general approach of computer simulation of human cognition then the issue of defining an acceptable match between computer and human outputs cannot be ignored.

The problem of specifying the criteria of a reasonable match between humans and computers becomes excessively complex when ordinary language serves as the output. Ideas can be expressed in an infinite variety of forms in common language. Machine translation of one language into another has not been as effective as initially anticipated because of the difficulties computers have with dealing with idiomatic expressions. An amusing example that highlights this problem comes from a program designed to translate English into Russian (Lachman, Lachman, & Butterfield, 1978). The English sentence, "The spirit is willing but the flesh is weak" was translated into Russian essentially as, "The vodka is fine, but the meat is tasteless." Perhaps it would be strategic for computer simulation of intellectual tasks to restrict their outputs to highly structured behavioral measures such as choice responses, reaction times, and so on.

The second problem involved in the effort to simulate cognitive behavior by computer programs is the extreme specificity of the interpretations. The program applies to a single empirical result, or at best, a limited set of related findings. This specificity encourages the conclusion, no matter how successful the simulation is, that the computer operations do not necessarily reflect underlying psychological processes. Such a conclusion can be best refuted by demonstrating a general explanatory capacity for a given computer model. If a program that simulates human performance in problem A can be successfully applied to problem B, then the confidence in the validity of the computer interpretation of problem A, as well as for B increases.[7] The more phenomena the general program can explain the more compelling will the position be that the similarity obtained between the outcomes of the computer program and human performance is an expression of common underlying processes. In other words, computer simulation of human cognition must be treated as a theoretical endeavor and judged in the same way as any other theoretical effort.

7. The similarity of an epistemological criterion of a general theoretical explanation and a psychological criterion of understanding should be noted. Wertheimer (1945) insisted that a child's ability to discover the area of a particular rectangle did not necessarily imply that he understood the problem. However, if the child was able to indicate how the area of a parallelogram was to be computed, then one could have confidence that he really understood the area of a rectangle. In sum, a transfer criterion is appropriate for both theoretical and psychological conceptions of understanding.

The extreme specificity of computer simulation programs encouraged Simon and Newell (1964, 1971) to formulate a program known as the General Problem Solver to cope with three major cognitive tasks: chess playing, discovering proofs in logic, and solving cryptarithmetic puzzles (e.g., discover numerical equivalent of letters in words when DONALD + GERALD = ROBERT where $D = 5$). The General Problem Solver contained programmed instructions that are assumed to be equivalent to common problem-solving processes that guide human thought. The General Problem Solver operates serially, coping with one major process at a time. For example, one process is to organize the problem-solving task into a set of subgoals that ultimately will lead to problem solution. Once a particular subgoal is selected then a means-end analysis begins to operate that specifies the difference between the existing situation (e.g., the position in a chess game at the end of the sixth move) and the desired situation (e.g., the control of the four center squares) so that the relevant heuristic procedure can be employed to reach the subgoal. The solution is not guaranteed; it may prove impossible to gain control of the center of the board from a particular position. If that be the case, a new subgoal is selected (e.g., secure the safety of one's king) and a means-end analysis of that subgoal is begun.

Proponents of the strategy of simulating human thought with general conceptions, such as the General Problem Solver, that contain no reference to the content of specific tasks viewed their efforts as a major breakthrough in cognitive psychology. Twenty years ago these efforts were considered to "have already produced a rigorous, detailed explanation of a significant area of human symbolic behavior" (Newell & Simon, 1961). Although much unfinished business still had to be completed, an optimism reigned that the goal of a general theory of human thought and problem solving would inevitably be achieved in the near future. This optimism proved to be unjustified. Nevertheless, the computer simulation research program, in spite of its failure to achieve its stated goal, is nevertheless defended as being more successful than competing research programs (e.g., phenomenological and behavioristic interpretations). However, even this defense can be called into question by raising the issue of whether the General Problem Solver is really a theory.

Weizenbaum (1976) argues that the General Problem Solver is not really a general theory but instead "is nothing more than a programming language in which it is possible to write programs for certain highly specialized tasks." That is, the GPS does not have any independent status that enables it, in some logical fashion, to generate specific programs for the different cognitive tasks. Cannot, however, the general theory be abstracted from the programs that are employed for the various cognitive tasks? Smith is skeptical:

> Anyone who has tried to read a theory embedded in a program knows how difficult it is to arrive at the general principles of the theory. More likely than not, whatever general principles there are, are buried in the mass of details needed to make the theory sufficient, i.e., to make the program run. More generally, as theories become increasingly sufficient they must by nature contain more details, and consequently become less transparent (1978, p. 49).

A theory expressed in the form of a computer program, Smith notes, may be so inaccessible that it becomes impossible to know what constitutes inconsistent evidence. If this be the case then some method must be developed to extract the major theoretical assumptions of a computer theory from the coordinated procedures that are needed to make the program sufficient. Perhaps this will prove difficult or impossible, or new epistemological procedures will be developed to evaluate general theories embedded in computer programs. For the moment, at least, the capacity of computer theories to interpret a comprehensive range of human cognition has yet to be demonstrated.

The problem of theoretical specificity versus generality is not limited to the segment of the information-processing approach that employs simulation techniques. It appears to be a core problem within the entire information-processing approach. The goal of an all-encompassing global theory was initially rejected by the information-processing paradigm for apparently good reasons

(Lachman, Lachman, & Butterfield, 1978). Psychologists were notoriously unsuccessful in formulating comprehensive theories of behavior, and it appeared sensible to limit theorizing to circumscribed empirical areas until a level of success was achieved to justify a broader conception. Although the impression prevails that the information-processing approach has generated a comprehensive interpretation of cognitive behavior, the actual theoretical achievements deny it. A common paradigmatic language is not equivalent to a core set of assumptions with a wide range of implications. In essence, the information-processing conceptions are not strictly theories in the sense that they coherently organize a factual domain but instead are "experiments in conceptualization. Their authors are stretching the limits of the information-processing paradigm to see if it provides the conceptual tools with which to attack the timeless questions humankind has raised about its own mental functioning" (Lachman, Lachman, & Butterfield, 1978).

The work of Kintsch and Van Dijk (1978), modestly entitled "Toward a model of text comprehension and production," is an example of a conceptual experiment, or what has been described as a pretheory that aims to interpret text comprehension and production. In concluding their article they acknowledge serious limitations and omissions: "It deals only with semantic representation not with the text itself," "The model stops short of full comprehension," "The component that interprets clusters of propositions as facts . . . is . . . missing," "General world knowledge organized in terms of frames . . . is another missing link."

Acknowledging, "these serious limitations" Kintsch and Van Dijk justify their efforts by the conviction that as long as "comprehension" is considered "as one undifferentiated process . . . it is simply impossible to formulate precise, researchable problems." In sum, specific hypotheses that would generate research are needed.

One can fault neither the efforts of Kintsch and Van Dijk (1978) nor general strategy that they have adopted. But their "conceptual experiment" does highlight the problem of theoretical breadth currently confronting the information-processing paradigm. In light of the obvious failures of global theories in the past, it appeared strategic to eschew general theories of information processing. As a consequence of this strategy a plethora of specific models were created that threw little light upon cognitive functioning in any complex real-life task because of the absence of any general conception as to how the specific processes and structures were integrated. When the limitations of these specific models became apparent, the conceptual tools within the information-processing paradigm, mainly a large set of assumed processes and mental structures that appeared to be intuitively valid, allowed for the ready formulation of general theories that opened up a "wealth of interesting significant research problems" and made up "in promise for what it [lacked] . . . in completeness" (Kintsch & Van Dijk, 1978).

The key problem is whether the promises will be realized. Is a general information-processing theory possible, or will the cognitive approach suffer the fate of predecessors that attempted to formulate a natural-science type theory for a broad range of behavior? One factor that dampens the optimism is the inability of research within the information-processing paradigm to resolve fundamental issues such as whether information is processed in a serial or parallel fashion. This difficulty might appear insignificant because a broad theory of cognition could be formulated that permits some assumptions to remain indeterminate. If physicists need not resolve the issue of whether light should be represented as waves or corpuscles, why must psychologists be forced to choose between serial and parallel processing? Although such a defense may provide some comfort, the difference between the explanatory capacities of the physical theory of light and of general information-processing models destroys the appropriateness of the analogy. The fundamental issue is whether there are ceilings to the explanatory powers of black-box theories, regardless of the research program in which they are embedded. Although information-processing conceptions have provided broader insights into human memory than previous associationistic theories, their potential, like all environmental-behavioral conceptions, are severely limited by the lack of direct control over the events and processes that are basic to the phenomena that are to be explained. The ingenuity of human reasoning to spin out a variety of pretheoretical models combined with this lack of control effectively prevents a choice between competing assumptions. Consequently fundamental theoretical problems remain unresolved and broad theories unattainable.

If the possibility of an explanatory limitation is acknowledged, then alternatives to broad theories of cognition based on environmental-behavioral laws should be considered. One, already suggested (page 316), is that the unresolved theoretical disputes be transformed into neurophysiological problems. If this can be accomplished then the more direct control that is exerted over the phenomenon increases the likelihood of resolving the theoretical issue. It does not follow that all theoretical disputes can be recast into neurophysiological questions. Before this can be accomplished additional knowledge about neurophysiology, or even environmental-behavioral events, will be required. In some cases the transformation may never be accomplished. The important methodological point is that black-box theorists need to reconsider the optimistic notion that their methods will lead ultimately to broad-range theories of the sort that have been achieved in physics and biology. By acknowledging the possibility of intrinsic limitations they can cope more productively with the type of theoretical debates that in the past have generated much research but not theoretical determinate outcomes. By recognizing theoretical limits one may be in a better position to identify when a particular controversy has reached a point where additional research will prove fruitless in resolving the theoretical issues. Rather than embark on a wild-goose chase that ultimately leads to discarding theoretical issues on the scrap-heap of history, it would be wise to put aside the problem until further knowledge and advanced technology provide the means by which the questions can be answered. Perhaps, if this strategy were followed significant theoretical issues and related research would not be so rapidly forgotten from one generation to the next.

What does the future hold for the information-processing paradigm? Will it be more successful than its predecessors in the arena of natural-science behavioral theories? Yes, if success is judged in terms of longevity. The life span of the information-processing conception will most likely exceed those of other paradigms because of its greater theoretical flexibility, its capacity to generate a wide range of questions, and the availability of an apparently infinite number of experimental tasks to answer them. Longevity, however, is not the only criterion that can be applied to behavioral theories, and certainly not the most important. Can the information-processing paradigm produce a coherent theory of cognition or even of the basic subareas of cognition such as memory or language? The history of black-box theories encourages a pessimistic view that broad-gauged theories of information processing, especially those that do justice to the capacities of human intelligence in real life, will achieve any compelling success. And by implication, the hope of extending the information-processing conception to other fields of psychology (e.g., personality, psychopathology, motivation) appears at best remote. Some may convince themselves that information processing is at the core of all human activities; it is questionable that such an assumption, even in its broadest sense, is sufficient to account for affective and motivational events, as well as personality development.

Anticipating possible difficulties that the information-processing conception might encounter can serve constructive purposes. In this attempt to read the future, however, one should not forget that information processing, in the final analysis, "is a paradigm, an approach to constructing theories, a style of theorizing. It cannot be correct or incorrect, only more or less productive" (Hayes, 1978). A final evaluation will depend both on the productivity of the information-processing paradigm and competing paradigms.

Postscript

The unity of psychology has all but collapsed. Psychology is a multidisciplinary field with different segments employing irreconcilable orientations. As a result bitter disputes have occurred concerning the proper methodological position that psychology should adopt. Inevitably, these disputes have spilled over into controversies about the appropriate professional roles of psychologists. These differences are unavoidable considering the fundamental nature of psychology. A choice of competing methodological alternatives cannot be made by purely rational means although society may encourage one form of psychology at the expense of others because of the manner in which society interprets its social responsibilities. The best that can be hoped for within psychology is a mutual understanding of the competing methodological positions and an appreciation of the decisions that led to their adoption. The purpose of this inquiry has been to achieve that goal.

References

Abel, T. The operation called *verstehen*. *American Journal of Sociology*, 1948, *54*, 211–218.

Albee, G. The protestant ethic, sex, and psychotherapy. *American Psychologist*, 1977, *32*, 150–161.

Alper, S., Beckwith, J., Chorover, S. L., Hunt, J., Inouye, H., Judd, T., Lange, R. V., & Sternberg, P. The implications of sociobiology. *Science*, 1976, *192*, 424–427.

Anglin, J. M. *Word, object, and conceptual development*. New York: Norton, 1977.

Asch, S. E. Studies of independence and conformity: I. A minority of one against a unanimous majority. *Psychological Monographs*, 1956, *70*, No. 9 (Whole No. 416).

Attneave, F. Some informational aspects of visual perception. *Psychological Review*, 1954, *61*, 183–193.

Atkinson, R. C. Reflections on psychology's past and concerns about its future. *American Psychologist*, 1977, *32*, 205–210.

Back, K. W. *Beyond words. The story of sensitivity training and the encounter movement*. New York: Basic Books, 1972.

Baker, J. J. W., & Allen, G. E. *The study of biology* (2nd ed.). Reading, Mass.: Addison-Wesley, 1971.

Beach, F. A. Evolutionary changes in the physiological control of mating behavior in mammals. *Psychological Review*, 1947, *54*, 279–315.

Bellow, S. *Humboldt's gift*. New York: Viking, 1975.

Bergmann, G. Psychoanalysis and experimental psychology: A review from the standpoint of scientific empiricism. *Mind*, 1943, *52*, 122–140.

Bergmann, G. Sense and nonsense in operationism. *Scientific Monthly*, 1954, *79*, 210–214.

Bergmann, G. The contributions of John B. Watson. *Psychological Review*, 1956, *63*, 265–276.

Bergmann, G., & Spence K. W. Operationism and theory construction. *Psychological Review*, 1941, *48*, 1–14.

Berkeley, G. *The principles of human knowledge*. Dublin: Jeremy Pepyat, 1710.

Berkowitz, L. *Social Motivation.* In G. Lindzey & E. Aronson (Eds.), *The Handbook of Social Psychology* (Vol. 3, 2nd ed.). Reading, Mass.: Addison-Wesley, 1969.

Berkowitz, L. The contagion of violence: An S-R mediational analysis of some effects of observed aggression. In W. J. Arnold & M. M. Page (Eds.), *Nebraska Symposium on Motivation.* Lincoln: University of Nebraska Press, 1970.

Berlyne, D. E. Humanistic psychology as a protest movement. Paper prepared for the 4th Banff Conference on Theoretical Psychology. Conceptual Issues in Humanistic Psychology. Centre for Advanced Study in Theoretical Psychology, Banff, Alberta, October 12–16, 1975.

Bernstein, L. *The unanswered question: Six talks at Harvard.* Cambridge: Harvard University Press, 1976.

Blodgett, H. C. The effect of the introduction of reward upon the maze performance of rats. *University of California Publications in Psychology,* 1929, *4,* 113–134.

Boring, E. G. *A history of experimental psychology.* New York: Appleton-Century, 1929.

Boring, E. G. *A history of experimental psychology* (2nd ed.). Englewood Cliffs, N.J.: Prentice-Hall, 1950.

Bousfield, W. A. The occurrence of clustering in the recall of randomly arranged associates. *Journal of General Psychology,* 1953, *49,* 229–240.

Bower, G. H. Organizational factors in memory. *Cognitive Psychology,* 1970, *1,* 18–46.

Breland, K., & Breland, M. The misbehavior of organisms. *American Psychologist,* 1961, *16,* 681–684.

Bridgman, P. W. *The logic of modern physics.* New York: Macmillan, 1927.

Bridgman, P. W. Remarks on the present state of operationalism. *Scientific Monthly,* 1954, *79,* 224–226.

Brodbeck, M. Explanation, prediction, and "imperfect" knowledge. In H. Feigl & G. Maxwell (Eds.), *Minnesota Studies in the Philosophy of Science* (Vol. 3). Minneapolis: University of Minnesota Press, 1962.

Bruner, J. S., & Postman, L. On the perception of incongruity: A paradigm. *Journal of Personality,* 1949, *18,* 206–223.

Bush, R. R., & Mosteller, F. A. A mathematical model of simple learning. *Psychological Review,* 1951, *58,* 313–323.

Cahn, E. Jurisprudence. *New York University Law Review,* 1955, *30,* 150–169.

Cain, W. S. To know with the nose: Keys to odor identification. *Science,* 1979, *203,* 467–470.

Campione, J. C. Optional intradimensional and extradimensional shifts in children as a function of age. *Journal of Experimental Psychology,* 1970, *84,* 296–300.

Carmichael, L., Hogan, H. P., & Walter, A. A. An experimental study of the effect of language on the reproduction of visually perceived form. *Journal of Experimental Psychology*, 1932, *15*, 73–86.

Chein, I. *The science of behavior and the image of man.* New York: Basic Books, 1972.

Chein, I., Cook, S. W., & Harding, J. The field of action research. *American Psychologist*, 1948, *3*, 43–50.

Chernoff, P. R. Understanding mathematical proofs: conceptual barriers. *Science*, 1976, *193*, 276.

Chomsky, N. Review of Skinner's *Verbal behavior. Language*, 1959, *35*, 26–58.

Chomsky, N. *Language and mind.* New York: Harcourt, Brace and World, 1968.

Chomsky, N. *Reflections on language.* New York: Pantheon, 1975.

Christy, P., Gelfand, D. M., & Hartmann, D. P. Effects of competition-induced frustration on two classes of modeled behavior. *Developmental Psychology*, 1971, *5*, 104–111.

Conant, J. *On understanding science.* New Haven: Yale University Press, 1947.

Courant, R., & Robbins, H. *What is mathematics?* (4th ed.). New York: Oxford University Press, 1941.

Cummings, N. A. The anatomy of psychotherapy under national health insurance. *American Psychologist*, 1977, *32*, 711–718.

D'Amato, M. *Experimental psychology.* New York: McGraw-Hill, 1970.

Darwin, F., & Seward, A. C. (Eds.). *More letters of Charles Darwin* (Vol. 1). London: John Murray, 1903.

Darwin, F. *The life and letters of Charles Darwin,* including an autobiographical chapter (3 vols.). London: John Murray, 1887.

Deutscher, M., & Chein, I. The psychological effects of enforced segregation: A survey of social science opinion. *Journal of Psychology*, 1948, *26*, 259–287.

De Valois, R. L., Abramov, I., & Jacobs, G. H. Analysis of response patterns of LGN cells. *Journal of the Optical Society of America*, 1966, *7*, 966–977.

De Valois, R. L., & Jacobs, G. H. Primate color vision. *Science*, 1968, *162*, 533–540.

Diamond, S. S., & Morton, D. R. Empirical landmarks in social psychology. *Personality and Social Psychology Bulletin*, 1978, *4*, 217–221.

Driesch, H. *The Science and Philosophy of the Organism.* London: A. and C. Black, 1908.

Dunn, L. C. *Heredity and evolution in human populations* (Rev. ed.). Cambridge: Harvard University Press, 1965.

Ehrenfreund, D. An experimental test of the continuity theory of discrimination with pattern vision. *Journal of Comparative Psychology*, 1948, *41*, 408–422.

Elesh, D., Ladinsky, D., Lefcowitz, M. J., & Spillerman, S. The New Jersey-Pennsylvania experiment: A field study in negative taxation. In L. L. Orr, R. E. Hollister, & M. J. Lefcowitz (Eds.), *Income maintenance: Interdisciplinary approaches to research.* Chicago: Markham, 1971.

Estes, W. K. Toward a statistical theory of learning. *Psychological Review*, 1950, *57*, 94–107.

Feigl, H. The *"mental"* and the *"physical."* Minneapolis: University of Minnesota Press, 1967.

Feigl, H. The "orthodox" view of theories: Remarks in defense as well as critique. In M. Radner & S. Winokur (Eds.), *Minnesota Studies in the Philosophy of Science* (Vol. 4). Minneapolis: University of Minnesota Press, 1970.

Feldman, S. E. Probabilistic hierarchies to ambiguous concept classes. *Journal of Experimental Psychology*, 1963, *65*, 240–247.

Ferster, C. B. Positive reinforcement and behavioral deficits of autistic children. *Child Development*, 1961, *32*, 437–456.

Festinger, L., & Carlsmith, J. M. Cognitive consequences of forced compliance. *Journal of Abnormal and Social Psychology*, 1959, *58*, 203–210.

Frank, J. D. The bewildering world of psychotherapy. *Journal of Social Issues*, 1972, *22*, 27–43.

Gallo, P. S., Jr. Meta-analysis—A mixed meta-phor? *American Psychologist*, 1978, *33*, 515–516.

Garcia, J. What lies ahead after Bakke ruling? *Los Angeles Times*, January 7, 1978, Part II, p. 4.

Gardiner, P. Vico, Giambattista, S. V. In P. Edwards (Ed.), *The Encyclopedia of Philosophy* (Vol. 8), New York: Macmillan & The Free Press, 1967.

Garner, W. R. *Uncertainty and structure as psychological concepts.* New York: Wiley, 1962.

Gesell, A., Halverson, H. M., Thompson, H., Ilg, F. L., Costner, B. M., Ames, L. B., & Amatruda, C. S. *The first five years of life: a guide to the study of the preschool child.* New York: Harper & Row, 1940.

Gesell, A., Ilg, F. L., Ames, L. B., & Bullis, G. E. *The child from five to ten.* New York: Harper, 1946.

Ghiselin, M. T. *The triumph of the Darwinian method.* Berkeley: University of California Press, 1969.

Goble, F. *The third force.* New York: Pocket Books, 1971.

Goldstein, K. *The organism.* New York: American Book, 1939.

Gross, J. *Learning readiness in two Jewish groups.* New York: Center for Urban Education, 1967.

Gurr, T. R. A comparative study of civil strife. In H. D. Graham & T. R. Gurr (Eds.), *The history of violence in America* (Rev. Bantam ed.). New York: Bantam, 1970.

Guthrie, E. R. *The psychology of learning* (Rev. ed.). New York: Harper, 1952.

Hall, C. S., & Lindzey, G. *Theories of personality.* New York: Wiley, 1957.

Hanson, N. R. *Patterns of discovery.* Cambridge: Cambridge University Press, 1958.

Harlow, H. F. The formation of learning sets. *Psychological Review,* 1949, *56,* 51–65.

Harlow, H. F. The nature of love. *American Psychologist,* 1958, *13,* 673–685.

Harré, R. *The principles of scientific thinking.* London: Macmillan, 1970.

Hayes, P. J. Cognitivism as a paradigm. *The Behavioral and Brain Sciences,* 1978, *1,* 238–239.

Hebb, D. O. *The organization of behavior.* New York: Wiley, 1949.

Heston, L. L. The genetics of schizophrenic and schizoid disease. *Science,* 1970, *167,* 249–255.

Hilgard, E. R., & Bower, G. H. *Theories of Learning* (4th ed.). Englewood Cliffs, N.J.: Prentice-Hall, 1975.

Honig, W. K. Prediction of preference, transposition, and transposition-reversal from the generalization gradient. *Journal of Experimental Psychology,* 1962, *64,* 239–248.

Howe, I. *World of our fathers.* New York: Harcourt Brace Jovanovich, 1976.

Hull, C. L. Quantitative aspects of the evolution of concepts. *Psychological Monographs,* 1920, *28,* 123.

Hull, C. L. The mechanism of the assembly of behavior segments in novel combinations suitable for problem solution. *Psychological Review,* 1935, *42,* 219–245.

Hull, C. L. *Principles of behavior.* New York: Appleton-Century, 1943.

Hull, C. L. Autobiography. In C. A. Murchison (Ed.), *A history of psychology in autobiography* (Vol. 4). New York: Russell & Russell Press, 1952.

Hull, C. L., Hovland, C. I., Ross, R. T., Hall, M., Perkins, D. T., & Fitch, F. B. *Mathematico-deductive theory of rote learning.* New Haven: Yale University Press, 1940.

Hunter, J. E., & Schmidt, F. L. Critical analysis of the statistical and ethical implications of various definitions of test bias. *Psychological Bulletin,* 1976, *83,* 1053–1071.

James, W. A. *The principles of psychology* (Vol. 1). New York: Holt, 1890.

Jensen, A. R. How much can we boost IQ and scholastic achievement? *Harvard Educational Review,* 1969, *39,* 1–123.

Jensen, A. R. *Educability and group differences.* New York: Harper & Row, 1973.

Jensen, A. R. What is the question? What is the evidence? In T. S. Krawiec (Ed.), *The psychologists* (Vol. 2). New York: Oxford University Press, 1974.

Jensen, A. R. Race and mental ability. In F. J. Ebling (Ed.), *Racial varia-tion in man*. New York: Halsted Press, 1975.

Jensen, A. R. Cumulative deficit in IQ of blacks in the rural south. *Developmental Psychology*, 1977, *3*, 184–192.

Kamin, L. J. *The science and politics of IQ*. Potomac, Md.: Erlbaum, 1974.

Kanner, J. H. A test of whether the "nonrewarded" animals learned as much as the "rewarded" animals in the California latent learning study. *Journal of Experimental Psychology*, 1954, *48*, 175–183.

Kaplan, A. *The conduct of inquiry*. San Francisco: Chandler, 1964.

Kemelman, H. *Wednesday the Rabbi got wet*. New York: Morrow, 1976.

Kendler, H. H. Some comments on Thistlewaite's perception of latent learning. *Psychological Bulletin*, 1952, *49*, 47–51.

Kendler, H. H. Learning. In P. R. Farnsworth & Q. McNemar (Eds.), *Annual review of psychology*. Stanford: Annual Reviews, 1959.

Kendler, H. H. *Basic psychology*. New York: Appleton-Century-Crofts, 1963.

Kendler, II. II. *Basic psychology* (2nd ed.). New York: Appleton-Century-Crofts, 1968.

Kendler, H. H. The unity of psychology. *The Canadian Psychologist*, 1970, *11*, 30–47.

Kendler, H. H. *Basic psychology* (3rd ed.). Menlo Park, Cal.: Benjamin, 1974.

Kendler, H. H. A seductive paradigm. In J. Cotton & R. L. Klatzky (Eds.), *Semantic Factors in Cognition*. Hillsdale, N.J.: Lawrence Erlbaum, 1978.

Kendler, H. H. Behaviorism and psychology: An uneasy alliance. Paper delivered at the 1979 meeting of The American Psychological Association, September, 1979.

Kendler, H. H. Developmental changes in classificatory behavior. *Child Development*, 1980, *51*, 339–348.

Kendler, H. H., & Kendler, T. S. Vertical and horizontal processes in problem solving. *Psychological Review*, 1962, *69*, 1–16.

Kendler, H. H., & Kendler, T. S. From discrimination learning to cognitive development: A neobehaviorist odyssey. In W. K. Estes (Ed.), *Handbook of learning and cognitive processes* (Vol. 1). Hillsdale, N.J.: Lawrence Erlbaum, 1975.

Kendler, H. H., Kendler, T. S., & Ward, J. W. An ontogenetic analysis of optional intradimensional and extradimensional shifts. *Journal of Experimental Psychology*, 1972, *95*, 102–109.

Kendler, H. H., & Mencher, H. C. The ability of rats to learn the location of food when motivated by thirst—An experimental reply to Leeper. *Journal of Experimental Psychology*, 1948, *38*, 82–88.

Kendler, H. H., & Spence, J. T. (Eds.). *Essays in neobehaviorism*. New York: Appleton-Century-Crofts, 1971.

Kendler, T. S. Contributions of the psychologist to constitutional law. *The American Psychologist*, 1950, *5*, 505–510.

Kendler, T. S., & Kendler, H. H. Experimental analysis of inferential behavior in children. In L. P. Lipsitt & C. C. Spiker (Eds.), *Advances in child development and behavior* (Vol. 3). New York: Academic Press, 1967.

Kessel, F. S. The philosophy of science as proclaimed and science as practiced: "Identity" or "dualism"? *American Psychologist*, 1969, 24, 999–1005.

Kintsch, W., & Van Dijk, T. A. Toward a model of text comprehension and production. *Psychological Review*, 1978, 85, 363–394.

Koch, S. Psychology and emerging conceptions of knowledge as unitary. In T. W. Wann (Ed.), *Behaviorism and phenomenology*. Chicago: University of Chicago Press, 1964.

Koch, S. Psychology as science. In S. C. Brown (Ed.), *Philosophy of psychology*. New York: Barnes & Noble, 1974.

Koffka, K. *Principles of Gestalt psychology*. New York: Harcourt, Brace, 1935.

Kohlberg, L. Implications of developmental psychology for education—examples of moral development. *Educational Psychologist*, 1973, 10, 2–14.

Köhler, W. *The mentality of apes*. New York: Harcourt, Brace, 1925.

Köhler, W. Simple structural functions in the chimpanzee and in the chicken. In W. D. Ellis (Ed.), *A source book of Gestalt psychology*. London: Routledge & K. Paul, 1938.

Kolata, G. B. Mathematical proofs: the genesis of reasonable doubt. *Science*, 1976, 192, 989.

Krebs, D. Empathy and altruism. *Journal of Personality and Social Psychology*, 1975, 32, 1134–1146.

Krechevsky, I. "Hypotheses" versus "chance" in the pre-solution period in sensory discrimination-learning. *University of California Publications in Psychology*, 1932, 6, 27–44.

Kuhn, T. S. *The structure of scientific revolutions*. Chicago: University of Chicago Press, 1962.

Kuhn, T. S. *The structure of scientific revolutions* (2nd ed.). Chicago: University of Chicago Press, 1970.

Kuhn, T. S. Second thoughts on paradigms. In F. Suppe (Ed.), *The structure of scientific theories*. Urbana: University of Illinois Press, 1974.

Külpe, O. *Outlines of psychology* (E. B. Titchener, Trans.). New York: Macmillan, 1909.

Lachman, R. The model in theory construction. *Psychological Review*, 1960, 67, 113–129.

Lachman, R., Lachman, J. L., & Butterfield, E. C. *Cognitive psychology and information processing: An introduction*. Hillsdale, N.J.: Lawrence Erlbaum, 1978.

Lack, D. *Darwin's finches*. Cambridge: Cambridge University Press, 1947.

Lakatos, I. History of science and its rational reconstruction. In R. C. Buck

& R. S. Cohen (Eds.), *Boston Studies in the Philosophy of Science* (Vol. 8). Dordrecht, Netherlands: Reidel, 1970a.

Lakatos, I. Falsification and the methodology of scientific research programmes. In I. Lakatos & A. Musgrave (Eds.), *Criticism and the growth of knowledge.* Cambridge: Cambridge University Press, 1970b.

Lakatos, I., & Musgrave, A. *Criticism and the growth of knowledge.* Cambridge: Cambridge University Press, 1970.

Latané, B., & Darley, J. M. Group inhibition of bystander intervention in emergencies. *Journal of Personality and Social Psychology,* 1968, *10,* 215–221.

Latané, B., & Rodin, J. A lady in distress: Inhibiting effects of friends and strangers on bystander intervention. *Journal of Experimental Social Psychology,* 1969, 5, 189–202.

Levine, M. Scientific method and the adversary model: Some preliminary thoughts. *American Psychologist,* 1974, *29,* 661–676.

Lewin, K. *A dynamic theory of personality.* New York: McGraw-Hill, 1935.

Lewin, K., Lippitt, R., & White, R. K. Patterns of aggressive behavior in experimentally created "social climates." *Journal of Social Psychology,* 1939, *10,* 271–299.

Lewis, O. The culture of poverty. *Scientific American,* 1966, *215*(4), 19–25.

Luborsky, L., Chandler, M. Averbach, A. H., Cohen, J., & Bachrach, H. M. Factors influencing the outcome of psychotherapy: A review of quantitative research. *Psychological Bulletin,* 1971, 75, 145–185.

MacCorquodale, K., & Meehl, P. E. On a distinction between hypothetical constructs and intervening variables. *Psychological Review,* 1948, 55, 95–107.

MacCorquodale, K., & Meehl, P. E. On the elimination of cul entries without obvious reinforcement. *Journal of Comparative and Physiological Psychology,* 1951, *44,* 178–183.

McFarland, M. W. (Ed.). *The papers of Wilbur and Orville Wright* (Vol. 1). New York: McGraw-Hill, 1953.

McKinney, F. Fifty years of psychology. *American Psychologist,* 1976, *31,* 834–857.

MacNichol, E. F., Jr. Three pigment color vision. *Scientific American,* 1964, *211*(b), 48–56.

Maddi, S. The search for meaning. In M. Page (Ed.), *Nebraska Symposium on Motivation.* Lincoln: University of Nebraska Press, 1970.

Maier, N. R. F. Reasoning in white rats. *Comparative Psychology Monographs,* 1929, No. 29.

Maslow, A. H. *Motivation and personality.* New York: Harper & Row, 1954.

Maslow, A. H. "Eupsychia—the good society." *Journal of Humanistic Psychology,* 1961, *1*(2), 1–11.

Maslow, A. H. *Religions, values and peak experiences.* Columbus: Ohio State University Press, 1964.

Masterman, M. The nature of a paradigm. In I. Lakatos & A. Musgrave (Eds.), *Criticism and the growth of knowledge*. Cambridge: Cambridge University Press, 1970.

Matarazzo, J. D. *Wechsler's measurement and appraisal of adult intelligence*. Baltimore: Williams & Wilkins, 1972.

Medawar, P. B. Unnatural science. *The New York Review of Books*, 1977, *24*(1), 13–18.

Meehl, P. E. Some methodological reflections on the difficulties of psychoanalytic research. In M. Radner & S. Winokur (Eds.), *Minnesota Studies in the Philosophy of Science* (Vol. 4). Minneapolis: University of Minnesota Press, 1970.

Meehl, P. E. Schizotaxia, schizotypy, schizophrenia. *American Psychologist*, 1962, *17*, 827–838.

Meyer, M. *Psychology of the other-one*. Columbia, Missouri: Missouri Book Co., 1921.

Milgram, S. Behavioral study of obedience. *Journal of Abnormal and Social Psychology*, 1963, *67*, 371–378.

Miller, N. E. Experimental studies in conflict. In J. M. Hunt (Ed.), *Personality and the Behavior Disorders*. New York: Ronald Press, 1944.

Money, J., & Ehrhardt, A. A. *Man and woman, boy and girl*. Baltimore: Johns Hopkins University Press, 1972.

Mpitsos, G. J., Collins, S. D., & McClellan, A. D. Learning: A model system for physiological studies. *Science*, 1978, *199*, 497–506.

Murdock, G. P. Comparative data on the division of labor by sex. *Social Forces*, 1937, *15*, 551–553.

Murray, M. The treatment of autism: A human protest. *Journal of Humanistic Psychology*, 1974, *14*, 57–59.

Nafe, J. P. The psychology of felt experience. *American Journal of Psychology*, 1927, *39*, 367–389.

Nagel, E. Methodological issues in psychoanalytic theory. In S. Hook (Ed.), *Psychoanalysis, scientific method, and philosophy*. New York: New York University Press, 1959.

Nagel, E. Theory and observation. In E. Nagel, S. Bromburger, & A. Grünbaum (Eds.), *Observation and theory in science*. Baltimore: Johns Hopkins Press, 1971.

Neisser, U. Review of W. G. Chase (Ed.) *Visual information processing. Proceedings of a symposium. Science*, 1974, *183*, 402–403.

Newell, A., & Simon, H. The simulation of human thought. In *Current trends in psychological theory*. Pittsburgh: The University of Pittsburgh Press, 1961.

Olbrisch, M. E. Psychotherapeutic interventions in physical health. *American Psychologist*, 1977, *32*, 761–777.

Osgood, C. E. A behavioristic analysis of perception and language as cognitive phenomena. In J. S. Bruner et al. (Contributors), *Contemporary approaches to cognition: A symposium held at the University of Colorado.* Cambridge: Harvard University Press, 1957.

Passmore, J. A. Can the social sciences be value-free? In H. Feigl & M. Brodbeck (Eds.), *Readings in the Philosophy of Science.* New York: Appleton-Century-Crofts, 1953.

Patai, R. *Tents of Jacob: The diaspora—yesterday and today.* Englewood Cliffs, N.J.: Prentice-Hall, 1971.

Pavlov, I. P. *Conditioned reflexes* (G. V. Anrep, Trans.). London: Oxford University Press, 1927.

Pavlov, I. P. *Conditioned reflexes and psychiatry.* New York: International Publishers, 1941.

Pennington, L. A., & Finan, J. L. Operational usage in psychology. *Psychological Review,* 1940, *47,* 254–266.

Phillips, D. C. *Holistic thought in social science.* Stanford: Stanford University Press, 1976.

Piaget, J. What is psychology? *American Psychologist,* 1978, *33,* 648–652.

Polyani, M. *Personal knowledge.* Chicago: University of Chicago Press, 1958.

Popper, K. R. *The poverty of historicism.* London: Routledge & K. Paul, 1957.

Popper, K. R. *The logic of scientific discovery.* New York: Basic Books, 1949.

Postman, L. Organization and interference. *Psychological Review,* 1971, *78,* 290–302.

Pratt, C. C. *The logic of modern psychology.* New York: Macmillan, 1939.

Provine, W. B. Geneticists and the biology of race crossing. *Science,* 1973, *182,* 790–796.

Ratliff, F. *Mach bands.* San Francisco: Holden-Day, 1965.

Reeves, J. W. *Thinking about thinking.* New York: George Braziller, 1966.

Reichbenbach, H. *Experience and prediction.* Chicago: University of Chicago Press, 1938.

Reynolds, B. A repetition of the Blodgett experiment on "latent learning." *Journal of Experimental Psychology,* 1945, *35,* 504–516.

Roche, J. P. Constitutional law: Distribution of powers, s. v. In D. Sills (Ed.), *International Encyclopedia of the Social Sciences* (Vol. 3), pp. 300–307. New York: Macmillan & The Free Press, 1968.

Rosenbaum, M. Psychosomatic medicine. II. *Psychophysiological disorders.* In A. M. Freedman, H. I. Kaplan, & B. J. Saduck (Eds.), *Comprehensive textbook of psychiatry.* Baltimore: Williams & Wilkins, 1967.

Rychlak, J. F. *A philosophy of science for personality theory.* New York: Houghton Mifflin, 1968.

Rychlak, J. F. Personality theory: Its nature, past, present and future? *Personality & Social Psychology Bulletin,* 1976, *2,* 209–224.

Scarr-Salapatek, S. Review of L. J. Kamin's *The science and politics of IQ*. *Contemporary Psychology*, 1976, *21*, 98–99.

Schiller, B. Verbal, numerical and spatial abilities of young children. *Archives of Psychology*, 1934, No. 161, 69.

Schlesinger, I. M. *Steps to language*. Hillsdale, N.J.: Lawrence Erlbaum, in press.

Sears, R. R. *Survey of objective studies in psychoanalytic concepts*. New York: Social Science Research Council Bulletin (No. 51), 1943.

Sheehan, T. Italy: Behind the ski mask. *The New York Review of Books*, 1979, *26*(13), 20–26.

Shuey, A. M. *The testing of Negro intelligence* (2nd Ed.). New York: Social Science Press, 1966.

Sidman, M. *Tactics of scientific research*. New York: Basic Books, 1960.

Silverman, L. H. Psychoanalytic theory: "The reports of my death are greatly exaggerated." *American Psychologist*, 1976, *31*, 621–637.

Simon, H. A., & Newell, A. Information processing in computer and man. *American Scientist*, 1964, *52*, 145–159.

Simon, H. A., & Newell, A. Human problem solving: The state of the theory in 1970. *American Psychologist*, 1971, *26*, 145–159.

Simpson, G. G. An adversary view of sociobiology (Review of M. S. Ahlin's *The use and abuse of biology*). *Science*, 1977, *195*, 773–774.

Skinner, B. F. Are theories of learning necessary? *Psychological Review*, 1950, *57*, 193–216.

Skinner, B. F. John Broadus Watson, behaviorist. *Science*, 1959, *129*, 197–198.

Skinner, B. F. *Contingencies of reinforcement: A theoretical analysis*. New York: Appleton-Century-Crofts, 1969.

Skinner, B. F. *Particulars of my life*. New York: Knopf, 1976.

Smith, E. E. Theories of semantic memory. In W. K. Estes (Ed.), *Handbook of learning and cognitive processes* (Vol. 6). Hillsdale, N.J.: Lawrence Erlbaum, 1978, pp. 1–58.

Smith, M. B. Social psychology, science, and history, so what? *Personality and Social Psychology Bulletin*, 1976, *4*, 438–444.

Smith, M. L., & Glass, G. V. Meta-analysis of psychotherapy outcome studies. *American Psychologist*, 1977, *32*, 752–760.

Spence, K. W. The nature of discrimination learning in animals. *Psychological Review*, 1936, *43*, 427–449.

Spence, K. W. The differential response in animals to stimuli varying within a single dimension. *Psychological Review*, 1937, *44*, 430–444.

Spence, K. W. Cognitive versus stimulus-response theories of learning. *Psychological Review*, 1950, *57*, 159–172.

Spence, K. W. *Behavior theory and conditioning*. New Haven: Yale University Press, 1956.

Spence, K. W., & Lippitt, R. An experimental test of the sign-gestalt theory of trial and error learning. *Journal of Experimental Psychology,* 1946, 36, 491–502.

Spengler, O. *The decline of the West.* New York: Knopf, 1950.

Spoerl, D. T. Bilinguality and emotional adjustment. *Journal of Abnormal and Social Psychology,* 1943, 38, 35–57.

Stein, L., & Wise, C. D. Possible etiology of schizophrenia: Progressive damage to the noradrenergic reward system by 6-hydroxydopamine. *Science,* 1971, 171, 1032–1036.

Stellar, E. The physiology of motivation. *Psychological Review,* 1954, 61, 5–22.

Sternberg, S. Memory scanning: Mental processes revealed by reaction-time experiments. *American Scientist,* 1969, 57, 421–457.

Stoppard, T. *Travesties.* New York: Grove Press, 1975.

Suppe, F. *The structure of scientific theories.* Urbana: University of Illinois Press, 1974.

Symonds, P. M. The effects of attendance at Chinese language schools on ability with English language. *Journal of Applied Psychology,* 1924, 8, 411–424.

Tart, C. T. (Ed.). *Altered states of consciousness.* New York: Wiley, 1969.

Teitelbaum, P. The issue of operant methods in the assessment and control of motivational states. In W. K. Honig (Ed.), *Operant behavior: Areas of research and application.* New York: Appleton-Century-Crofts, 1966.

Terrace, H. S. Discrimination learning, the peak shift, and behavioral contrast. *Journal of Experimental Analysis of Behavior,* 1968, 11, 727–741.

Thorndike, E. L. Animal intelligence: An experimental study of the associative processes in animals. *Psychological Monographs,* 1898, 2(8).

Thurstone, L. L. *Vectors of the mind.* Chicago: University of Chicago Press, 1935.

Titchener, E. B. *An outline of psychology.* New York: Macmillan, 1899.

Titchener, E. B. *Lectures on the experimental psychology of the thought processes.* New York: Macmillan, 1909.

Titchener, E. B. *Text-book of psychology.* New York: Macmillan, 1910.

Tolman, E. C. *Purposive behavior in animals and men.* New York: Century, 1932.

Tolman, E. C. Operational behaviorism and current trends in psychology. Proceedings of the *25th Annual Celebration of the Inauguration of Graduate Studies, The University of Southern California.* Los Angeles: The University of Southern California Press, 1936, pp. 89–103.

Tolman, E. C., & Honzik, C. H. Introduction and removal of reward and maze performance in rats. *University of California Publications in Psychology,* 1930, 4, 257–275.

Toynbee, A. J. *A study of history* (Abridgement in two volumes by D. C. Somervell). London: Oxford University Press, 1946–57.

Tuddenham, R. D. The nature and measurement of intelligence. In L. Postman (Ed.), *Psychology in the making.* New York: Knopf, 1962.

Tulving, E., & Osler, S. Transfer effects in whole/part free-recall learning.
Canadian Journal of Psychology, 1967, *21,* 250–262.

Turner, M. B. *Philosophy and the science of behavior.* New York: Appleton-
Century-Crofts, 1965.

Vurpillot, E. The development of scanning strategies and their relation to
visual differentiation. *Journal of Experimental Child Psychology,*
1968, *6,* 632–650.

Wade, N. Sociobiology: Troubled birth for a new discipline. *Science,* 1976,
191, 1151–1155.

Wagoner, K. S., & Goodson, F. E. Does the mind matter? In M. H. Marx
& F. E. Goodson (Eds.), *Theories in comtemporary psychology*
(2nd ed.). New York: Macmillan, 1976.

Wallace, R. K., & Benson, H. The physiology of meditation. *Scientific
American,* 1972, *226*(2), 85–90.

Warren, J. M. Primate learning in comparative perspective. In A. M. Schrier,
H. F. Harlow, & F. Stollnitz (Eds.), *Behavior of nonhuman primates*
(Vol. 1). New York: Academic Press, 1965.

Watson, J. B. Experimental studies on the growth of the emotions. In
C. Murchison (Ed.), *Psychologies of 1925.* Worcester, Mass.: Clark
University Press, 1926.

Watson, R. I. *The great psychologists* (4th ed.). Philadelphia: Lippincott,
1978.

Weber, M. *The protestant ethic and the spirit of capitalism* (T. Parsons,
Trans.). New York: Scribner's, 1958 (Originally published 1904–05).

Weizenbaum, J. *Computer power and human reason.* San Francisco: W. H.
Freeman, 1976.

Wertheimer, M. Gestalt theory. In W. D. Ellis (Ed.), *A source book of
Gestalt psychology.* New York: Harcourt, Brace & World, 1938.

Wertheimer, M. *Productive thinking.* New York: Harper, 1945.

Whewell, W. *Novum organon renovatum, being the second part of the
philosophy of the inductive sciences* (3rd ed.). London: Parker &
Son, 1858.

Williams, B. Rationalism. In P. Edwards (Ed.), *The encyclopedia of philosophy* (Vol. 7). New York: Macmillan & The Free Press, 1967.

Wilson, E. O. *Sociobiology: The new synthesis.* Cambridge: Belknap Press
of Harvard University Press, 1975.

Wittig, M. A., & Petersen, A. C. (Eds.). *Sex-related differences in cognitive
functioning. Developmental differences.* New York: Academic Press,
1979.

Wolff, P. H. Ethnic differences in alcohol sensitivity. *Science,* 1972, *175,*
449–450.

Woodworth, R. S. *Experimental psychology.* New York: Holt, 1938.

Index